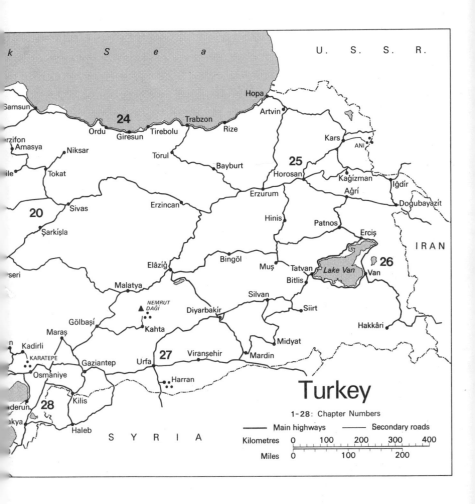

k S e a   U. S. S. R.

Samsun

Ordu   Giresun   Tirebolu   Trabzon   Rize   Hopa   Artvin

Hopa

Trabzon

24

rzifon
Amasya   Niksar   Torul   Bayburt   Kars   ANI

ile   Tokat   Horosan   Kağızman   Iğdır

25

Erzincan   Erzurum   Ağrı

20   Sivas   Hinis   Doğubayazit

Şarkişla   Patnos   Erciş

seri   Elâzığ   Bingöl   Muş   Tatvan   Lake Van   **26**   IRAN

Malatya   Bitlis   Van

NEMRUT
DAĞI   Silvan

Gölbaşi   ▲   Diyarbakir   Siirt

Maraş   Kahta   Hakkâri

n   Kadirli   Midyat

KARATEPE   Urfa   **27**   Viranşehir   Mardin

Osmaniye   Gaziantep

28   Kilis   Harran

derun

akya   Haleb   S Y R I A

Turkey

1-28: Chapter Numbers

—— Main highways   —— Secondary roads

Kilometres   0   100   200   300   400

Miles   0   100   200

THE COMPANION GUIDE TO
Turkey

THE COMPANION GUIDES

GENERAL EDITOR: VINCENT CRONIN

*It is the aim of these Guides to provide a Companion
in the person of the author, who knows intimately
the places and people of whom he writes, and is able to
communicate this knowledge and affection to his readers.
It is hoped that the text and pictures will aid them
in their preparations and in their travels, and will
help them to remember on their return.*

LONDON · EAST ANGLIA · KENT AND SUSSEX · DEVON AND CORNWALL
THE SHAKESPEARE COUNTRY · NORTHUMBRIA · NORTH WALES · SOUTH WALES
IRELAND · THE WEST HIGHLANDS OF SCOTLAND
PARIS · THE ILE DE FRANCE · BURGUNDY · THE LOIRE
THE SOUTH OF FRANCE · SOUTH WEST FRANCE
ROME · FLORENCE · VENICE
UMBRIA · TUSCANY · SOUTHERN ITALY
MADRID AND CENTRAL SPAIN · THE SOUTH OF SPAIN
MAINLAND GREECE · SOUTHERN GREECE · THE GREEK ISLANDS
JUGOSLAVIA · SOUTH AFRICA

In preparation
EDINBURGH AND THE BORDER COUNTRY
NORMANDY

THE COMPANION GUIDE TO

Turkey

❧

JOHN FREELY

COLLINS
ST JAMES'S PLACE, LONDON
1979

William Collins Sons & Co. Ltd
London · Glasgow · Sydney · Auckland
Toronto · Johannesburg

First published 1979
© John Freely 1979

ISBN 0 00 216116 8

Set in Monotype Times Roman
Maps by Brian Elkins
Made and printed in Great Britain by
William Collins Sons & Co. Ltd, Glasgow

For Toots
In Memory of Anatolian Journeys

Acknowledgements

❦

During the years of travel and research which led up to this book I received the generous help and stimulating encouragement of many friends, particularly my colleagues at the University of the Bosphorus (formerly Robert College) in Istanbul. In particular, I would like to express my gratitude to Dr Aptullah Kuran, Rector of the University, for having answered my many questions on Ottoman architecture, and to Godfrey Goodwin, who was my companion-guide on my first strolls through Istanbul. I would also like to thank Mrs Mary Hoffman, Librarian of the University, for her constant help in making readily available to me the unique resources of the Near East Collection of the Van Millingen Library. Other colleagues and friends who were of great assistance to me in providing information on the history, art, architecture and archaeology of Turkey are: Professor Bahadír Alkím, Dr Robert Betts, Dr Robert Hardy, Professor Heath Lowry, Professor Bruce McGowan, Mr Dimitri Nesteroff, Professor Lee Striker, and the late Professor Lee Fonger, the former Librarian of the University. I am greatly indebted to Professor Ayfer Bakkalcioğlu, Mr Ergün Çağatay, and the Turkish Ministry of Tourism for having provided me with the photographs used to illustrate this guide. Ergün Çağatay kindly gave me many of his own photographs, as did Ersin Alok, Henry Angelo-Castrillon, S. Peter Fay Jr, Şemsi Güner, E. Hakaran, Sedat Pakay, Ozan Sağdiç, and Zeynel Yeşilay. I would also like to express my deep appreciation to the Honorable Mr William Macomber, former Ambassador from the United States of America to Turkey, and to his wife Phyllis, whose warm hospitality in Ankara made the writing of the chapter on that city such a pleasure.

But my principal debt is to the late Professor Hilary Sumner-Boyd, whose death in 1976 deprived Istanbul of one of its most distinguished scholars. Professor Sumner-Boyd was both mentor and colleague during our years of work together studying the monuments of Istanbul, and much of what I know of the antiquities of the city I learned from him. I hope that whatever merits my book possesses will add honour to his illustrious memory.

Contents

❧

	LIST OF ILLUSTRATIONS	*page* 11
	MAPS AND PLANS	13
	INTRODUCTION	15
1	Istanbul I: Haghia Sophia	19
2	Istanbul II: Topkapí Sarayí	33
3	Istanbul III: Around the Hippodrome	47
4	Istanbul IV: Central Stamboul	57
5	Istanbul V: Along the Golden Horn	70
6	Istanbul VI: The Modern Town	81
7	Bithynia: Iznik and Bursa	92
8	Thrace and the Dardanelles	103
9	The Northern Aegean Coast	114
10	The Aeolian Coast and Pergamum	125
11	Izmir and its Environs	140
12	The Ionian Coast	151
13	Caria	166
14	The Lycian Shore	177
15	The Maeander and the Taurus	186
16	The Pamphylian Coast	196
17	The Cilician Coast	208
18	Karamania	220
19	Cappadocia	234
20	Central Anatolia I	246
21	Central Anatolia II	259
22	Ankara	272
23	Western Anatolia	283
24	The Black Sea Coast	297
25	North-Eastern Anatolia	312
26	The Eastern Borderlands	326
27	The Arab Borderlands	340
28	Southern Anatolia and the Hatay	353

APPENDICES

A Turkish Primer 367
Practical Suggestions 369
Hotels 370
Restaurants and Turkish Cooking 370
Shops and Markets 371
Holidays 371
Glossary 372
Chronological Table 373
Byzantine Emperors 379
Ottoman Sultans 380
Some Books on Turkey 381

INDEX 387

Illustrations

❧

Galata Bridge   *facing page* 64
Haghia Sophia [*Zeynel Yeşilay*]   65
Topkapí Sarayí [*H. Angelo-Castrillon*]   65
The nave of Haghia Sophia [*Ergün Çağatay*]   80
Dining-room, Topkapí Sarayí   80
The Alexander Sarcophagus [*Istanbul Archaeological Museum*]   81
The Süleymaniye [*Ergün Çağatay*]   112
The Covered Bazaar [*Zeynel Yeşilay*]   112
Palace of the Sweet Waters of Asia [*Sedat Pakay*]   113
Fortress of Rumeli Hisar [*Şemsi Güner*]   113
Mosque of Selim II, Edirne   128
Kütahya: the tea house [*S. P. Fay Jr*]   129
Aphrodisias: village square [*Ergün Çağatay*]   129
Wrestlers at the Kirkpinar festival, Edirne [*S. P. Fay Jr*]   129
Miletos: the theatre [*Şemsi Güner*]   176
Ephesus: the Street of the Curetes [*Şemsi Güner*]   176
Antalya: the Fluted Minaret [*Şemsi Güner*]   177
The harbour of Marmaris [*Şemsi Güner*]   177
The Cotton Castle at Pamukkale   192
Didyma: the Temple of Apollo [*Ergün Çağatay*]   192
Mevlana shrine, Konya [*Şemsi Güner*]   193
A Laz from Trabzon [*H. Angelo-Castrillon*]   288
Mevlevi dervishes [*S. P. Fay Jr*]   288
Karanlik Kilise, Cappadocia [*Ergün Çağatay*]   289
The Church of St Gregory in Ani [*Zeynel Yeşilay*]   304
Doğubeyazít: the Castle of Ishak Pasha [*H. Angelo-Castrillon*]   304
Boğazkale: the Lion Gate   305
Relief on Armenian church, Isle of Akhtamar   305
The Hierotheseion at Nemrut Daği [*Ersin Alok*]   305

Maps and Plans

❧

Maps

Istanbul and its Environs	*page* 68–9
Thrace, Bithynia and the Troad	90–1
The Aegean Coast	138–9
The Mediterranean Coast	194–5
Cappadocia	232–3
Central Anatolia	244–5
Western Anatolia	284–5
The Black Sea Coast	298–9
North Eastern Anatolia	310–11
South Eastern Anatolia	338–9
Southern Anatolia and the Hatay	354–5

Town Plans

Istanbul	20–1
Izmir	141
Ankara	270–1

Ground Plans

Haghia Sophia	26
Topkapí Saraýi (Topkapi Palace)	34–5
Sultan Ahmet Camii (Blue Mosque)	50
The Süleymaniye	63
Kariye Camii (Church of St Saviour in Chora)	77
Troy	116–17
Pergamum	126–7
Pergamum: the Acropolis	130
Ephesus	154–5

Ephesus: the Hellenistic Theatre 157
Didyma: Temple of Apollo 164
Bodrum: Castle of St Peter 172
Theatre at Aspendos 202
Konya: Alâeddin Camii 225
Kayseri: Çifte Medrese 248
Sultan Hani near Kayseri 252
Ani 320–1
Ulu Cami in Diyarbakír 342

KEY TO THE SYMBOLS USED IN THE MAPS

Church or monastery

Underground city

Archaeological site

Castle

Caravanserai

Introduction

❧

Foreign travellers in times past came to Turkey primarily in order to see its rich heritage of archaeological sites and historical monuments, which represent the numerous cultures that have flourished there over a span of ten millennia. More recently many have gone there to see the country itself, for it is a vast subcontinent with an enormous variety of topography and scenery, ranging from the white sand beaches and green rivieras along the Aegean and Mediterranean coasts, the rain forests and tea plantations of the Black Sea coast, the stark barrenness of the great Anatolian plateau, the eroded lunar landscape of Cappadocia, out to the rugged mountains of the eastern provinces. As all writers on Turkey have remarked, this is a nation that stands astride two continents and two worlds. And so the Turks are influenced by both East and West, often leaving them with one foot in the oriental past and the other in the western present, a cultural schizophrenia that adds still more to the interest which this country has for travellers. Thus this guide will not look upon Turkey as an outdoor museum of antiquities, but will try to describe its monuments in the context of the extraordinary land in which they stand and the fascinating people who dwell there.

I have chosen to start the tour in Istanbul, one of the truly great cities of the world, adorned with the monuments of the Byzantines and the Ottomans, the two world empires that had their capital there at the confluence of the Bosphorus and the Golden Horn. From there we will cross the eastern end of the Sea of Marmara to see Iznik and Bursa, the two historic cities of ancient Bithynia. Returning to Istanbul, we will then cross Thrace to visit Edirne, the ancient Adrianople, after which we will drive out along the Gallipoli peninsula, crossing the Dardanelles to the Asian shore at Çanakkale. There we begin a tour of the Aegean and Mediterranean coasts of Turkey, followed by a swing through central Anatolia to Ankara, the capital.

After visiting Ankara, those with limited time at their disposal can return through western Anatolia to Istanbul, while those on a longer

15

stay can drive eastwards along the Black Sea coast and then make the immensely long circuit of the eastern and southern borderlands. This is a lengthy journey, not only in space but in time, for in Anatolia one finds the ruins and monuments of civilizations ranging from the Neolithic and Bronze Ages through those of the Hurrians, Assyrians, Hattians, Hittites, Phrygians, Carians, Lydians, Urartians, Armenians, Greeks, Romans, Byzantines, Crusaders, Arabs, Selcuks, Mongols, and finally the Ottoman Turks, making this country a veritable palimpsest of history. (Appendix 8, on p. 373, gives a chronological table of these various cultures, while Appendices 9 and 10, on pp. 379–81, give lists of the Byzantine Emperors and Ottoman Sultans.)

The best way to travel is by car, and the cross-country itineraries are so designed. (Advice on other means of transport is given in Appendix 2, p. 369.) Each of these chapters is intended to correspond to a day's journey, leaving time for sightseeing en route. (This ideal may be somewhat difficult to realize in eastern Anatolia, where the distances between towns are often so great that those who wish to see out-of-the-way places might have to spend several days on the itinerary described in a single chapter.)

But in the cities, especially Istanbul, it is much more fun to stroll through the old quarters of the town on foot, and each of these chapters is designed so that it can be accomplished in a morning or an afternoon, allowing time for lunch. (Advice on restaurants and Turkish cooking is given in Appendix 4.) Street names are seldom used in describing itineraries in Istanbul and other Turkish cities, nor are street maps any help, for the neighbourhoods in which most of the monuments are found are labyrinths of narrow, winding byways with names like the Elephant's Path, the Street of the Chicken That Could Not Fly, the Avenue of the White Mustache, and the Street of Ibrahim of Black Hell. (The last two streets actually intersect in Istanbul, joining to form the Street of the Bushy Beard.) If you wander down such streets on your own you will learn more about Turkey than you would on any tour bus, for they never traverse such eccentric alleyways as the Street of Nafi of the Golden Hair.

Besides those already mentioned, the appendices at the back of the guide are meant to be helpful advice to the traveller in Turkey. You might start by reading the first appendix, which is a simple introduction to the pronunciation of Turkish words, and perhaps before you set out on your journey you should study a primer on modern Turkish. (The best is *Teach Yourself Turkish*, by Geoffrey Lewis.) A little knowledge of Turkish will add greatly to the enjoyment of your trip and it will be much appreciated by your Turkish hosts. (When they ask you if you speak Turkish you can then answer, '*Evet, çat patça, Tarzanca.*' ('Yes, bits and pieces, like Tarzan's language.')

Modern Turkey may at first strike the traveller as a sombre and troubled country. Turkey in recent years has suffered from severe economic, social and political problems, which have given rise to considerable violence in its cities. (More than one thousand people were killed in urban warfare between political extremists in 1978, yet not even a single foreigner was injured.) But this has not in the least diminished the genuine warmth and friendliness of the Turks, whose hospitality to travellers is proverbial. We have had poor labourers and shepherds offer to share with us their scant lunch of bread and goat's cheese, and our whole family has been given food and shelter in the home of a fisherman who moved his own large family into a single room in order to accommodate us, refusing all offers of payment. '*Hoş geldiniz!*' (Welcome!) they said to us in greeting, to which we responded, '*Hoş bulduk!*' (We are pleased to be here!) You will undoubtedly have the same experience and feel the same pleasure in your own trip to Turkey. So *iyi Yolculuklar!*, have a good journey!

C.G.T.   17   B

CHAPTER ONE

Istanbul I: Haghia Sophia

❧

The Galata Bridge – The New Mosque – The Mosque of Rüstem Pasha – The Çağaloğlu Baths – The Basilica Cistern – Haghia Sophia

Procopius, court chronicler in the reign of Justinian the Great, described his beloved city as being surrounded by a garland of waters. Much has changed in the fourteen centuries since he wrote his paean of praise for Constantinople, and even the name of the city is no longer the same, but the beauty of modern Istanbul still owes much to the waters which bound and divide it. The loveliest branch in this garland is the Bosphorus, the incomparable strait which flows from the Black Sea to the Sea of Marmara, separating the main part of the city in Europe from its Asian boroughs and suburbs. At its southern end the Bosphorus is joined by the Golden Horn, the historic stream which flows seaward from the Sweet Waters of Europe, now an open sewer of industrial waste and pollution. The left bank of the Golden Horn on its lower reaches is formed by the Levantine port quarter of Galata, and on its right bank is the seven-hilled imperial city which some still prefer to call Stamboul.

The best place from which to begin a tour of the city is the **Galata Bridge**, which spans the Golden Horn between Galata and Stamboul. Here you can orientate yourself and begin to sense something of the true character of Istanbul, for the bridge and the adjacent shores of the Golden Horn are at the centre of the city's daily life. Fleets of ferries sail to and from their berths at and around the bridge, dodging caiques carrying cargo for the riotous fruit and vegetable markets on the Stamboul shore, while fishermen fry their catch in braziers and sell them from their rowboats to hungry passers-by. Pedlars hawk their wares to the passing crowds, producing umbrellas for sale when clouds threaten and sunglasses when it clears. They are ready with hooks and lines to sell when fish are running in the Golden Horn, and when you see them peddling stovepipes you know winter is near.

From the bridge you have a middle-distance view of the **First Hill**, the wooded acropolis above the confluence of the Bosphorus and the

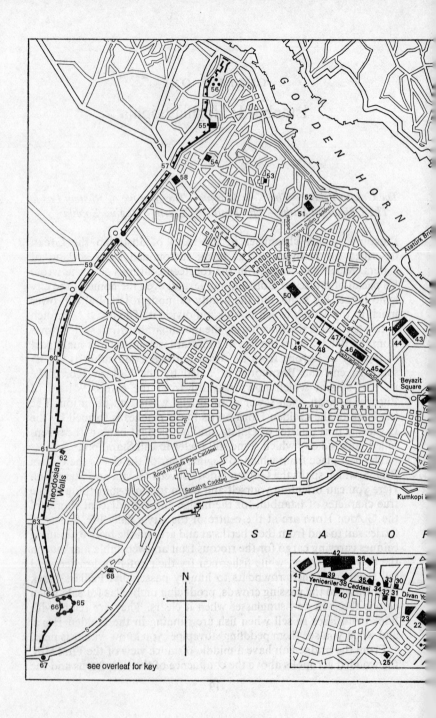

GOLDEN HORN

Atatürk Br

Beyazıt
Square

Kumkopi

SEA O

Theodosian
Walls

Koca Mustafa Paşa Caddesi

Samatya Caddesi

Divan Yo

Yeniçeriler 38 Caddesi

N

see overleaf for key

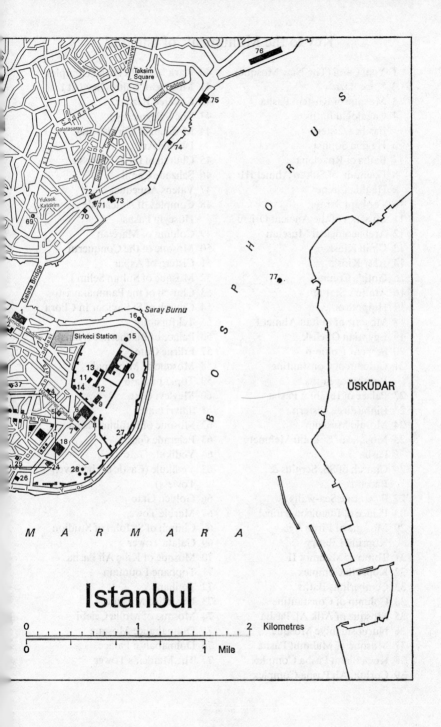

Taksim
Square

İnönü Caddesi

Cumhuriyet Caddesi

76

75

74

Galatasaray

72

73
71
70

Yüksek
Kaldirim

69

Galata Bridge

Haliç

77

BOSPHORUS

Saray Burnu

16

Sirkeci Station

15

13
11
10
14
12
9
8
6
5
7

37

Haliç

Divan Yolu

18

25
24
28
26

27

BOSPHORUS

ÜSKÜDAR

MARMARA

Istanbul

| 0 | | 1 | | 2 | Kilometres |

| 0 | | 1 | Mile |

Key to the Monuments of Istanbul

1 Yeni Cami (The New Mosque)
2 Spice Bazaar
3 Mosque of Rüstem Pasha
4 Çağaloğlu Baths
5 Basilica Cistern
6 Haghia Sophia
7 Baths of Roxelana
8 Fountain of Sultan Ahmet III
9 Haghia Eirene
10 Topkapí Sarayí
11 Museum of the Ancient Orient
12 Archaeological Museum
13 Çinili Kiosk
14 Alay Kiosk
15 Goth's Column
16 Atatürk Statue
17 Hippodrome
18 Mosque of Sultan Ahmet I
19 Egyptian Obelisk
20 Serpent Column
21 Column of Constantine
   Porphyrogenitus
22 Palace of Ibrahim Pasha
23 Binbirdirek Cistern
24 Mosaic Museum
25 Mosque of Sokollu Mehmet
   Pasha
26 Church of SS. Sergius &
   Bacchus
27 Byzantine Sea-walls
28 Palace of Bucoleon (ruins)
29 Mosque of Firuz Ağa
30 Köprülü Library
31 Tomb of Mahmut II
32 Köprülü Complex
33 Çemberlitaş Baths
34 Column of Constantine
35 Mosque of Atik Ali Pasha
36 Nuruosmaniye Mosque
37 Mosque of Mahmut Pasha
38 Koca Sinan Pasha Complex
39 Çorlulu Ali Pasha Complex
40 Kara Mustafa Pasha Complex
41 Mosque of Sultan Beyazit I
42 Covered Bazaar
43 The Súleymaniye
44 Museum of Turkish and
   Islamic Art
45 Church of the Kyriotissa
46 Şehzade Camii
47 Valens Aqueduct
48 Complex of Amcazade
   Hüseyin Pasha
49 Column of Marcian
50 Mosque of the Conqueror
51 Cistern of Aspar
52 Mosque of Sultan Selim I
53 Church of the Pammakaristos
54 Church of St Saviour in Chora
55 Tekfursaray
56 Palace of Blachernae (ruins)
57 Edirne Gate
58 Mosque of Mihrimah
59 Topkapí Gate
60 Mevlevi Gate
61 Silivri Gate
62 Mosque of Ibrahim Pasha
63 Belgrade Gate
64 Yedikule Gate
65 Yedikule (Castle of the Seven
   Towers)
66 Golden Gate
67 Marble Tower
68 Church of St John of Studion
69 Galata Tower
70 Mosque of Kílíç Ali Pasha
71 Tophane Fountain
72 Tophane
73 Nusretiye Mosque
74 Mosque of Molla Çelebi
75 Dolmabahçe Mosque
76 Dolmabahçe Palace
77 The Maiden's Tower

Golden Horn. According to tradition, this is the site where Byzas the Megarian founded the Greek colony of Byzantium in the seventh century BC. Ancient Byzantium comprised little more than the acropolis itself, protected on its landward side by a defence-wall which ran from the Golden Horn to the Sea of Marmara. The town was enlarged somewhat and surrounded by a longer line of walls after its capture in AD 196 by the Roman Emperor Septimius Severus. Then, in the year 330, Constantine the Great made Byzantium capital of the Roman Empire and rededicated the city as New Rome, soon after to be called Constantinople, the City of Constantine. The new capital was far greater in size and in grandeur than old Byzantium, enclosed by a much longer line of walls whose course was traced out by the Emperor himself, led on, so the legend goes, by a vision of Christ. During the century after Constantine the city grew rapidly and soon expanded beyond the limits set by its founder. In the first half of the fifth century a new and much stronger line of defence-walls was built nearly a mile farther out into Thrace, replacing the walls of Constantine. These walls delimited the size of the city up to the present century.

For more than a thousand years Constantinople was capital of what came to be called the Byzantine Empire, the eastern remnant of the dominions of Old Rome. For nearly five centuries after that it was capital of the Ottoman Empire, the vast and powerful warrior-state that succeeded Byzantium with the Turkish conquest of Constantinople in 1453. After the Conquest, Turks began to call their capital Istanbul, their version of the Greek *Stin Poli*, meaning 'in (or to) The City', 'city' being so capitalized because in those days it was indeed beyond compare.

Istanbul served as capital of the Ottoman Empire from 1453 until the establishment of the Turkish Republic in 1923, at which time Ankara became the seat of government. And so for the first time in sixteen centuries the ancient city on the Golden Horn was no longer reigning over a world empire, with only the presence of its magnificent monuments to remind one of its imperial past.

Eminönü, the neighbourhood around the Stamboul end of the Galata Bridge, has been a market quarter since the earliest days of the city, and if you have the courage to wander through its cobbled alleys you will find it tumultuous and colourful. Its vast square is dominated by **Yeni Cami**, the **New Mosque**, one of the most familiar landmarks in the city. The first mosque on this site was commissioned in 1597 by the Valide Sultan (Queen Mother) Safiye, wife of Sultan Murat III and mother of Mehmet III. Construction was halted in

1603 when Sultan Mehmet III died, for his mother then lost her power in the Harem and was unable to complete her mosque. The half-finished building stood desolate on the shore of the Golden Horn for more than half a century, until it was eventually destroyed by fire in 1660. Later that year Turhan Hadice, mother of Mehmet IV, decided to rebuild the mosque. It was finally completed in 1663 and dedicated on 6 November of that year as the 'New Mosque of the Valide Sultan'. The French traveller Grelot was present at the opening ceremonies and wrote that Turhan Hadice was 'one of the greatest and most *spirituelle* ladies who ever entered the Saray', and also that it was fitting that 'she should leave to posterity a jewel of Ottoman architecture as an eternal monument to her generous enterprises'.

Yeni Cami, like all of the great Ottoman mosques, was the centre of a *külliye*, a complex of religious and philanthropic institutions. The original *külliye* of Yeni Cami included a hospital, a primary school, a mausoleum, two public fountains, a public bath and a market, with the revenues from the latter two going towards the support of the mosque and the other branches of the pious foundation. The hospital, primary school and public bath have been destroyed, but the other structures are still standing. The market of the Yeni Cami complex is the handsome L-shaped building whose main entrance is just across from the outer courtyard of the mosque. It is known locally as the Mísír Çarşísí, or Egyptian Market, but to foreigners it has always been famous as the **Spice Bazaar**, because of the spices and medicinal herbs which are sold there. A great variety of other commodities are now found there as well, however, for many of the spice and herb merchants have moved elsewhere in the quarter. But this is still one of the most colourful markets in the city, retaining vestiges of its former oriental atmosphere. In the domed rooms above the entrance to the Spice Bazaar there is an excellent restaurant called Pandelis; there you can dine well while enjoying a view of the Galata Bridge and the Golden Horn.

A short distance to the north-west of Yeni Cami you see **Rüstem Pasha Camii**, one of the most beautiful of the smaller mosques designed by Sinan, the architect who built so many magnificent structures in Istanbul and elsewhere in the Ottoman Empire. Rüstem Pasha was twice Grand Vezir in the reign of Süleyman the Magnificent and husband of the Sultan's favourite daughter, the Princess Mihrimah. His mosque is deservedly famous for its beautiful tiles, which were made in Iznik, the ancient Nicaea, in the greatest period of Ottoman ceramic art, *c.* 1555–1620. In every conceivable floral and geometric design, they cover not only the walls and columns of the interior, but also the *mimber*, or pulpit, and the façade of the porch.

When walking along the market streets between Yeni Cami and Rüstem Pasha Camii you come across many picturesque old *hans* or caravansarais with arcaded courtyards. Most of these are Ottoman structures, but a few are Byzantine in origin, and one or two may date back to the time when this area belonged to the various Italian city-states that had been given concessions here in the late Byzantine period. The area around the present site of Rüstem Pasha Camii belonged to the Venetians, and downstream from that along the shore of the Golden Horn were the concessions of the Amalfians, the Pisans and the Genoese.

The area where Yeni Cami now stands was in earlier centuries a Jewish quarter, wedged in between the concessions of the Venetians and Amalfians. The Jews who resided here were members of the schismatic Karaite sect, who broke off from the main body of orthodox Jewry in the eighth century. The Karaites seem to have settled in this quarter as early as the eleventh century, at about the time when the Italians first obtained their concessions here. The Karaites continued to live in the area until 1660, when they were evicted to make room for the final construction of Yeni Cami. They were resettled in the village of Hasköy, some four kilometres up the Golden Horn, where their descendants remain to this day.

The most direct approach to the First Hill from Eminönü begins on **Hamidiye Caddesi**, the street which passes between Yeni Cami and the Spice Bazaar. The area behind the mosque is the principal flower market of the city, and the kerbside is lined with the desks of professional scribes typing letters for illiterate Anatolian peasants.

Hamidiye Caddesi soon brings you to the square before **Sirkeci Station**, built in 1888 as the terminus of the Orient Express, which made its first through-run to Istanbul that year. Across the street is the Konyalí Lokantasí, one of the finest restaurants in the city.

Here you turn right on to Ankara Caddesi, which is thought to follow the course of the defence-walls built in AD 202 by Septimius Severus. The third street to the left off Ankara Caddesi, Hilaliahmer Caddesi, leads straight towards the broad summit of the First Hill. A short distance down this street and on the left stands the **Çağaloğlu Hamamí**, one of the most handsome public baths in Istanbul. The *hamam* was founded in 1741 by Sultan Mahmut I, and is a particularly fine example of Turkish baroque architecture. Like most of the larger *hamams* in Istanbul it consists of two separate baths, each with its own entrance, for men and women.

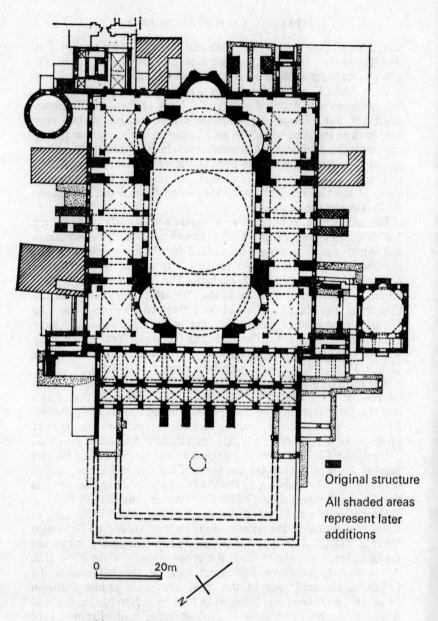

Original structure

All shaded areas represent later additions

0   20m

Haghia Sophia

Towards the end of the street and on the right is a small building which is the entrance to Yerebatan Saray, the Underground Palace. This is an immense and splendid subterranean cistern. In Byzantine times it was known as the **Basilica Cistern**, for it was beneath the Stoa Basilica, one of the main public squares of Constantinople. The cistern was built in 532 by the Emperor Justinian the Great, possibly as a reconstruction of an earlier cistern due to Constantine. It is 140 metres long and 70 metres wide, and its 336 columns are arrayed in 12 rows of 28 each. But only a small part of this vast structure is visible from the landing at the bottom of the stairs below the entryway, for the lights there illuminate only the first few ranks of the colonnade, leaving the rest in absolute darkness. It is no wonder that this place has excited the romantic imagination of travellers and writers ever since its rediscovery in 1545 by the French scholar Petrus Gyllius.

After emerging from the cistern you continue along the last stretch of the street, which ends in the great square at the top of the First Hill. Off to the right you see the imperial mosque of Sultan Ahmet, and to the left the venerable **Haghia Sophia**.

The present Haghia Sophia, known in Turkish as 'Aya Sofya', is the third church of this name to stand upon the site, both its predecessors having been destroyed by fire during riots. The destruction of the second church, founded in 415 by Theodosius II, occurred during the famous Nika Revolt in January 532, when Justinian the Great nearly lost his throne. Shortly after the revolt was finally crushed the Emperor set out to rebuild the church on an even grander scale, bringing in workmen and artisans from throughout his vast empire. He appointed as head architect Anthemius of Tralles, the most distinguished mathematician and physicist of the age, and as his assistant named Isidorus of Miletos, the greatest geometer of late antiquity and former head of the Platonic Academy in Athens. Isidorus was placed in charge after Anthemius died in 532. The new church was formally opened by Justinian on 26 December 537, St Stephen's Day, and in a moving ceremony that evening it was dedicated to Haghia Sophia, the Divine Wisdom.

Although Haghia Sophia was restored several times during the Byzantine and Ottoman periods the present edifice is essentially that of Justinian's reign. The only major structural additions are the huge buttresses that support the building on its north and south sides. These were originally erected in 1317 when the church seemed in danger of collapsing, and were restored by Sinan in the mid-sixteenth century. The four minarets at the corners of the building were erected at various times after the building had been converted into a mosque in 1453. The last extensive restorations were commissioned by Sultan Abdül Mecit and carried out in the year 1847 by the Swiss architects, the brothers Fossati.

The present entrance to Haghia Sophia is at the north-west corner. The vault of the long, narrow **vestibule** glitters with gold mosaic tesserae – part of the original decoration of Justinian's church, in which a total surface area of four acres was revetted with gleaming designs. Much of the original mosaic decoration still survives, particularly in the vault of the narthex, the side aisles, the galleries, and on that part of the great dome which dates from Justinian's time.

There were almost certainly no figural mosaics in Justinian's church, and none would have been allowed during the Iconoclastic Period, when the veneration of icons was banned. The figural mosaics that one sees today, therefore, date from after the mid-ninth century. They were covered over with plaster and whitewash after the Turkish Conquest; later, during the nineteenth-century restoration, they were briefly exposed and then plastered over again. After the mosque was closed in 1933 Thomas Whittemore of the Byzantine Institute of America began work on locating, uncovering and restoring what was left of the mosaics, a project which was finally completed in the 1960s. The surviving figural mosaics represent only a small fraction of those with which the church was once decorated throughout, but nevertheless they do evoke something of the vanished splendour of Haghia Sophia in the days of Byzantium.

The first mosaic one sees is in the lunette above the doorway at the far end of the vestibule. This depicts two emperors paying court to the enthroned Mother of God and the Christ Child. The figure on the left is Constantine; he is offering the Virgin the model of a towered medieval town, signifying his founding of Constantinople, while on the other side Justinian holds a model of Haghia Sophia. This mosaic has been dated to the last quarter of the tenth century, in the reign of Basil II Bulgaroctonus, the Bulgar-Slayer.

One now enters the **narthex**, a long and lofty hall of nine vaulted bays. Five great doors on the left lead to the exonarthex and nine on the right, one in each bay, lead to the nave. The monumental central door to the nave was known as the **Imperial Gate**, and was used only by the Emperor and those who accompanied him in procession.

In the lunette above the Imperial Gate there is a mosaic portrait depicting Christ seated upon a bejewelled throne, receiving an emperor in suppliant attitude. Above there are two roundels, the one over the Emperor containing a bust of the Blessed Virgin, and the other an angel with a wand. The penitent Emperor is thought to be Leo VI, the Wise, who ruled from 886 till 912, and the mosaic has been dated tentatively to the early part of his reign.

The **nave** is an immense space pierced by oblique shafts of moted sunlight falling from the circlet of forty windows at the base of the dome. The central area is defined by four enormous piers standing in a square measuring thirty-one metres on each side. From them rise four great arches between which four pendentives make the transition to the almost circular cornice. Above this rises the majestic dome, which the Byzantines pictured as being suspended from heaven by a golden chain, with its crown fifty-six metres above the floor. To east and west pairs of subsidiary piers support the two great semi-domes. These give the nave its vast length, about eighty metres, and allow one to see from the very threshold the soaring, hovering dome. The central arches to north and south are filled with tympanum walls pierced by twelve windows. Between each of the main piers on the north and south four monoliths of verd antique support the galleries, while about six similar columns support the tympana. At the eastern and western ends, to north and south, semi-circular exedrae prolong the nave, with two massive columns of porphyry below and six of verd antique above, on which rest smaller semi-domes. (The capitals of the columns are famous and splendid, many of them bearing the monogram of Justinian and his Empress Theodora.) Thus the central area of the nave is flanked by a two-tiered colonnade of noble monoliths, a rhythmical procession which Procopius likened to a line of dancers in a chorus. At the east, beyond the subsidiary piers, a semi-circular *apse* projects beyond the east wall; it too is covered by a semi-dome or conch.

The largest and most striking mosaic is in the conch of the apse. This depicts the enthroned Mother of God holding in her lap the Christ Child. At the bottom of the arch which frames the apse there is a colossal figure of the Archangel Gabriel, but the portrait of the Archangel Michael on the other side has been almost completely obliterated. On the face of the arch before the apse a fragmentary inscription commemorates the commissioning of the mosaic by two 'pious emperors'; these were Michael III, the Sot, and his protégé and co-emperor, Basil I, a former stable-boy. The apse mosaic was unveiled by the Patriarch Photius on Easter Sunday 867. This was a most historic occasion, for it signified the final triumph of the Orthodox party over the Iconoclasts and marked the permanent restoration of images to the churches of Byzantium. Six months later Basil brutally murdered the drunken Emperor and usurped the throne, thus beginning the illustrious dynasty which was to rule Byzantium for nearly two centuries.

Three other mosaic portraits are located in niches at the base of the north tympanum wall and are visible from the nave. These depict the brilliantly-robed figures of three saints of the early Orthodox Church; on the western end stands Ignatius the Younger, in the centre John Chrysostomos, and to his left Ignatius Theophorus.

The only other mosaics visible from the nave are the six-winged angels which decorate the eastern pendentives. (Those in the western pendentives are painted imitations done during the nineteenth-century.) These are the latest of the mosaics in the church, probably dating from the middle of the fourteenth century. They were never covered over as were the other figural mosaics.

At the north end of the narthex an incline leads up to the galleries. In the **central gallery** is the spot where once stood the throne of the Empress of Byzantium; it is marked by a disc of green Thessalian marble and a coupled pair of green marble columns.

You might now return to the left, or **north gallery**, to see the only mosaic there: a full-length portrait of the Emperor Alexander, who succeeded his elder brother Leo VI in May 912. 'Here comes the man of thirteen months,' said Leo with his dying breath, seeing his despised brother coming to pay his last respects. This prophecy was fulfilled in June of the following year, when Alexander died of apoplexy during a drunken game of polo.

All the remaining mosaics are in the **south gallery**. Part way down that gallery one passes through a marble screen in the form of two pairs of false double doors with elaborately decorated panels, the so-called **Gates of Heaven and Hell**. The screen was apparently erected in later times to shut off that part of the south gallery which was reserved for the royal family.

After passing through the screen turn right around the inward extension of the south-west buttress. There you find the latest in date of the gallery mosaics, the magnificent **Deesis**. This mosaic, one of the greatest works of art ever produced in Byzantium, is dated to the first half of the fourteenth century. It is a striking illustration of the cultural renaissance which took place in Constantinople after the restoration of the Byzantine Empire in 1261. Christ is shown flanked by the Virgin and St John the Baptist, pleading, so the iconographers inform us, for the salvation of mankind.

Set into the pavement opposite the Deesis there is a cracked sarcophagus lid inscribed with the proud name of Henricus Dandolo. Dandolo, Doge of Venice, was one of the leaders of the Fourth

Crusade; although over ninety years old and nearly blind he personally led the final assault in which Constantinople was conquered and savagely sacked on 17 April 1204. After the Latin Conquest three-eighths of Constantinople, including Haghia Sophia, was awarded to the Venetians and ruled by Dandolo. The old Doge now added the title of Despot to his name and thereafter styled himself 'Lord of the fourth and a half [i.e. 3/8] of all the Roman Empire'. Dandolo lorded it over his fractional kingdom until his death on 16 June 1205, when he was buried in the gallery of Haghia Sophia, then a Latin cathedral. Dandolo's tomb seems to have remained undisturbed after the recapture of the city by the Byzantines in 1261, but, according to tradition, his sarcophagus was broken open after the Turkish Conquest and his bones thrown to the dogs.

There are two more mosaic portraits at the south-west end of the gallery, flanking a window which once gave entrance to a private stairway leading down to the Great Palace of Byzantium. *The Book of Ceremonies*, the Byzantine manual of court rituals, tells us that the Emperor and Empress always paused here when leaving Haghia Sophia privately, kneeling with lighted tapers in hand to say a last prayer before descending to the palace.

The mosaic panel to the left of the window depicts a royal couple kneeling on either side of Christ enthroned. On Christ's left stands the notorious Empress Zoe, one of the few women to rule Byzantium in her own right, and on the other side is her third husband, Constantine IX. The Emperor's head is obviously a later addition, probably replacing the heads of one or both of her previous husbands, Michael IV and Romanus III. This portrait was probably completed in its final form soon after Zoe's marriage to Constantine in 1042. Zoe died at the age of seventy-two in 1050, mourned by the common people of Constantinople, who called their beloved empress 'Mama'. Michael Psellus, in his *Chronographica*, has left us a description of the bawdy empress in her last years, saying that Zoe was still youthful in form and straight of limb, and that 'her face had a beauty altogether fresh'.

The mosaic to the right of the window shows another royal couple presenting gifts to the Virgin and Christ Child, while on the narrow panel of side wall perpendicular to the main composition there is the portrait of a young prince. These are the figures of John II Comnenus, his wife Eirene, daughter of King Ladislaus of Hungary, and their eldest son, who died not long after this portrait was completed, in about 1122. The Emperor, who ruled from 1118 till 1143, was known in his time as Kalo Yanis, or John the Good. The Byzantine historian Nicetas Choniates wrote of John that 'he was the best of all the emperors from the family of the Comneni who ever sat upon the Roman throne'. His Empress Eirene was noted for her piety and charity and is venerated as a saint in the Greek Orthodox Church.

During the centuries when Haghia Sophia served as an imperial mosque it was held in great reverence by the Ottoman sultans, so much so that five of them are buried in its precincts. These **royal Ottoman sepulchres** are in the garden just to the south of the church. The oldest of these is the tomb of the two mad Sultans, Mustafa I and Ibrahim, who ruled Turkey in the first half of the seventeenth century. This building, which was formerly the baptistery of Justinian's church, stands just to the right of the inner entrance to Haghia Sophia. Evliya Efendi, the seventeenth-century Turkish chronicler, tells us that in his day the tomb was a place of pilgrimage popular among the women of Istanbul, who flocked there because 'Ibrahim was particularly addicted to the fairer sex'. At present the baptistery is not open to the public.

The other imperial tombs, or *türbe*, stand in the garden beyond the baptistery. The earliest in date is the *türbe* of Selim II, the Sot, who died in 1574; it is important because it is a work of Sinan and also because both the exterior entrance façade and the whole of the interior are decorated with superb Iznik tiles. On either side of Selim's *türbe* are those of his two immediate successors, his son Murat III, and his grandson Mehmet III who died in 1603, their catafalques surrounded by those of their favourite concubines and the tiny coffins of their many children. The majority of the little princelings buried here were murdered when their elder brother succeeded to the throne, a practice intended to prevent the wars of succession which troubled the Ottoman Empire in earlier years.

The **garden** to the west of Haghia Sophia contains an array of columns, capitals and other architectural fragments discovered in excavations around the city in recent years. At the far end of the garden is the excavation which in 1935 unearthed the entry way to the original Theodosian church. From the fragments which remain one can see that this must have been a vast building. In its time it was known as *Megale Ekklesia*, the 'Great Church', a name which was passed on to the magnificent edifice one sees today.

CHAPTER TWO

Istanbul II: Topkapí Sarayí

❧

Topkapí Sarayí – The Harem – Haghia Eirene – The Museum of the Ancient Orient – The Archaeological Museum – The Çinili Kiosk – The Alay Kiosk

Topkapí Sarayí, the great palace of the Ottoman sultans, stands on what was once the acropolis of the ancient town of Byzantium, with the palace proper on the high ground and its gardens and terraces covering the slope of the hill leading down to the seashore. The palace was enclosed by a massive defence-wall around the landward side of the acropolis, while along the shore it was protected by the Byzantine sea-walls which terminate at Saray Burnu, the point below the acropolis where the Bosphorus and the Golden Horn meet and flow together into the Marmara. As Evliya Efendi described the situation of this fabulous pleasure-dome: 'Never hath a more delightful residence been erected by the art of man; it seems not just a palace but a town situated on the confluence of two seas.'

The main plan of the palace was laid out by Sultan Mehmet II in the years 1459–65, though most of the present structures date from the second half of the sixteenth century, with restorations and additional building going on into the last century. Topkapí Sarayí served as the principal imperial residence and administrative centre of the Ottoman Empire for nearly four centuries, a strange and sequestered world which in time became the subject of voluptuous legend and romance throughout Europe and Asia. Topkapí Sarayí continued as the seat of empire until 1853, when Sultan Abdül Mecit moved his entire household to the new palace of Dolmabahçe on the Bosphorus, abandoning the old palace on the Golden Horn. Thenceforth the Saray was used to house the unwanted women of departed sultans and the old palace began to decay and die, along with its forlorn occupants. Even these last pathetic survivors were evicted in 1909, when the imperial Harem was officially disbanded. After that only a few forgotten eunuchs continued to live on among the ruins, until they too were evicted when the palace was converted

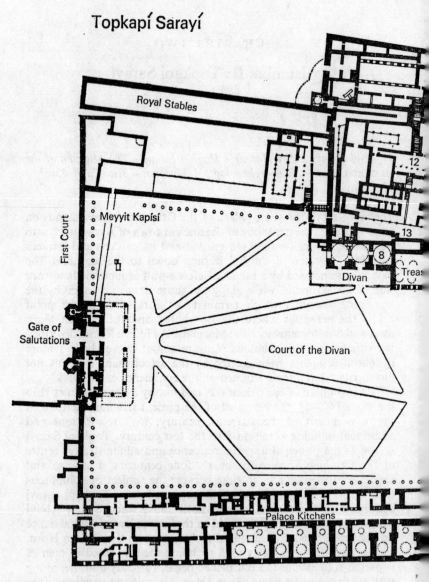

Topkapí Sarayí

Royal Stables

First Court

Meyyit Kapísí

Gate of Salutations

Court of the Divan

Divan

Treas

12

13

8

Palace Kitchens

1 Cümle Kapisi
2 Çeşmeli Oda
3 Hall of the Emperor
4 Salon of Murat III
5 Library of Ahmet I
6 Fruit Room

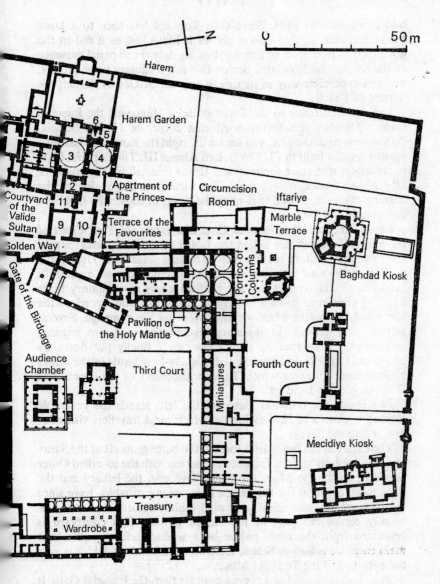

0   50 m

Harem

Harem Garden

6
5
.3   4

Circumcision
Room

Iftariye

Apartment of
the Princes

Marble
Terrace

2

Courtyard
of the
Valide
Sultan

11

Terrace of the
Favourites

Portico of
Columns

Baghdad Kiosk

9   10

7

Golden Way

Gate of the Birdcage

Pavilion of
the Holy Mantle

Audience
Chamber

Third Court

Miniatures

Fourth Court

Mecidiye Kiosk

Treasury

Wardrobe

7 Place of Consultation of the Jinns   11 Ocaklí Oda
8 Grand Vezir's Office   12 Courtyard of the Cariyeler (Women Slaves)
9,10 Suites of the First and Second Kadins   13 Hall of the Black Eunuchs

into a museum in 1924. Since then Topkapí has been to a large extent restored, so that now much of it looks just as it did in the great days of the Ottoman Empire, lacking only the imperial presence of the Sultan and his court. Seeing this extraordinary palace today, one can appreciate why in its time it was called Dar-us Saadet, the 'House of Felicity'.

The main entrance to the Saray is **Bab-i Hümayun**, the **Imperial Gate**, which is opposite the north-east corner of Haghia Sophia. As you approach the gate, you see on the right the handsome baroque street-fountain built in 1728 by Sultan Ahmet III. The Imperial Gate is actually a miniature fortress, and it was manned by a garrison of fifty armed *kapíci*, or gatemen. The niches on either side of the entrance were often used to display the heads of those who had been executed in the Saray.

Passing through the Imperial Gate one enters the **First Court** of the Saray. This was also called the Court of the Janissaries, named after the élite military corps which once assembled here. During the decline of the Ottoman Empire in the seventeenth and eighteenth centuries the Janissaries lost their effectiveness as a military force but they continued to be a heavily armed group, and terrorized the town and the palace whenever they went on the rampage. Several sultans were deposed in Janissary insurrections and two reigning sultans were murdered by them. They were finally put down by Mahmut II in 1826 and annihilated in a day-long battle in the centre of Stamboul, an event which Turkish historians of the time called 'The Auspicious Incident'.

Just inside the Imperial Gate, on the left, stands the venerable Byzantine church of Haghia Eirene, which most travellers visit after first seeing the Saray.

The Court of the Janissaries formed the outer grounds of the Saray and was used for various facilities connected with the so-called Outer Service, such as the Mint, the Outer Treasury, the bakery and the storehouse of wood for the palace furnaces, all of which have since disappeared. It was of a somewhat public nature and was not usually considered part of the palace proper. This courtyard is separated from the inner palace by a second defence-wall whose main entrance is **Bab-us Selam**, the **Gate of Salutations**, which is now the entrance to the Topkapí Museum.

The Gate of Salutations is even grander than the Imperial Gate. It too is a small fortress and is flanked by two conical-topped towers, giving it a quaint medieval appearance. The gatehouse here was the residence of the Chief Executioner of the Saray, a post usually held by the Head Gardener. Set into the wall to the side of the gate is Cellat Çeşmesi, the Executioner's Fountain, where the Head Gardener washed his hands and cleaned his sword after a beheading.

After passing through the Gate of Salutations one enters the **Court of the Divan**. This pleasant courtyard takes its name from the Hall of the Divan, one of the chambers beneath the tower in the far left corner. The Divan was once the administrative centre of the Empire, where four times a week the Grand Vezir and other high officials of the realm met to settle affairs of state.

The **Grand Vezir's Office**, which now has a separate entrance under the portico, is today used to display the interesting collection of antique clocks from the Saray. Adjacent to this is the **Treasury**, a long room covered with four pairs of double domes; this was used to store the taxes and tribute money that came in from various parts of the Empire. Four times a year this was distributed by the Council of the Divan for salaries and other state expenses, and the residue was then transferred to the Inner Treasury in the Third Court. The Treasury now houses the Saray's collection of antique arms and armour.

The present public entrance to the Harem, the Carriage Gate, is beneath the Divan Tower, the most conspicuous landmark in the Saray. Most travellers defer a visit to the Harem until after they have seen the rest of the palace.

After leaving the Divan walk back along the portico to the gate at the far end. This is called **Meyyit Kapísí**, for through it were carried for burial outside the bodies of those who died in the Saray. This leads to the **Royal Stables**, which once sheltered the horses of the Sultan and his pages. These were built by Mehmet the Conqueror and are among the oldest structures in the Saray. The building consists of two parts: the long stables themselves, and at the far end two smaller chambers, one for the Master of the Horse and the other the Harness Treasury, where the bejewelled harnesses and trappings were stored. Both rooms are now used to display a collection of these harnesses, while in the former stables are shown a number of imperial carriages, most of them from the nineteenth century.

Now take the path which leads to the far right-hand corner of the court. This brings you to the **palace kitchens**, which, together with the quarters of the kitchen staff, take up that entire side of the court. Once inside you find yourself on a long cobbled walk, with ten double kitchens on the left and on the right a series of domed chambers which once housed the kitchen staff. Eight of the kitchens are now used to display the Saray's incomparable collection of

Chinese porcelain and other china and glassware. The first two kitchens near the entrance have been restored to their original appearance and contain a collection of antique Turkish kitchenware and utensils once used in the Saray. The small building to the left of the entrance was the **Confectioner's Mosque**; displayed here is a collection of eighteenth- and nineteenth-century Turkish glassware.

The main entrance from the Court of the Divan to the inner palace is through **Bab-us Saadet**, the **Gate of Felicity**. This was not a military gate, as were the entrances to the first two courts, but a more ornamental entryway. But it was guarded even more closely than the other gates, since it gave entrance to the House of Felicity, the strictly private quarters of the Sultan and his household. The Gate of Felicity was guarded by the white eunuchs, and their chief had his apartment in the gatehouse. The Chief White Eunuch was in charge of the Inner Service of the Saray, except the Harem, which was guarded by the Chief Black Eunuch and his staff.

Immediately inside the Gate of Felicity is the **Arz Odasí**, or **Audience Chamber**, a handsome building with an overhanging roof supported by ancient marble columns. This was the only part of the inner palace to which persons from outside the Saray were normally admitted. Here, at the end of each session of the Divan, the Grand Vezir and the other members of the Council reported to the Sultan and obtained his formal approval for the decisions which they had taken. Ambassadors of foreign powers were also presented here upon their arrival in Istanbul.

Most of the chambers which line the **Third Court** were given over to the Inner Service: the palace pages, the students in the Palace School and the various departments in the male household staff of the inner palace. The former chambers of the Palace School are now used to house the three most famous collections in the Topkapí Museum. These are the **Wardrobe**, where are displayed imperial costumes spanning the entire period from the Conquest to the end of the Empire (notice the blood-spattered robe of Osman II, which he was wearing when he was executed by the Janissaries in 1622); the **Treasury** – an astonishing collection of precious objects owned by the sultans; and the **Miniature Exhibition**, the world's finest and most extensive collection of Turkish and Persian miniatures which are incorporated in the Books of Accomplishments and the Books of Festivals. The first two of these collections are in chambers on the right side of the court and the third is at the far end. Then at the far left corner of the court one enters the **Hírka-i Saadet Dairesi**, the **Pavilion of the Holy Mantle**, where are preserved relics of the

Prophet Mohammed.

Passing through the Pavilion of the Holy Mantle, you enter the **Portico of Columns**. At the east end of this portico you find the Rivan Kiosk, built in 1636 by Murat IV to commemorate his capture of Rivan, now the Russian Eriven. At the other end of the portico is the Sunnet Odasí, the **Circumcision Room**, used for the circumcision of young princes; this handsome chamber was constructed in 1641 for the mad Sultan Ibrahim.

Ibrahim succeeded his brother Murat IV to the throne in 1640, at which time he was the last surviving male in the royal Ottoman line. The dynasty seemed in danger of extinction, for Ibrahim had no children of his own and it was rumoured in the Harem that he was impotent. His mother Kössem sought to remedy this by dosing him with aphrodisiacs and by bringing to his bed the most desirable women she could buy in the Istanbul slave market. Finally, in 1642, Ibrahim fathered a son and soon the Harem was swinging with cradles. Ibrahim spent the remaining six years of his short life in what from all accounts seems to have been an almost continual orgy. The most vivid description of Ibrahim's escapades is that given by Demetrius Cantemir in his *History of the Growth and Decay of the Othoman Empire* (London, 1756):

As Murat was wholly addicted to wine so was Ibrahim to lust. They say he spent all his time in sensual pleasure and when nature was exhausted with the frequent repetition of venereal delights he endeavoured to restore it with potions or commanded a beautiful virgin richly habited to be brought to him by his mother, the Grand Vezir, or some other great man. He covered the walls of his chamber with looking-glass so that his love battles might seem to be enacted at several places at once. He ordered his pillows to be stuffed with rich furs, so that the bed designed for the imperial pleasure might be the more precious. Nay, he put whole sable skins under him in a notion that his lust would be inflamed if his love toil were rendered more difficult by the glowing of his knees. In the palace gardens, he frequently assembled all the virgins, made them strip themselves naked, and neighing like a stallion ran among them and . . . ravished one or the other, kicking or struggling by his order. Happening once to see the privy parts of a wild heifer he sent the shape of them in gold all over the Empire with orders to make enquiry whether a woman made just in that manner could be found for his lust. At last such a one was found and received into the women's apartments. He made a collection of great and voluminous books of pictures expressing the various ways of coition whence he even invented some new and previously unknown postures. Thus the public treasury, earlier diminished by Murat's drunkenness, was quite exhausted by Ibrahim's luxury and lust, and the sinews of the Empire which were applied by his ancestors to repulse their enemies and enlarge their domains, were by him used to the destruction of his body.

After leaving the Circumcision Room you go out on to a marble terrace which affords a marvellous view of the Golden Horn. Half-way along the balustrade of the terrace a little balcony with a superb bronze canopy projects outwards. This is called **Iftariye**, and it was constructed in 1640 for Ibrahim the Mad. The balcony takes its name from the *iftar*, the meal which is taken just after sunset to break the fast during the holy month of Ramazan. A miniature in the Saray collection shows the mad Sultan seated there playing with his numerous children, in one of the very few intimate views of the Sultan's private life within the palace.

At the far end of the marble terrace stands the **Baghdad Kiosk**. This was built in 1639 by Murat IV to commemorate his recapture of Baghdad, one of the last great triumphs of Ottoman arms. The kiosk is superbly decorated within and must have given pleasure to the terrible Murat, who spent the last year of his short life there carousing with his favourites.

The marble terrace is common ground between the Third and Fourth Courts, the latter of which is not really a courtyard but a garden adorned with kiosks and pavilions. At the far end of the garden is the nineteenth-century **Mecidiye Kiosk**; the lower floor of the kiosk now serves as a restaurant, with a splendid view out over the Sea of Marmara to the Asian shore.

One now returns to the Second Court to visit the **Harem**, entering through the Carriage Gate. Only a small part of this labyrinthian inner palace has been restored, and one must accompany a museum guide on a conducted tour of those rooms which are open to the public.

After passing through the Carriage Gate and the guardrooms beyond you will find yourself on a mosaic walk called the **Golden Way**, which runs along the entire length of the Harem. Just inside the gateway on the left you pass a colonnade behind which is the **Hall of the Black Eunuchs**. Generally the younger black eunuchs were employed in guarding and attending to the women of the Harem, while the older ones dominated the hierarchy of the Inner

Service, with the Chief Black Eunuch sometimes becoming the most powerful figure in the Empire.

The Chief Black Eunuch had his apartment at the end of the courtyard inside the Carriage Gate, just beyond the Hall of the Black Eunuchs. The floor above his apartment was used as the **Princes' School**. From their fifth to their eleventh year the young princes received their schooling under the supervision of the Chief Black Eunuch, during which time they lived with their mothers in the Harem. Later, after their circumcision rites, the princes moved to the Selamlík, the male quarter of the palace, and continued their education at the Palace School.

Just beyond the apartment of the Chief Black Eunuch the Golden Way passes **Cümle Kapísí**, the main entrance to the Harem proper in Ottoman times. You then come to a guardroom, from the left side of which a long corridor leads to the **Courtyard of the Cariyeler**, the women servants who did the housekeeping chores in the Harem. From the guardroom a gate opens into the **Courtyard of the Valide Sultan**, the mother of the reigning Sultan and titular head of the hierarchy in the Harem; her extensive apartments occupied most of the west side of the court on two storeys. Crossing the courtyard diagonally, you enter the **Ocaklí Oda**, a tiled chamber which takes its name from the *ocak*, or bronze chimney, which dominates the room. This is an antechamber where the Harem quarters met those of the Sultan, and on the right a door leads to the **Suites of the First and Second Kadíns**, the first two of the sultan's four wives. On the left you pass into another tiled antechamber, Çeşmeli Oda, the Room with a Fountain, named for the elegant wall-fountain which is its principal adornment.

You enter now the **Hünkâr Sofasí**, the **Hall of the Emperor**, the largest and grandest room in the Saray. This was also called the Throne Room Within, for here the Sultan had his private court within the House of Felicity itself.

From the Hünkâr Sofasí another antechamber leads into the **Salon of Murat III**. This is the most splendid room in the Saray, particularly since it retains the whole of its original decoration. The walls are sheathed in Iznik tiles at the apogee of their greatest period, and the room is adorned with a handsome bronze *ocak* on one side and on the other an elaborate three-tiered cascade fountain of carved polychrome marble set into a marble embrasure. This beautiful room with its superb decoration was completed by Sinan in 1578, in the early years of Murat's reign. Although Murat may have been a weak and ineffective ruler, he was potent enough in the Harem and was the most prolific of all the Sultans, fathering one hundred and three children.

At the far end of Murat's Salon you find two very small but exquisite rooms. The first of these is the **Library of Ahmet I**, built in 1608-9, and the second is the **Yemiş Oda**, or **Fruit Room**, so called because of the painted panels of fruit and flowers with which the room is decorated. The room was created in 1705-6 for Ahmet III, and the paintings are the earliest known examples of Turkish rococo art. The period of Ahmet III's reign is known as Lale Devrisi, the 'Age of Tulips', for the annual blossoming of the tulip was celebrated by a festival of flowers in the palace gardens. All affairs of State ceased while the court enjoyed these revels presided over by the Sultan himself, who used to be known as the Tulip King.

You now retrace your steps through the Salon of Murat III and the anterooms beyond. This brings you to an apartment which until recent years had been identified as the infamous Kafes, or Cage, the place of confinement of the Sultan's younger brothers. This custom was instituted early in the seventeenth century, after the abolition of the bloody code by which the younger brothers of a sultan were slaughtered at the time of his accession. The Kafes is now thought to have been situated elsewhere, perhaps in the dark congeries of rooms across the way from the splendid apartment one sees here. This suite of two rooms, now called the **Apartment of the Princes**, is thought to date from the beginning of the seventeenth century. It has been superbly restored in recent years and is the most attractive set of rooms in the Saray.

The colonnaded passageway which leads past the Apartment of the Princes is known as the **Place of Consultation of the Jinns**. The origins of this name are lost in the mists of Harem traditions, but one can easily guess why it was so called, for in the silent shadows of late afternoon the dark rooms that line the colonnade do indeed seem haunted. The passageway leads out on to a large open terrace from which one can look down on to the now forlorn gardens of the Saray, the scene of the Tulip King's festivals. This is called **Gözdeler Taşliği**, the **Terrace of the Favourites**, whose apartments were in the suite of rooms on the upper floor of the building at the rear of the terrace. These rooms are not open to the public, for they have not been changed or restored since the last women of the Harem left in 1909.

Guided tours of the Harem end here, and one is led back along the Golden Way to the exit. Halfway along you pass the stairway where in 1809 the slave girl Cevri Kalfa fought off the assassins who were trying to kill Prince Mahmut, the future Sultan Mahmut II. You then pass through Cümle Kapísí and come to **Kuşhane Kapísí**, the **Gate of the Birdcage**, where in 1651 the Valide Sultan Kössem was murdered by the Chief Black Eunuch, Tall Süleyman. Here one leaves the Harem and enters the Third Court, having completed a tour through the House of Felicity.

You can now return to the First Court to visit **Haghia Eirene**, the church which you passed on first entering the Saray. This church is another of Justinian's foundations, replacing an earlier one of the same name which was destroyed during the Nika Revolt. The building was completed in 537, at about the same time as Haghia Sophia, and the Emperor rededicated it to Haghia Eirene, the Divine Peace. Haghia Eirene is one of only two Byzantine churches in Istanbul which was never converted into a mosque, owing to the fact that it was taken over by the Janissaries after the Conquest and used by them as an arsenal. After the dissolution of the Janissaries in 1826 it was used for a time as a storehouse for antiquities and later as a military museum, an ironic fate for a church dedicated to the Divine Peace.

Haghia Eirene is basically a basilica, but one of a very unusual design. The wide nave is divided from the side aisles by the usual columned arcade, but this is interrupted towards the west by the great piers that support the dome to the east and the smaller elliptical vault to the west. The eastern dome is supported by four great arches which are expanded into deep barrel-vaults on all sides except the west. The apse has a semi-dome above and seats for the clergy below. In the semi-dome there is a mosaic of a cross in black outlined against a gold ground with a geometrical border; it is thought that this is part of the original mosaic decoration from the time of Justinian. Within the past decade Haghia Eirene has been very well restored, and the serene old nave makes a superb setting for the presentation of musical performances at the annual Istanbul Festival, which usually begins in late June.

After leaving Haghia Eirene, take the path which leads towards the gate in the left side of the First Court. This portal was called **Kíz Bekçiler Kapísí**, the **Gate of the Watchmen of the Girls**, a reminder that one is leaving the confines of the palace proper for the more public gardens on the west side of the acropolis.

A short distance down on the right you come to a courtyard around which stand three of the most important museums in the city: the Museum of the Ancient Orient, the Archaeological Museum, and the Çinili Kiosk.

As you enter the courtyard, the first building you see on the left is the **Museum of the Ancient Orient**, which houses a distinguished collection of Sumerian, Babylonian, Assyrian, Hittite and pre-historic Anatolian antiquities. The museum has recently reopened after extensive reorganization, and its unique exhibits are attractively displayed. Perhaps the most important exhibit, historically, is a clay tablet with an inscription giving part of the Treaty of Kadesh. This is history's oldest-known peace pact, dated to 1269 BC, signifying the end of the war between the armies of Ramses II of Egypt and Hattusilas, the Hittite Emperor. A second interesting monument from the Hittite period is a limestone column with hieroglyphic inscriptions dating from the tenth century BC. Other remarkable exhibits are the votive statuettes and sculptured head from a necropolis in southern Arabia; dated to the first century BC, these are among the very rare examples of the pre-Islamic art of that region. Perhaps the most striking of all the antiquities in the museum are the coloured tile panels containing the figures in low relief of lions and mythological beasts from Babylon. These panels date from the reign of Nabuchadrezzar II (605–562 BC); they formed part of the monumental processional way which led from the Ishtar Gate to the sanctuary where the New Year's festival was held.

The entire right side of the courtyard is taken up by the **Archaeological Museum**, in front of which are arrayed a line of Byzantine sarcophagi found in Istanbul in the last century. A new museum building is now under construction behind the old one, and it is expected that the museum's collection of antiquities will be re-housed there and opened to the public in the near future. Since the museum is presently being reorganized, only a summary account of some of its most important exhibits will be given here.

The museum is world famous for its extraordinary collection of sarcophagi, many of them discovered towards the end of the last century by Hamdi Bey, the founder of the modern museum. The most famous of these is the Alexander Sarcophagus, discovered in 1887 by Hamdi Bey in the royal necropolis at Sidon. The sarcophagus is so called not because it was that of Alexander himself but because it is decorated with sculptures in deep, almost round relief, showing Alexander in scenes of hunting and battle. This magnificent work, one of the masterpieces of Hellenistic art, has been dated to the last quarter of the fourth century BC. Other famous and splendid sarcophagi in the museum are those known as the Mourners, the Meleager, the Sidamara, the Lycian, the Sarígüzel, and the Tabnit. The last of these is actually an alabaster mummy-case, made to contain the remains of Tabnit, father of the Pharaoh Eshmounazar II.

The most spectacular of the museum's exhibits is a colossal **statue of Bes**, the Cypriot Hercules, who is shown holding up a headless lioness by her hind legs; the great gap in his loins may have served as the spout of a very phallic fountain.

Another great work of art is the famous **Ephebos of Tralles**. This statue represents a youth resting after exercise; he is standing in a relaxed attitude with a cape draped over his shoulder to protect him from the cold, a wistful half-smile on his downcast face. This masterpiece, which probably once adorned a gymnasium in Tralles, is dated to the third century BC.

Another famous work from the same period is the **head of Alexander**, a third-century BC copy of the original by Lyssipus. Alexander is here represented in the pose which became the archetype for all later representations, with what Plutarch called his swimming eye and lion's mane of hair, his mouth slightly open and his head inclined to the left, looking remarkably like Marlon Brando playing Alexander. Standing nearby (as it surely will in the new museum too) is a full-length statue of Alexander in which he is shown as a youthful Hercules, another archetypal representation of the young god-king. This fine work is dated to the second century BC.

Another of the museum's well-known exhibits is a charming **head of the Emperor Arcadius** (395–408), found in Istanbul a generation ago. Arcadius is represented as a handsome young man with delicate features, and is crowned with a simple diadem formed from two circlets of large pearls. This is perhaps the finest extant example of the late Roman sculpture of Constantinople.

Other important monuments are the two large pedestals from the Hippodrome of Constantinople. These once supported bronze statues of Porphyrios, the famous charioteer; they were commissioned by the Emperor Anastasius (491–508), one of his greatest patrons. The pedestals are particularly interesting because they are decorated with reliefs depicting the chariot races and other activities in the ancient Hippodrome.

After leaving the Archaeological Museum, cross over to the handsome and very Persian-looking building in the corner of the courtyard; this is the **Çinili** ('Tiled') **Kiosk**. The Çinili Kiosk is one of the few buildings in the Saray dating from the time of the Conqueror, built by him in 1472 as an outer pavilion of the palace. The kiosk was originally used by the Conqueror as a review pavilion from which he could watch the young princes and pages playing *cirit*, the Turkish form of polo. The building is now used to house a collection of

Turkish tiles and ceramic works of all periods.

Now take the road that leads downhill from the museum court-yard to Gülhane Park. Beside the entrance to the park you see a baroque gazebo built into the outer defence-walls of the Saray. This is the **Alay Kiosk,** the Kiosk of the Processions, so called because the Sultan from there reviewed military parades and the processions of the guilds which were held from time to time in the Ottoman period, the only place in his walled-in palace from which he could look out on to the passing life of his city.(Ibrahim the Mad used it to pick off passers-by with his cross-bow.) The Alay Kiosk is now used to display a collection of Turkish carpets and embroideries.

CHAPTER THREE

Istanbul III: Around the Hippodrome

❧

The Blue Mosque – The Hippodrome – The Palace of Ibrahim Pasha –
The Binbirdirek Cistern – The Mosaic Museum – The Mosque of
Sokollu Mehmet Pasha – The Church of SS Sergius and Bacchus –
The Palace of Bucoleon

The great square beside Haghia Sophia was the centre of Byzantine
Constantinople. This square occupies the site of the ancient
Augustaeum, the public forecourt to the Great Palace of Byzantium.
On its northern side the Augustaeum gave access to Haghia Sophia
and the Patriarchal Palace, and at its south-eastern corner stood
Chalke, the Brazen House, the monumental vestibule to the Great
Palace. To the west of the Augustaeum was the Stoa Basilica, a
porticoed square surrounded by some of the most important public
buildings in the city, and to the south-west was the famous Hippodrome. This area continued to be the centre of the city's life even
after the Conquest, particularly after the sultans took up residence
in Tcpkapí Sarayí. But after the abandonment of the Saray halfway
through the nineteenth century this area declined in importance, the
life of the city moving elsewhere in Stamboul and across the Golden
Horn in Pera. Today the square before Haghia Sophia is a centre only
of tourism, lined with Pullman buses and crowded with groups of
tourists, guides and pedlars of postcards and trinkets, drawn there
by the great monuments on the First Hill.

Just opposite Haghia Sophia, at the end of the garden between it
and the mosque of Sultan Ahmet I, there is an important building
which most tourists fail to notice, perhaps because it is dwarfed by
the imposing monuments on either side. This is the **Hamam of
Haseki Hurrem**, built by Süleyman the Magnificent in honour of his
wife, who is better known in the west as Roxelana. The *hamam*,
which was completed in 1556, is another master work of Sinan, and
is perhaps the finest public bath he built in his long and illustrious
career. The *hamam* has recently been restored, and it is hoped that in
the near future it will be reopened to the public as a museum.

The **Mosque of Sultan Ahmet I**, with its six stately minarets and its harmonious cascade of domes and semi-domes, is one of the most imposing monuments on the skyline of Stamboul. Better known to foreigners as the **Blue Mosque**, it was founded by Ahmet I and constructed by the architect Mehmet Ağa between 1609 and 1616. According to tradition, the young Sultan was so enthusiastic about his mosque that he often worked on the site himself in order to hurry along the construction, and at the dedication ceremony he wore a turban shaped like the Prophet's foot in token of his humility. But he was allowed little time to enjoy his new building, for he died the year after its opening.

Like all the imperial mosques in Istanbul, that of Ahmet I resembles Haghia Sophia both in plan and interior design. It is preceded by a colonnaded courtyard patterned on the now-vanished atrium of Haghia Sophia, and in the middle of the courtyard there is a handsome *şadirvan*, or 'ablution fountain', corresponding to the *phiale* of a Byzantine church. Within, the central dome of the mosque is supported by four huge free-standing columns – again as in Haghia Sophia – and the transition to the circular cornice is made through four pointed arches and four pendentives, while at the ends of the building there are semi-domes flanked by smaller satellite domes. But instead of tympanum walls on the other axis, as in Haghia Sophia, there are two more semi-domes, making it a quatrefoil design. This is a variation of the so-called 'centralized plan' characteristic of classical Ottoman mosques, in which the architect tries to create a contained centralized space unobscured by piers and colonnades, as far as is possible, so that from virtually everywhere in the mosque one can see the whole of the interior.

The furnishings of Sultan Ahmet Camii are typical of those in the other imperial mosques in Istanbul. The most important element in the interior of any mosque is the *mihrab*, a niche set into the centre of the front wall. The purpose of the *mihrab* is to indicate the *kible*, the direction of Mecca, towards which the faithful must face when they perform their prayers. To the right of the *mihrab* is the *mimber*, or pulpit, where the *imam* stands when he is delivering the noon prayer on Friday or on holy days. To the left of the *mihrab*, standing against the main pier on that side, is the *Kuran kursu*, where the *imam* sits when he is reading the Kuran to the congregation. Against the opposite pier on the right is the *müezzin mahfili*, a raised marble platform where the choir of *müezzin* kneel when they are chanting the responses to the prayers of the *imam*. And at the far corner of the left gallery is the *hünkâr mahfili*, the royal loge, where the Sultan and his party worshipped when they attended services.

The lower walls of the mosque and those of the gallery are revetted with original Iznik tiles of great beauty. The magnificent floral designs display the traditional lily, carnation, tulip and rose motifs, along with cypress and other trees, subtle greens and blues predominating. The painted arabesques in the dome and upper part of the walls are inferior modern imitations of the original decoration, and the mosque takes its popular name from their predominant colour, a vivid blue. The *mihrab* and *mimber* are of white marble and are part of the original decor of the mosque; they are particularly fine examples of the Ottoman stonework of that period. Notice also the superb bronzework of the great courtyard doors, and the woodwork, encrusted with ivory and mother-of-pearl, of the doors and window-shutters within the mosque. Under the royal loge the wooden ceiling is painted with floral and geometrical arabesques in rich and gorgeous colours, one of the few surviving examples of that exquisite early style.

The square in front of the Blue Mosque is situated on the site of the ancient Hippodrome, and the street which runs around it follows the course of the original chariot track. The history of the Hippodrome goes back to the very early years of the city. Its construction was begun by Septimius Severus in AD 203, and it was later rebuilt and considerably enlarged by Constantine the Great; according to one estimate it could seat one hundred thousand spectators. During the early centuries of the Byzantine Empire the Hippodrome was the centre of the turbulent and often violent public life of Constantinople. Many of the great events in the history of Byzantium took place here, beginning with the inaugural rites of the city of New Rome on 11 May 330. Here were celebrated in Roman fashion the triumphs of victorious generals and emperors, and here too patriarchs and emperors were executed.

The principal sport in the Hippodrome was chariot-racing, while between events the crowd was entertained with music, dancing and various circus acts. (Justinian's wife, the Empress Theodora, was the daughter of a bear-keeper in the Hippodrome, and she began her notorious career as a dancer there.) The mob in the Hippodrome was divided along social, economic and political lines into four factions – the Whites, Reds, Blues and Greens – with the latter two achieving dominance early on and absorbing the others. It was a dispute between the Blues and Greens which led to the Nika Revolt in 532, with both factions eventually joining together and turning on the Emperor. The revolt was finally put down when Belisarius, Jus-

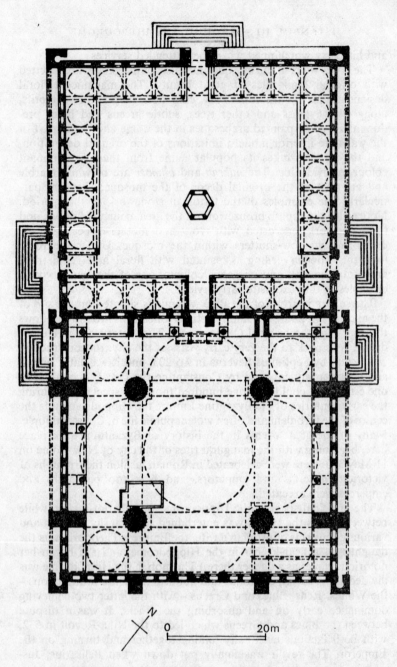

Sultan Ahmet Camii (Blue Mosque)

0   20m

tinian's general, trapped the insurgents in the Hippodrome and there slaughtered thirty thousand of them. There was long a legend in Constantinople that the partisans were buried in a mass grave in the arena, and that their ghosts haunted the site.

The Hippodrome, like so many other monuments in Constantinople, was pillaged and destroyed in the Latin occupation of 1204–61. At the time of the Turkish Conquest it was in ruins, and then it was demolished completely between 1609 and 1616, when it was used as a quarry for the construction of Sultan Ahmet's mosque. The site of the arena then became a public square, the **At Meydaní**, or **Square of Horses**, a name stemming from the fact that it was used as a *cirit* (polo) field by the palace pages. Today little remains of this historic structure except its foundations and three ancient monuments standing along the *spina*, the central axis of the arena.

The most prominent of the ancient monuments on the *spina* is the **Egyptian Obelisk**. This was originally due to the Pharaoh Thutmose III (1549–03 BC), who erected it opposite Thebes in upper Egypt. What one sees here is only the top third of the original obelisk; it was brought to Constantinople early in the fourth century and erected on its present site in 390 by Theodosius the Great. The obelisk is mounted on four brazen blocks which rest on a marble basis decorated with low reliefs. These represent the Emperor Theodosius and his family in the Kathisma, the royal enclosure: on the south side he is watching the races; on the east he is crowning the winner with a laurel wreath; on the north he is supervising the erection of the obelisk; and on the west he is receiving homage from vanquished enemies. Inscriptions in Greek and Latin on the base praise Theodosius and his prefect Proclus for erecting the obelisk; the Latin inscription says that thirty days were required to do this, while that in Greek says that it took thirty-two.

Beyond the obelisk stands the **Serpentine Column**, in the form of three intertwined bronze serpents. This once formed the base of a trophy which stood in the Temple of Apollo at Delphi, presented as a token of thanksgiving by the thirty-one cities that fought together in the Greek victory over the Persians at the battle of Plataea in 479 BC. The column was brought from Delphi to Constantinople by Constantine the Great and later erected in the Hippodrome. The three serpent heads were broken off and lost at various times after the Conquest, although one of them has since been rediscovered and is now on display in the Archaeological Museum.

The third monument on the *spina* is the roughly-built pillar of squared stones that stands at the southern end of the Hippodrome.

It is sometimes called the **Column of Constantine Porphyrogenitus**, but only because an inscription on its base records that it was repaired and sheathed in bronze by that emperor in the tenth century. It is quite possible that its erection dates back to the reign of Constantine the Great, and that it was one of the monuments that he built on the *spina* at the time when he reconstructed the Hippodrome. One of the surviving mosaic pavements from the Great Palace seems to show that this column formed the turning-point of the chariot-track at the southern end of the arena.

Much of the west side of the At Meydaní is occupied by the remains of a vast Ottoman palace, some of which is concealed from view by a nineteenth-century building on the street front. This is the once-famous **Palace of Ibrahim Pasha**, the grandest private residence ever erected in the Ottoman Empire. Its founder, Ibrahim Pasha, was a Greek convert to Islam who became a favourite of Süleyman the Magnificent and afterwards served as the Sultan's Grand Vezir. Later in Süleyman's reign his wife Roxelana persuaded him that Ibrahim Pasha was becoming too powerful. That year, 1536, after an intimate dinner in Süleyman's private chambers, Ibrahim retired to an adjacent room and was murdered while he slept. His possessions were then confiscated by the State, including his palace on the Hippodrome. The great hall, which fronts on to the Hippodrome, seems to have been used for some time as a review pavilion, where the Sultan and his court could observe the public displays and festivals which were held in the At Meydaní. The most noteworthy of these was the fabulous circumcision feast of Prince Mehmet, son of Murat III, which went on for forty (some say fifty-two) days and nights in the summer of 1583. Ibrahim Pasha's palace is now being restored and will be reopened some years hence as a museum.

If you take the street which leads off the Hippodrome to the west and around behind Ibrahim Pasha's palace you arrive at a large open space, on one side of which there is a small building. This is the entrance to another of the city's ancient underground cisterns, known as **Binbirdirek Sarnící**, the **Cistern of a Thousand-and-One Columns**. Binbirdirek is the second largest structure of its type in the city, and although it is only about one-third the area of the Basilica Cistern it actually seems far more extensive. For, unlike the Basilica, Binbirdirek is dry and one can walk about among its colonnade of 224 columns and appreciate how vast it really is. It is thought that this cistern was originally built during the reign of Constantine the Great, although some of the structure, at least, seems to be from the fifth or sixth century.

Retracing your steps, take the street which leads off from the south end of the Hippodrome and round behind the Blue Mosque. This brings you to the so-called **Mosaic Museum**, in the garden of which there are strewn columns, capitals, sarcophagi and other fragments of ancient structures. Together with the mosaic pavements on exhibit inside the museum, these were unearthed in excavations which began in 1935. They were once part of the Great Palace of Byzantium, whose buildings and gardens covered the whole slope leading down from the summit of the First Hill to the Marmara. After passing through the gate you find yourself in a quaint little alley with an arcade of arched booths on either side. This is part of **Kabasakal Sokaği**, the **Street of the Bushy Beard**, which was built as part of the *külliye* of Sultan Ahmet Camii. Some of the booths – once shops whose rents went towards the upkeep of the rest of the foundation – are now used to exhibit panels of mosaic pavement unearthed in the surrounding area. At the end of the alley you descend into a shed that has been erected over a large area of pavement which is still *in situ*. This is the north-east corner of a pavilion of the Great Palace, the **Mosaic Peristyle**. The mosaics here have been dated to the second quarter of the sixth century, that is, in the reign of Justinian the Great. It is quite probable that the mosaic decoration here was done after the Nika Revolt of 532, when Justinian rebuilt and enlarged the Great Palace.

Returning once again to the Hippodrome, you now take the street which leads off towards the Marmara from its south-western corner. Follow this street as it turns right and winds downhill till you approach **Sokollu Mehmet Pasha Camii**, one of the finest of Sinan's smaller mosques. It was built in 1571–2 for Esmahan Sultan, daughter of Selim the Sot and wife of Sokollu Mehmet Pasha, after whom the mosque is generally named. Sokollu Mehmet was one of the most outstanding Grand Vezirs in the history of the Ottoman Empire. Born in Bosnia as the son of an Orthodox priest, he was taken up in the *devşirme*, or levy of Christian youths, and educated at the Palace School in Topkapí Sarayí. His outstanding genius brought him early preferment and he rose rapidly through the highest posts in the Ottoman Empire, finally becoming Grand Vezir in 1564 under Süleyman the Magnificent. He continued to hold that post under Süleyman's son and successor, Selim the Sot, and married the Sultan's daughter Esmahan, a dwarf. After Selim's death Sokollu continued as Grand Vezir under Murat III, until in 1579 he was killed in the Divan by a mad soldier from the frontier. The courtyard of the mosque is one of the most attractive in

Istanbul, with a portico bordering three sides and a handsome *şadirvan* in the centre. As in the case of many mosques, the chambers under the portico served as a *medrese*, or theological school, with each domed cell equipped with its own window, fireplace and wall recesses for the books and bedding of the students who lived there. Classes were held in the *dershane*, the large room over the staircase at the main entrance, and also in the mosque itself. In form the mosque is a hexagon inscribed in a rectangle, and the whole is covered by a dome, counterbalanced at the corners by four small semi-domes. Around three sides of the mosque there extends a low gallery supported on slender columns with Ottoman lozenge capitals. The polychrome of the arches, with voussoirs of alternate green and white marble, is characteristic of the classical period of Ottoman architecture. The mosque is particularly noted for its superb decoration of Iznik tiles, particularly those in the pendentives of the dome, the exquisite *mihrab* section of the east wall, and a frieze of floral designs under the galleries. Above the entrance portal there is a small specimen of the wonderful painted decoration of the period, with elaborate arabesque designs in rich and vivid colours. Also above the door, surrounded by a design in gold, is a fragment of black stone from the holy Kaaba in Mecca; other fragments can be seen in the *mihrab* and *mimber*, themselves fine works in carved marble and faience.

After leaving the mosque by the main gate in the courtyard, turn left and then left again, and continue generally south towards the Marmara. This is one of the most picturesque neighbourhoods in the city: the winding cobbled lanes are lined with venerable wooden houses of the last century and even earlier, a scene reminiscent of an older and more serene Stamboul. Looking back uphill, you can now see the massive substructure of the *sphendone*, the curved southern end of the Hippodrome, as it marches in a great circular arc across the Marmara slope of the First Hill.

Finally you come to SS **Sergius and Bacchus**, one of the most beautiful and historic of the surviving Byzantine churches in the city. Known locally as Küçük Aya Sofya Camii, the church was begun by Justinian in 527, the first year of his reign, and was dedicated to the patron saints of Christians in the Roman army, two centurions who had been martyred for their faith. Justinian's devotion to these saints was due to his belief that they had saved his life some years before he ascended the throne, in the reign of Anastasius. It seems that Justinian had been accused of plotting against the Emperor and was under sentence of death, but Sergius and Bacchus appeared in a dream to Anastasius and interceded for him. As soon as Justinian himself became Emperor he expressed his gratitude to the saints by dedicating to them this church, the first of many with which he adorned the city.

Its plan is a complicated one: an irregular octagon inscribed somewhat off-axis in a very irregular rectangle. The octagon has eight polygonal piers between which are pairs of columns, alternately of verd antique and red marble both above and below; these are arranged straight on the axes but curved out into the exedrae at each corner so as to create a colourful and harmonious arcade on two levels. The space between the colonnade and the exterior walls of the rectangle becomes an ambulatory below and a gallery above. The capitals and the classic entablature are exquisite examples of the elaborately carved and deeply undercut style of the sixth century; on a few of the capitals on the ground floor one can make out the monograms of Justinian and Theodora. The frieze consists of a long and finely-carved inscription honouring Justinian, Theodora and St Sergius, though for some odd reason St Bacchus is not mentioned.

If you now leave the church courtyard by its southern gate and once outside turn right and then left you will find a winding lane which passes under the railway line and out on to the Marmara shore. Here turn left and follow the ancient Byzantine sea-walls towards Saray Point.

These sea-walls were originally constructed by Constantine the Great, and when the Theodosian walls were built in the following century the Marmara sea-walls were extended to meet them. During the second quarter of the ninth century the Marmara walls were re-built by the Emperor Theophilus, who sought to strengthen the city's defences against the Arabs. Although much of the fortifications along the Marmara has been destroyed in recent years what remains is grand and impressive, particularly the walls and towers between SS Sergius and Bacchus and Saray Point.

About three hundred metres beyond SS Sergius and Bacchus is the ruined façade of a palatial building which forms part of the sea-wall there. This is part of **Bucoleon**, the magnificent sea-pavilion of the Great Palace of Byzantium, and now all that remains of that fabled pleasure-dome. The Great Palace was first built by Constantine when he established his new capital here. The palace was largely destroyed during the Nika Revolt, but was soon after rebuilt and enlarged by Justinian, and the surviving façade of Bucoleon appears to date from his reign. Later emperors restored and extended the palace and adorned it with works of art, luxurious furnishings and ingenious mechanical inventions. The most famous of these was the fabulous golden tree with its mechanical song-birds, of which medieval travellers have left awed descriptions, and which in Yeats's 'Sailing to Byzantium' becomes a symbol of that lost empire.

Bucoleon and the other pavilions of the Great Palace were wrecked during the Latin occupation and never rebuilt. After the restoration of the Empire in 1261 the emperors took up residence in the newer Palace of Blachernae, just inside the Theodosian walls and above the Golden Horn, and that became the principal imperial residence during the last two centuries of Byzantium. The Great Palace decayed even further, and by the time of the Turkish Conquest it was completely in ruins. Shortly after he entered the city Mehmet the Conqueror walked through the halls of Bucoleon and was so saddened he recited a melancholy distich by the Persian poet Saadi:

The spider is the curtain-holder in the Palace of the Caesars
The owl hoots its night-call on the Towers of Aphrasiab.

CHAPTER FOUR

Istanbul IV: Central Stamboul

᭡

The Mosque of Firuz Ağa – The Palace of Antiochus – The Tomb of Mahmut II – The Köprülü Complex – The Column of Constantine – The Mosque of Atik Ali Pasha – The Complex of Koca Sinan Pasha – The Complex of Çorlulu Ali Pasha – The Mosque of Kara Mustafa Pasha – The Covered Bazaar – The Süleymaniye

Divan Yolu, the avenue which runs from the summit of the First Hill to that of the Third, follows almost exactly the course of the ancient Mese, the main thoroughfare of Byzantine Constantinople. This continued to be the main road of the city in Ottoman times, for it led directly from Topkapí Sarayí to Beyazit Meydaní, the second of Stamboul's great squares. Consequently, Divan Yolu is lined with monuments of the imperial Ottoman centuries, as well as with some ruined remnants from the days of Byzantium.

Walking down Divan Yolu you pass on the left a small but elegant mosque, **Firuz Ağa Camii**. This was built in 1491 for Firuz Ağa, Chief Treasurer in the reign of Beyazit II. This is one of the very few examples in Istanbul of the so-called 'pre-classical' mosques – that is, those built before 1500. The founder is buried under a marble sarcophagus beside his mosque.

Just beyond the mosque is the site of an archaeological excavation made some years ago. The ruins have been identified as being mostly the remains of the **Palace of Antiochus**, a Roman nobleman of the fifth century. Two centuries later the palace was converted into a martyrium for the body of St Euphemia of Chalcedon, a virgin martyred for her faith in 303. St Euphemia's body is now preserved in the Greek Orthodox Patriarchal church of St George.

About two hundred metres farther along on the right you pass the large **Türbe of Sultan Mahmut II**, who ruled from 1803 till 1839. Mahmut spent the latter years of his reign, after the dissolution of the Janissaries in 1826, trying to reform the institutions of the Ottoman State and to modernize them along Western lines. But the Empire had declined so far that his reforms were too little and too late to

57

save it from its eventual destruction in the following century.

A short way past the *türbe* on the left is a handsome **library**. This is one of the buildings of a *külliye* founded in 1659–60 by two members of the renowned Köprülü family, Mehmet Pasha and his son, Fazil Ahmet Pasha. The Köprülüs are generally considered to have been the most distinguished family in the history of the Ottoman Empire, with five of them serving as Grand Vezir in the late seventeenth and early eighteenth centuries. The library houses an important collection of books and state papers which belonged to the Köprülüs. One block beyond the library and on the same side of the street are two other institutions of the Köprülü *külliye*, the mosque and the family graveyard. Among those buried there are the two founders of the *külliye*, Mehmet the Cruel and Ahmet the Statist.

Directly across the street from the Köprülü mosque is one of the most famous public baths in Istanbul, the **Çemberlitaş Hamamí**. Founded some time before her death in 1583 by the Valide Sultan Nur Banu, wife of Selim the Sot and mother of Murat III, it was originally a double bath, but today only the men's section survives. Although the exterior is shabby and obscured by a modern façade, you discover once inside that this is one of the most beautiful Turkish baths in existence.

Just beyond the *hamam* you come to one of the most historic monuments in the city, the **Column of Constantine**. This is known locally as Çemberlitaş, the Hooped Column, because of the iron bands which hold together the six porphyry drums of which it is principally made. In English it is usually called the Burnt Column, because of its black scars left by the great fire which destroyed the surrounding neighbourhood in 1779. The column marks the centre of what was once the Forum of Constantine the Great, and was erected by him to commemorate the dedication of the city as capital of the Roman Empire on 11 May 330. At the top of the column there was originally a statue of Constantine in the guise of Apollo, but this was toppled during a hurricane in 1106.

Across the street from Çemberlitaş stands a handsome old mosque, **Atik Ali Pasha Camii**. This was built in 1496 for Atik Ali Pasha, a white eunuch who became Grand Vezir in the reign of Beyazit II.

Continuing along the thoroughfare, which now changes its name to Yeniçeriler Caddesi, the Avenue of the Janissaries, you pass on the right the **Külliye of Koca Sinan Pasha**. This complex, which is enclosed by a picturesque marble wall with iron grilles, consists of a *medrese*, the handsome *türbe* of the founder, and a *sebil*, a fountain for distributing free water to passers-by. Koca Sinan, who died in

1595, was Grand Vezir under Murat III and Mehmet III and is renowned in Turkish history as the conqueror of the Yemen.

Just beyond Sinan Pasha's *külliye* you pass that of **Çorlulu Ali Pasha**. This Ali Pasha was Grand Vezir in the reign of Ahmet III, the Tulip King, on whose orders he was beheaded in 1711 while on campaign in the Aegean. Ali Pasha's head was afterwards brought back to Istanbul and buried in the cemetery of his *külliye*, which had been completed three years before; it consists merely of a *mescit*, or small mosque, and a *medrese*, now used as a residence for university students.

Just across the avenue from Ali Pasha's *külliye* is that of **Kara Mustafa Pasha of Merzifon**. This little complex consists of a mosque, a *sebil*, and a cemetery – in which the head of its founder is buried. Kara Mustafa was Grand Vezir in the reign of Mehmet IV; he was beheaded by the Sultan for his failure to capture Vienna in the siege of 1683, an event which is generally taken to be a turning-point in Ottoman military history. The *külliye* was founded by Kara Mustafa in 1669 and was finally completed by his son in 1690. Today the *medrese* serves as a library and research institute commemorating the famous Turkish poet Yahya Kemal (1884–1958), whom one admirer has termed the G. K. Chesterton of Turkish letters.

About a hundred metres or so farther on is **Beyazit Meydaní**, the crowded and chaotic centre of modern Stamboul. This has been one of the main squares of the city since the early years of Constantinople. In Byzantium it was known as the Forum of Theodosius I, after the emperor who in 393 constructed the square and the triumphal arch which bore his name. Colossal fragments of the Arch of Theodosius have been unearthed in recent years; they now are piled beside the avenue which leads off from the far end of the square.

Beyazit Meydaní takes its name from the Beyazidiye, the imperial mosque complex of Sultan Beyazit II, whose various pious foundations are to be found around the northern side of the square. Founded by the son and successor of Mehmet the Conqueror and constructed between 1501 and 1506, the complex consists of the imperial mosque itself, plus a *medrese*, an *imaret*, or public kitchen, a *mektep*, or a primary school, a *hamam*, a market, and several mausolea. Most of these institutions have been restored in recent years and are now functioning once again, mostly as libraries and research institutes.

The **Mosque of Beyazit II** marks the beginning of classical Ottoman architecture, which for the next two hundred years was to give rise to some of the finest buildings in the Empire. The mosque is preceded by a colonnaded inner courtyard which is perhaps the most beautiful in Istanbul, with its noble portico of ancient columns and its handsome *şadirvan*. The mosque itself is a much smaller and greatly simplified version of Haghia Sophia. The great central dome and the semi-domes along the main axis of the building create a kind of nave, which is flanked by the two side aisles. But here, unlike Haghia Sophia, there are no galleries over the aisles; these open wide into the nave, being separated from it only by a pair of piers on either side and a single column between them, a step towards the realization of the 'centralized plan' characteristic of classical Ottoman architecture.

The founder, Sultan Beyazit II, lies buried in a splendid *türbe* that stands in the garden behind his mosque. The first sultan to ascend to the throne in Istanbul, Beyazit reigned there for thirty-six years and died in 1512 at the age of sixty-six. He was quite different in character and disposition from his warrior father, the Conqueror, and during his long reign the Ottoman Empire enjoyed a welcome period of prosperity and peace. In his time he was known to his people as Sufi, or 'the Mystic'.

The north-east exit from the outer courtyard of the Beyazidiye is called the **Gate of the Spoonmakers**, after the guild which once had its workshops there. This leads into the **Sahaflar Çarşísí**, the **Market of the Booksellers**. This is one of the most picturesque byways in the city, a vine-shaded, sun-dappled courtyard lined with old-fashioned bookshops. The Sahaflar is one of the most ancient markets in the city, occupying the site of the main book and paper market of Byzantine Constantinople.

You leave the Sahaflar Çarşísí through the **Gate of the Engravers**, named for the artisans who had their shops here before the market was taken over by the booksellers at the beginning of the eighteenth century. You then turn right and a few steps farther on you find yourself at one of the entrances to the **Kapalí Çarşí**, the **Covered Bazaar**.

The Kapalí Çarşí is one of the largest and most fascinating marketplaces in the world. It is a city in itself, with thousands of shops, stalls, ateliers and warehouses, along with half a dozen restaurants, scores of cafés and teahouses, two banks, a police station, a tomb, and an information centre for lost tourists. At first sight it would seem inevitable that a newcomer must get lost in this enormous labyrinth. But after wandering through the Kapalí Çarşí for a while you will find that it is really a well-planned town, with streets and squares laid out in a generally regular grid pattern. Shops selling the same kind of goods tend to be congregated on the same streets, and indeed the streets themselves are named after the guilds which for centuries have carried on their activities there. Some of these names, such as the Street of the Turban Makers, commemorate long-vanished trades and remind one that much of the oriental atmosphere of the Covered Bazaar has vanished in recent decades. Nevertheless it still retains its fascination for both tourists and locals, who flock there to window-shop and bargain over cups of coffee and glasses of tea every day of the week except Sunday.

The Kapalí Çarşí was established on its present site by Sultan Mehmet II shortly after the Conquest, and the original market seems to have occupied much the same area that it does today. Although it has been destroyed several times by fires, the most recent in 1954, the Kapalí Çarşí is essentially the same in structure and appearance as it was when it was first built five centuries ago. The great antiquity of the market is especially evident in the **Old Bedesten**, the domed hall at the centre of the Bazaar. This is one of the original structures remaining from the time of the Conqueror; then, as now, it was used to house precious goods, for it can be securely locked and guarded at night. Some of the most interesting and valuable objects in the Bazaar are sold here, including all kinds of brass and copper and antiques of every description, many of them authentic.

The Bedesten has four gates, one in the centre of each wall, and each of these is named after one of the guilds which had their shops in the streets immediately outside. One of these is the **Gate of the Goldsmiths**, which leads to a glittering street lined with shops selling the finest gold and silver jewellery in the Bazaar. The streets around the Bedesten are lined with some of the best shops in the Bazaar, particularly the colonnaded street of the rug-merchants and those of the jewellers and antique dealers.

There are also a number of interesting old *hans* in the Bazaar which one should not fail to visit. The oldest is the **Sandal Bedesten**, a huge domed hall near that gate of the Bazaar which leads to Nuruosmaniye Camii. The hall was built early in the sixteenth century, when the great increase in trade and commerce during the reign of Beyazit II required an additional market and storehouse for valuables. The Sandal Bedesten is the scene of the bi-weekly rug-auction, one of the most interesting spectacles in the Bazaar. Nor should one miss seeing the **Zincirli Han**, which is almost hidden away off a little passage near one of the lower exits from the Bazaar. The courtyard of this lovely sixteenth-century *han* is surrounded by a double arcade whose walls are of fading pink and ochre, and fragments of ancient statuary are scattered here and there. The scene is exceptionally picturesque, and the shops around the arcade sell some of the finest antiques in the Bazaar.

After returning to Beyazit Square you may wish to walk to the grounds of Istanbul University and ascend the **Beyazit Tower**. This was built in 1828 by Mahmut II as a fire-observation tower, a function which it still performs. The way up is by a wooden staircase of 150 steps, which reaches to a height of 50 metres; the view from the observation deck is stupendous, with almost the whole of Istanbul and its surrounding waters spread out below.

The best way to leave the grounds of the University is by the gate to the west. Turn right on the street outside, and walk around the University grounds and past the buildings on its northern end, where you come to the **Süleymaniye**, the mosque and pious foundations of Sultan Süleyman the Magnificent.

The Süleymaniye is the most splendid of the imperial mosque complexes in the city. It is a fitting monument to its founder and a masterwork of one of the world's greatest architects, the extraordinary Sinan. The construction of the Süleymaniye began in 1550 and the mosque itself was completed in 1557, but it was some years later before all the buildings of the *külliye* were finished. The mosque itself is surrounded by a vast outer courtyard, with its auxiliary foundations lining the adjoining streets. In front of the mosque there is a porticoed inner courtyard of exceptional grandeur, with minarets rising from each of the four corners. According to tradition these four minarets symbolize the fact that Süleyman was the fourth sultan to reign in Istanbul, while the ten *şerife*, or *müezzin*'s balconies, denote that he was the tenth monarch of the imperial House of Osman.

The interior design of the mosque is yet another original variation on the basic plan of Haghia Sophia; that is, a central nave covered by a dome and extended on either end by semi-domes. The dome rests on a circular cornice which is carried on four great arches and pendentives, and these in turn are supported by four huge piers. On each side two enormous porphyry monoliths standing between the piers support the tympana of the transverse arches. The side aisles are separated from the nave only by the graceful arcade formed by the piers and columns; thus the whole interior of the mosque is visible as one vast and self-contained space, virtually uninterrupted by barriers.

The interior furnishings and decoration of the mosque are classi-

The Süleymaniye

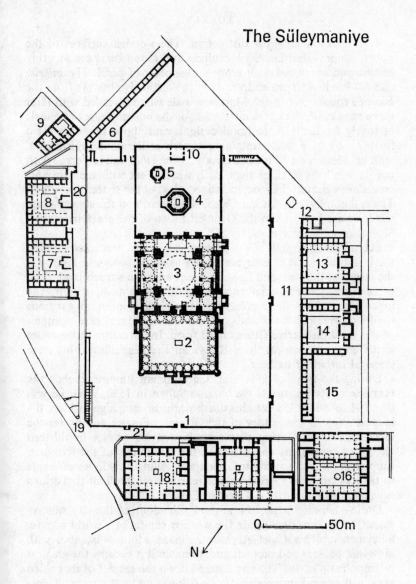

0 ⊢————————⊣ 50m

N

1 Entrance
2 Inner Courtyard
3 Mosque
4 Tomb of Süleyman
5 Tomb of Roxelana
6 Dar-ul-Hadis
7 Salis Medrese
8 Rabi Medrese

9   Hamam
10 Dar-ül Kura
11 Tiryaki Carsísí
12 Mektep
13 Evvel Medrese
14 Sani Medrese
15 Tip Medrese
16 Dar-üs Sifa

17 Imaret (museum)
18 Caravansarai
19 Tomb of Sinan
20 Avenue of Sinan the Architect
21 Sifahane Sokagi

cally simple and of great distinction. The wooden surfaces of the doors, window shutters, book cabinets and *Kuran kursu* are superbly carved and encrusted with ivory and mother-of-pearl. The *mihrab* and *hünkâr mahfili* are sculptured in the distinctive marble from the Isle of Proconnesus in the Marmara, pale white threaded with faint wavy streaks of black. On either side of the *mihrab* there are panels of lovely Iznik tiles with floral designs, and above them are set a further pair of panels containing superb calligraphic inscriptions, with gold letters on a blue background. The *kíble* wall is pierced with twenty windows in three tiers, each window set with the rare and exceedingly beautiful Ottoman stained glass of the sixteenth century. The calligraphy is by Hasan Çelebi Karahísarí and the stained-glass windows are by Ibrahim the Drunkard, two of the great artisans of Süleyman's golden age.

Behind the *kíble* wall of the mosque is a walled garden containing the beautiful **tombs of Süleyman and Roxelana**. Süleyman's *türbe* is the larger of the two, and its walls are revetted in superb Iznik tiles, twice as many in this small room as in the whole mosque itself. The inner dome of the *türbe* preserves its original painting in gorgeous shades of wine-red, black and gold, another of the very rare examples of this most distinctive Ottoman art form. In the centre of the room is the enormous cenotaph of Süleyman the Magnificent, his huge imperial turban at its head.

During the reign of Süleyman the Ottoman Empire reached the pinnacle of its greatness. He became Sultan in 1520, when he was twenty-five, and ruled until his death while on campaign in 1566, the longest reign in the history of the Ottoman Empire and by far the most illustrious. During that time he led his armies in thirteen victorious campaigns and extended the dominions of the Ottoman Empire as far as Baghdad and Budapest, failing only in his attempts to take Vienna and Corfu, which thereafter set the limit to Turkish expansion to the north and west in Europe.

During his reign, too, the ancient splendour of the city was restored, to become once again the wealthy capital of a world empire. Süleyman and his Chief Architect, Sinan, adorned Istanbul with mosques, palaces and pious foundations until it became the greatest metropolis on earth. The city entered upon the second of its golden ages, a thousand years after its first flowering in the reign of Justinian.

Galata Bridge

Beside the Sultan lies his favourite daughter, Mihrimah, the most famous princess in Ottoman history. Also buried in this *türbe* are two later sultans, Süleyman II and Ahmet II. These two insignificant brothers spent most of their lives locked up in the infamous Kafes, emerging to rule briefly and ineffectually at the end of their days, after which they were stuffed away in the tomb of their great ancestor because they had no *türbe* of their own.

Roxelana's *türbe* is smaller and simpler than Süleyman's, but it is decorated with Iznik tiles even finer than his. Here, too, one inevitably reflects upon the person who is buried here, one of the most powerful and sinister women in the history of the Saray. Süleyman fell in love with Roxelana in the early years of his reign and soon made her his legal wife, putting aside the other women in the Harem. At that time the heir-apparent was Prince Mustafa, Süleyman's eldest son. Mustafa was a highly intelligent and vigorous prince and promised to be a worthy successor to his father. But Roxelana and her son-in-law, the Grand Vezir Rüstem Pasha, persuaded Süleyman that Mustafa was plotting to usurp the throne. Süleyman was eventually swayed by their arguments and finally, in the autumn of 1553, he had Mustafa strangled by his mutes. Roxelana's own son, Selim the Sot, then succeeded to the throne after the death of Süleyman. Historians consider this to be the turning-point in the history of the Ottomans, for with the alcoholic reign of Selim II began the long and almost uninterrupted decline of the Empire.

The pious foundations of the Süleymaniye stand on the streets which border the outer courtyard of the mosque. Some of the most interesting of these are on the street which runs past the entrance to the courtyard. This is called **Tiryaki Çarşísí**, the **Market of the Addicts**. This curious name comes from the fact that the teahouses along the street were once frequented by the members of the Ulema, the religious hierarchy of Islam, who liked a puff of hashish or opium to further the enjoyment of their *keyíf*, or 'contemplative day-dream'.

Turning left on to Tiryaki Çarşísí, you walk to the far end of the arcade. There you find the former **mektep**, where the children of the Süleymaniye staff received their primary education. One-roomed schoolhouses such as this were in use until the end of the last century and were one of the most characteristic elements in the life of

---

Haghia Sophia, the former Church of the Divine Wisdom.

Topkapí Sarayí, the great palace of the Ottoman Sultans.

Ottoman Stamboul. The *mektep* here has been very well restored and now serves as a children's library.

As you walk back along Tiryaki Çarşísí you come to the Evvel and Sani *medreses*, two of the four schools of Islamic law which were part of the *külliye*. These now house the renowned **Süleymaniye Library**, one of the most important collections of ancient Islamic books and manuscripts in the city.

Just beyond the law schools you pass the former **Tip Medresesi**, the **Medical College**, which was once the finest institution of its kind in the Ottoman Empire. All that remains of the *medrese* today is the row of chambers along the street-front; the other three sides of the original structure have long since vanished and have now been replaced by a modern building. This, too, is serving the people of Istanbul much as it did in the past, for it now houses a modern maternity clinic.

At the end of Tiryaki Çarşísí stands what was once the *daruşşifa*, or hospital. The **Süleymaniye Hospital** had a separate ward for the care of mental patients, and early travellers to Istanbul commented favourably on the humane treatment given there. As Evliya Efendi describes the care given to the madmen of his day: 'They have excellent food twice a day; even pheasants, partridges and other birds are supplied. There are musicians and singers who are employed to amuse the sick and insane and thus to cure their madness.'

You now turn right on to Şifahane Sokağí, which runs along the western end of the mosque courtyard. The first building you come to is the former *imaret*, or soup kitchen, which now houses the **Museum of Turkish and Islamic Art**. Among the exhibits there are: Selcuk and early Ottoman pottery and glass; medieval Turkish carpets, metalwork and gold and silver jewellery, inlaid Kuran covers, and old albums with beautiful calligraphy and miniatures. The courtyard of the *imaret* is most attractive, with a lovely marble fountain in its centre surrounded by plane trees and palms.

Next to the *imaret* stands the former *tabhane*, or caravansarai. It is built to the same general plan as are the other institutions of the *külliye*; that is, an open square with an arcade of chambers opening on to an interior courtyard. In its time it included a kitchen, bakery, olive-press, refectory, dormitories for travellers, stables for their horses and camels, and storage rooms for their belongings. According to Islamic tradition, all accredited travellers were given free food and shelter for three days at this and other hostels upon their arrival in Istanbul.

The remaining buildings of the Süleymaniye *külliye* stand on

Mimar Sinan Caddesi, the **Avenue of Sinan the Architect**, which borders the mosque courtyard to the north. One side of this street consists of an arcade of shops built into the vaulted substructure of the courtyard. They were also part of the *külliye* and their rents were used to pay for the upkeep of the mosque and its dependencies. At the far end of the street are the Salis and Rabi *medreses*, the other pair of the four schools of Islamic law. These are among the most attractive and original structures in Istanbul, but, unfortunately, they are not presently open to the public. Beyond them, at the corner, is the former *hamam*, now dilapidated and used as a storehouse. And above, at the corner of the mosque courtyard, stands the *dar-ul hadis*, the school of sacred tradition, yet another of the educational institutions of the Süleymaniye *külliye*.

This, then, is the great mosque complex of Süleyman the Magnificent. Surely there can be in the world few, if any, civic centres to compare with it in extent, in grandeur of conception, in the ingenuity of its design, or in the harmony of its parts.

Before leaving the Süleymaniye, pause for a moment at the tomb of its architect, which stands in a little triangular graveyard garden at the corner of Şifahane Sokağí and Mimar Sinan Caddesi. Sinan lived on this site for many years and when he died he was buried in his garden, in a tomb which he had designed and built himself. On the wall of the *türbe* garden there is a long inscription written by Sinan's friend, the poet Mustafa Sa'i, which commemorates this Renaissance man. Sinan was born of Greek parents in the central Anatolian region of Karamania in about 1491. As a youth he was caught up in the *devşirme*, the levy of Christian youths for the Sultan's service, whereupon he became a Moslem and was sent to one of the palace schools in Istanbul. He was assigned to the Janissaries as a military engineer and rose rapidly through the ranks, until in 1538 he became Chief of the Imperial Architects. During the course of the next half-century he was to adorn the Ottoman Empire with more than three hundred structures of every conceivable kind, of which eighty-four still remain standing in Istanbul alone. Sinan died in 1588 at the age of ninety-seven – one hundred, according to the Moslem calendar – still building until the very last day of his life. He was the architect of Süleyman's golden age, and his memory will endure as long as do the magnificent buildings with which he adorned Istanbul and the other cities of what was once the Ottoman Empire.

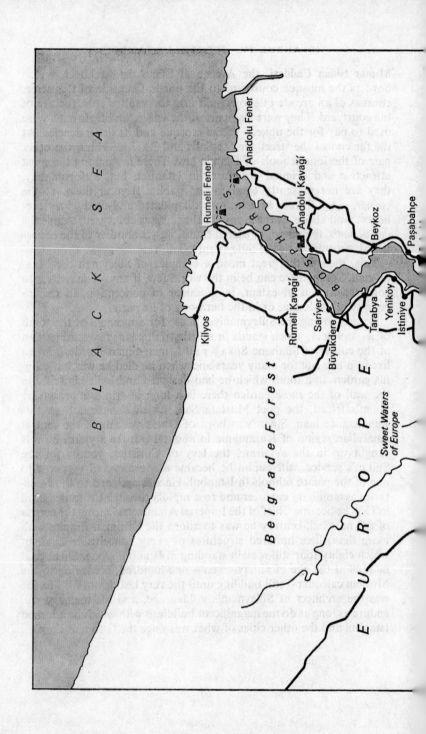

BLACK SEA

Rumeli Fener

Anadolu Fener

Anadolu Kavağı

Beykoz

Paşabahçe

Rumeli Kavağı

Sarıyer

Büyükdere

Tarabya

Yeniköy

İstiniye

Kilyos

Belgrade Forest

Sweet Waters of Europe

EUROPE

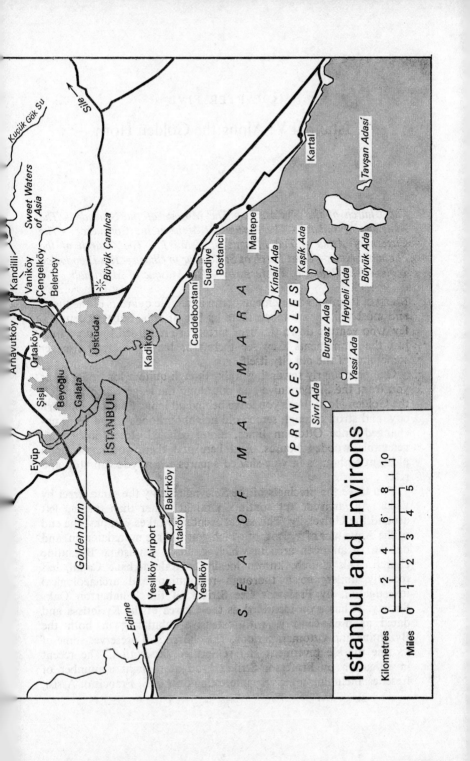

Istanbul and Environs

Kilometres
0 | 2 | 4 | 6 | 8 | 10
Miles
0 | 1 | 2 | 3 | 4 | 5

Küçük Gök Su

Şile

Sweet Waters
of Asia

Kandilli
Vaniköy
Çengelköy
Belerbey

Büyük Çamlıca

Kartal

Tavşan Adası

Arnavutköy

Ortaköy

Üsküdar

Maltepe

Suadiye
Bostanci

Caddebostani

Kaşık Ada

Kınalı Ada

Şişli

Beyoğlu

Galata

Kadiköy

PRINCES' ISLES

Burgaz Ada

Heybeli Ada

Büyük Ada

Eyüp

İSTANBUL

Sivri Ada

Yassi Ada

S E A   O F   M A R M A R A

Golden Horn

Bakirköy

Ataköy

Yesilköy Airport

Yesilköy

Edirne

CHAPTER FIVE

Istanbul V: Along the Golden Horn

✣

The Church of the Kyriotissa – The Mosque of the Şehzade – The Aqueduct of Valens – The Mosque of Mehmet the Conqueror – The Cistern of Aspar – The Mosque of Selim I – The Church of the Pammakaristos – The Church of St Saviour in Chora – The Theodosian Walls – The Palace of Tekfursaray – The Mosque of Mihrimah

Many of Istanbul's monuments stand in remote quarters of the town, and most visitors are taken there by bus or taxi. But the fortunate few who venture down the back streets are rewarded by more than just the monuments they see there, for they inevitably discover something of the old city itself.

One particularly rewarding walk, though quite a long one, takes you from the Süleymaniye and out along the ridge which parallels the Golden Horn. Here you leave behind all indications of a modern city, and stroll through serene old neighbourhoods which seem unchanged since Ottoman times, along cobbled streets lined with venerable wooden houses. And here and there you come upon pleasant teahouses in vine-shaded squares where you can stop and rest.

You leave the precincts of the Süleymaniye by the same street by which you arrived, but continue straight rather than turning left around the University. This street eventually takes you past the end of the Aqueduct of Valens, of which you will see more later on, and out on to an open area in which stands a handsome Byzantine church. This church, known locally as **Kalenderhane Camii**, has recently undergone a thorough restoration and archaeological investigation by Professor Lee Striker of the Dumbarton Oaks Society. It has been identified as the **Church of the Kyriotissa** and dated as ninth-century, with extensive rebuilding in both the Byzantine and Ottoman periods. The church still preserves some of its fine marble revetment and sculptured decoration. The recent investigation by Professor Striker brought to light a number of frescoes, including some very interesting ones of St Francis of Assisi,

70

apparently done only a few years after his death in 1226. These have been identified as works of the court-painter of King Louis of Jerusalem, and have been dated to the latter part of the Latin occupation of Constantinople (1204–61).

You now turn right on to Şehzadebaşí Caddesi. This avenue, which changes its name several times en route, follows the same course as did the north-west branch of the ancient Mese, the principal thoroughfare of Byzantine Constantinople. In the near distance can be seen the imposing edifice of **Şehzade Camii**, the **Mosque of the Prince**. This great mosque and its extensive pious foundations were built by Süleyman the Magnificent in memory of his favourite son, Prince Mehmet, who died in 1543 at the age of twenty-one. The architect was the great Sinan; he completed this immense project in 1548, his first imperial mosque on a truly monumental scale.

The mosque is preceded by a handsome courtyard surrounded on all four sides by a portico, with the usual *şadirvan* in the centre. The two minarets which rise from the corners of the *kíble* wall are probably the most beautiful in Istanbul; notice the elaborate geometrical sculpture in low relief, the intricate tracery of the *müezzin*'s balconies, and the occasional terracotta inlay. Altogether this is one of the very finest mosque exteriors ever created by Sinan.

The interior of the mosque is covered by a great dome, with pairs of semi-domes on both axes, Sinan's first attempt at creating a centralized interior. Except for the four piers which support the great dome there is not a single column within the mosque, nor are there galleries. The general effect of the interior is of an austere simplicity that is not unattractive.

Behind the mosque there is a walled garden with several very handsome and unusual *türbe*. Unfortunately these superb tombs are not open to the public, although one can obtain special permission to visit them by applying to the Antiquities Commission. The largest *türbe* is that of the Şehzade himself; it is adorned with the most beautiful Iznik tiles in existence.

If you leave the Şehzade courtyard by its eastern gate you will see immediately opposite a *medrese* with an exceptionally handsome *sebil* at the corner. This charming *külliye* was built in 1720 by Nevşehirli Ibrahim Pasha, Grand Vezir and son-in-law of Ahmet III. Ibrahim Pasha was executed by the Janissaries in 1730 at the time when they deposed the Sultan, thus bringing the gay Tulip Period to a sad end.

Continue walking along Şehzadebaşí Caddesi past Şehzade Camii, and just beyond the outer courtyard of the Şehzade complex

71

you will see a small mosque with a striking spiral minaret. This is **Burmalí** (Spiral) **Cami**, built about 1550 by Emin Nurettin Osman Efendi, Cadi (Chief Judge) of Egypt in the reign of Süleyman the Magnificent. The spiral minaret is the only one of its kind in Istanbul, and is a late survival of an older archITectual tradition, of which several examples are still extant in Anatolia.

You now come to Atatürk Bulvarí, the highway which begins at the Golden Horn and cuts straight across the spine of Stamboul to the Marmara. Off to the right you now see the **Valens Aqueduct** at its grandest, with its two tiers of arches striding majestically across the deep valley between the Third and Fourth Hills. This immense structure was built by the Emperor Valens about AD 375, and was designed to take water across this valley and ultimately to the *nymphaeum maximum*, the central cistern near the Forum of Theodosius. The aqueduct was kept in repair by both the Byzantine emperors and the Ottoman sultans and continued in use until the last century.

Just beneath the aqueduct, where it crosses Atatürk Bulvarí, there is a small *medrese* built in 1599 by Gazanfer Ağa. He was the last of the Chief White Eunuchs to dominate affairs in Topkapí Sarayí; after his time the Chief Black Eunuch became the dominant figure. The *medrese* now serves as the **Municipality Museum**, where are displayed various interesting oddments from old Ottoman Istanbul.

Continuing along and crossing Atatürk Bulvarí, you see on the left the archaeological site where a few years ago was unearthed the ancient **Church of St Polyeuctes**. This church was completed in 527 for the Princess Ancina Juliana; it was one of the largest and grandest churches in Constantinople, surpassed only by Haghia Sophia and the Church of the Holy Apostles, of which not a trace remains. The fragments of columns, capitals and carved entablature show that this must have been a very impressive edifice indeed.

Just beyond the archaeological site is the little *külliye* built in 1698 by **Amcazade Hüseyin Pasha**, Grand Vezir in the reign of Mustafa II. This is one of the most elaborate and picturesque of the smaller classical complexes, including a small mosque as well as a *medrese*, library, primary school, *şadirvan* and public fountain, plus a row of shops and two cemeteries. The founder, 'Hüseyin the Wise', was yet another of the Köprülü Grand Vezirs who served the Ottoman Empire so well.

Two blocks beyond this, to the left, is an ancient column standing in the centre of a small square. This is one of the two Roman commemorative columns still standing in the city; an inscription states that it was erected for the Emperor Marcian, who ruled from 450 till

457. The Turks call this monument **Kíz Taşí**, or the **Maidens' Column**, because of the reliefs of the two Winged Victories which appear on the pedestal.

Two blocks farther along on the left is another small *külliye* built at about the same time as that of Amcazade Hüseyin Pasha. This is the *medrese* founded in 1700 by Feyzullah Efendi, who was Şeyh-ul Islam, or head of the religious hierarchy, and one of the most enlightened scholars in Ottoman history. He went completely against the mystical, obscurantist tendency of Ottoman times and actually built an observatory at the top of the Galata Tower so he could see for himself what was going on in the heavens rather than reading the same nonsense everyone else did in the astrological treatises. His observatory was destroyed by the Ulema and he himself was publicly disgraced for his efforts. The present *medrese* now serves as the **People's Library of Istanbul**.

You are now opposite the enormous mosque complex of Sultan Mehmet the Conqueror, or Fatih, as he is known in Turkish. **Fatih Camii** was built by the Conqueror between 1463 and 1470 and was the most extensive and elaborate mosque complex ever founded in the Ottoman Empire. The original mosque was destroyed by earthquake in 1766; the present structure dates from 1771 and is of little architectural interest. Most of the other buildings of the complex date from Fatih's time; they include eight *medreses* and their annexes, as well as a hospice, public kitchen, caravansarai, primary school, library and *hamam*. The whole complex I find one of the grandest and most impressive monuments in Istanbul.

You leave the outer courtyard of Fatih Camii by the gate at the north-eastern corner; this leads into Daruşşafaka Caddesi, which in turn leads northwards towards the summit of the Fifth Hill. This avenue takes you through the lively district of **Çarşamba**, or 'Wednesday', so named for the boisterous street-market which throngs its streets every week on that day. This is a travelling street-market which sets up its stalls and barrows in various parts of the town on different days; thus there are neighbourhoods in Istanbul named after all the days of the week.

About four hundred metres along you turn right on to Yavuz Selim Caddesi, where you see looming ahead the imperial mosque complex of Sultan Selim I. As you approach the mosque you pass an immense open cistern, the largest of the three Roman reservoirs in the city. This is the **Cistern of Aspar**, named after a Gothic general put to death in 471 by the Emperor Leo I. The cistern has been dry since late Byzantine times and today is the site of a picturesque little village, the tops of whose houses barely reach up to the level of the surrounding streets. The Turks call this lovely place Çukurbostan, or the Sunken Garden.

You now enter the precincts of the **Mosque of Selim I**, which stands on a high terrace overlooking the middle reaches of the Golden Horn. The mosque was completed in 1522 by Süleyman the Magnificent and dedicated to his father, Selim I. The courtyard is one of the most attractive mosque enclosures in the city, with its superb colonnade and its *şadirvan* surrounded by slim cypresses. The interior of the mosque is severely simple in plan – just a square room surmounted by a dome – but it is impressive because of its size, its harmonious proportions, and its decoration of very beautiful Iznik tiles.

The **Türbe of Selim I** stands in the garden behind the mosque. Selim, son and successor of Beyazit II, was forty-two when he became Sultan and ruled for only eight years. During his brief reign he doubled the extent of the Ottoman Empire, conquering western Persia, Syria, Palestine, Arabia and Egypt. After his capture of Cairo in 1517 Selim took for himself the title of Caliph, and thenceforth the Ottoman sultans assumed the titular leadership of Islam. The Sultan was known to his people as Yavuz Selim, Selim the Grim, perhaps because he beheaded his Grand Vezirs at the rate of one a year. The last two years of his reign were spent preparing for a great campaign into Europe, which was cut short by his sudden death in 1520. For long afterwards a cynical Turkish proverb maintained that: 'Yavuz Selim died of an infected boil and thereby Hungary was spared.'

You should now retrace your steps and return to Daruşşafaka Caddesi, where you continue in the same direction as before. A short walk along this winding street, which changes its name several times en route, brings you to one of the most interesting Byzantine churches in the city. This is the former **Church of the Theotokos Pammakaristos**, known as the Mosque of the Conquest to commemorate the conquest of Georgia by Sultan Selim I.

The Pammakaristos was originally built in the twelfth century and a parecclesion, or funerary chapel, was added in the fourteenth century. The parecclesion has now been admirably restored and has revealed a series of mosaics second only to those in Kariye Camii, which you will see presently. The chapel was originally adorned throughout with mosaics, of which some thirty-five figures and one scene mosaic remain. In the dome Christ Pantocrator (the Almighty) is surrounded by Prophets, and in the apse Christ appears with the

Blessed Virgin, St John the Baptist and angels. The scene mosaic is that of the Baptism of Christ, and the remaining figures are saints of the Greek Orthodox Church. Like those in Kariye Camii, these mosaics date from the first half of the fourteenth century and belong to the last great renaissance of Byzantine art.

Before you leave the precincts of the Pammakaristos you might walk out on to the terrace behind the church, from where there is a sweeping view of the upper reaches of the Golden Horn. Just below you see the buildings and grounds of the **Greek Orthodox Patriarchate**, the residence of the Ecumenical Patriarch and the spiritual centre of the Greek Orthodox Church. Nearby is the ancient **Chapel of St Mary of the Mongols**, a thirteenth-century church which is the last Byzantine sanctuary still in the possession of the Greek Orthodox Patriarchate. The neighbourhood below is called the **'Fener'**, meaning 'lighthouse', and hidden away down its picturesque streets are dozens of little Greek churches, many of which were founded before the Conquest. Although most of the present structures date only from the eighteenth or nineteenth century they evoke something of the vanished past of Byzantium, with their gleaming oil-lamps and their sacred icons black with age, their dwindling but still faithful congregations worshipping there as they have for centuries past. Farther up the Golden Horn, near the Theodosian walls, is the venerable quarter of **Balat**. Here one finds many more of these old Greek churches as well as several Armenian sanctuaries of considerable antiquity. Here and there in the cobbled back streets of Balat one also comes upon a number of ancient synagogues, some of which go back to Byzantine times, and whose congregations still speak Ladino, the medieval language which the Sephardic Jews brought with them from Spain five centuries ago.

Leaving the Pammakaristos and returning to the avenue, here called Fethiye Caddesi, you continue in the same direction as before. The avenue soon changes its name again, to Draman Caddesi, and eventually brings you to the vicinity of **Kariye Camii**.

Kariye Camii, the former church of St Saviour in Chora ('in the country'), is, after Haghia Sophia, the second most important Byzantine monument in the city, and its art treasures surpass even those of the Great Church. In recent years a superb series of mosaics have been uncovered and restored by the Byzantine Institute of America, and today the church is a museum of Byzantine art at the culmination of its existence. Although the church in its first form was constructed in the eleventh century its present structure and its works of art date from the years 1315–21. At that time the church was completely rebuilt and redecorated by Theodore Metochites, Lord High Treasurer in the reign of Andronicus II Palaeologus.

The mosaics and frescoes in Kariye Camii are far and away the most important and extensive series of Byzantine art works in the city and among the most interesting in the world. The mosaics fall naturally by position and theme into six groups dealing with the life of Christ and the Blessed Virgin; these are found in the outer and inner narthex and in the nave. The frescoes are all in the parecclesion, the side chapel to the south of the church.

The first mosaic which you see on entering the church is that of **Christ Pantocrator**, which is in the lunette over the door between the outer and inner narthex. This is one of six dedicatory or devotional panels which form the first iconographic series. The second mosaic in this group is the **Virgin with Angels**, which is opposite the above, over the entrance door to the church. The third, over the door leading from the inner narthex to the nave, is a portrait of **Theodore Metochites** presenting his church to Christ. This mosaic is flanked by full-length portraits of **St Peter**, to the left, and **St Paul**, to the right. And to the right of the door is the sixth and last mosaic in this series, the **Deesis**, a portrait of Christ flanked by the Blessed Virgin and St John the Baptist.

The second iconographic series, the **Genealogy of Christ**, consists of just two mosaics. The first is in the southern dome of the inner narthex; in the crown there is a medallion of Christ Pantocrator and in the flutes two rows of his ancestors. The second mosaic is in the northern dome of the inner narthex. In the crown there is a medallion of the Blessed Virgin with the Christ Child; below this in the upper zone are sixteen figures of the House of David; and in the lower eleven figures representing 'other figures outside the genealogy'.

The third series is the **Cycle of the Life of the Blessed Virgin**, which consists of nineteen extant mosaics in the central bay of the inner narthex and the two bays to the right. The fourth series is the **Cycle of the Infancy of Christ**. This consists of thirteen extant or partly extant scenes, each of which occupies a lunette of the outer narthex, starting at the centre of the far left bay and proceeding clockwise around all seven bays. The fifth series is the **Cycle of Christ's Ministry**, which occupies the domical vaults of all seven bays of the outer narthex as well as parts of the south bay of the inner narthex. Unfortunately all but one of the vaults in the inner narthex are badly damaged, many being totally lost or reduced to fragments. This series begins in the far left bay of the outer narthex and consists of nineteen extant scenes and a few fragmentary mosaics. The sixth

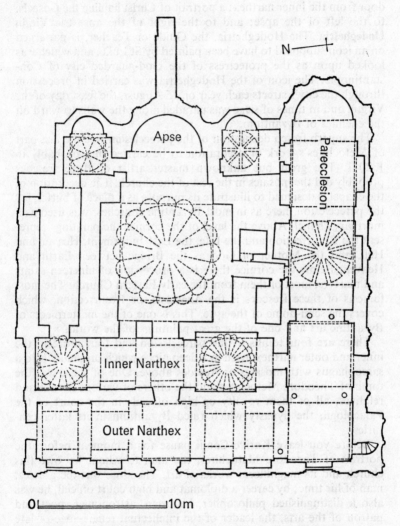

Apse

Parecclesion

Inner Narthex

Outer Narthex

0   10 m

Kariye Camii (Church of St Saviour in Chora)

N

and final series of mosaics consists of three panels in the nave. These are: the **Koimesis** (Dormition) **of the Virgin**, over the central door from the inner narthex; a portrait of **Christ holding the Gospels**, to the left of the apse; and to the right of the apse the **Virgin Hodeghetria**. The Hodeghetria, the Guide or Teacher, is patterned on an icon supposed to have been painted by St Luke, and which was looked upon as the protectress of the God-guarded city of Constantinople. The icon of the Hodeghetria was carried in procession through the city's streets each year on 15 August, the feast day of the Virgin, and in times of siege was paraded along the walls to ward off the enemies of Byzantium.

The superb fresco decoration of the **parecclesion** was the last part of Metochites's work of decoration to be carried out, probably in 1320–1. The great but unknown master artist of these frescoes probably did the mosaics in the rest of the church. The decoration of the chapel is designed to illustrate its purpose as a place of burial, for the parecclesion, here as in most Byzantine churches, was used as a mortuary chapel. Above the level of the cornice the paintings represent the Resurrection and the Life, the Last Judgement, Heaven and Hell, and the Mother of God as the Bridge between Earth and Heaven. Below the cornice there is a procession of nineteen saints and martyrs, most of them from the early Eastern Church. The most famous of these frescoes is the **Anastasis**, or Resurrection, which covers the semi-dome of the apse. This is one of the masterpieces of Byzantine art and one of the great paintings of the world.

There are four tombs in the parecclesion and four more in the inner and outer narthex, each in a deep niche which originally held a sarcophagus with mosaics or frescoes above. One of these was the tomb of Theodore Metochites and the others of various friends and relatives, all of them royalty or high officials in the court of the Palaeologii, the dynasty which ruled Byzantium in its latter centuries.

Before you leave Kariye Camii pause for a moment before the portrait of Theodore Metochites, the man to whom we owe this church and its magnificent works of art. Theodore was the greatest man of his time; by career a diplomat and high court official, he was also a distinguished philosopher, historian, astronomer, poet and patron of the arts, the leader of the intellectual renaissance of late Byzantium. Shortly before he died, on 13 March 1331, Theodore spoke of his hope that his church and its works of art would secure for him 'a glorious memory among posterity to the end of the world'. They have indeed, for Theodore's church is a monument not only to him but to the times in which he lived, the last flowering of Byzantium.

From Kariye Camii it is only a short stroll out to the **Theodosian walls**. These great walls stretch from the Sea of Marmara to the Golden Horn, a total distance of about seventeen kilometres. Although in ruins they are still a splendid and impressive sight, with towers and battlements marching across the hills and valleys of Thrace. The main section of the walls from the Marmara to the top of the Sixth Hill was constructed in the middle of the fifth century under Theodosius II. The section leading down from the Sixth Hill to the Golden Horn was built at various times from the seventh to the tenth century, replacing the older Theodosian walls in that region. The impressive shell of a Byzantine palace still stands at the junction of these two stretches of wall; this is known in Turkish as **Tekfursaray**, the **Palace of the Sovereign**. It is thought to date from the thirteenth century and to have been part of the Palace of Blachernae, the principal imperial residence in the last two centuries of Byzantine rule.

The neighbourhood just inside the walls in the north-west corner of Stamboul is one of the most picturesque in the city, with country lanes wandering through gardens in the shadow of the ruined walls, and here and there an ancient column serving as a doorstep or a Corinthian capital as a well-head.

Nearly all of the Byzantine city gates are still in use; indeed, until the present century they were the only entrances to this walled city. A short distance to the west of Kariye Camii is the historic **Edirne Gate**, through which Mehmet the Conqueror made his triumphal entry after taking Constantinople.

Beside the Edirne Gate you see the imperial **Mosque of Princess Mihrimah** standing atop the Sixth Hill, the highest point in Stamboul. This is another masterwork of the great Sinan, built in the period 1562–5 for Süleyman's favourite daughter, whose premature death saddened the Sultan's last years. Besides the mosque, the *külliye* consists of a *medrese*, a primary school, *türbe*, double *hamam*, and a long row of shops in the substructure of the terrace on which it is built.

The central area of the mosque interior is a square, covered by a great dome resting on smooth pendentives. The tympana of all four dome arches are filled with three rows of windows. To north and south high triple arcades, each supported on two great granite columns, open into side aisles with two galleries above, each of three domed bays, thus giving the sense of an enormous light-filled space.

Mihrimah Camii is one of the finest mosques in Istanbul, and is all the more impressive standing as it does on the peak of the highest hill in the old city.

There is still a great deal more to see in old Stamboul; beautiful and historic Byzantine churches and Ottoman mosques with their pious foundations, many of them hidden away down back streets in remote quarters of the town. I can think of no more pleasant way to spend a day in Istanbul than to seek out one of these antiquities down the cobbled streets of the old city, and then to picnic in the courtyard of a Roman basilica or in the garden of a dervish monastery. But the visitor with limited time may want to postpone such pleasant strolls for another visit: there is so much yet to see in Istanbul and elsewhere in this vast and historic country.

The nave of Haghia Sophia.

CHAPTER SIX

Istanbul VI: The Modern Town

※

*Galata – The Galata Tower – Beyoğlu – Eyüp – Üsküdar – The Princes'
Isles – The Bosphorus*

Although most of the major monuments of Istanbul are located in
the old city there are a number of interesting places to see in other
parts of the town. This is particularly true of Galata and Pera, the
old Levantine quarters which face Stamboul across the Golden
Horn.

The historic origins of Galata and Pera go back as far in time as
those of Constantinople itself. When Constantine founded his new
capital there was already a settlement of some size on the opposite
side of the Golden Horn. This town, which was called Sykae, was
incorporated within the civic boundaries of Constantinople by the
middle of the fourth century AD. In the course of time the name
'Sykae' was gradually abandoned and those of 'Galata' and 'Pera'
came into use; Galata comprising the maritime quarter along the
Golden Horn and the Bosphorus, and Pera including the region on
the hills above the port. These regions have been renamed in the past
half-century; Pera is now known officially as 'Beyoğlu' and Galata
as 'Karaköy', but by force of habit many residents still refer to these
quarters by their old names.

The port quarter of **Galata** first came into prominence with the
settlement there of Genoese merchants in the eleventh century.
During the latter centuries of Byzantine rule Galata was virtually an
autonomous city-state, ruled by a Podestat appointed each year by
the mother-city of Genoa. After the Conquest the citizens of Galata
and Pera continued to retain some measure of autonomy under the
Turks up until the late seventeenth century, calling themselves 'The
Magnificent Community of Pera'.

The Dining-Room of Sultan Ahmet III, the Tulip King, in the Topkapí
Sarayí.
The Alexander Sarcophagus. Istanbul Archaeological Museum.

About all that now remains of the medieval Genoese town is the **Galata Tower**, the most familiar landmark on that side of the Golden Horn. The tower, over fifty metres tall, stands on the highest point of the old town of Galata. Originally known as the Tower of Christ, it was built in 1348 as the focal point of the defence-walls of the Genoese colony. At the time of the Conquest the Genoese town consisted of six fortified enceintes surrounded by an outer defence-wall and a moat. A section of the moat is still visible near the tower itself, and several of the defence-towers and a section of wall still stand behind the houses on Galata Kulesi Sokaği; these can best be seen by looking down from the tower itself. The Galata Tower has been restored in recent years and there is now a restaurant on its upper floor; from there one commands the finest of all views of Istanbul and its surrounding waters.

After leaving Galata you ascend to Beyoğlu, or old **Pera**. The most direct approach on foot is via Yuksek Kaldírím, a lively street which climbs up the hill from the main square before the bridge, passing close to the Galata Tower halfway along. But you can ride up in a minute and ten seconds on the Tunel, the venerable underground funicular which old Periotes still refer to as the 'Mouse's Hole'. Either way, you find yourself in Tunel Meydaní, the main intersection at the top of the hill. Here you begin walking down **Istiklal Caddesi**, the main thoroughfare of Beyoğlu. This is the once-famous avenue known in Ottoman times as the 'Grande Rue de Pera', of which the distinguished historian Joseph von Hammer wrote: 'It is as narrow as the comprehension of its inhabitants and as long as the tapeworm of their intrigues.'

The area which later came to be called Pera was still open country-side until the second half of the sixteenth century. At that time the European ambassadors began to move from the crowded confines of Stamboul to the rustic suburbs in the hills above Galata, building their palatial residences along the road which would soon be known as the Grande Rue. Several of these old embassy buildings (now demoted to the status of consulates) can still be seen along the right side of the avenue, along with the churches which were built to serve the Christian citizens of the various European 'Nations', as they were called. The first you come to, just beyond the exit of the Tunel, is the **Swedish Embassy**, established in its present building towards the end of the seventeenth century. Next is the **Russian Embassy**, built in 1837 by the brothers Fossati, who a decade later would restore Haghia Sophia. Just past the grounds of the Russian Embassy is the

Roman Catholic **Church of St Mary Draperis**; this was founded in 1678 and its present building dates from 1789.

Postacílar Sokaği, the street which leads downhill past the side of the Russian Embassy, leads to the **Palazzo Venezia**, once the Embassy of the Serene Republic of Venice. The present structure dates from 1695, though the Venetian Embassy was established here long before that. We learn from his *Memoirs* that Giacomo Casanova was a guest here in the summer of 1744; in his three months in the city the great lover made not a single conquest, although he was himself seduced by one Ismail Efendi.

Returning to Istiklal Caddesi, you pass next the **Dutch and French Embassies**, founded in 1612 and 1580 respectively, though the present buildings date from the first half of the nineteenth century. Two blocks farther on you pass a large church in a courtyard below the street level; this is the Franciscan **Church of St Anthony of Padua**, founded on this site in 1725. The present building dates from 1913 and is a good example of Italian neo-Gothic.

You now come to **Galatasaray**, the main square of downtown Beyoğlu. The square takes its name from the Galatasaray Lisesi, whose ornate gateway can be seen across the square to the right. The Galatasaray Lisesi was originally a branch of the Palace School of Topkapí Sarayí. Then in the middle of the nineteenth century it was reorganized along European lines as the first modern secondary school in the Ottoman Empire, and it produced many of the writers, scholars and political figures who were responsible for creating the new Turkish Republic.

The avenue which leads off left from the square takes you to the old **British Embassy**, a handsome building dating from the middle of the nineteenth century. It looks out on to the **Galatasaray fish market**, the most interesting and picturesque part of Beyoğlu. This is the only neighbourhood in Beyoğlu which still retains the Levantine atmosphere of old Pera, and along its squalid streets are innumerable lively taverns crowded with the rough but friendly people of the quarter. The best of these drinking-places are in the **Çiçek Pasají**, the **Passage of Flowers**, a rowdy alleyway which leads off to the left from Istiklal Caddesi just beyond Galatasaray Square. The Passage is lined with boisterous *meyhanes*, raffish kerbside taverns where one can enjoy an informal meal washed down with draught beer served in giant glasses called Argentines. In good weather the customers drink at marble-topped beer-barrels in the alleyway itself, dining on titbits bought from passing pedlars, occasionally serenaded by street-musicians. Since the Passage is common ground to the local fish and flower markets it is a real museum of Istanbul sights and sounds and smells, and every odd and interesting character in town is sure to pass through there during the course of an evening.

Past Galatasaray Square the avenue is lined with shops, cinemas, theatres, restaurants and cafés, for this is the heart of downtown Istanbul. Next comes **Taksim Square**, the featureless centre of the modern town, whose drabness is relieved only by the glittering façade of the new **Opera House**. Inönü Caddesi goes off to the right and leads down to the Bosphorus near Dolmabahçe Palace. Straight ahead is Cumhuriyet Caddesi, which leads off to the more modern quarters of Harbiye, Şişli and Nişantaş. The beginning of this avenue is lined with cafés, travel agencies, smart restaurants and hotels, the most luxurious of which is the Hilton. Just beyond the Hilton is the **Military Museum**, with an interesting collection of Ottoman armaments and military costumes. Outside the museum on most afternoons there are performances of Ottoman martial music by the famous Mehter Band, which dates back to 1830 when it was formed by Donizetti Pasha, an older brother of the famous composer Gaetano Donizetti. And on Halaskargazi Caddesi, the continuation of Cumhuriyet Caddesi, one finds the **Atatürk Museum**, which was once the home of Kemal Atatürk, the Father of modern Turkey and the first President of the Turkish Republic.

Many of the interesting maritime suburbs of Istanbul are best reached by ferry-boat; routes and schedules are posted at the various piers under the Galata Bridge and on the nearby banks of the Golden Horn.

Ferries leave from the upstream side of the bridge for **Eyüp**, a quiet and very conservative village some distance up the Golden Horn. This is one of the most sacred places of pilgrimage in the Moslem world, for it is the reputed burial-place of Eyüp Ensari, standard-bearer for the Prophet Mohammed, who is said to have died there during the Arab siege of Constantinople between 674 and 678. Eyüp's grave was miraculously discovered by Sultan Mehmet II during the siege in 1453, and the Conqueror afterwards erected a mosque and *türbe* dedicated to the saint. The original mosque was destroyed in the earthquake of 1766 and the present structure dates only from 1800. The two courtyards of the mosque are delightful and picturesque, with gnarled old plane trees inhabited by lame storks unable to make the journey to Africa, and crowds of pious pilgrims and pedlars of religious trinkets. In the inner courtyard you find the *türbe* of the saint, revetted in superb Iznik tiles. In the hills above the shrine is the great cemetery of Eyüp, with its slopes covered with turbaned tombstones and shaded with spectral cypresses. At the top of the hill is the famous teahouse associated with Pierre Loti, the French novelist. From here the view is particularly romantic at sunset, when the foul waters of the Golden Horn are tinted with the changing pastels of twilight.

The ferries on the downstream side of the Galata Bridge leave for the Asian suburbs and the Princes' Isles.

The most interesting of the Asian suburbs is **Üsküdar**, which stands directly opposite Stamboul at the mouth of the Bosphorus. Üsküdar was known in Byzantine times as Chrysopolis, the City of Gold; according to tradition, it was founded early in the seventh century BC, some two decades before the original settlement of Byzantium. Throughout the Byzantine period Chrysopolis was a suburb of Constantinople, and thus had much the same history as the capital. However, its site was not as well-suited for defence, and it was on several occasions occupied and destroyed by invading armies, while Constantinople remained safe behind its great walls. Consequently, no monuments from the Byzantine period remain in modern Üsküdar. The town was taken by the Turks in the fourteenth century, more than a hundred years before the fall of Constantinople. During the Ottoman period several members of the royal family adorned Üsküdar with splendid mosques and pious foundations, most of which are still to be seen there today.

As you approach Üsküdar you pass the fabled Maiden's Tower, better known in English as **Leander's Tower**. During the Byzantine period this was the site of a small fortress; in times of siege a chain was stretched from there to Saray Burnu, so as to close off the harbour of Constantinople. Since then it has been used variously as a lighthouse, semaphore station, lazaretto, and customs control station. The present building dates from the eighteenth century.

The ferry-landing in Üsküdar is dominated by an imposing mosque standing on a high terrace; in Turkish this is known as **Iskele Camii**, the **Mosque of the Landing-Place**. This fine mosque was built in 1547–8 by Sinan for the Princess Mihrimah. (The other mosque which bears Mihrimah's name, the one atop the Sixth Hill, was founded by Süleyman to honour the memory of his beloved daughter, who died prematurely in 1562.) Standing in the square before the mosque is the handsome baroque **Fountain of Ahmet III**, built in 1726. On the other side of the square is the large complex of **Yeni Valide Camii**; this was built by Ahmet III between 1708 and 1710 and dedicated to the memory of his mother, the Valide Sultan

Gülnus Emetullah.

There are several other distinguished old mosques to the right of the ferry-landing. The most beautiful is **Şemsi Pasha Camii**, which Evliya Efendi aptly described as 'a little pearl of a mosque on the lip of the sea'. This was built by Sinan in 1580 for the famous Vezir, Şemsi Pasha, who is buried in a most unusual *türbe* housed in a side chamber of the mosque itself.

The largest and most impressive monument in Üsküdar is **Atik Valide Camii**, which stands in the hills above the lower town. This great mosque complex was built by Sinan in 1583 for the Valide Sultan Nur Banu, wife of Selim II and mother of Murat III. After the Süleymaniye this is the most splendid and impressive of all of Sinan's works in Istanbul. Beside the mosque itself the *külliye* includes a *medrese*, Kuran school, public kitchen, hospital, *hamam* and caravansarai, all of which remain standing and in good repair. Altogether, this is one of the most outstanding monuments of Ottoman architecture in all Turkey.

The most famous of all the beauty spots in the vicinity of Istanbul are the **Princes' Isles**, the little suburban archipelago in the Sea of Marmara. The group consists of nine isles, four of them of a certain size, the others tiny. Ferries from the Galata Bridge call first at Kínalí, then at Burgaz, Heybeli Ada, and finally at Büyük Ada, about an hour's ride on the express. Büyük Ada, the Greek Prinkipo, is the largest and most beautiful of the isles, and it has several good hotels and restaurants. On all four of these isles there are lovely pine groves and other forests, wild cliffs plunging down to the sea, and secluded sandy coves for bathing, a pleasant relief from the great but maddening city on the Golden Horn.

The Bosphorus ferries leave from the Stamboul shore of the Golden Horn, a short distance downstream from the Galata Bridge. The various ferries follow rather erratic itineraries, flitting back and forth between the continents as they go up and down the strait. For that reason it is wise to study the schedules posted at the terminals before departing; perhaps the best approach is to choose a ferry which goes up the Bosphorus along the European shore, then disembark for a while, and return later along the Asian shore.

The **Bosphorus** is one of the most historic waterways in the world, and for centuries travellers to this city have praised its beauties. Both its shores are indented by frequent bays and harbours, most of which shelter picturesque little villages nestling in the folds of the green hills behind them. The hills above the Bosphorus are wellwooded, especially with cypresses, umbrella-pines, horse-chestnuts, terebinths and judas trees. The red-pink blossoms of the flowering judases in spring, mingled with the mauve flowers of the wisteria and the red and white candles of the chestnuts, give the Bosphorus at that season an even greater beauty.

A number of interesting mosques line the European shore of the lower Bosphorus, though you will catch only a fleeting glance of them from the ferry. The first is **Kílíç Ali Pasha Camii**, which stands about half a kilometre up the Bosphorus from the Galata Bridge. This was Sinan's last mosque on a monumental scale; he completed it in 1580 on the eve of his ninetieth birthday. The founder, Kílíç ('The Sword') Ali Pasha, was one of the great pirate-admirals in Ottoman history. He twice captured Tunis from the Spaniards, the second time permanently, and while he was in command there he freed Cervantes from prison and arranged for his return to Spain. When Kílíç Ali died in 1587 he was one of the wealthiest men in the Ottoman Empire and a voluptuary to the very end. 'Although ninety years of age,' says the historian von Hammer, 'he had not been able to renounce the pleasures of the harem, and he died in the arms of a concubine.'

A short distance beyond Kílíç Ali's mosque you pass the **Nusretiye Cami**, built between 1822 and 1826 by Mahmut II. The Sultan named his mosque 'Nusretiye' – 'Victory' – because it was completed just after his liquidation of the Janissaries.

Eight hundred metres beyond the Nusretiye is the **Molla Çelebi Camii**, built in 1561–2 for one of Süleyman's Chief Justices. The mosque is at the water's edge, and its position as well as its graceful lines make it very picturesque.

The most imposing monument along the first stretch of the Bosphorus is **Dolmabahçe Palace**, about two kilometres from the Galata Bridge along the European shore. Dolmabahçe was built in 1852 for Sultan Abdül Mecit, and was the principal residence for most of the latter sultans. Kemal Atatürk, the great Turkish leader, died in Dolmabahçe on 10 November 1938 and lay there in state before his burial in Ankara, while his country mourned for him.

About three kilometres farther along the ferry passes under the new **Bosphorus Bridge** (officially known as the Atatürk Bridge), the fourth longest suspension bridge in the world. The bridge opened on 30 September 1973, on the fiftieth anniversary of the founding of the Turkish Republic.

Just past the bridge and on the Asian side stands the **Palace of Beylerbey**, built in 1865 for Sultan Abdül Aziz. Abdül Hamit II, the last of the autocratic sultans of the Ottoman Empire, died here in

1918, deposed and a virtual prisoner.

You are now in the middle Bosphorus, bordered by hills clad in pines and cypresses, with a succession of seaside villages sheltered in coves on either side of the strait. The first of those at which you stop on the European shore is **Arnavutköy**, the Village of the Albanians, whose waterfront is graced with some of the most picturesque wooden houses along the Bosphorus. Rounding the cape past Arnavutköy the ferry enters **Bebek Bay**, the most beautiful haven on the Bosphorus. Lush rolling hills with groves of pines and cypresses form a dramatic backdrop to the bay, a green frieze of hills between the blues of sea and sky.

This is the most beautiful and historic part of the Bosphorus, and is well worth a pause in mid-journey. The best view of it is from the terrace of Boğaziçi Universitesi, the **University of the Bosphorus**, which is perched atop a hill between Bebek and Rumeli Hisar, the next village up the Bosphorus. This distinguished Turkish university is the descendant of the old Robert College, which in its time was the finest institution of higher learning in Turkey. Robert College was founded in 1863 by Cyrus Hamlin, an American missionary who baked bread and washed clothes for Florence Nightingale at her hospital in Üsküdar.

From the University terrace you look out across the strait to the famous **Sweet Waters of Asia**, a surpassingly beautiful valley which was a famous resort of the *beau monde* in late Ottoman times. **Küçüksu**, the little seaside palace in the centre of the Sweet Waters, was built by Sultan Abdül Mecit in 1856. A few hundred metres to the right of the palace you see three of the few surviving Bosphorus *yalís*, the waterfront mansions which once lined both banks of the strait. The first on the right is the Kíbríslí Yalí, built in 1760. Beside that is the Hüseyin Bey Yalísí, built in about 1790, and beyond that is the red Ostrorog Yalísí, dating from the beginning of the nineteenth century.

Beyond Bebek the Bosphorus suddenly diminishes to its narrowest width. The fortress on the Asian side is **Anadolu Hisarí**, the **Castle of Anatolia**, built in about 1390 by Sultan Beyazit I. In Turkish it is known as 'Güzelce Hisar', the 'Beautiful Castle', and one can well see why, for the old fortress and its picturesque setting make this one of the loveliest sights along the Bosphorus. The narrows are dominated on the European side by **Rumeli Hisarí**, the **Castle of Rumelia**, built by Sultan Mehmet II in 1452; between them these two fortresses cut off Constantinople from the Black Sea in preparation for the siege of 1453. Rumeli Hisarí is a splendid late medieval fortification; it spans a steep valley with two massive towers on opposite hills and a third at the bottom of the valley at the water's edge, where the sea gate is protected by a barbican. A curtain wall, defended by three smaller towers, joins the three major defence-towers, forming an irregular figure some 250 metres long by 125 broad at its maximum. The castle was restored in 1953 in connection with the five hundredth anniversary of the Turkish Conquest, and the area inside has been made into a park with a theatre. Plays and performances of Turkish folk-dances are presented here in summer; the setting is spectacular, with the stunning background of the castle walls and towers, and across the Bosphorus the glittering lights of the villages on the Asian shore.

Beyond the two castles the Bosphorus widens again, and the ferry passes a succession of seaside villages on either shore. The most famous of those on the European shore is **Tarabya**, with its crescent bay crowded with luxurious yachts which never seem to sail and its waterfront lined with excellent but expensive restaurants. The large village across the way from Tarabya on the Asian shore is **Beykoz**, where one can take a taxi to the Black Sea resort village of **Şile**, which has the finest beaches in the vicinity of Istanbul. Farther up the European shore the ferry calls at **Sarıyer**, a very lively village which is the main port for the Black Sea fishing fleet. Here one can debark and take a taxi through the Belgrade Forest to the Black Sea resort village of **Kilyos**, which has the best beaches on the European shore of the Black Sea.

The last ferry-stop on the European side is **Rumeli Kavağí**, where there are several good and inexpensive fish restaurants clustered around an old Turkish fortress beside the sea. Across the way is **Anadolu Kavağí**, the last ferry-stop on the Asian side. On the hill above Anadolu Kavağí are the ruins of the ancient **Castle of Yoros**, constructed in late Byzantine times and later used in turn by the Genoese and the Turks. Those wishing to explore the upper Bosphorus beyond this point must hire a boat and take to the sea. The excursion is one of extreme delight, for the scenery is wild, rugged and desolate, and exceptionally beautiful.

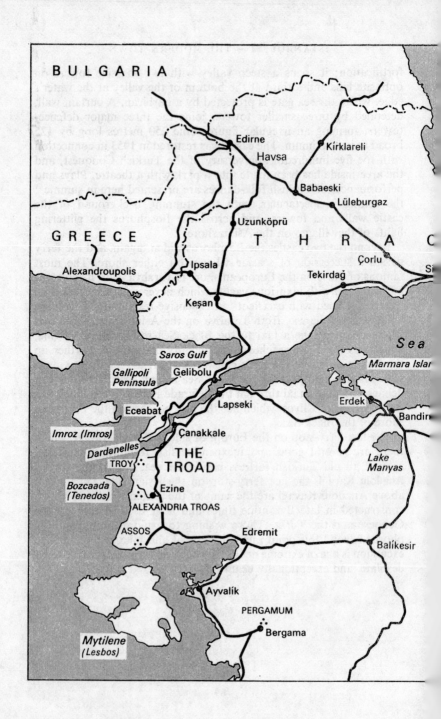

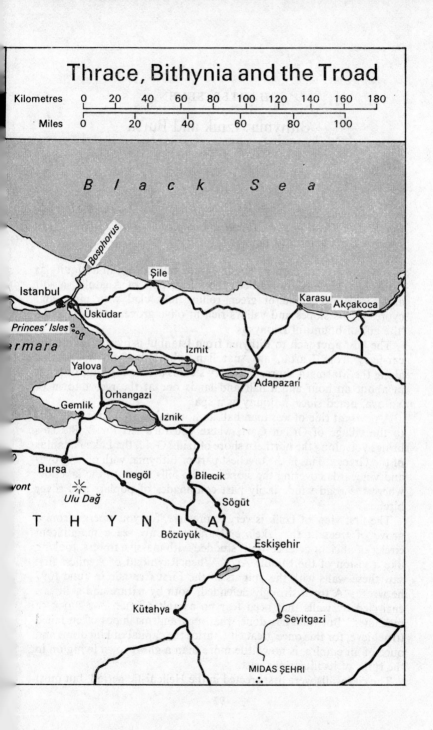

Thrace, Bithynia and the Troad

Kilometres 0   20   40   60   80   100   120   140   160   180

Miles 0   20   40   60   80   100

B l a c k   S e a

Bosphorus

Şile

Istanbul

Karasu   Akçakoca

Üsküdar

Princes' Isles

Izmit

rmara

Yalova

Adapazarí

Orhangazi

Gemlik

Iznik

Bursa

Inegöl   Bilecik

Ulu Dağ

vont

Söğüt

T H Y N I A

Bözüyük

Eskişehir

Kütahya

Seyitgazi

MIDAS ŞEHRI

CHAPTER SEVEN

Bithynia: Iznik and Bursa

✣

*Iznik: Haghia Sophia – The Zaviye of Nilufer Hatun – Yeşil Cami
Bursa: Ulu Cami – The Muradiye Complex – Yeşil Cami – Yeşil
Türbe – The Complex of Beyazit I*

The north-western corner of Asia Minor was known in antiquity as
Bithynia. This has always been the fairest part of Anatolia, a soft
and temperate region of green rolling hills clad with pines and
cypresses, its slopes and valleys rich in olive groves and vineyards,
'the gift of bountiful Dionysus'.

The best approach to Bithynia from Istanbul is by sea, taking the
car-ferry from Kartal, an Anatolian suburb half an hour's ride
along the Marmara shore. The ferry steams across the Gulf of Izmit
in about an hour and a half and lands one at the resort town of
Yalova, noted since antiquity as a spa.

A pleasant ride of less than half an hour takes you across the hills
to the village of Orhan Gazi, where you turn left for Iznik. This
brings you along the northern shore of Iznik Gölü, the Lake Ascanius
of the Greeks. This is the loveliest part of Bithynia, with olive groves
and vineyards covering the slopes of the hills down to the lakeside,
where the road winds lazily past colonnades of poplars and silver
birches.

The first view of Iznik is very impressive, for you emerge from a
grove of trees at the lake's end and suddenly see a magnificent
circlet of ancient defence-walls studded with massive towers, looking
like a vision of the Middle Ages. When Raymond of Aguilers first
saw these walls with the knights of the First Crusade in June 1097
he wrote: 'A town strongly defended, both by nature and skill . . .
encircled by walls that need fear no assault of man nor shock of
machines.' But time has done what men and machines often failed
to achieve, for this once great city, thrice the capital of kingdoms and
once of an empire, is now little more than a ghost town living on in
the ruins of its illustrious past.

The city walls were first erected in the Hellenistic period, but most of the present fortifications date from late Byzantine times, with repairs by both the Selcuk and Ottoman Turks. The city itself was founded in 316 BC by Antigonus the One-Eyed, one of Alexander's generals and later ruler of much of his empire. Around 300 BC the city came under the control of Lysimachus, King of Thrace, and at that time he named it Nicaea after his deceased wife, a daughter of Antipater. Soon after the death of Lysimachus in 281 BC Nicaea was captured by Nicomedes I of Bithynia, and for a time it served as the capital of his kingdom. Two centuries later the city was willed to the Roman people by Antiochus, the last king of Bithynia, at which time it became capital of the Roman province of that name. Thereafter Nicaea became one of the leading cities of the eastern Roman Empire and later of Byzantium. Valentinian I and Valens were elevated as Emperors of Rome while in Nicaea; Diocletian resided here, as did Constantine and Justinian. The first Ecumenical Council of the Church was convened in Nicaea by Constantine in 325 and the Seventh Council by the Empress Eirene in 787, both of them landmarks in the history of Christianity.

But those were violent times, and on several occasions Nicaea fell victim to the invading armies that ravaged Asia Minor during the Middle Ages, captured in turn by the Goths, Persians, Mongols and Turks. Nicaea was taken by the Selcuk Turks in 1081, after which it served as the capital of the Sultanate of Rum until the Selcuks were dislodged in 1097 by an allied force of Byzantines and Crusaders. Then, after the capture of Constantinople by the knights of the Fourth Crusade in 1204, Nicaea became capital of one of the surviving fragments of the Byzantine Empire, ruled by Theodore I Lascarides. The Lascarid dynasty ruled brilliantly in Nicaea for the next half-century, and through their efforts Byzantium was finally restored to its ancient capital in 1261.

The period of Lascarid rule was the golden age of Nicaea, but it did not long outlast their reign, for in 1331 the city was captured by Orhangazi, the first Sultan of the Ottoman Turks. The Turks renamed the city Iznik and for a time Orhan Gazi made it his capital. Iznik was sacked by Tamerlane in 1402, a catastrophe it shared with most other cities in Anatolia at that time. But Iznik quickly recovered and once again took its place as one of the most important cities in western Anatolia, now dominated by the Ottoman Turks. For the next two centuries Iznik was celebrated for its beautiful ceramic tiles, which adorned the mosques, palaces and pious foundations of the Ottoman Empire, and which remain as one of its greatest contributions to Islamic art. But in later centuries the city began to decline, along with so much else in the Ottoman Empire, until at the beginning of the present century it was just an Anatolian farm village, dozing on amid the remnants of its almost forgotten past. Then came the final catastrophe in 1922, when the town was almost totally destroyed during the last days of the Greco-Turkish War, leaving the melancholy ruins which one sees today.

The modern road enters the city through a breach in the walls beside **Istanbul Kapísí**, one of the four main gateways in the defence-walls. This is a double gate, for the city was surrounded by two concentric walls, each guarded by more than a hundred defence-towers. Between the two walls there is a triumphal arch, erected to commemorate the Emperor Hadrian's visit to Nicaea in AD 123.

Like most Hellenistic towns, Nicaea was laid out and built by city-planners, and its streets form a graph oriented along the meridians of the compass. Atatürk Caddesi, the main avenue of the town, leads south from Istanbul Kapísí to Yenişehir Kapísí, while Mazharbey Caddesi forms the east-west axis between the Lake Gate and Lefke Kapísí.

At the centre of the town, where Mazharbey Caddesi intersects Atatürk Caddesi, are the ruins of the former **Church of Haghia Sophia**, the principal Byzantine monument of Iznik. Excavations in 1935 revealed that the first church on this site was probably built in the reign of Justinian and destroyed by an earthquake in 1065, and that the present edifice was erected soon afterwards. When Orhan Gazi captured the city for the Ottomans in 1331 Haghia Sophia was converted into a house of Islamic worship, and thereafter it was known as Ulu Cami, the Great Mosque. The building was wrecked by Tamerlane in 1402 and was badly damaged again in the middle of the sixteenth century, after which it was restored by Sinan on Süleyman's orders. But in late Ottoman times the structure fell into disrepair and was finally destroyed completely during the fighting in 1922. The ruins of Haghia Sophia are of some interest, particularly the mosaic pavement and the fresco of the Deesis; but more significant are the historical memories this place evokes, for here were crowned five emperors in the years when Nicaea was capital of what was then left of the Byzantine Empire.

The principal Turkish monuments of Iznik are in the eastern quarter of the town; you approach them by taking Mazharbey Caddesi eastwards toward Lefke Kapísí, a monumental gate erected at the time of Hadrian's visit. At the last intersection before the gate turn left; then at the next corner you see on your left the Zaviye of Nilufer Hatun and on your right Yeşil Cami.

Yeşil Cami, or the **Green Mosque**, was built in the years 1378–91 in honour of Çandarlí Halil Pasha, Judge of Iznik under Orhan Gazi, and Grand Vezir in the reign of Sultan Murat I. The mosque takes its name from the turquoise ceramic tiles which once adorned its splendid Selcuk minaret; they were among the finest products of the Iznik kilns, but the ones which you see today are poor imitations from Kütahya.

The **Zaviye**, or **Dervish Hospice of Nilufer Hatun**, was built in 1388 by Murat I in honour of his mother. Nilufer Hatun had been born a Greek princess, a daughter of the Emperor John VI Canta-cuzenos, and was married to Orhan Gazi in order to cement a Byzantine-Ottoman alliance. Nilufer Hatun was one of the most able women in Ottoman history, and she often administered the Empire while the Sultan was off on campaign. Her *zaviye* today serves as the local archaeological museum, which houses antiquities found in Iznik and the surrounding area. (The museum keeper has the keys to the painted Roman tomb outside the Istanbul Gate; apply to him if you wish to see it.)

You now turn back along Mazharbey Caddesi and continue past the town centre to what was once the Lake Gate. Here you can walk out along the shore of Lake Iznik, where there are some good but simple restaurants serving freshly-caught lake fish.

You should now make your way back to the town centre, turning right on to Atatürk Caddesi and heading south towards the Yenişehir Gate. About halfway along towards the gate turn left and you will soon come to the **Zaviye of Yakub Sultan**, dating from the end of the fourteenth century. The founder of this dervish hospice was a younger brother of Beyazit I, murdered by the Sultan at the time of his accession to the throne. Beyazit justified the fratricide by stating that he had acted to avoid a possible war of succession, quoting the appropriate words of the Kuran: 'Death is better than disquiet.'

Retracing your steps, you now go back across Atatürk Caddesi and continue for a way on the other side, stopping at the vast ruins of an **ancient theatre**. This was built by Pliny the Younger when he was governor of Bithynia in AD 111–12, and was designed to seat fifteen thousand spectators. Today the theatre is a total ruin, almost completely covered with grass, and only here and there can one see remnants of its structure.

If you return to Atatürk Caddesi and turn right and you will finally reach **Yenişehir Kapísí**, the main gate at the southern end of the city. This is a monumental gate built, according to an inscription, by the Emperor Claudius in AD 268. The ruinous condition of this gate is due to the fact that it was the focal point of two violent assaults on the city, by the Selcuks in 1081 and the Ottomans in 1331. Through here the Emperor Alexius I Comnenus passed in triumph in 1097, after recapturing the city from the Selcuks, as did Orhan Gazi in his turn after taking the city from the Byzantines. The modern road bypasses this historic gateway, and today it is used only by the villagers who have farms outside the walls in its vicinity.

After leaving Iznik by the Yenişehir Gate you drive along the south shore of the lake. The scenery here is even lovelier than on the north shore, as the lake road winds along through groves of olive trees, cypresses, poplars and silver birches, taking one deeper into the ancient kingdom of Bithynia.

Soon after leaving the western end of the lake you come to **Gemlik**, a small seaport standing at the end of an immense fiord. In antiquity the town was known as Cius, named after its legendary founder, an Argonaut who settled here after his return from the land of Colchis.

You pass Gemlik and then head up into the hills. After a drive of half an hour or so you come down into the broad plain below **Ulu Dağ**, the **Great Mountain**, whose lofty peaks now loom ahead. This is the ancient Mount Olympus of Bithynia (one of about a dozen mountains in the ancient Greek world which bore the same name, the one in Thessaly being the most famous), and at its foot stands the beautiful and historic city of **Bursa**.

This city was known to travellers of an older generation as Prusa, named after King Prusias I of Bithynia, who founded the town in 183 BC. Following a distinguished history in antiquity, Bursa came into prominence again in the fourteenth century, when the Ottoman Turks established their capital there after taking the city from the Byzantines in 1326. It remained the capital until the early years of the fifteenth century, when the central government of the expanding Ottoman Empire was transferred to Edirne. But Bursa was still the heart of the old Ottoman homeland in Anatolia, and it retained its eminence during the early centuries of the Empire; Osman Gazi, the founder of the Ottoman dynasty, is buried there, as are the first five sultans. Their imperial mosques, mausoleums and pious foundations still adorn the green hills of this lovely old town, reminding one of its imperial past.

The road from Gemlik brings you to Cumhuriyet Meydaní, the centre of the modern town. From there you might begin by walking west along Atatürk Caddesi; this soon leads to **Ulu Cami**, the **Great**

Mosque, which stands in the old market area at the base of the citadel hill.

Ulu Cami was built in the years 1396–9 by Sultan Beyazit I, known in his time as Yíldírím, or Lightning. The Sultan financed the construction with the loot from his victory at the battle of Nicopolis on 24 September 1396, when he defeated a Crusader army led by King Sigismund of Hungary. This is the grandest of all the Great Mosques constructed in Anatolia during the two centuries preceding the Conquest, and represents the ascendancy of the Ottomans over their rivals among the Turkish emirates.

Twelve great piers divide the vast interior of the mosque into twenty equal domed areas. One of these, the second in from the main door, contains a *şadirvan* pool with a cascade fountain at its centre. As in other Bursa mosques, the top of the dome above the *şadirvan* was originally left open to the elements, but in recent years this oculus has been covered over with a glass window. Nevertheless, the effect remains most attractive, giving the impression of an interior court filled with light, ringed by the faithful, busy at their ablutions.

Before you leave the mosque notice its superb walnut *mimber*, the finest of its type in existence. Afterwards it is worth standing back in the courtyard to admire the handsome exterior, with its façade of honey-coloured limestone from Mount Olympus. The impressive main gateway is apparently not part of the original construction, and there is reason to believe that it was built by Tamerlane during his occupation of Bursa in 1402–3. During that time Beyazit was suffering through the last year of his life as Tamerlane's captive, after having been defeated at the battle of Ankara in 1401. As wrote Arabshah, the chronicler of the Mongol conqueror's career: 'The son of Osman fell into a hunter's snare, and became confined like a bird in a cage.'

If you return down Atatürk Caddesi for a short way past Ulu Cami you soon come to the oldest of the royal Bursa mosques, **Orhan Gazi Camii.** This was built in 1336 by Orhan I, conqueror of Bursa. The mosque has been twice destroyed and subsequently restored – once in the fifteenth century and again in the eighteenth – but nevertheless it retains its original form. It is the earliest example of a cross-axial *eyvan* mosque, an *eyvan* being a vaulted or domed space recessed from a central court or hall. Here the two side *eyvans* flank the central hall, while the main *eyvan*, raised by three steps, constitutes the prayer room with the *mihrab* and *mimber*. In addition, there are two small rooms on either side of the entrance; these are *tabhane* or *zaviye*, used as hospices for wandering dervishes.

The principal market of Bursa lies behind the two mosques we have just seen. The entire area was gutted by fire in 1955, but since then most of it has been restored to its original form. Something of its old charm and character has been lost, but nevertheless, one still gets the feeling here of being in an old Ottoman market town, and one could easily spend the better part of a day wandering through its labyrinthian arcades in search of a bargain.

The core of the market, here as in Istanbul, is the **Bedesten**. The Bursa Bedesten was built during the reign of Yíldírím Beyazit and was used to store and display only the most valuable goods, such as brocades, jewellery and objects of gold and silver. Beside the Bedesten is the **Sipahilar Çarşísí**, a covered bazaar built by Mehmet I in the first half of the fifteenth century. And beyond these two buildings there are about a dozen splendid old *hans*, most of them dating from the fifteenth century. The most handsome of these is the **Koza Han**, built in 1451 and recently restored.

Beyond Ulu Cami the avenue divides into two branches, one skirting the acropolis and the other, Yiğitler Caddesi, leading to the heights along the ramparts of the Citadel. Along the first, steep stretch of Yiğitler Caddesi lie the massive remnants of the ancient defence-wall of the Citadel; this was originally constructed in Hellenistic times and rebuilt during both the Byzantine and Ottoman periods.

At the top of the acropolis you come to an enclosed area where stand the **tombs of Osman Gazi and Orhan Gazi**. Osman Gazi, the eponymous founder of the Ottoman dynasty, died in the nearby town of Söğüt in 1324 and his body was brought here only after the capture of Bursa two years later. At that time his son Orhan buried him in what had been the baptistery of the former church of St Profitis Elias, then converted into a mosque. When Orhan himself died in 1359 he was buried in what had been the nave of the church. Both buildings have been destroyed and rebuilt several times, and now all that remains of the original church are some fragments of mosaic pavement around the catafalque of Sultan Orhan. Behind the tombs there is a broad esplanade from which one has a sweeping view out over the lower town of Bursa and its surrounding hills.

From there the avenue continues on around the ramparts, and soon you see in the valley below the domes of the Muradiye complex, the next stop on your tour. But before you leave the Citadel you might stroll along some of its picturesque back streets to see some of the prettiest houses in Turkey. These old Bursa houses are usually built of stone and are painted sky blue, green, ochre or pink, with the upper floor projecting out over the street. Occasionally an open kitchen door allows you a peep inside into a garden bright with flowers growing in petrol tins, or you glance up to see an ancient taking his ease in a vine-shaded balcony, enjoying his *keyf* like a sultan in his palace.

The grandest of these old Ottoman houses stands just around the corner from the Muradiye. Built in the early eighteenth century, it has been well restored and is now open as a museum, with some of its rooms furnished as they were in Ottoman times.

The **Muradiye** was built during the years 1424–6 by Sultan Murat II, father of Mehmet the Conqueror. This was the last imperial complex to be built in Bursa; besides the mosque itself it included an *imaret*, a *medrese*, and the *türbe* of the founder. The mosque is of the cross-axial *eyvan* type, similar in design to Orhan Gazi Camii, and it too has a pair of *tabhane*, or dervish hospices, situated on either side of the entrance.

The **Mausoleum of Murat II** stands in the garden behind his mosque, surrounded by another dozen *türbe* that were built during the following century. The great warrior died in Edirne in 1451 and soon afterwards he was laid to rest here, the last sultan to be buried in the old capital of Bursa. His tomb has a simple grandeur about it, with his earth-filled marble catafalque lying along under the open oculus of the dome.

There are three other imperial mosque complexes in Bursa, and all are in outlying sections of the town. During the first century and a half of the Ottoman Empire, in Bursa and later in Edirne, the sultans generally built their palaces and mosques outside the crowded town centre, preferring instead the peace and privacy of the suburbs.

The oldest of these complexes is that of **Murat I Hüdavendigâr**. (Hüdavendigâr is a pompous imperial title meaning literally the Creator of the Universe.) This mosque complex, constructed during the years 1365–85, stands in the pleasant suburb of Çekirge, on the heights to the north-west of the town. The reason why it took so long to build is that the Sultan spent most of his long reign at war and had little time to spare for his mosque. In 1361, the year before he succeeded his father Orhan Gazi as Sultan, Murat captured Edirne, and in the next three decades he led his armies to a series of important victories in the southern Balkans. His last and greatest triumph came at the battle of Kossova on 27 August 1389, when the Turkish forces crushed the allied armies led by King Lazarus of Serbia and annexed his kingdom to the Ottoman Empire. But the Sultan was assassinated on the field of battle and died hours after his victory, to be buried soon after beside his mosque in Bursa.

The Hüdavendigâr is a two-storeyed building with a mosque-hospice on the ground floor and a *medrese* above – a design without parallel in Ottoman architecture. Besides the mosque all that remains of the pious foundations are the Sultan's *türbe* and a little *hamam* called the Bath of the Bereft.

The oldest of all the thermal baths in Bursa, the famous **Eski Kaplíca Hamam**, stands at the foot of the Çekirge hill, a short distance below the Hüdavendigâr. According to tradition, these baths were first built by Justinian and Theodora. In their present form they are due to Murat I, but the ancient columns and capitals used in their construction indicate that the original structure may have been founded in Byzantine or even Roman times.

On the way back to town you see in the fields below the road the **Yeni Kaplíca Hamam**, built in the middle of the sixteenth century by Rüstem Pasha. Evliya Efendi says that Süleyman was cured of his gout by bathing at a hot spring there, whereupon he commanded his Grand Vezir to build a *hamam* on the site.

Then on your left you pass the **Culture Park**, where the people of Bursa come in summer to enjoy themselves at outdoor cafés, casinos and the amusement park. Within the park is the new **Archaeological Museum**, which houses a collection of antiquities found in and around Bursa, including a large number of funerary stelae from the Roman and Byzantine periods.

The other two imperial mosque complexes stand on the hillside to the south-east of the town centre. The best approach is to return to Cumhuriyet Meydaní and walk east along Atatürk Caddesi. This will take you across a bridge over the Gök Dere, a stream which flows down from Ulu Dağ. Once across the bridge take the second left into Yeşil Caddesi, which soon brings you to **Yeşil Cami**, the **Green Mosque**.

Yeşil Cami was commissioned by Mehmet I Çelebi in 1413, the year in which he finally became Sultan after the long civil war which followed the death of his father, Yíldírím Beyazit. The mosque was not finished when Mehmet himself died in 1421, and although work continued for another three years thereafter it was never completed, lacking its entrance portico. Nevertheless Yeşil Cami is the grandest and most beautiful of the imperial mosques in Bursa, both in the harmony of its design and the richness of its interior decoration.

The design is yet another variation of the cross-axial *eyvan* type. You enter through a small, barrel-vaulted *eyvan* into the interior court, in the centre of which there is a *şadirvan* pool which is illuminated by daylight from the oculus in the dome above. To left and right there are side *eyvans* elevated by a single step above the central court, while the main *eyvan*, the prayer area, is reached by a marble stairway of four steps. This is surely the most beautiful mosque interior in Bursa, with the magnificent *mihrab* framed in the great arch of the prayer *eyvan*, and the still water of the pool mirroring the brilliant colours of the stained-glass windows in the *kible* wall.

After examining more closely the fine ceramic tiles on the walls of the main *eyvan*, look back towards the entryway. Above the entrance *eyvan* you see the beautifully tiled imperial loge, and to either side of it the screened balconies which were reserved for the royal family; below these are the private pews used by the courtiers. Finally there are the two pairs of *zaviye* flanking each of the side *eyvans*.

Yeşil Türbe, the **Mausoleum of Sultan Mehmet I**, stands at the top of a hill across the street from the mosque. Originally its exterior walls were revetted in the turquoise tiles from which the *türbe* and the mosque took their names, but these were destroyed in the earthquake of 1855 and replaced by modern Kütahya tiles. The interior decoration of the *türbe* rivals that of the mosque itself, particularly the finely-carved doors, the tile revetment of the walls, the beautifully-decorated *mimber*, and the Sultan's sarcophagus with its ornate inscription in golden calligraphy on a blue ground.

The mosque complex of Mehmet I also included a *medrese*, an *imaret* and a *hamam*, but of these only the *imaret* remains intact. The *imaret* has been used in recent years to house the **Museum of Turkish and Islamic Art**, in which are exhibited, among other things, Ottoman armaments, kitchen utensils, jewellery, calligraphy, and antique books handwritten in Osmanlí script. At the time of writing, however, the *medrese* is undergoing restoration and so the museum is temporarily closed.

The fourth of Bursa's imperial mosque complexes is that of Yíldírím Beyazit, which stands on the top of a hillside to the northeast of Yeşil Cami. The best approach is to sight on it from the outer courtyard of Yeşil Cami and then follow the streets which lead generally in that direction. It is a fair walk, but the quarter through which you stroll is full of interest, with cobbled lanes lined with lovely old Bursa houses like those in the Citadel.

The **Mosque Complex of Yíldírím Beyazit** was begun in 1391 and completed in 1395. Like most Bursa mosques, it was badly damaged in the earthquake of 1855; since then it has been restored twice, once in 1878 and again in 1948, yet it seems to have retained its original form and character. This was one of the first extensive mosque complexes in the Ottoman Empire. The *külliye* consisted of the mosque with its dervish hospice, along with two *medreses*, an *imaret*, a hospital, a palace, and the *türbe* of its founder. Today all that remains are the mosque, the *türbe* and one of the *medreses*, which now serves as a dispensary. The mosque itself is of the now-familiar cross-axial *eyvan* design, with pairs of *zaviye* flanking each of the side *eyvans*. The exterior of the mosque is particularly handsome, with its strong portico of five arches and its shining façade of marble and cut stone.

The best time to visit Bursa is in spring, when the broad plain below Ulu Dağ turns a virginal green and the hillsides are bright with wild flowers and blossoming trees. By then the winter clouds and mists are gone and you can see the majestic slopes and peaks of Ulu Dağ looming over the town. And of course no visit to Bursa is complete without an ascent of the Great Mountain itself. Those without transport can take the cable car which starts from the hillside to the east of town, not far from Yeşil Cami, otherwise one can drive or take a taxi up the mountain road which ascends from Çekirge. The view from the summit is awesome, with all of Bithynia spread out before your feet, and on a clear day you can see the domes and spires of Istanbul shining in the distance.

CHAPTER EIGHT

Thrace and the Dardanelles

❧

Istanbul to Edirne – Edirne: Üç Şerefeli Cami – The Selimiye – Mosque of Murat II – Mosque of Beyazit II – Mosque of Murat I – Edirne to Gallipoli – The Dardanelles – The Gallipoli War Cemetery

The main highway for Thrace, the infamous Londra Asfalt, leaves Istanbul just to the right of the Edirne Gate, passing through a breach in the Theodosian walls. The road follows the course of the ancient Via Egnatia, the main Roman route between Constantinople and the West. Once you are safely past Istanbul Airport conditions improve to the point where you can occasionally glance at the scenery, seeing here and there old bridges which were once part of the Via Egnatia and its descendants. Some of these are Roman, some Byzantine, and others Ottoman, for this has been the highroad through Thrace for two thousand years. The finest of these structures is a very handsome Ottoman bridge of four spans just past Küçük Çekmece, a village at the mouth of an inlet of the Marmara. This was built by Sinan for Süleyman in 1563.

Soon afterwards you pass by Silivri, the Greek Selembria, which in antiquity was the largest town outside Byzantium on the northern coast of the Marmara.

About ten kilometres past Silivri the highway divides in two. The left branch, which follows what was once the main branch of the Via Egnatia, leads out along the Marmara shore as far as Tekirdağ, where it turns inland towards the Greek border. Here you take the right fork, which heads directly across Thrace to Edirne and the Greek-Turkish frontier.

The towns you pass on the way to Edirne were originally founded in Roman times as stations on this branch of the Via Egnatia. During the Ottoman period they once again became important as garrison posts, for they stood along the only road leading to the European provinces of the Empire. The first one you come to is Çorlu, the Roman Cenopurio, where in AD 275 the Emperor Aurelian was murdered. After that comes Lüleburgaz, the ancient Arcadiopolis, and then Babaeski and Havsa. Sinan built a number of mosques in these towns late in his career, while he was working on the great Selimiye complex in Edirne. In Lüleburgaz he built a mosque for Sokollu Mehmet Pasha; in Babaeski for Semiz Ali Pasha; and in Havsa for Kasím Pasha. These fine old mosques give character and distinction to what would otherwise be little more than outposts on the lonely Thracian downs.

Finally you arrive in **Edirne**, where the highway brings you down Mithat Pasha Caddesi to Cumhuriyet Meydaní, the centre of the town. As you enter the square you can see straight ahead the Üç Şerifli Cami, on the left Eski Cami and the Bedesten, and some distance off to the right the Selimiye, the principal adornment of Edirne, the ancient Adrianople.

Adrianople, the city of Hadrian, was founded by that great emperor in AD 125, and from that time it has always been the main town of Thrace. During Byzantine times the city appears principally in connection with the great battles which were fought in its vicinity. Constantine the Great defeated Licinius near Adrianople in 323, the year before his final victory outside Byzantium. The Emperor Valens was killed here in battle against the Goths in 378; and in 811 Nicephorus I lost his life fighting against Krum of the Bulgars, who afterwards fashioned the Emperor's skull into a goblet from which he served beer to his officers at the victory feast. During the following five centuries the town was fought over and captured in turn by the Byzantines, Avars, Bulgars, Crusaders and Turks, until it finally fell to Murat I in 1361. Edirne, as it was then called, soon afterwards became capital of the expanding Ottoman Empire, a position it held until the Conquest of Constantinople in 1453. Edirne retained its prominence long after the transfer of the capital, for several of the sultans and their pashas looked upon the city as their second home, and continued to adorn it with splendid buildings. However, the decay of the Ottoman Empire in later centuries brought about a decline in the fortunes of Edirne, and the city suffered terribly at the hands of invading armies in the nineteenth and twentieth centuries. It was occupied by the Russians in 1829 and 1878, the Bulgars in 1913 and the Greeks in 1919–22, after which it was formally awarded to Turkey in the Lausanne Treaty of 1923. The wounds of war have healed in the years since then, and today Edirne is a lively and cheerful market town, distinguished by its many imperial Ottoman monuments.

Eski Cami, the **Old Mosque**, was built during the years 1402–13 by three sons of Yíldírím Beyazit: the Emir Süleyman, Musa Çelebi and Mehmet Çelebi, who fought one another for control of the Otto-man Empire after their father's death as Tamerlane's captive in 1402. The struggle was eventually won by Mehmet Çelebi, who in 1413 became sole ruler of the Empire as Mehmet I. In that same year he celebrated the beginning of his reign by dedicating the mosque which had been begun by his dead brothers.

The building is a perfect square, divided into nine equal sections covered by nine domes which are supported internally by four massive piers. Because of the smaller number of piers and the larger spans, the interior appears more spacious than the Ulu Cami of Bursa, which is built to the same general design.

Before crossing the square to see Üç Şerifli Cami you might wander through the market around Eski Cami. This is not as ex-tensive or colourful as the market area in Bursa, but nevertheless has three old Ottoman buildings well worth visiting.

Just to the south-west of Eski Cami is the **Caravansarai of Rüstem Pasha**, built by Sinan in about 1560. This is an imposing structure of two storeys surrounding two arcaded courtyards, the smaller of which was once used to stable the horses and camels of the travellers who were accorded hospitality there. The caravansarai has been restored in recent years and now serves as a modern tourist hostelry, the Hotel Caravansaray.

Just beside Eski Cami you see the Edirne **Bedesten**, built by Mehmet I immediately after the completion of the mosque. As in the case of most Ottoman markets, the revenues from its shops went to pay for the upkeep of the mosque and the support of its staff. The Bedesten, which has been restored in recent years, consists of two rows of seven domed areas flanking a central hall.

Another old Ottoman market building stands at the end of Saraçlar Caddesi, the first main street to the west of Eski Cami. This is the **Market of Semiz Ali Pasha**, built by Sinan in 1568 for one of Süleyman's grand vezirs. Then, just across the avenue Talat Pasha Asfaltí, stands the tower known as Kule Kapísí. This is the last remnant of a defence-tower which once guarded the main gate of the Citadel of Adrianople, built by Hadrian when he founded the city. The tower was reconstructed by John II Comnenus in 1123, at the time when he rebuilt the outer defence-walls of the city. Parts of the Byzantine fortifications are to be seen scattered in the streets to the west of Ali Pasha's market.

You now return to Cumhuriyet Meydaní to visit **Üç Şerefeli Cami**. This imperial mosque was built by Murat II in the years 1437–47; it was the most monumental building erected in the Empire before the

Conquest of Constantinople, and represents the culmination of early Ottoman architecture. The mosque is preceded by a great porticoed courtyard centring on a *şadirvan* pool, and at the four corners of the building rise the four minarets. The minaret at the south-west corner has the three *müezzin*'s balconies, called in Turkish *üç şerif*, from which the mosque takes its name. When it was built this was the tallest minaret in the Ottoman Empire, more than sixty-seven metres in height, a record subsequently exceeded only by the minarets at the Selimiye.

The mosque itself consists of a domed prayer room flanked by side areas each covered by a pair of domes. The central dome is twenty-four metres in diameter, the largest span achieved in the Ottoman Empire up to that time; internally its only supports are two huge hexagonal piers. They are the only obstructions within the mosque and so there is a feeling of vast spaciousness, in which the faithful have from almost everywhere in the interior a clear view of the *mihrab* and *mimber*. This was a great advance towards the centrally-planned classical mosques of the sixteenth century, when Ottoman architecture reached the pinnacle of its greatness.

The culmination of classical architecture came with the **Selimiye Mosque**, which stands only a few hundred metres away down Mimar Sinan Caddesi, named after the great architect who created it. Sinan built the mosque for Selim II in the period 1569–75, completing it when he was in his eighty-fifth year, and till the end of his days he held that this was the masterwork of his career, surpassing even the Süleymaniye in its grandeur.

The mosque is surrounded on three sides by a vast outer courtyard. From within this courtyard there is an unimpeded view of the magnificent edifice framed by its four slender minarets, each over seventy metres tall and each fringed with three balconies adorned with stalactite corbelling. Then within the inner courtyard one sees a regal portico of Byzantine columns, the voussoirs of the arches in alternating red stone and white marble, the whole centring on a graceful *şadirvan* pool.

From there you pass through the lofty front portico and enter the great doorway to look upon the mosque interior, the supreme achievement of Ottoman architecture, rivalling even Haghia Sophia in its beauty and its grandeur. The great dome, whose diameter is slightly greater than that of Haghia Sophia, is supported by eight huge independent piers. Two of them flank the entrance and two frame the *mihrab*, which is recessed from the nave under a semi-dome, giving it the appearance of a sanctuary and heightening its religious importance. Directly beneath the great dome stands the *müezzin*'s gallery, a marble platform carried on rectangular columns, surmounting a marble patio with a pretty fountain at its centre. The *mihrab* is also of marble, as is the *mimber*, perhaps the finest in all of Turkey, with its sides carved in a striking openwork design. The lower walls of the *mihrab* apse are revetted in fine Iznik tiles above which there is a calligraphic inscription with flowing white letters on a blue ground. In the south-west corner the imperial loge is carried out from the east gallery on a portico with four arches. This is one of the most gorgeous chambers in all of Turkey, for its tile decoration is absolutely unsurpassed, even in Topkapí Sarayí. The *mihrab* in the imperial loge is extraordinary too, for at its centre two superb wooden shutters open to reveal a window looking out over the town and the surrounding countryside.

The pious foundations of the Selimiye are surprisingly few considering the immense dimensions of the complex. Its entire western side is taken up by the **Kavaflar Arasta**, or **Cobbler's Arcade**. This market of 124 shops for cobblers and shoe merchants was built a decade after the completion of the mosque by Davut Ağa, Sinan's student and his successor as Chief Architect. Attached to the market at its centre there is a primary school with a handsome loggia. The southern end of the market abuts a Kuran school, which stands beside a graveyard. On the other side of the graveyard there is a *medrese*, which now houses the **Antiquities Museum**. Across the way from the *medrese* in a new building is the **Archaeological and Ethnographical Museum**, which includes an interesting collection of Turkish embroideries, *kilims*, household utensils, antique armaments and coins, along with some Roman statuary and ancient jewellery and pottery.

The other imperial mosques of Edirne are all located in outlying areas of the city, in keeping with the early Ottoman practice of building royal mosques and palaces away from the crowded town centres. This served a dual purpose, for not only did it give the Sultan more quiet and privacy, but also the new imperial mosque complexes soon became civic centres for the suburbs which grew up around them, a particularly enlightened example of Ottoman town-planning.

The first of these that we will visit is the **Muradiye**, which stands on a hill to the north-east of town. It is best approached along Mimar Sinan Caddesi. The Muradiye was originally founded by Murat II in 1435 as a *zaviye* for Mevlevi dervishes, whose founder, Celattin Rumi, appeared one night to the Sultan in a dream and asked him to build this hospice. Later in his reign Murat converted the *zaviye* into a mosque, housing the dervishes in a separate *tekke* in the garden. The mosque is of the cross-*eyvan* type, with two rooms opening off from the main interior court and the prayer room approached by a flight of six steps. The *mihrab* is particularly worthy of inspection, for it is revetted with some of the finest surviving examples of early fifteenth-century Iznik tiles.

The remaining imperial mosques are on the other side of the Tunca, one of the two rivers which nearly encircle Edirne. You approach them by returning to Mimar Sinan Caddesi and following its continuation as it winds to the north-east towards the river. The Tunca here divides into two branches, the first of which you cross on the **Bridge of Süleyman the Magnificent**, built by Sinan in 1554. This brings you to **Sarayiçi**, an island in the Tunca where once stood the famous Edirne Sarayí, the palace which was begun by Murat II in 1450 and afterwards completed by Mehmet the Conqueror. Unfortunately, the palace was destroyed in 1877 and not a trace of it remains.

For the past half-century Sarayiçi has been the site of the famous Kírkpínar Wrestling Matches, an annual festival held in mid-June. The origins of this festival go back six centuries; according to tradition, they commemorate the wrestling bouts held by Süleyman Pasha, son of Orhan Gazi, so that his forty heroes could amuse themselves between battles. As many as a hundred thousand spectators attend the matches, and for a week Edirne is thronged with excited crowds and the roads around are lined with gypsy caravans, giving the whole scene the flavour and atmosphere of a medieval fair.

After leaving Sarayiçi, you cross the second branch of the Tunca on the **Bridge of the Conqueror**, built by Mehmet II to provide access to the countryside from his palace. Once across you turn left and follow the road or any of the paths which run parallel to the river. This eventually brings you to the **Mosque of Beyazit II**, built for the Sultan by the architect Hayrettin in the years 1484–8. This is the most extensive of the mosque complexes in Edirne, reflecting the greatly increased prosperity of the Empire during Beyazit's reign, when the Sultan for the most part refrained from war to consolidate the gains made by his predecessors.

The pious foundations of the complex line the vast outer courtyard, where once were tethered the horses and camels of the caravans which stopped here. Along the west side of the courtyard stands the *imaret* and the food-store; these served the needs of the travellers who put up here and also supplied food for the patients and staff of the hospital. The various institutions of the hospital are on the west side of the courtyard. Just beside the mosque you see a domed structure which was used as the hospital proper. Adjoining that is the *timarhane*, or asylum for the insane, and set back at the end of that is the *tip medrese*, or medical school. Evliya Efendi tells us that music was played at the hospital thrice weekly as a 'cure for the sick, a medicine for the afflicted, spiritual nourishment for the mad, and a remedy for the melancholy'.

The mosque itself is preceded by a porticoed courtyard centred on a *şadirvan*. From there you pass through the entrance portico of seven bays into the mosque, a square room surmounted by a dome. The two hospices which flank the mosque on either side are here totally isolated from the prayer room, and are entered either from the outside or from the fountain-court.

The oldest of Edirne's imperial mosques stands to the south-east of Beyazit's complex, some distance downstream and on the same side of the Tunca. Until recently this mosque was attributed to Yíldírím Beyazit and dated from the period of his reign, but now it has been shown to be a foundation of **Murat I, the Hüdavendigâr,** probably constructed not long after the capture of Edirne in 1361. The mosque was undoubtedly built on the ruins of a Greek church, for the foundations and lower walls are obviously of Byzantine construction. The building is sadly neglected and in need of repairs, but is still open as a mosque, serving the faithful of the surrounding area as it has now for more than six centuries past.

Leaving the mosque, you head back to town along the road which comes from the Bulgarian frontier. When you reach the Tunca you see on your right the **Mosque of Mihal Gazi,** built in 1421 by a Greek nobleman who became a Moslem and a 'Warrior for the Faith' (Gazi). The bridge across the Tunca at this point is also named after Mihal Gazi, but it was originally built by the Byzantines in the second half of the thirteenth century. **The Bridge of Mihal Gazi** was repaired on several occasions by the Turks, most extensively by the Grand Vezir Kara Mustafa Pasha in the seventeenth century.

On the far side of the bridge, on the left, is the ruined **Hamam of Mihal Gazi.** And on the right is the little **Mosque of Şahmelek Pasha,** built in 1428. You then continue east on Talat Pasha Asfaltí, which brings you back to Cumhuriyet Meydani and the centre of town.

After a day of walking around Edirne you will probably be in the mood for a relaxing Turkish bath at one of the many *hamams* in town. The most famous of these is the recently-restored **Sokullo Mehmet Pasha Hamamí**, which stands just beside the Üç Şerefeli Cami. This grand *hamam* was built by Sinan in 1579 and is the most beautiful in Edirne.

Refreshed and cleansed, you might then be inclined to stroll down the back streets of town, for there are more than fifty other antiquities besides those you have seen, including Ottoman mosques, *medreses*, *hamams*, caravansarais, bridges and fountains, as well as the scattered remnants of Byzantine and Roman walls, monuments of the long and illustrious history of Edirne.

From Edirne you return along the Istanbul highway as far as Havsa; there, if you are going on to Gallipoli (Gelibolu in Turkish), you turn right and drive parallel to the Greek border as far as Keşan. From Keşan it is a pleasant drive over the pine-clad hills and down into the plain below, where the road winds through vineyards and orchards around the head of the Saros Gulf.

At **Bolayír** you come to the neck of the Gallipoli peninsula, so narrow here that on one side you can see the gulf and on the other the beginning of the Dardanelles. At the far end of the village there is a large *türbe* standing in a copse of cypresses high above the plain below. This is the **Tomb of Prince Süleyman**, eldest son of Orhan Gazi, who in 1354 captured the fortress of Gallipoli on the Dardanelles. This established the first Turkish foothold in Europe, and within the following half-century their armies swept throughout the Balkans and up into central Europe. However, Prince Süleyman did not live to inherit his father's empire, for he died on this spot in 1359, killed by a fall from his horse while falconing. Buried in the garden beside his *türbe* is the poet Namík Kemal, one of the leaders of the Young Ottomans, the group who strove to reform and revive the Empire in the latter part of the nineteenth century.

The road soon comes down to the sea at **Gelibolu**, the former Gallipoli, the principal port on the European side of the strait. The port itself is cheerful and picturesque, with brightly-coloured fishing-boats anchored under the walls of the medieval fortress. The ruined tower beside the inner port is now all that remains of the fortifications which once enclosed Gallipoli and its harbour. According to Greek tradition, the original Castle of Gallipoli was constructed by Philippicus Bardanes, an Armenian who was Emperor of Byzantium from 711 to 713. After the capture of Gallipoli in 1354, the fortress was rebuilt by the Turks and used by them to guard the straits, a control which they continued to maintain through the long history of the Ottoman Empire and down to the present day.

Across the way from Gelibolu on the Asian shore you see the town of **Lapseki**, the Greek Lampasacus. There is a regular car-ferry between Gelibolu and Lapseki, and many travellers prefer to cross here rather than at Eceabat, the port directly across from Çanakkale. The drive from Lapseki to Çanakkale is very pleasant and the countryside is lovely, with the road winding along through the rich vineyards for which this region has been famous since antiquity.

On the European side, the road leaves Gelibolu and at first runs along the peninsula at some distance from the sea. Thirteen kilometres past Gelibolu the road crosses over a little stream and then comes down to a cove called **Ince Liman**, the **Port of the Pearl**. The stream was known in antiquity as the Aegospotamos, and the cove into which it flows was the site of one of the most historic battles in naval history. There in August 405 BC a Spartan force led by Lysander decisively defeated an Athenian fleet commanded by Conon and Pericles, in what would be the last battle of the long and bitter Peloponnesian War.

The promontory at the far end of the cove is the **site of ancient Sestos**, celebrated in poetry as the setting of the legendary romance between Hero and Leander. Hero, a priestess at the temple of Aphrodite in Sestos, met and fell in love with Leander at a festival of the goddess, and afterwards he swam the Hellespont nightly from his home across the straits in Abydos, guided by the lamp which she lit for him on the shore. But during a winter storm the lamp was extinguished; Leander lost his way and drowned, and when his dead body was eventually washed up at Sestos his heartbroken lover drowned herself too. Byron swam the straits here on 3 May 1810, a feat which he commemorated six days later with the completion of his poem, *Written after Swimming from Sestos to Abydos*.

The **site of ancient Abydos** is at the top of Maltepe, the promontory just across the strait from Sestos. This was where the Persian army crossed the Hellespont in May of 480 BC, while Xerxes watched from a throne of white marble on the heights of Abydos. According to Herodotus: 'The King watched the spectacle below, and when he saw the whole Hellespont hidden by ships, and the beaches of Abydos and all the open ground filled with men, he congratulated himself – and the moment afterwards burst into tears . . . "I was thinking," Xerxes replied (to his uncle Artabanus), "and it came into my mind how pitifully short is human life, for all these many thousands of men not one will be alive in a hundred years' time".'

After Akbaşi Liman the road runs inland for some distance and returns to the sea at Kilia Liman. From here another road leads inland to two Anzac cemeteries of the Gallipoli campaign: the Australian memorial at Lone Pine and the New Zealand monument at Çanuk Bair. Then, a little farther along, you come to Eceabat, where there is a car-ferry across to Çanakkale.

After Eceabat the road comes to **Kilitbahir**, the **Key to the Sea**, a village directly across the narrows from Çanakkale. The village takes its name from the medieval Ottoman fortress which guards the narrows here. Kilitbahir was one of the castles built by Mehmet the Conqueror in 1452 to cut off the straits in preparation for his siege of Constantinople; it remains the best-preserved and most picturesque of the old fortresses along the Dardanelles.

The strait between Kilitbahir and Çanakkale is only 1300 metres wide, and because of its strategic importance it has been contested by all of the powers who have fought one another in these waters. The headland above Kilitbahir was known to the Greeks as Cynossema, and it gave its name to the naval battle in the narrows in 411 BC in which Athens won an important victory over Sparta. With his account of that battle Thucydides suddenly breaks off his *History of the Peloponnesian War*, six years before the final defeat of Athens a few miles farther up the strait. And it was here in the narrows that the Allied fleet was repulsed by Turkish batteries on 18 March 1915, when they first tried to force their way through the straits, with the loss of several French and British warships and the death of hundreds of their crew.

Once past Kilitbahir the road continues along the sea for some distance, passing several memorials to Turkish soldiers who died at their guns during the Gallipoli campaign. Then you head inland and up into the hills through a pine forest to drive down the spine of the peninsula. You soon come to the village of **Alçítepe**, where signposts at a crossroad indicate the various British and Commonwealth war cemeteries which are to be found in the vicinity; to the right are the cemeteries at Twelve Tree Copse, Pink Farm and Lancashire Landing; and to the left the Beach Cemetery, the Redoubt, Skew Bridge, and the Cape Helles War Memorial.

The main road turns left at the crossroad and goes down to the end of the peninsula, to the Turkish War Memorial at Abide and the British and Commonwealth Memorial at Cape Helles. Visitors

---

The Süleymaniye, as seen from the Galata shore of the Golden Horn. The smaller mosque in the left foreground is Rüstem Pasha Camii.

Kapalí Carsí, the Covered Bazaar.

THRACE AND THE DARDANELLES

rarely come to visit the war cemeteries here, in this haunted battle-field where more than a hundred thousand men of both sides lie buried where they fell. A party of British and Anzac veterans landed once again on Cape Helles on 25 April 1975, just sixty years to the day after they had fought their way ashore from the collier *River Clyde*. This time they found waiting for them on the beach only a handful of stooped and white-haired Turkish veterans, and the old men embraced and wept on the same beach where they had tried to kill one another in their youth.

This is surely one of the world's oldest battlefields, for its ruins, memories and legends cover a span of more than three millennia. The headland near the Turkish monument is known as Eski Kale, the Old Castle. This is the **site of ancient Elaeus**, the scene of several naval battles in the Peloponnesian War and the legendary burial-place of Protosilaus, the first warrior in Agamemnon's army to fall in the siege of Troy. Alexander the Great came to offer sacrifice at the tumulus of the Argive hero before he crossed the Hellespont in 334 BC, at the beginning of his great campaign into Asia. Arrian, his biographer, informs us that 'his purpose in performing the ceremony was to ensure for himself better luck than Protosilaus had'.

You now return to **Eceabat** to take the car-ferry across to Çanak-kale. Alexander embarked from here after returning from his visit to the tomb of Protosilaus, launching the expedition which would change the history of the ancient world. Arrian wrote that: 'half-way over he slaughtered a bull as an offering to Poseidon and poured wine from a golden cup into the sea to propitiate the Nereids ... Fully armed, he was the first to leave the ship and set foot upon the soil of Asia, and he built an altar on the spot where he had left the shore of Europe and another when he landed on the other side of the strait, both of them dedicated to Zeus, the Lord of Safe Landings, and to Athena and Heracles.'

The Palace of the Sweet Waters of Asia.

The fortress of Rumeli Hisar. The modern buildings above it house the University of the Bosphorus, the former Robert College.

C.G.T.   113   H

CHAPTER NINE

The Northern Aegean Coast

❧

Çanakkale – Troy – Alexandria Troas – Assos – Edremit – Ayvalík

Most travellers use **Çanakkale** as a base for visiting Troy and the northern Aegean coast, but they pay little heed to the town itself. So before starting out you might take a stroll around Çanakkale, for it is an attractive and unusual place, particularly the quarter around the port. Some of the handsome but decaying old mansions one sees there date from the turn of the century or even earlier, when Çanakkale was a customs and immigration station and the flags of many nations waved from their consulates along the quay. Today the town looks run-down and has lost whatever international flavour it might have had, but the port quarter would seem to be as lively and colourful as ever. From the cafés and restaurants along the seafront you see an endless armada of ships steaming into and out of the strait, while caiques and ferries are continually docking at and departing from the cobbled quays around the port: it makes an exhilarating scene.

The road from Çanakkale follows the shore of the Dardanelles as far as Güzel Yalí, where there are several pleasant hotels by the sea. Then the road winds uphill through a pine forest, passing on the way several memorials to Turkish heroes who died at their guns during the Gallipoli campaign. The road reaches the crest of the hill at Intepe, from where you have your first view of the Trojan plain. From there the road descends to the Dümrek Su, the Simois of Homer, and thence to the hamlet of Gökçalí, where there is a turn-off to **Hisarlík**, the **site of ancient Troy**.

There are many who profess to be disappointed with their first sight of Troy, for the acropolis on which the ancient city stood is now a shapeless mound carved up by the trenches of archaeologists, a midden-heap littered with the confused remains of three millennia of human existence. Nevertheless, the site has enormous historical importance, and for those who have read Homer a visit to Troy is a spiritual pilgrimage to the beginnings of Western literature. One need only browse through the *Iliad* while sitting out on the ruined ramparts of the ancient town, and the windy plains of Troy will come alive again with the gods and heroes of whom Homer wrote.

That Hisarlík is in fact the site of Homer's Troy is now established almost beyond doubt. The city which stood here was known as Ilium Novum throughout classical times and remained inhabited until the fourth century of the Christian era. Despite this, a number of scholars in the nineteenth century, basing their arguments largely on topographical evidence from the *Iliad*, sought to prove that Homer's Troy stood on the heights of Bunarbaşí, some ten kilometres to the south of Hisarlík. It remained for Heinrich Schliemann, in his pioneering archaeological excavations which began in 1870, to prove conclusively that Hisarlík was the site of Homeric Troy, and subsequent investigations by Dörpfeld, Blegen and others have fully substantiated his claim.

What emerges from the archaeological work of the past century is a stratigraphical picture, a historical palimpsest, as it were, of a site inhabited more or less continuously from the Early Bronze Age until late antiquity, with each successive settlement resting on the rubble and ashes of the city that came before it, some destroyed by fire, some by earthquake, some by besieging armies. Even an amateur observer can detect the discontinuities from one level to another, and although to an untrained eye the picture is a confused one, archaeological evidence has established nine main levels of habitation, most of which have several sub-strata. (The latest publication by the University of Cincinnati team recognizes some forty-six strata in all.) Troy I to V have been assigned to the Early Bronze Age, that is, from about 3000 to 1800 BC; Troy VI lasted through the Middle and Late Bronze Ages, i.e., from 1800 to 1300; while the various sub-levels of Troy VII have been dated to the period 1300–1100 BC. After that the site seems to have been uninhabited for about four centuries, the Dark Ages of the ancient Greek world, until it was settled again by Hellenic colonists in about 700 BC. This is the city labelled Troy VIII, while Troy IX is the Ilium Novum of Hellenistic and Roman times. The findings of the Cincinnati expedition led Professor Blegen to maintain that Troy VIIa was the city of Priam, destroyed in about 1260 BC, at about the same time as Mycenae, Tiryns, Pylos and other sites of the Mycenean age, those places which Homer mentions in his chapter in the *Iliad* 'The Catalogue of Ships' as having fought under Agamemnon at the siege of Troy. (Turkish archaeologists disagree to a certain extent and hold that Priam's city is to be identified as a sub-level of Troy VI,

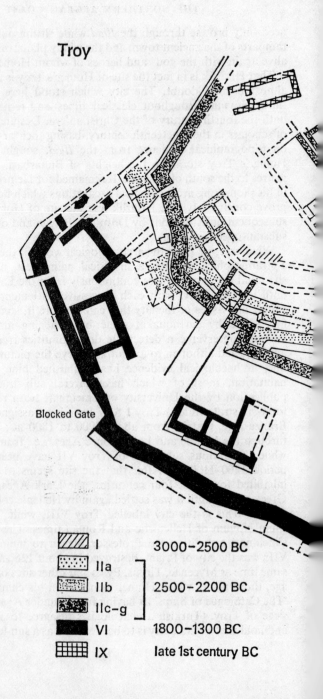

Troy

Blocked Gate

▨	I	3000–2500 BC
⣿	IIa	⎫
⣿	IIb	2500–2200 BC
⣿	IIc–g	⎭
■	VI	1800–1300 BC
▦	IX	late 1st century BC

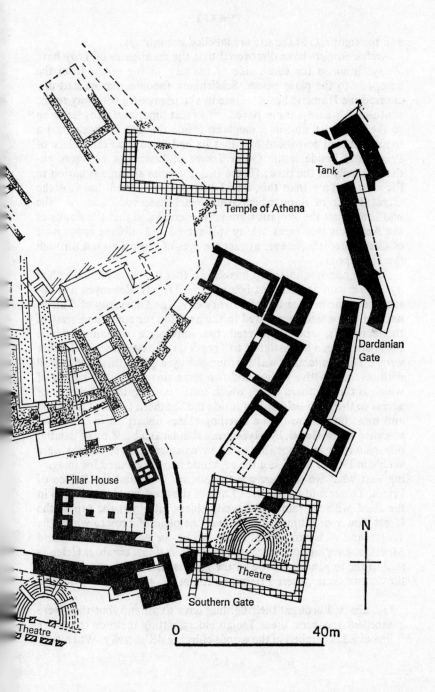

Tank

Temple of Athena

Dardanian
Gate

Pillar House

Theatre

Southern Gate

Theatre

N

0   40m

and the signposts at the site are labelled accordingly.

Archaeologists have discovered that the main gates of Troy have always been on the south side of the city, giving access from the acropolis to the plain below. Schliemann thought that he had discovered the Homeric Scaean Gate in the impressive entryway to the south-east, where a ramp paved with great limestone slabs leads up to the acropolis, and in a megaron inside the gate he unearthed a treasure which convinced him that he had discovered the Palace of Priam and beside it the Great Tower of Ilium. As he wrote enthusiastically at the time: 'There is not a more sublime situation in the area of Troy than this, and I therefore presumed that it is the Great Tower of Ilium which Andromache ascended because "she had heard that the Trojans were hard-pressed and that the power of the Achaeans was great". May this sacred and sublime monument of Greek heroism for ever attract the eyes of those who sail through the Hellespont!'

Alas, modern scholarship has shown that the structure unearthed by Schliemann at that spot belonged to Troy II, destroyed a thousand years before the fall of Priam's city. The University of Cincinnati team has since excavated in the area farther south and west of the acropolis, and discovered the impressive structures which Professor Blegen has assigned to Troy VIIa, the city of which Homer wrote. This settlement was surrounded by a powerful defence-wall with several massive towers and two large entry ways, the largest of which is the Southern Gate, which today is the principal means of access to the plain below. Just inside the Southern Gate is the largest and most impressive of the dwelling-places unearthed in Troy, the so-called **Pillar House,** by Mycenaean standards a building of palatial dimensions. It is impossible to know whether these structures were visible in Homer's day, but the romantic may be excused for imagining that what we see here are the Scaean Gate and the Palace of Priam. This would be the site of one of the most moving passages in the *Iliad*, where Priam and the city elders, sitting at the top of the Great Tower of Ilium, look out over the plain of Troy to where the Trojan and Achaean armies stand facing one another as Paris and Menelaus prepare to engage one another in single combat. Helen is told of the impending battle by the goddess Iris and rushes down to the Scaean Gate, where Priam and the others marvel at her beauty.

Old age had brought their fighting days to an end, but they were excellent speakers, these Trojan elders, sitting there on the tower like cicadas perched in the woods chirping delightfully. When they saw Helen coming to the tower they lowered their voices. 'Who on earth,' they asked one another, 'could blame the Trojan and Achaean men-at-arms for suffering so long for such a woman's sake? Indeed she is the very image of an immortal goddess. All the same, and lovely as she is, let her sail home and not stay here to vex us and our children after us.' Meanwhile Priam had called Helen to his side. 'Dear child,' he said, 'come here and sit in front of me, so that you can see your former husband and your relatives and friends. I bear you no ill will at all. I blame the gods; it is they who brought this terrible Achaean war upon me'.

From the crest of the mound one commands a view of the entire Trojan plain and the background of the Homeric epic. On a clear day you can see far to the south-east the peaks of Mount Ida, where Zeus sat enthroned as a spectator during the siege of Troy. Off to the south-west is the Aegean isle of Tenedos, home of Apollo the Mouse-God; to the north-west is the island of Imbros, and behind that is the mountainous Samothrace, from whose summit Poseidon the Earth-Shaker watched the battle. Across the plain you see glinting here and there the meandering streams of the Scamander, which Achilles once fought with furiously after the river god tried to drown him in anger for having polluted its waters with the corpses of slain Trojans. The Scamander flows into the Dardanelles at the very end of the strait, just before it merges with the Aegean at Kumkale, the Achillaeum of antiquity. The foreshore north of Achillaeum was the site of the Achaean camp, where they beached their beaked ships during the nine-year siege of Troy. This is where Homer begins his tale, writing of the quarrel between Achilles and Agamemnon over the beautiful slave-girl Chryseis: 'The wrath of Achilles is my theme, that fateful wrath which, in fulfilment of the Will of Zeus, brought the Achaeans so much suffering and sent the souls of many noblemen to Hades, leaving their bodies as carrion for the dogs and passing birds.'

A mile or so to the south of Kumkale along the Aegean shore is the promontory known in antiquity as **Cape Sigeum**, just north of which are the two mounds which have traditionally been called the **Tumuli of Patroclus and Achilles**. The burial of Achilles is described in the last book of the *Odyssey*, where the shade of Agamemnon addresses that of Achilles in the underworld meadow of asphodel:

For seventeen days and seventeen nights we mourned you, immortal gods and men alike; and on the eighteenth day we committed you to the flames, with a rich sacrifice of fatted sheep and shambling cattle at your pyre . . . When the sacred flames had consumed you we gathered your white bones at dawn, Achilles, and laid them by in unmixed wine and oil. Then your mother gave us a golden urn, a gift she said was from Dionysus made by the great Hephaestus. In this your white bones lie, my lord Achilles, and mingled with them the bones of Menoetius's son Patroclus, dead before you, and separately those of Antilochus, who was your closest friend after the death of Patroclus. Over them all, we soldiers of the Argive force built up a great and glorious mound, on a promontory jutting out over the broad waters of the Hellespont, so that it might be seen far out to sea by the sailors of today and future ages.

From Troy the highway heads south through the region known in antiquity as the Troad. The highway follows approximately the route of a Roman road, laid down soon after the establishment of the Roman province of Asia in 133 BC. Driving along around the heavily wooded spurs and foothills of Mount Ida, you will notice how different is this verdant countryside from that of Thrace, though the two regions are separated only by the thin strait of the Dardanelles. The Romans were similarly impressed with this bountiful province when they first acquired it, for as Cicero said in one of his orations: 'In the richness of its soil, in the varieties of its products, in the extent of its pastures, and in the number of its products it surpasses all other lands.'

The main town of the central Troad is Ezine, where a road to the right leads off to the coast. The road comes to the sea at the hamlet of Odun Iskelisi, the local port for the isle of Tenedos, known in Turkish as Bozcaada. From there it is only a short drive to the **site of Alexandria Troas**, whose extensive ruins flank the road as it approaches the sea once again.

The city was founded shortly before the end of the fourth century BC by Antigonus the One-Eyed, King of Thrace, who named it Antigonia in his own honour, populating it with the residents of the surrounding towns in the Troad. Antigonus was defeated and killed at the battle of Ipsus in 301 BC by Lysimachus, King of Macedonia, who annexed the Troad to his own dominions and renamed its principal city Alexandria Troas, after his former emperor. During Hellenistic times this was one of the richest and most important commercial centres in Asia Minor, for its strategic position near the entrance of the Hellespont gave it control of all the trade passing between the Aegean, the Propontus and the Euxine. Many of the monumental structures one sees today date from the Roman period, most notably the enormous public baths endowed in about AD 135 by Herodes Atticus, who later built the theatre in Athens which still bears his name.

Alexandria Troas declined in importance after the transfer of the capital of the Roman Empire to Constantinople, and little is heard of it after that time. During the Ottoman period it was known as Eski Stamboul, the Old City, and travellers in the nineteenth century reported that by then it had degenerated into a miserable village huddled among the scattered ruins. The baths of Herodes Atticus and the other buildings of the city were used as a quarry to supply stone for several of the imperial mosques in Istanbul, principally that of Sultan Ahmet I and Yeni Cami. If you walk down to what was once the harbour you will see a number of huge monoliths lying on the beach, abandoned there when they broke while being loaded aboard the ships which were to have taken them to Istanbul.

A drive of half an hour past Ezine brings one to Ayvacík, where a turn-off to the right leads to **Behram Kale**, the **site of ancient Assos**. The approach to Behram Kale is very impressive, as you pass a hog-backed Ottoman bridge of the fourteenth century and see the village clinging to the side of the acropolis, a huge flat-topped cone of basalt rising from the coastal ridge. The road then winds around the town to the west, where you see the necropolis of Greek and Roman times, with a number of sarcophagi scattered around where they were left by grave-robbers. Sarcophagus means literally 'body-eater', since the stone from which they were made was reputed to consume the flesh of the deceased; they were the principal export of Assos and are found all over Asia Minor.

Assos was founded early in the first millennium BC by settlers from Methymna, an Aeolian city on the island of Lesbos. In early times the town was a landing-place for cargoes which were shipped overland to avoid the currents and head-winds of the Hellespont. Later, however, with the improvement of navigation and the establishment of a harbour at Alexandria Troas, Assos declined in importance and became primarily an agricultural community.

The most brilliant period in the history of Assos came in the middle of the fourth century BC, when the Troad and Lesbos were ruled for a time by the eunuch Hermeias, Tyrant of Atarneus. Hermeias had been a student at the renowned Academy in Athens, and he obtained Plato's advice in designing his principality as an ideal city-state. Two of Plato's assistants, Erastas and Coriscus, established a branch of the Platonic Academy in Assos and invited there several of the outstanding scientists and philosophers of the age, the most renowned of whom were Aristotle and Theophrastus. Aristotle remained in Assos through the years 347–4, and while there he and Theophrastus carried out their pioneering researches in zoology, botany and biology, thus laying the foundations for those branches of the life sciences. Aristotle also became an intimate friend and adviser of his first patron, the eunuch Hermeias, and before long married the tyrant's neice, the lady Pythia, who bore him a daughter the following year.

The walls of Assos have been dated to the fourth century BC, and were probably built in the reign of Hermeias. Three kilometres in length, they are among the most impressive in Asia Minor, particularly the stretch leading to the west side of the acropolis. The large gate beyond the necropolis was the entrance to the lower town; this was where most of the public buildings of Assos stood, including the agora, the theatre, the gymnasium and the bouleuterion, or senate chamber. The ruined structures which you see there today date from the third or second century BC.

The citadel on the acropolis was protected by an inner defence-wall, built at about the same time as the outer fortifications. Within these walls, on the highest level of the acropolis, are the ruins of the **Temple of Athena**, built in about 530 BC. All that remains of this once-famous temple is its stylobate, or platform, as well as some scattered Aeolic capitals, columns, and other architectural fragments. Much of the sculptural decoration in relief was still visible until the late nineteenth century, but it has since been removed; some is now on exhibit in the Istanbul Archaeological Museum. It is a pity that no attempt at restoration has been made, for this is the only archaic Doric temple which has survived in all Asia Minor.

To the north of the acropolis there are the ruins of an early Ottoman mosque, built after the capture of Assos by the Turks in 1306. The mosque is believed to have been founded by Sultan Murat I; the cross and Greek inscription over the door indicate that it was constructed from the stones of a Byzantine church on the acropolis, which in turn may have been made from the ruins of the Temple of Athena.

From the acropolis there is a magnificent view out across the Aegean and the Gulf of Edremit. Across the strait is the Greek island of Lesbos, from which the men of Methymna set sail three millennia ago to settle in Assos. And to the south-east across the Gulf is the land which was known in Greek times as Aeolia, the next region on your journey around the Aegean coast of Turkey.

You now return to Ayvacík to rejoin the main road. Those fortun- ate enough to pass through Ayvacík in late April will see the most extraordinary festival in all of Turkey, the annual **paniyir**. This is a market-fair and carnival which brings together all the country people of the Troad in a week-long celebration with music, dancing, song, and drinking – something one hardly expects to find in a sober Moslem country. This *paniyir*, a corruption of the Greek *panaghia*, is the survival of a primitive festival of the Great Earth Mother, the fertility goddess of prehistoric Anatolia. As might be expected the festival attracts gypsies from throughout Anatolia, and all the roads and meadows around are filled with their colourful caravans. The *paniyir* also brings down from the hills thousands of nomads who since time immemorial have made their living cutting timber on the slopes of Mount Ida. They are a proud and independent clan who have little contact with modern civilization, and who move from one mountain encampment to another on horseback, setting up their black goatskin tents in a forest clearing. They are fine-looking people who dress in distinctive native costumes, their unveiled women adorned with necklaces of golden coins, their hardy men mounted on horseback and armed with rifles and bandoliers, looking like klepht warriors from an old print. They are called *yürük*, or wanderers, the last survivors of an ancient Anatolian culture which is rapidly vanishing.

After leaving Ayvacík the highway approaches the Gulf of Edremit, and the forests of pine and valonia oak give way to un- dulating groves of olive trees. Then the road crests the coastal ridge and heads down a splendid gorge where one is suddenly confronted with a magnificent panorama of the Gulf of Edremit and the rolling hills on its far side, with the blue-green mountains of Lesbos rising out of the turquoise Aegean to the west.

The scenery along the Gulf is beautiful, as the road runs along the shore through olive groves, past pink sand beaches and pine-clad promontories. On the left the majestic peaks of Mount Ida loom over the road, with white villages perched high up on its soaring flanks, looking like the mountain towns one sees out on the Aegean isles.

Along the shore there are a succession of small towns with good hotels, as well as bungalows by the sea and facilities for camping, for this is becoming one of the most popular areas along the Aegean coast. The largest of these resorts is Akçay, a village near the head of the Gulf, which is believed to stand on or near the **site of Antandros**, one of the ancient cities of the Troad. Antandros is famous in literature as the place from which Aeneas and the other Trojan survivors embarked on their own odyssey after the fall of Priam's city. Book Three of Virgil's *Aeneid* runs: 'Lordly Ilium had fallen and all Neptune's Troy lay a smoking ruin on the ground. We the exiled survivors were forced by divine command to search the world for a home in some uninhabited land. So we started to build ships below Antandros, the city by the foothills of Phrygian Troy, with no idea where destiny would take us or where we should be allowed to settle.'

At the head of the Gulf the road continues inland for some distance to enter **Edremit,** whose public gardens are the prettiest in Turkey. Edremit stands on the site of ancient Adramyttium, of which not a trace remains. This was one of the cities sacked by Achilles in his raid along the coast in the ninth year of the Trojan War, an event which takes place just prior to the opening of the *Iliad,* and it was here that he captured Chryseis of the lovely cheeks, whom he later presented as a prize to Agamemnon. But when Chryseis was reclaimed by her father Agamemnon demanded that he be given Achilles's prize, the beautiful Briseis, thus touching off the quarrel which is the main theme of Homer's epic poem.

After you pass Edremit the road turns south-west to run along the southern shore of the Gulf, from which there is a panoramic view of the whole range of Mount Ida mirrored in the Aegean. There are several turn-offs along the way to beach resorts, the most popular of which is **Ören**, a short way past Edremit. However, most foreign travellers prefer **Ayvalík**, the large resort town at the end of the peninsula, where there are miles of excellent beaches and scores of good hotels and restaurants.

The scenery around Ayvalík is superb, with a string of green islets set like pieces of jade around the luminescent waters of the bay. The largest of these is Ali Bey Adasí, a sybaritic isle which looks out across the narrow strait to Lesbos, so near but so very far away because of the political gulf separating these two countries which share the beautiful Aegean. As we were sitting in a café there on a moonlit evening years ago, one of our company lifted his glass and recited a fragment of the poem which Sappho wrote, looking on this same scene twenty-five centuries before:

> The glow and beauty of the stars are nothing near the splendid moon
> When in her roundness she burns silver about the world . . .

CHAPTER TEN

The Aeolian Coast and Pergamum

Pergamum – The Asklepieion – Çandarlí – Foça – Izmir

After leaving Ayvalík you continue south, driving through the land known in antiquity as Aeolia. This region, which extended from the Gulf of Adramyttium to that of Smyrna, was first settled in about the tenth century BC by Aeolians from Thessaly and Boetia, forced from their homeland by the Doric invasion from the north. Twelve Aeolian cities were founded in this migration, and you will pass the sites of several along the northern Aegean coast of Turkey. The names of most of these places are today familiar only to historians and archaeologists, for Aeolia never achieved anything like the extraordinarily brilliant and creative civilization of the Ionian cities farther south. The reason may lie in the different backgrounds from which these two peoples came, for the Ionians were seafarers and merchants while the Aeolians had been mostly farmers in their homeland and settled in the most fertile region along the coast of the eastern Aegean. As Herodotus wrote: 'The soil of Aeolia is better than that of Ionia, but the weather is not so good.' And as the humorist Athenaeus added, in his *Doctors at Dinner*: 'And that is why the Aeolians are so given to wine, women and luxurious living.'

The most important centre of civilization in this region was not Aeolian, but a Hellenized Anatolian city-State – **Pergamum** – which stood some distance inland from the coast. You approach the site of ancient Pergamum by turning left off the main road about a half-hour's drive beyond Ayvalík, where you drive up the valley of the Bakír Çayí, the River Caicus of antiquity.

Most of the ruins of ancient Pergamum stand on the acropolis above the modern city of Bergama, although a few important monuments are to be found in the plain below. The setting of the ancient city is spectacular, for the acropolis rises precipitously on three sides to a height of nearly a thousand feet above the plain, flanked by twin tributaries of the Caicus, with the Selinus sweeping around the acropolis to the west and the Caicus to the east. One can appreciate how

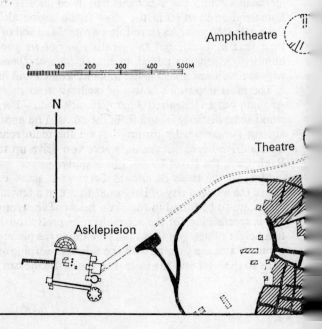

Pergamum

1 Temple of Demeter
2 Upper Gymnasium
3 Lower Gymnasium
4 Lower Agora
5 Great South Gate

0 100 200 300 400 500M

N

Amphitheatre

Theatre

Asklepieion

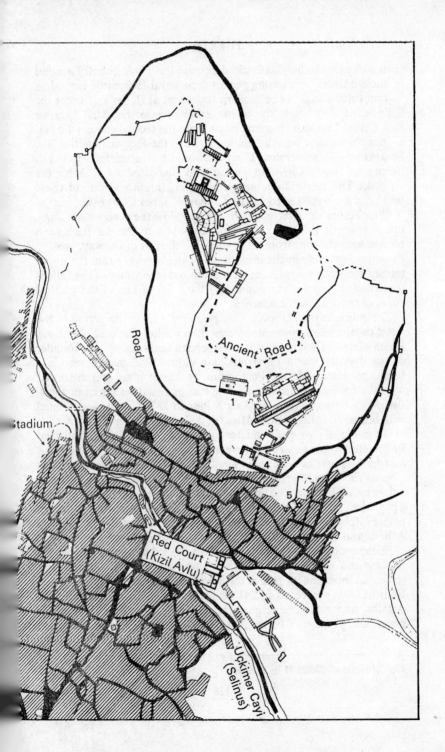

Road

Ancient Road

Stadium

1

2

3

4

5

Red Court
(Kızıl Avlu)

Üçkimer Çayi
(Selinus)

such a city on the heights could dominate the whole country around in ancient times, in a setting perfect for a royal Hellenistic capital.

You drive through the modern town and at its far end cross the Selinus, passing beside the monumental ruins of the **Kízíl Avlu,** or **Red Court.** This vast structure dates from the second century BC and is thought to have been a temple sacred to the Egyptian deities Isis, Serapis and Hermocrates. The edifice was converted into a church during the early Christian period and dedicated to St John the Apostle. The Christian community in Pergamum was one of those to whom John addressed his *Letters to the Seven Churches.*

Once across the river you turn left to follow the road which winds uphill towards the acropolis. This takes you to the car park on a terrace near the top; from there you walk the rest of the way, passing through a gateway in the inner walls of the citadel. From the upper terrace there is a magnificent view down over the valley of the Caicus towards the Aegean, surrounded by the ruins of one of the greatest cities of the Hellenistic age.

The ruins on the acropolis date principally from the period of the Attalids, the kings who ruled Pergamum during the most illustrious epoch of its history, in the third and second centuries BC. The founder of the dynasty was a Paphlagonian named Philetaeros, who had been appointed ruler of Pergamum by Lysimachus and entrusted with the enormous treasure that he had amassed on his campaigns. But when Seleucus invaded Asia Minor in 281 BC Philetaeros sided with him against his master. After the defeat and death of Lysimachus at the battle of Corupedium later that same year Seleucus confirmed Philetaeros in his control of Pergamum and its treasure. Philetaeros and his successors used their wealth wisely. They made enormous gifts to the neighbouring Greek cities on the coast, thus cementing alliances with them and eventually dominating the whole region. They also used their money to endow Pergamum with splendid palaces, temples and other public buildings, so that it rivalled even Athens and Alexandria in the brilliance of its culture.

Philetaeros died in 263 BC, and was succeeded two years later by his nephew and adopted son, Eumenes, who soon after established himself as an independent prince by defeating Antiochus, King of Syria. Eumenes was succeeded in 241 BC by his kinsman and adopted son, Attalus, who in his long reign of forty-four years greatly enhanced the power and prestige of Pergamum. His proudest exploit was his great

The Mosque of Selim II in Edirne.

triumph over the Gauls in a battle near Pergamum in 230 BC. As a result Attalus assumed the titles of King and Saviour, and established his position as a defender of Hellenism against the barbarians. Shortly after his victory over the Gauls Attalus entered into an alliance with Rome, an event which was to have profound effects on the history of Pergamum and the other cities in Asia Minor.

Attalus was succeeded by his eldest son, Eumenes II, who in his reign of thirty-eight years extended the boundaries of the Pergamene kingdom to include virtually all of western Asia Minor. He also expanded the city, which up to that time included only the top of the acropolis, and built great public buildings there and on other terraces farther down the slope, including the lower agora, the great gymnasium, the world-famous altar of Zeus and the renowned library.

When Eumenes died in 159 BC he was succeeded by his eldest son, Attalus II. Although Attalus was over sixty when he came to the throne he ruled for twenty-one years, a period during which he was almost continually at war. Attalus is remembered today principally through the stoa which he endowed in the Agora in Athens and which still bears his name; it has been restored in recent years and stands as a monument to the power and culture of Pergamum in its golden age.

But the golden age did not long outlive the last of the great Attalids. Attalus II was succeeded in 138 BC by his eccentric nephew, Attalus III, who neglected the affairs of state for alchemy and botany and allowed his kingdom to become increasingly dominated by Rome. Towards the end of his life the power of Rome grew so strong in Asia Minor that it seemed inevitable that Pergamum would eventually be absorbed, so in his last will and testament Attalus made the Roman people heir to all his possessions. When Attalus finally died in 133 BC his bequest was quickly accepted, and the Kingdom of the Attalids became the Roman province of Asia, with Pergamum as its capital. Pergamum would continue to be a rich and powerful city through the Roman period and on into the early

---

A gentleman smoking his narghilah in a teahouse in Kütahya.

Two gentlemen taking their ease under the Tree of Idleness, in the village square of Aphrodisias.

Wrestlers performing their ritual march at the Kírkpínar festival in Edirne.

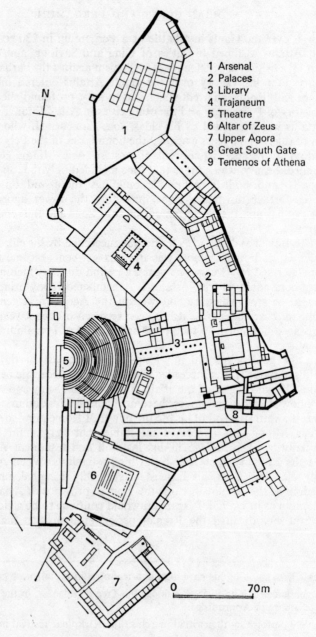

1 Arsenal
2 Palaces
3 Library
4 Trajaneum
5 Theatre
6 Altar of Zeus
7 Upper Agora
8 Great South Gate
9 Temenos of Athena

N

0   70m

Pergamum: the Acropolis

centuries of the Christian era, but its culture was never again as brilliant as in the days of the Attalids.

The oldest part of the city of the Attalids is to be found among the ruins at the very top of the acropolis. The citadel gate there gives entrance to a street which runs from south to north along the ridge of the acropolis. On the right of the street as you ascend are what remains of the royal palaces of the various kings, with that of Eumenes II at the south end, followed by those of Attalus II, Eumenes I, Attalus I, and finally that of Philetaeros.

On the left side of the street at its southern end are the ruins of the temenos, or **Sacred Precinct of Athena Polias Nikephorus**, the Bringer of Victory, with what remains of the temple at its south-west corner. This is one of the two oldest temples in Pergamum, and it may date back to the reign of Philetaeros. About a century later Eumenes II added a stoa and a monumental entryway on the east side and another stoa to the north (the south stoa was added in the second century BC). At that time Eumenes II also built a **library** adjoining the north-eastern side of the temenos, the ruins of which can be seen alongside the temple precinct. This library was one of the most renowned cultural institutions in the Hellenistic world, rivalling the great library of the Ptolemys in Alexandria.

To the north of the temenos of Athena are the monumental remains of the **Trajaneum**, the largest temple in Pergamum. This was built for the deified Emperor Trajan (98–117) and was completed during the reign of Hadrian (117–28), who was worshipped here along with his imperial predecessor. Colossal statues of both emperors stood within the temple precinct. The Trajaneum occupies the highest point of the acropolis, standing on a vast terrace supported by a massive retaining wall, and in Roman times, seen from the plain below, it dominated the city.

The most prominent structure on the Pergamene acropolis today is the great **theatre**, one of the most impressive monuments in Asia Minor remaining from the Hellenistic age. The auditorium is built into the slope of the acropolis, at the top of which the principal sanctuaries of the upper city fan out at either end, the temple of Athena to the south and the Trajaneum to the north. The theatre is exceptionally steep, with eighty rows of seats ascending the slope through an elevation of 118 feet; because of the lie of the land it forms an arc much more acute than is usual in Greek and Roman theatres. The seats are arranged in three tiers separated by broad horizontal passages, or diazomata, with narrow stairways dividing each of these into six or seven sectors. The orchestra extends out on to a long and narrow terrace, once bordered on both sides by stoas. At the northern end of the terrace there are the massive remains of an Ionic temple, believed to have been a sanctuary of Dionysus, god of the theatre. In the days of the Attalids this terrace must have been a favourite place for the Pergamenes to promenade at the end of the day. On one side their theatre, the palaces of their kings, and the temples of their gods rose above them, and on the other their fertile domains spread out below in the broad valley of the Caicus.

From the southern end of the theatre terrace you walk back to what was once the court of the great **Altar of Zeus**, of which only the foundation now remains. This altar was constructed by Eumenes II in about 190 BC, at a time when Pergamum was at the peak of its power and prosperity. The Great Frieze which once adorned its sides and the stair wells of its podium represent the culmination of Pergamene art. Eumenes and his artists chose as the principal theme for the decoration of the altar the Gigantomachy, the mythical battle of the gods and giants, symbolizing thus the victory of Pergamum over the Gauls and commemorating the glory of the Attalids as the saviours of Hellenism in its battle against the barbarians. Unfortunately there is nothing left today in Pergamum of the altar except its foundations, for the surviving figures from the frieze and the remaining architectural fragments were removed during the German excavations which began in 1878. The altar of Zeus may now be seen in the Pergamum Museum in Berlin, where it has once again been reconstructed in all its former grandeur.

The **upper agora** of Pergamum stood on a terrace just below the altar of Zeus, connecting with the south end of the theatre terrace. This was the principal gathering-place of ancient Pergamum, where the townspeople from the lower city mingled with those who dwelt in the upper citadel. You can still see the marks of an ancient road, rutted with wagon tracks, that led down from the gate of the citadel and passed through the upper agora. The road leads down to the lower part of the acropolis, ending in the Great South Gate of Eumenes II. From there you can walk back up to see the monuments on the lower acropolis before returning to the car park.

Starting back from the Great South Gate along the ancient road, you pass along two sides of the **lower agora**, another construction of Eumenes II. Within the courtyard of the agora stand neatly stacked piles of catapult missiles which were found in an arsenal at the top of the acropolis. The neighbourhood around the lower agora must have been where the wealthy Pergamenes lived, for the remains of several Hellenistic mansions have been unearthed there. These are

built on the peristyle plan, where the rooms open out on to a courtyard surrounded by a stoa. The grandest of these is called the **House
of Attalus**: an inscription identifies it as belonging to a Roman consul
of that name.

Beyond the House of Attalus the road ascends to the north-east
and soon brings you to the substructure of the **gymnasium**, whose
entrance was just to the west of the monumental city fountain. The
gymnasium, the largest secular structure in Pergamum, was built on
three separate terraces, each one larger and more elaborate than the
one below. The lower terrace served as a playground for children,
the middle was reserved for ephebes, youths in training for the
military, and the grand upper gymnasium was for young men. All
three gymnasia were part of a unified complex that included two
stadia, exercise grounds, dressing-rooms, baths, classrooms and
lecture-halls, and an auditorium, with most of the institutions
located on the upper terrace. There were also two temples attached
to the complex; on the east end of the middle terrace stood a
sanctuary of Hermes, Heracles and the deified Emperor, while to the
west of the upper gymnasium there was a temple of Asklepios, of
which only the foundations remain. The upper gymnasium was
surrounded by a stoa which housed some of the institutions associated with the gymnasium. The most important of these was the
Ephebion, at the centre of the north stoa, where all of the religious
and civic ceremonies connected with the activities of the gymnasium
were held. The structures you see in the gymnasium today date in
foundation to the first half of the third century BC, with extensive rebuilding in the Roman period.

Above the gymnasium stood the temple of Hera Basileia, built in
the reign of Attalus II. And over to the north-west is the oldest of all
the sanctuaries in Pergamum, the **Temple of Demeter**, whose origins
go back to the beginning of the Attalid dynasty. The cult of Demeter
and her daughter Persephone, celebrated in the Eleusian Mysteries,
was particularly popular among the women of Pergamum. As the
poet Lasus of Hermione wrote in his Hymn to Demeter, echoing the
songs sung in the nocturnal ceremonies here: 'I sing of Demeter and
the maiden Persephone, wife of Klymenos, leading a honey-voiced
hymn in the deep mode Aeolian.'

The most important monument in lower Pergamum is the
Asklepieion, which is about a kilometre outside the town to the
north-west. You approach the shrine along a splendid colonnaded
way known in Roman times as the Via Tecta. This was once a
bazaar catering for the pilgrims and patients who came to the

Asklepieion, which was one of the most famous shrines and thera-peutic centres in the ancient world. The cult of Asklepios, the god of healing, seems to have spread from Epidauros early in the fourth century BC, when the first sanctuary was erected on this site. The sanctuary was extended and rebuilt at various times, and the ruins one sees today date principally from the first half of the second century AD.

The Pergamene Asklepieion reached the peak of its popularity in the second half of the second century BC, when it surpassed Epi-dauros as the principal shrine of healing in the Graeco-Roman world. Its fame in this period was largely due to the eminence and reputation of the physician Galen, who was born in Pergamum in AD 129. Galen, the greatest physician and medical writer of antiquity, received his first training in medicine at the Asklepieion, and after the completion of his studies returned for a time to practise in Pergamum, acting as surgeon for the gladiators in the arena. Galen's writings were to form the basis for medical science up to the time of the Renaissance, earning for him the title by which he was known in the Middle Ages, the 'Prince of Physicians'.

You enter the Asklepieion through what was once the propylon courtyard, the forecourt to the monumental entryway. Just to the right of the entrance are the foundations of a square room which once served as the medical library and as a cult room for the deified Emperor Hadrian. To the left of the entryway are two round build-ings, the first of which was the **Temple of Zeus-Asklepios**, built about AD 150 as a small replica of the Roman Pantheon. The second build-ing, which is in a much better state of repair, appears to have been the main **hospital**. From this building a long tunnel leads to the centre of the main courtyard, to the **sacred well** whose waters were believed to have both physical and spiritual value in the cure of illness. (A recent analysis has shown the water to be mildly radio-active.)

The treatment at the hospital consisted of both a physical regimen, which stressed good diet, mud baths and freezing dips into the sacred spring in winter, and also psychotherapy, which included an imagin-ative analysis of dreams, two millennia before Freud. Among the psychic complaints which were recognized by Galen was that of love-sickness, which he believed to be the principal cause of in-somnia. In his clinical analysis he wrote: 'The quickening of the pulse at the name of the beloved gives the clue.'

The courtyard of the Asklepieion was bounded on three sides by a stoa, of which only part of the north colonnade is now standing.

Behind the western end of the colonnade there is a handsome Roman **theatre**, the best-preserved structure in the Asklepieion. According to an inscription, it was dedicated to Asklepios and Athena Hygieia. The theatre could seat three and a half thousand spectators, so it must have been used by the townspeople as well as the patients and staff at the institute. For the Asklepieion at Pergamum, like that at Epidauros, was very much a spa in the nineteenth-century sense, and while the patients awaited their recovery they were entertained by dramatic performances in the theatre as well as by gladiator combats and other shows in the arena.

Before leaving Bergama one should not fail to visit the local **Archaeological Museum**. This was the first local museum in Turkey devoted to housing antiquities found in the city and surrounding area, and it remains one of the more attractive small museums in the country.

The old **Turkish quarter** of Bergama is well worth a visit, for along its picturesque back streets there are a number of historic Ottoman buildings. The most important of these is the Yíldírím Camii, built in 1399 by Sultan Beyazit I.

You should now return to the main coastal highway, and then continue driving south towards Izmir. If there is time it may be of interest to make a few brief excursions to look at some of the ancient Aeolian cities which you pass along the way. But after the splendours of Pergamum the Aeolian sites are a disappointment, for in most cases there is nothing left beyond a few ruined walls and some scattered fragments of marble columns and capitals. Nevertheless the coast itself is lovely, and the sites are often on promontories by the seaside, perfect places for a picnic or a swim.

You approach the first of these Aeolian sites by turning right for **Çandarlí**, about sixteen kilometres after regaining the coastal highway. A drive of ten kilometres along this good side road brings you to Çandarlí, a simple little coastal village at the end of a sandy cove. The village is dominated by a handsome and very well-preserved Genoese fortress dating from the late thirteenth or early fourteenth century, with five main towers connected by a line of curtain walls. The fortress stands at the neck of a long and narrow peninsula where the Aeolian city of Pitane once stood. Almost nothing now remains of the ancient city, although bits and pieces of it are built into the castle and the village houses.

If you return to the main highway and continue south along the coast for about eight kilometres you will pass the village of Yenişakran, just beyond which you see a little peninsula jutting out into the sea. This is **Temaşalik Burnu**, the **site of** the Aeolian city of **Gryneum**, renowned in antiquity for its temple of Apollo and its resident oracle. All that remains today is a flat-topped mound in the farmland near the tip of the peninsula, around which there are a number of fluted column drums. The great Greek traveller Pausanias passed this way in the middle years of the second century AD, and has left this description of the sanctuary: 'Gryneum, where Apollo has a most beautiful grove of fruit trees and others which are pleasant to smell and look upon.' At the time of our last visit to Gryneum, in April 1975, the little peninsula looked just as Pausanias described it eighteen centuries before, with blossoming fruit trees and a few gnarled olive trees shading the ancient sanctuary of Apollo.

A few kilometres farther along you cross a bridge over the Güzelhisar Çayí, the Stream of the Beautiful Castle. This is the ancient River Pythicus, which flows into the Aegean just to the south of the **site of Aeolian Myrina**. The site is difficult to reach and would seem hardly worth the visit, for there is little left of the ancient city except some sarcophagi scattered around what was once its acropolis; but if you are romantic you might still wish to while away an hour or so there, for this is one of the towns which Strabo tells us was founded by Queen Myrina of the Amazons.

You now pass a beautiful bay at the south end of which is Ali Ağa, a town built from the ruins of Myrina and Cyme, another Aeolian city. The **site of ancient Cyme** is also difficult to reach, requiring a six-kilometre drive from the coastal highway to Namurtköy, a coastal hamlet on Namurt Limaní, the Harbour of Nimrod. Here, too, there is almost nothing left to see of the ancient settlement, which Strabo called 'the largest and best of the Aeolian cities'.

After passing Ali Ağa the highway loses contact with the coast, which now turns westwards to join the peninsula at the north side of the Gulf of Izmir. Sixteen kilometres past Ali Ağa a turn-off to the right leads to the pleasant seaside villages of Eski Foça and Yeni Foça, near which there is a holiday village run by the Club Méditerranée. On the way to Eski Foça you will pass on the right a striking and unique monument known locally as the **Taş Kule**, or **Stone Tower**. This has been identified with some certainty as being a Phrygian tomb dating from as early as the eighth century BC, perhaps from the time of King Midas.

The town of **Eski Foça** stands on the site and preserves the name of **ancient Phocaea**. Although Phocaea was located in a region otherwise settled by Aeolians it was always an Ionian city, one of the original confederacy. Diogenes Laertius describes it as 'a city of moderate size, skilled in nothing but to rear brave men'. And Herodotus wrote of them in Book One of his *Histories*: 'The Phocaeans were the pioneer navigators of the Greeks, and it was they who showed their countrymen the way to the Adriatic, Tyrrhenia and the Spanish peninsula as far as Tartessus. They used to sail not in deep, broad-beamed merchant vessels but in fifty-oared galleys.' The Phocaeans founded more than a dozen colonies in the Black Sea, the Hellespont and the Mediterranean, one of which, Massalia, developed into the present-day city of Marseilles. Phocaea continued as an important port throughout antiquity and the Middle Ages, and it was held in turn by Greeks, Romans, Byzantines, Mongols, Italians, and finally by the Ottoman Turks, who captured the city from the Genoese in 1455. The harbour fortress which you see today was built by the Genoese late in the thirteenth century, and aside from that almost nothing remains of the old city. However, perhaps it is fitting that the Phocaeans have left no monuments other than the memory of their exploits, for as the poet Alcaeus wrote, describing the Phocaeans of his time: 'Not houses finely roofed nor the stones of walls well-builded a city make, but men able to use their opportunity.'

After returning to the main highway you should continue south for another two kilometres to come to Buruncuk, a small village standing at the foot of a steep, rocky eminence. On the top of the hill are ruins which are thought to be those of **ancient Larisa**, the southernmost of the Aeolian settlements. Those who take the trouble to climb the hill will find the remains of defence-walls dating from the fourth century BC, as well as the foundations of two temples and a palace. Larisa is one of the very few Aeolian cities mentioned by Homer, when he lists among the Trojan allies 'the warlike Pelasgians who dwelt around fertile Larisa'. According to tradition the town was named after a daughter of one of these legendary Pelasgian kings, of whom Strabo has this tale to tell: 'Piasus . . . was ruler of the Pelasgians and fell in love with his daughter Larisa, and, having violated her, paid the penalty for the outrage; for, observing him leaning over a cask of wine, they say, she seized him by the legs, raised him, and plunged him into the cask. Such were the ancient accounts.'

Shortly after leaving Larisa you pass over the Gediz Çayí, the River Hermus of the Greeks. In ancient times this was taken to be the southern boundary of Aeolia, separating it from the lands of the Ionians. Soon you pass the town of Menemen, and within half an hour the highway brings you to the outskirts of Izmir, which you see shining on the hillside at the head of its magnificent bay.

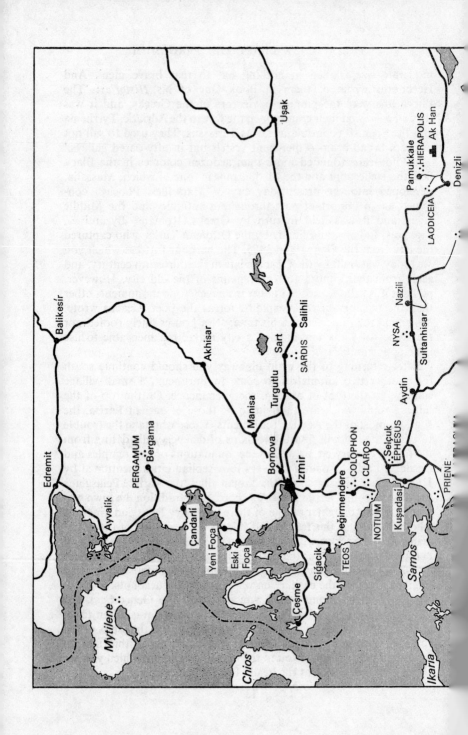

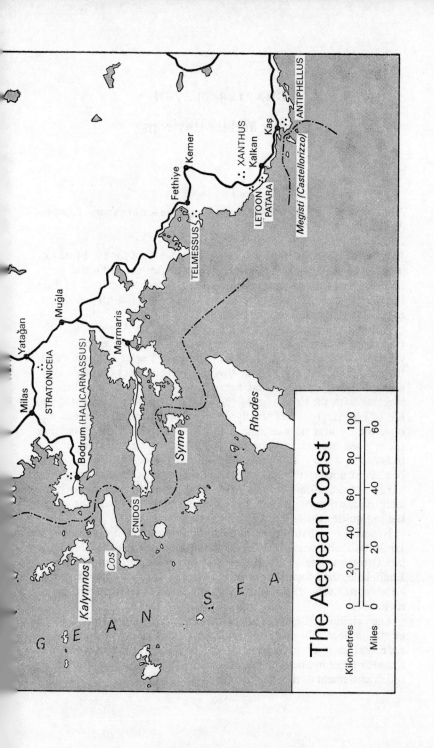

The Aegean Coast

TURKEY

ANTIPHELLUS

Kaş

XANTHUS   Kalkan

Kemer

Fethiye   LETOON   PATARA

TELMESSUS   *Megisti (Castellorizo)*

Muğla

Yatağan

Milas   STRATONICEIA   Marmaris

Rhodes

Bodrum (HALICARNASSUS)   *Syme*

CNIDOS

Cos

Kalymnos

A E G E A N   S E A

| Kilometres | 0 | 20 | 40 | 60 | 80 | 100 |
| Miles | 0 | 20 | 40 | 60 |

CHAPTER ELEVEN

Izmir and its Environs

❧

Izmir – Sardis – Teos – Clazomenae – Çeşme – Colophon – Claros – Notium

Izmir, the Greek **Smyrna**, has long been celebrated for the beauty of its setting. The city lies at the end of the long Aegean gulf which bears its name, stretching for miles along a sun-drenched seafront and up the slopes of Kadifekale – the Velvet Castle – the flat-topped mountain that dominates Izmir to the south.

Although Izmir is as old as any city along the Aegean coast the ravages of time and of its turbulent history have severed almost all tangible connections with its past. The most recent of these catastrophes happened in 1922, at the end of the Greek-Turkish War, when a great fire destroyed nearly all the old city. This disaster, together with the expulsion of the Greeks who once dominated the life of old Smyrna, has totally changed the character of what was once the liveliest port in Asia Minor. During the past half-century the city has been almost completely rebuilt and repopulated, so that today it is a very busy port and tourist centre, with its seafront boulevard lined with luxury hotels and apartment houses, revealing hardly a trace of its colourful past. And so most travellers to Izmir visit the town only incidentally, using it mainly as a base for seeing the antiquities along the Aegean coast.

Nevertheless there are a number of interesting things to see in Izmir itself, and one can still catch glimpses of the Levantine town of late Ottoman times. Perhaps the best way to begin is to drive up to **Kadifekale**, the **Mount Pagus** of the Greeks, for there one can enjoy a panoramic view of the whole city and begin to learn something of its history.

The original settlement from which the city developed was located at the present village of **Bayraklí**, just across from Mount Pagus near the far northern corner of the bay. An Aeolian colony was founded there in about the tenth century BC, on the site of an Anatolian settlement dating back to the first half of the third millennium.

140

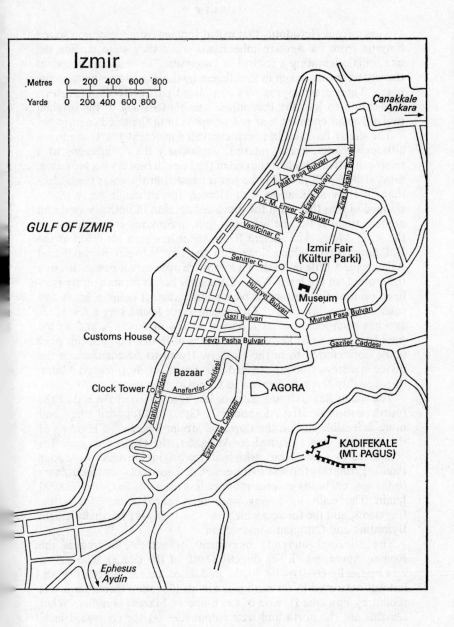

Izmir

Metres 0 200 400 600 800

Yards 0 200 400 600 800

GULF OF IZMIR

Çanakkale
Ankara →

Talat Pasa Bulvari

Ziya Gökalp Bulvari

Sair Esref Bulvari

Dr. M. Enver Bulvari

Vasifcinar C.

Sehitler C.

Izmir Fair
(Kültur Parki)

Hürriyet Bulvari

Museum

Gazi Bulvari

Mursel Pasa Bulvari

Customs House

Fevzi Pasha Bulvari

Gaziler Caddesi

Bazaar

Anafartlar Caddesi

Clock Tower

Atatürk Caddesi

Esref Pasa Caddesi

AGORA

KADIFEKALE
(MT. PAGUS)

Ephesus
Aydin

We learn from Herodotus that exiled Ionians from Colophon seized Smyrna from its Aeolian inhabitants while they were outside the city walls celebrating a festival of Dionysus. The original citizens of the city were then taken in as refugees by the Aeolian colonies to the north. Thereafter Smyrna was considered part of Ionia, though its application to join the Panionium, the confederacy of the original twelve Ionian colonies, was not accepted until the third century BC.

The site at Bayraklí has been excavated in recent years; the ruins, although scanty, are of interest, particularly the foundations of a temple of Athena built at the end of the seventh century BC. However, most visitors will probably be less interested in the ruins themselves than in their association with Homer, for although many places claimed him as their own the prevalent opinion in both classical and modern times is that he was born here in Smyrna, on the banks of the River Meles. The ancient River Meles has been identified as the Halkpínar Suyu, which flows into the bay between Bayraklí and Aslanacak. A little more than a kilometre upstream it passes through the grounds of the Izmir Water Company; here it forms a pretty tree-lined pool at the bottom of which some ancient column bases and squared stones are visible. An ancient statue found here a few years ago has been identified as a representation of Artemis, and so the pool has come to be known as the **Baths of Diana**. Perhaps this pool is the one referred to in the Homeric Hymn to Artemis, where the divine huntress, 'having washed her horses in deep-reeded Meles, drove swiftly through Smyrna to Claros rich in wines'.

The site at Bayraklí was more or less abandoned at the end of the fourth century BC after Alexander the Great had founded a new and more defensible city on the slopes of Mount Pagus. The building of the new city was entrusted to Antigonus the One-Eyed, and was completed by Lysimachus, who built the original fortress on Mount Pagus. From this fortress two lines of defence-walls stretched down to the sea, enclosing an area more or less the same as that of central Izmir. The walls have long since disappeared except for a few fragments, and the fortress which one sees today is principally of late Byzantine and Ottoman construction.

The principal surviving monument of ancient Smyrna is the Roman **Agora**, which lies directly south of the citadel. The Agora was originally constructed in the middle of the second century AD, but was destroyed by an earthquake in AD 178; soon thereafter it was rebuilt by Faustina II, wife of the Emperor Marcus Aurelius. What remains are the north and west colonnades on the courtyard level and a splendid vaulted basement on the north side. At the north-west corner a small enclosure shelters the figures in high relief of Poseidon and Demeter. These were reconstructed from fragments found during the excavations of 1932–41; they are believed to have been part of a group of deities which adorned an altar to Zeus in the centre of the Agora.

A story connected with the Agora provides a picture of what life was like in ancient Smyrna. It seems that in the second half of the third century BC a fleet from Chios set sail to attack Smyrna. On landing the Chians found the town deserted, for the Smyrnians were celebrating the annual festival of Dionysus on the heights of Mount Pagus. However, as soon as they learned of the invasion the men of Smyrna rushed down to the shore and routed the Chians, capturing their vessels. Then, the battle over, the Smyrnians resumed their festival on Mount Pagus, revelling in their Bacchic dances and carousing with even greater abandon than before. This victory was celebrated for centuries afterwards at the annual festival of Dionysus, when the men of Smyrna carried aloft a trireme from the sea to the Agora, with the high priest of Dionysus acting as the symbolic helmsman.

Most of the remaining antiquities in Izmir are housed in the **Archaeological Museum**, which is located in the Izmir Fair Grounds. The antiquities exhibited here are mostly from archaeological sites along the southern Aegean coast, but there are some from ancient Smyrna, most notably from the excavation at Bayraklí.

The most interesting quarter of modern Izmir is the **Bazaar**, where one can see what little there is left of the old town of late Ottoman times. The best approach is to begin on the waterfront at the **Clock Tower**, one of the most familiar landmarks in Izmir. Across the square from the Tower is the beginning of the main street of the Bazaar; this takes one on a winding course through the entire length of the market quarter. The Izmir Bazaar is not nearly as interesting as that in Istanbul, but is still colourful and lively, especially in some of the side streets and mosque courtyards near its upper end.

One of the most interesting archaeological sites in the vicinity of Izmir is Sardis, a drive of about an hour and a half along the main highway leading east to Ankara.

Eighteen kilometres along the Ankara highway you approach the small town of Kemalpaşa, the ancient Nymphaeum. Just before entering the town you see on the left the ruins of the Byzantine palace from which the ancient city took its name. This is the historic **Palace of Nymphaeum**, built by Andronicus I Comnenus during his brief reign (1183–5). The Nymphaeum served as one of the imperial residences of the Lascarids, the dynasty which ruled the Byzantine Empire from Nicaea during the Latin occupation of Constantinople.

The next town of any size which you pass is Turgutlu, set in lush orchards to the left of the road. Once past Turgutlu the road runs in an almost straight line up the plain of the Gediz Nehri, the River Hermus of antiquity. Then, ninety-four kilometres out of Izmir, you cross the Ecelkapíz, the Greek Pactolus, and come to the hamlet of Sart, in and around which are the ruins of **ancient Sardis.**

Sardis was once capital of the ancient kingdom of Lydia. At the height of its power, from about 650 to 550 BC, the dominions of Lydia comprised most of western Asia Minor, and during that time Sardis was the richest city in the world. The source of this wealth was the gold washed down from Mount Tmolus by the Pactolus; Herodotus tells us that the Lydians obtained this gold by catching it on sheepskins placed in the shallows of the stream, a practice which may have given rise to the legend of the golden fleece. The Lydians used this gold to great advantage in their commercial activities by the invention of coinage, the earliest examples of which date to about 600 BC.

The golden age of Lydia coincided with the illustrious rule of the Mermnad dynasty, beginning with Gyges (680–45) and ending with Croesus (561–46). The Lydian kingdom reached the pinnacle of its greatness under Croesus, who succeeded in subjugating the Greek cities of Asia Minor and placing them under his benevolent and enlightened rule. As a result, the wealthy capital of this powerful neighbour began to fascinate the writers and scholars of the awakening Greek world. Herodotus devotes almost the whole of Book One of his *Histories* to the rise of Croesus and his eventual defeat in 546 BC by Cyrus, King of Persia. This brought to an end the Lydian kingdom and its benign rule over the Ionian cities, and within a few years they and the rest of Asia Minor were included within the Persian Empire. The Ionians revolted in 499 BC and captured Sardis, which by then had become the capital of the local Persian satrapy, after which they sacked and destroyed the golden city. The Persians finally crushed the revolt five years later, setting the stage for their invasion of Greece and the ultimate Greek victory of 479 BC.

Sardis rose from its ashes after its destruction by the Ionians and before long it was once again a wealthy commercial centre. It owed this status principally to its position at the western terminus of the Royal Road, the great highway which began at the Persian capital of Susa. Sardis was captured by Alexander the Great in 334 BC and thereafter became a thoroughly Greek city, its old Lydian culture vanishing almost without a trace. It continued to prosper through the Hellenistic, Roman and Byzantine periods, and in the Christian era it became an important bishopric, one of the Seven Churches of Revelations. The end finally came for Sardis in 1401, when it was sacked and totally destroyed by Tamerlane, as were so many of the great cities of Anatolia. During the latter centuries of the Ottoman Empire the site was practically deserted, for the hamlet of Sart came into being only at the beginning of the present century. By that time even the ruins had almost vanished, buried under the soil and rocks that had fallen down from the acropolis. Excavations began in the years 1910–14 and were resumed in 1958 by Professor G. M. A. Hanfman and his team; their work has now completely transformed the site and the golden city of Croesus is once again coming into view.

The most famous monument remaining from ancient Sardis is the Temple of Artemis, just over a kilometre to the south along the valley of the Pactolus. As you drive along you pass on your right a Byzantine church of the thirteenth century. The deep trench beside the road is part of the recent excavations and has yielded much interesting information about ancient Sardis. In the centre of the dig there is a rectangular structure which has been identified as an altar to Cybele, the Phrygian mountain goddess who was worshipped in Lydian Sardis. The excavations here have also unearthed some of the workshops in which Lydian workmen smelted and refined the gold which had been fleeced out of the Pactolus.

The **Temple of Artemis** is a very impressive sight, with its ruined colonnade standing starkly against the background of the tawny acropolis to the east. Until the excavations of 1910–14 all that remained visible above ground were two columns, at the south-east corner of the temple, both crowned with beautiful Ionic capitals. Since that time an enormous mass of earth and rock has been removed to a depth of thirty feet in some places, thirteen additional columns have been re-erected, and part of the cella wall has been unearthed, so the form of the temple is now clearly visible.

A careful study shows that its construction can be dated to three periods. The original sanctuary on the site was apparently an altar to Artemis; this has been identified as the structure made of red sandstone blocks adjoining the temple to the west and goes back to the fifth century BC. The first stage of the temple proper was begun in about 300 BC, when Sardis was being Hellenized after Alexander's conquest. The second stage of building has been dated to the second quarter of the second century BC, and the third and final stage to the middle of the second century AD, during the reign of Antoninus Pius. At that time the cella or central chamber of the sanctuary was divided into two halves, with the western side remaining sacred to Artemis and the eastern half devoted to the worship of the deified Empress Faustina I, wife of Antoninus Pius, who died in AD 141. The ruined structure standing beside the temple at its southeast corner is a Christian church erected in the fourth century, at a time when Christianity began to supplant the older religions of Anatolia.

One now returns to Sart to visit the more recent excavations, the most interesting of which are just north of the highway to the east of the bridge. The most important structure unearthed in this area is a huge complex made up of a **gymnasium, baths and shops**; inscriptions indicate that this was built between AD 166 and 211. The centre of this complex is the so-called Marble Court, which was once the palaestra of the gymnasium. The handsome south hall of this palaestra was apparently used as a synagogue, and it remained in use from the third century AD up until the time of the Persian sack of Sardis in 616. Altogether this is one of the most splendid and interesting examples of the Roman architecture of that period in Asia Minor.

Just across the highway from this complex is an excavation site known as the **House of Bronzes** area. This so-called House of Bronzes was a large structure dating from about AD 550; it is thought to have been the residence of an important Christian cleric, perhaps the Bishop of Sardis. Also on this site is the 'Lydian Trench', an area which has been identified as the market of Sardis in the period 700–300 BC.

There are remains of other ancient buildings on either side of the road farther to the east. The most prominent of these is a large structure which is thought to have been a **Roman baths**, probably part of the great civic centre of Roman Sardis. To the south of the road, below the acropolis, there are other unexcavated ruins which were undoubtedly part of this complex, principally the Roman stadium and the theatre.

Finally there remains the **acropolis** itself, which you should approach from the Temple of Artemis. The climb takes about forty-five minutes from the temple and is not difficult, although there are one or two giddy spots which make one realize how nearly impregnable this fortress must have been. The extant fortifications on the acropolis date from the Byzantine period, although much of the building material has been taken from more ancient structures. Excavations on the acropolis have revealed structures from the Lydian, Greek and Roman periods, as well as terraced Byzantine houses from as late as the seventh century AD, altogether giving evidences of human occupation spanning fifteen centuries. And now this great capital has been dead for five hundred and seventy-five years at the time of writing, with only these fragmentary ruins to show that it was once the wealthiest city in the world. As the poet Bacchylides wrote after the Ionian sack of Sardis: 'Lo, how it hath ceased, the golden city!'

There are a number of ancient sites along the peninsula which forms the southern shore of the Gulf of Izmir. While these cannot begin to compare in interest with those more famous sites farther south, they do make pleasant destinations for short excursions out of Izmir.

Five kilometres west of Izmir along the shore road there is a turn-off to the right for Inciraltí, a very popular beach resort. And to the left is a turn-off for the thermal establishment called the Baths of Agamemnon, which has been used by local hypochondriacs since ancient times.

Nineteen kilometres west of Izmir you come to Güzelbahçe, near where a road turns off south for Siğaçik. This is a seaside village of medieval aspect which is near the **site of ancient** Teos, another of the Ionian cities. Although the ruins here are not particularly important the scene is exceptionally beautiful, with the ruined Temple of Dionysus set romantically in an olive grove, and with fragments of ancient walls, columns and capitals scattered about the harbour and superb sand beach. In its time Teos surpassed even Smyrna as a port, and until the fifteenth century it remained an important town.

The most famous son of Teos was Anacreon, one of the greatest lyric poets in the ancient Greek world. Anacreon was born in Teos about 572 BC and died there eighty-five years later after a rich and varied life, drawing his last breath at a banquet where he choked upon a grape-pip. As Critias of Athens wrote of Anacreon after the old poet had sung his last poem of love: 'Teos bore thee, thou sweet old weaver of womanish song, rouser of revels, couzener of dames, rival of the flute, lover of the lyre, the delightful, the anodyne; and never shall love of thee, Anacreon, grow old and die, as long as serving lads bear round bumpers above board, so long as band of maidens does holy night-long service of the dance . . .'

And so one might sit beneath an olive tree in the Temple of Dionysus at Teos, and after a picnic washed down with white wine read one or two of those fragments of Anacreon's poems that have survived, perhaps beginning with his *To a Virgin*.

My Thracian foal, why do you glare with disdain and then shun me absolutely as if I knew nothing of this art?
I tell you I could bridle you with tight straps, seize the reins and gallop you around the posts of the pleasure course.
But you prefer to graze on the calm meadows, or frisk or gambol gaily – having no manly rider to break you in.

Seven kilometres past the turn-off for Teos one comes to the site of ancient Clazomenae, another member of the Ionian Confederacy. This ancient city stood on a little island just off the coast, and was later connected to the mainland by a causeway built by Alexander the Great. Some stones of Alexander's causeway can still be seen, and also some fragmentary remains of ancient structures on the island itself, but the site has not been excavated and is of interest mainly for its historical connections. For Clazomenae is immortalized as the birthplace of Anaxagoras, one of the greatest and most influential philosophers in the ancient Greek world. Anaxagoras was born in Clazomenae at the beginning of the fifth century BC, the last of those extraordinary Ionian physicists who began mankind's first attempt to understand and explain the physical universe in rational terms. As Plutarch wrote of him: '. . . Anaxagoras the Clazomenian, whom men of that day used to call *"Nus"* ["Mind"], either because they admired that comprehension of his, which proved of such surpassing greatness in the study of nature; or because he was the first to enthrone in the universe, not Chance, nor yet Necessity, as the source of its orderly arrangement, but Mind pure and simple, which distinguishes and sets apart, in the midst of an otherwise chaotic mass, the substances which have like elements.'

Sixteen kilometres farther along a road branches off to the right to Karaburun at the northern extremity of the peninsula. The ride is long and tortuous but well worth it, for the scenery is superb. The main road continues on to the resort town of Çeşme at the western tip of the peninsula, just across the strait from the Greek island of Chios. The handsome fortress on the seafront was built by the Genoese in the fourteenth century and captured by Beyazit I in about 1400. The last time this fortress played a role in history was on 5 July 1770, when it was shelled by the Russian navy during its destruction of the Ottoman fleet in Çeşme harbour.

There are several beach resorts out along the end of the peninsula in the vicinity of Çeşme. The most popular of these is at Ilíca, some five kilometres back along the main highway to Izmir. From Ilíca a road turns off to follow the coast to the north-west for eight kilometres, ending at the seaside village of Ildír. This is the **site of ancient Erythrae**, still another city of the Ionian Confederacy. Here again the ruins are scant but the site is quite lovely.

Still another excursion from Izmir leads you to the southern part of the peninsula to see three more ancient cities of Ionia: Colophon, Claros and Notium. You approach these sites by taking the main highway to the south and turning right fifteen kilometres out of Izmir. A drive of twenty kilometres along this road brings you to the village of Değirmendere; just beyond it is the **site of ancient Colophon**, of which only a few ruined walls remain.

Colophon was famous in antiquity for its cavalry, which ranged over the broad plain south of Smyrna, using fierce dogs as auxiliaries. The city also had a powerful navy, as evidenced by its seizure of Smyrna from the Aeolians. These forces and its fertile land soon brought Colophon great wealth. But at the same time the Colophonians lapsed into a voluptuous life-style which so softened them as to make their city an easy prey for King Gyges of Lydia. The decadent ways of the Colophonians are eloquently described by the lyric poet Xenophanes, who was born in Colophon in 565 BC and fled from there to southern Italy to escape the invading Persians. In one of his surviving poems, *Gay Days in Asiatic Colophon*, he criticizes his fellow citizens for their corrupt ways. 'They acquired useless luxuries out of Lydia while still free from her odious tyranny; paraded to the marketplace in sea-purple robes, often in bright swarms of a thousand. They were proud and pleased in their elaborate coiffures, and hid their body odours with rare perfumes.'

Another source of Colophon's wealth was the famous shrine at nearby Claros, which brought thousands of pilgrims each year to the city. Claros itself was never a city, but consisted merely of the temple and oracle of Apollo and their associated buildings. Nevertheless there is far more left of Claros than of Colophon, particularly since the excavation in recent years of the Temple of Apollo.

The **site of Claros** is approached by continuing on the same road seventeen kilometres past Değirmendere; the ruins are in a river valley some few hundred metres to the left of the road. Since they are below the level of the water table the remains of the temple are kept visible only by constant pumping; nevertheless the site of these splendid ruins half-submerged in the water is impressive. One notices in particular the gigantic fragments of the huge cult-statue of Apollo, the enormous number of massive column drums, the great altar-

149

table, nearly twenty metres long, and the subterranean chambers where the oracle delivered his ambiguous responses to the questions and petitions of the suppliants. We read in Tacitus a description of a visit to the oracle made in AD 18 by Germanicus, the adopted son of Tiberius: 'There is no woman there as at Delphi, rather a priest, after hearing merely the number and name of the clients, goes down into a cave; there he drinks from a secret fountain and, though generally illiterate, issues responses in verse concerning the various questions in the consultants' minds.'

The Temple of Apollo dates from the late fourth or early third century BC, and is one of the very few Doric monuments in Ionia. As in the case of many of his shrines Apollo shared the sanctuary with Dionysus, and there is also on the site a smaller temple of Apollo's sister Artemis. The shrine is far older than any of the extant structures, though, for it is mentioned in one of the Homeric hymns as 'gleaming Claros', one of the sacred places where Leto sought refuge before giving birth to Apollo and Artemis.

You now drive on down to the sea at a pretty sand beach some three kilometres beyond Claros, to the **site of ancient Notium**. The ruins here are extensive, sprawling across the peaks and slopes of the two hills to the left side of the beach as you face the sea. They include the ruins of a temple to Athena and two other sanctuaries, as well as an agora, a senate-house, a theatre and some remnants of a defence-wall which was originally four kilometres in length; all of them are poorly preserved. Throughout antiquity Notium was always the port for Colophon, and for long periods in their history the two formed part of one civic unit. Later, with the growth of sea-borne commerce, much of the population moved down to the port, which came to be called New Colophon, while the inland city was referred to as the Old Town.

This was undoubtedly where the Colophonian poet Xenophanes embarked when he fled from his native land at the age of twenty-five, a place of which he wrote with sadness as an old exile of ninety-two, in the last year of his long life: 'Three score and seven years have crossed my careworn soul up and down the land of Hellas, and there were then five and twenty years from my birth.' And one can sense the nostalgia in the old poet's soul as he reflects upon his long exile from far-away Ionia: 'Such things should be said beside the fire in wintertime when a man reclines full-fed on a soft couch drinking sweet wine and munching chick-peas, such things as who and whence art thou? And how old are thou good sir? And of what age was thou when the Mede appeared?'

CHAPTER TWELVE
The Ionian Coast

✤

Ephesus – Kuşadası – Priene – Miletos – Didyma

'Ionia enjoys the finest of climates and its sanctuaries are unmatched in the world . . . The wonders of Ionia are numerous, and not much short of the wonders of Greece itself.'

So said Pausanias in Book VII of his *Guide to Greece*. Although eighteen centuries have passed since he wrote those lines they are as true now as they were then. For Ionia has always been the most beautiful part of Anatolia, and not even mainland Greece has so many monuments of classical architecture. When driving along this coast one can easily appreciate how Ionia came to be the birthplace of so much of Greek culture. The mild but invigorating climate; the surpassingly beautiful landscape, with the blue Aegean constantly in view over gentle hills covered with pines, cypresses, olive groves and vineyards; its central position between the Mediterranean and Anatolia that made it a market place for ideas as well as goods; the newness and independence of its city-states, freeing them from the constraints of the conservative past – these were surely some of the factors which gave rise to the extraordinary flowering of culture in Ionia in the sixth and fifth centuries BC. Even today this is the most pleasant and progressive region in Turkey, and its sun-washed coastal towns are among the loveliest in the Aegean.

Once again you take the main road leading south from Izmir, but now continuing past the turn-off for Colophon. As soon as the urban sprawl of Izmir is left behind the countryside becomes increasingly lovely: the rich farmlands are dotted with groves of maritime pines, and the road is lined with colonnades of cypresses and silver birches. Camel caravans pass by, and shepherds dressed in sheepskin cloaks. The countryside becomes even more beautiful as the road turns south-west to run down the valley of the Küçük Menderes, one of the branches of the ancient Maeander River. As you begin driving down the green gorge at the end of the valley you will see high on a peak to the right the ruins of a Byzantine castle, a

151

fortress that once guarded the northern approaches to Ephesus.

The first sight of Ephesus is the huge Byzantine fortress crowning the acropolis of Ayasuluk above Selçuk, the town which stands near the ancient site. The structures on Ayasuluk are all from the medieval town of Ephesus, while the remains of the ancient city are to be found in the plain below and on the lower slopes of Paniyir Daği and Bülbül Daği, the two eminences off to the south-west.

The original Hellenic settlement of Ephesus was established by Ionians in about 1000 BC, and was situated on the northern slope of Paniyir Daği, the ancient Mount Pion, at a time when the sea came in as far as the modern town of Selçuk. The site was already occupied by Lydians and Carians who worshipped at an ancient shrine of Cybele, the Anatolian Mother-Goddess. The Ionians adapted the shrine to their own use and dedicated it to the Greek fertility-goddess, Artemis. Because of its excellent harbour and its location at the western terminus of trade routes leading into Anatolia, Ephesus soon became very prosperous, and as a result it was the first Ionian colony to attract the attention of King Croesus of Lydia. After taking the city in 550 BC Croesus destroyed the buildings and fortifications on the slopes of Mount Pion and resettled the Ephesians on the plain below. There it remained throughout the classical period and until the beginning of the third century BC. After Lysimachus gained control of western Asia Minor in 301 BC he moved the city yet again, to a fortified position on the seaward slope of Mount Pion and in the valley between it and Mount Coressos, the Turkish Bülbül Daği, the Mountain of the Nightingale. By that time the sea had retreated to the foot of the two mountains because of the silt carried down into the plain by the River Cayster.

After the end of the wars between Alexander's successors Ephesus became capital of the Roman province of Asia, and thereupon entered the period of her greatest prosperity. The city became the principal banking and commercial centre in Asia Minor and in time its population reached a peak of about a quarter of a million. Throughout the Hellenistic and Roman periods the pride of Ephesus continued to be its great Temple of Artemis, which attracted pilgrims from all over the Graeco-Roman world. But Christianity began to take root in Asia Minor very early on, particularly in Ephesus. When St Paul first arrived there in AD 53 he found that there was already a community of Christians, and in his two years in the city he laid the foundations of what would be the principal centre of Christianity in Asia Minor. St John the Apostle came here at about the same time, perhaps accompanied by the Blessed Virgin, beginning the tradition which would make Ephesus one of the greatest Christian shrines in the world, with the Mother of God eventually supplanting the ancient Anatolian Earth-Mother.

The ruins of the **Temple of Artemis,** the most ancient of the extant monuments of Ephesus, lie at the foot of Ayasuluk just to the right of the Kuşadasí road. The oldest sanctuary of which traces have been found at this site has been dated to the eighth century BC; this was apparently destroyed during the Cimmerian invasions of the seventh century. During the first half of the sixth century work was begun on a new and far more magnificent temple to Artemis; this was the first monumental building ever to be made entirely of marble, and at the time of its completion in about 550 BC it was the largest and most splendid structure in the Greek world. The temple was destroyed by fire in 356 BC; tradition says that the blaze was started by a lunatic named Herostratus who wished thereby to achieve everlasting fame. Work commenced soon after on another and still more monumental temple, four times greater in area than the Parthenon, which was eventually completed in the first half of the third century BC. This stupendous edifice, with its forest of 127 columns, each nearly 20 metres tall, was one of the most famous structures in antiquity, and Philo of Byzantium ranked it with the Pyramids among the Seven Wonders of the World. The Artemesium was destroyed by the Goths in their sack of Ephesus in AD 263, and though it was afterwards partially rebuilt its days of glory were drawing to a close. For the cult of Artemis was rapidly being eclipsed by Christianity, and by the beginning of the sixth century the temple had been demolished to provide building materials for the new cathedrals of the Byzantine Empire. By the beginning of modern times the temple had entirely disappeared, its ruins completely covered by silt washed down from the River Cayster. The first excavation at Ephesus was undertaken in 1863 by the English engineer J. T. Wood, whose life-long ambition it was to find the lost Temple of Artemis. He finally discovered the site of the temple in 1869, and in the years since then its remains have been unearthed, a task made difficult by the fact that its foundations lie under the water level of the Cayster. Although the ruins which one now sees are relatively insignificant they do evoke the splendour of this fabled temple of the dethroned goddess who once dominated the religious thought of ancient Greece and Anatolia.

If you continue on down the Kuşadasí highway for about a kilometre and then turn left on the road leading to the archaeological site, a short way along you will pass on your right the ruins of an

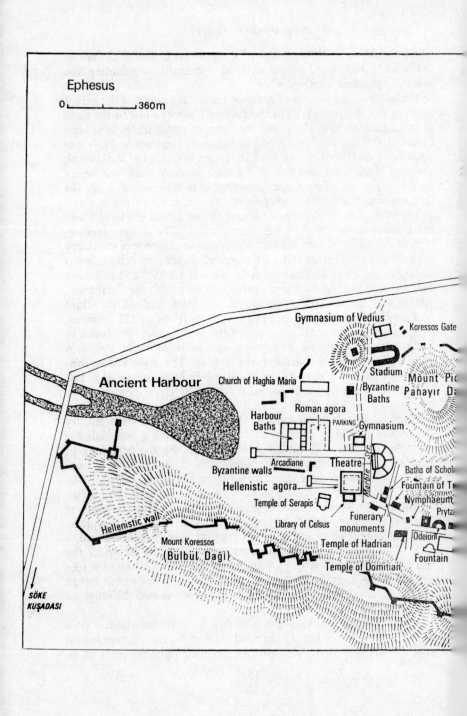

Ephesus

0 ⸻ 360m

Gymnasium of Vedius

Koressos Gate

Ancient Harbour

Church of Haghia Maria

Stadium

Mount Pic
Panayır Da

Byzantine
Baths

Harbour
Baths

Roman agora

PARKING

Gymnasium

Arcadiane

Theatre

Marble Str.

Byzantine walls

Baths of Schol

Hellenistic agora

Fountain of T

Temple of Serapis

Nymphaeum

Pryta

Library of Celsus

Funerary
monuments

Odeion

Hellenistic wall

Mount Koressos
(Bülbül Dağı)

Temple of Hadrian

Fountain

Temple of Domitian

SÖKE
KUŞADASI

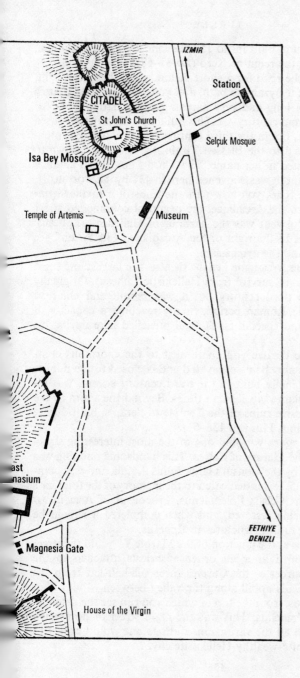

IZMIR

Station

CITADEL

St John's Church

Selçuk Mosque

Isa Bey Mosque

Temple of Artemis

Museum

ast
nasium

Magnesia Gate

FETHIYE
DENIZLI

House of the Virgin

enormous gymnasium, built in AD 150; beyond that is the stadium, constructed during the reign of Nero (AD 37–68).

Continue along the road for a short distance and then bear right, passing the ruins of a Byzantine bath, and you will reach the **Church of Haghia Maria**, a long and very narrow basilica dating from the first half of the second century AD. This building was originally used as a banking-house, but in the third century it was converted into a church and dedicated to the Blessed Virgin, the first one known to have been consecrated in her name. The Third Ecumenical Council of the Christian Church was convened here in 431 by Theodosius II.

Returning to the road, you now pass the ruins of a smaller gymnasium and come to the **Arcadiane**, the beautiful colonnaded street which runs down to what was the harbour of Hellenistic Ephesus. The huge structures to the right of the Arcadiane at its far end are the **harbour baths** and the **gymnasium**.

At the head of the Arcadiane lies the **theatre**, the largest and most impressive structure to survive from Hellenistic Ephesus. Originally constructed in the third century BC, it was rebuilt and enlarged several times in the Roman period, finally reaching a capacity of twenty-four thousand spectators. St Paul preached here during his stay in Ephesus.

After leaving the theatre you come next to the enormous commercial agora; it is now being excavated and is closed to the public. This, too, was originally built in the third century BC and was reconstructed and enlarged in Roman times. Beyond the agora to the west are the impressive ruins of the Temple of Serapis, built during the reign of Antoninus Pius (AD 138–61).

Just beyond the agora you find one of the most interesting structures in Ephesus, the **Library of Celsus**. This handsome building was founded in AD 110 by the Consul Gaius Julius Aquila and was completed in the year 135. It was dedicated to the memory of the founder's father, Gaius Julius Celsus Polemaenus, Proconsul of Asia in AD 106–7. It is now being restored, and when completed it should be one of the most beautiful structures in Ephesus.

The library stands at the junction of the Marble Way and the street called Curetes, named after an order of priests attached to the Artemesium. The street of the Curetes turns off half-left from the Marble Way and leads uphill along the valley between Mount Pion and Mount Coressos, from the top of which you can see the defence-walls built by Lysimachus. This was the main street of downtown Ephesus, lined with all the various institutions one would expect to find in the centre of a wealthy Hellenistic city.

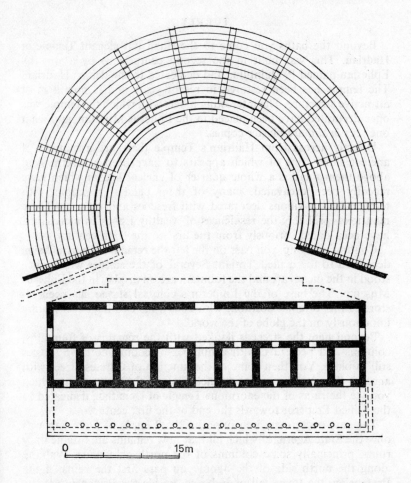

Restored Plan of the Hellenistic Theatre, Ephesus

At the beginning of Curetes Street on the left stand the **Baths of Scholastica**. This large complex was founded in about AD 200, and in the fourth century it was reconstructed by a Christian matron named Scholastica, whose headless statue can be seen in what was probably the entrance hall. Scholastica's foundation included public baths, latrines, a large dining-hall, and a dormitory on the upper floor. Graffiti on the walls of the baths indicate that at one time the building may have been used as a brothel.

Beyond the baths you come to the small but elegant **Temple of Hadrian**. This was built in the second century AD by a wealthy Ephesian named P. Quintilius and dedicated to the deified Hadrian. The temple has been restored in recent years and is now a most attractive structure. The interesting reliefs with which the temple was once decorated have been placed in the Ephesus Museum, and what one sees *in situ* are plaster copies.

Directly across from Hadrian's Temple there are a number of ancient shops, one of which appears to have been a tavern. And above them there is a whole quarter of **ancient houses** which have recently been excavated, many of them palatial mansions with terraces and pavilions decorated with frescoes and mosaics. These mansions, probably the residences of wealthy Ephesian merchants, have been dated variously from the first to the sixth century AD.

Continuing along, you pass on the left the remains of a **nymphaion** dedicated to the deified Trajan. Several of the statues which once stood in the niches around the fountain are on display in the Ephesus Museum. The base of the Emperor's colossal statue has been restored to its original position, with one of his two huge feet resting imperiously on the globe of the world.

Beyond here the street is flanked with the remains of fountains, columns and pedestals, with a number of commemorative statues still in place. You then come to the junction of Curetes Street with another thoroughfare which branches off to the right, along which you see the ruins of the enormous **Temple of Domitian**, dedicated to the deified Emperor towards the end of the first century AD.

The vast overgrown area opposite the Temple of Domitian was once the **State Agora**, of which all that now remains are fragmentary ruins, principally some columns of the north colonnade. Walking along the north side of the agora you pass first the ruins of the **Prytaneion**, the town-hall of Ephesus. Beside the Prytaneion is the **Odeion**, a structure centring on a theatre which was used for meetings of the Ephesian Senate and also for musical performances.

Directly opposite the Odeion on the other side of the agora are the ruins of a **monumental fountain** dating from the second century AD. And beyond the Odeion are the massive ruins of two more Roman buildings of the same period, a **public bath** and a **gymnasium**. Their vast size attests to the wealth of Ephesus in Roman times, when it was known as the Metropolis of Asia.

This brings you to the ruins of the **Magnesia Gate**, one of the two main entry ways to Hellenistic Ephesus. From here a colonnaded street led around the back of Mount Pion to the Artemesion, following more or less the route of the present track which leads in that direction; you can follow this to visit the monuments on the acropolis. These monuments all date from medieval times, a period when the old Hellenistic city was abandoned because of malaria and the continued silting-up of the harbour. Also, in those troubled times the acropolis was more easily defended than the crumbling old city on the plain.

At the foot of the acropolis you come to the huge **Mosque of Isa Bey**, built in 1375 by a prince of the Aydíníd Turks. The Aydíníds were the Turcoman clan which captured Ephesus in 1304 and ruled over much of western Asia Minor in the first half of the fourteenth century.

You now enter the portal called, for some unknown reason, the **Gate of Persecution**. This gives entrance to the precincts of the **Church of St John** who, according to tradition, lived here during his years in Ephesus; after his death a shrine was erected over his grave. This shrine was replaced by a larger church in the fourth century, and this in turn was torn down two centuries later to make room for the monumental edifice whose ruins one sees today. It was built by Justinian at about the same time as Haghia Sophia, and archaeological work in recent years has revealed that it was a domed basilica, comprising a central nave with two aisles on either side formed by two pairs of colonnades. The basilica ended in a semi-circular apse, and the main dome before the altar was flanked by two side domes to form a cross. This central dome covered the supposed grave of St John, a spot now marked by a slab of white marble enclosed by a grille. Excavation to the east of the basilica has revealed a structure which may have been the baptistery; the frescoes on the apse of this chapel have been dated tentatively to the tenth century.

If time permits, it is worth climbing to the **Citadel of Ayasuluk**. the defence-walls there were originally constructed by the Byzantines and rebuilt by the Turks. Excavations on the acropolis have unearthed Mycenaean pottery and other artifacts, indicating that this may have been the site of the indigenous Anatolian settlement before the arrival of the Ionians in Ephesus.

The Ephesus **Museum** is one of the most attractive and interesting of the small local museums in Turkey. Its prize exhibits are the two statues of Artemis which were found in the Prytaneion. The most famous of these is the beautiful alabaster statue of the goddess which stands opposite the entrance; this is the type called **Artemis Polymastros**, of the Many Breasts, symbolic of her role as a fertility-goddess. This was created during the reign of Domitian (AD 81–96)

159

and once stood in the middle of the central courtyard of the Prytaneion.

Ephesus is as popular a religious shrine today as it was in ancient times. This is due to the 'miraculous' discovery near Selçuk of the supposed **House of the Blessed Virgin**, known in Turkish as *Meryemana*. The House of the Virgin is at Panayia Kapulu, eight kilometres to the south of Selçuk, approached by a road which leads off to the right from the Aydín highway one kilometre from town. This was a sacred spot long before the discovery of the shrine, for the local Greeks celebrated a *panaghia* of the Virgin there on 15 August for centuries before their expulsion from Anatolia in 1923. This *panaghia* was undoubtedly a continuation of an ancient fertility-rite of the Anatolian Mother-Goddess, Cybele-Artemis, whose mythical birthplace was at the spot called Ortygia, just a short distance away from Panayia Kapulu on the slopes of Mount Coressos. As we read in the Homeric Hymn to Delian Apollo: 'Rejoice, blessed Leto, for you bear glorious children, the lord Apollo and Artemis who delights in arrows; her in Ortygia and him in rocky Delos . . .'

You should now take the road to Kuşadasí; this brings you down the valley of the Cayster to the sea, some five kilometres below Ephesus. You then cross a headland and come upon one of the most beautiful bays on the Aegean coast of Turkey. The bay is formed by two promontories; the nearer one is called **Kuşadasí**, the **Isle of Birds**, a name which in modern times has been given to the pretty town at the head of the bay, a major port of call for tourist ships in recent years. Kuşadasí itself has little in the way of monuments, just the picturesque Genoese fortress on an islet in the bay and the seventeenth-century caravansarai of Okuz Mehmet Pasha, which has been superbly restored and is now used as a hotel by the Club Méditerranée. There are a number of good fish restaurants down on the quay where one can dine under the stars beside the Aegean.

Once you are past Kuşadasí the road heads inland, through the most lyrically beautiful countryside in all Ionia. The road winds along past rolling hills covered with olive groves and verdant fields dotted with clusters of pines and spectral cypresses, with the great massif of Mount Mycale just to the south. You then come to Söke, where you turn south to round the eastern flank of Mycale. Once past the flank you turn right on to a dirt road which hugs the southern slope of Mycale and takes you to the village of Güllübahçe, the Rosy Garden. From there a short climb up the mountain brings you past ancient defence-walls to the **site of Priene**, another member of the Ionian Confederacy.

Priene has by far the most spectacular site of any of the ancient Ionian cities, standing on a narrow shelf of hillside high above the Maeander valley, with one of the mighty bastions of Mycale rising sheer above the ruins. The original site of Priene was farther inland. The citizens moved to the present location in the middle of the fourth century BC to follow the receding shoreline, which moved ever westwards with the silt carried down by the Maeander. Priene's main claim to fame in antiquity was that on its territory stood the Panionium, the central meeting-place and sanctuary of the Ionian Confederacy.

The most important monument in Priene is the **Temple of Athena**, which stands in the most dominant position in the city. The temple was designed by Pytheos, architect of the Mausoleum of Halicarnassus; it was begun in the second quarter of the fourth century BC, and after its completion it became the archetypal temple in Ionic architecture. The temple was still being built when Alexander the Great arrived with his army in 334 BC, whereupon he offered to defray the expenses of completing the sanctuary if his name was inscribed upon it as its founder. The dedicatory inscription was discovered during the nineteenth-century excavation; it reads: 'King Alexander presented this temple to Athena Polias.'

Below the temple there is a long stoa which must have been a favourite place of promenade, with its sweeping view out across the valley of the Maeander, in ancient times an inlet of the Aegean. At its eastern end the valley gave entrance to the Sacred Stoa; this formed the north side of the **agora**, the central market and communal meeting-place of the city. At the eastern end of the agora stood the **Temenos of Zeus Olympios**, the second most important sanctuary in Priene. Directly above the agora is the bouleterion, or council-chamber, the best-preserved monument in Priene, and above that the Roman gymnasium and the theatre. Below the agora, at the very edge of the cliff, are the lower gymnasium and the stadium. West of the agora there is a whole quarter of private houses, some of them quite grand. The largest of these is a mansion which seems to have served as a sanctuary; the discovery there of a marble statuette representing Alexander suggests that the house may have been dedicated to the deified Emperor. It is quite possible that Alexander stayed in it during his stay in Priene, while he was directing the siege of Miletos.

The only other monument of note in Priene is the **Sanctuary of**

Demeter and Kore, which can be reached by a short climb uphill from the Temple of Athena. This is the oldest temple in Priene, and it was the principal sanctuary before the completion of the Temple of Athena.

Since Priene had faded into relative insignificance by Roman times it has no buildings of note from that period. For this reason Priene is the finest extant example of a well-planned Hellenistic town, its grid-work of streets lined with majestic public buildings and private dwellings. This magnificent city stands deserted on its lofty site, a haunting reminder of the splendid civilization that once flourished along this beautiful coast.

After leaving Priene you should return to the main road, which now heads south across the flat delta of the Maeander. In classical times this was the Latmian Gulf, bounded on the north by Mount Mycale and on the south by the low hills which you see ahead. When you reach the hills turn right down the southern side of the Maeander valley. A short drive along this road brings you to the hamlet of Akköy; here turn right for the village of Balat, which is a short distance from the **site of ancient Miletos**.

Although Ephesus is more famous today Miletos was by far the greatest of the Ionian cities, as measured by its enormous contribution to the development of Greek civilization. It was the principal port and the richest emporium on the Aegean coast. The city's seaborne trade brought its mariners to every corner of the *oicumene*, the inhabited world known to the Greeks. During the eighth and seventh centuries BC Miletos established nearly one hundred colonies along the shores of the Mediterranean, the Marmara and the Black Sea, and thus was a major force in the Hellenization of Anatolia. Science and natural philosophy were born here at the beginning of the sixth century BC, when Thales of Miletos began to speculate about the nature of the physical world. Thales believed that there was a fundamental unity beneath the apparent disorder and complexity of nature, and he postulated that water was the material basis for all things. His ideas were further developed by his Miletian successors, Anaximander and Anaximenes, whose theories about the nature of matter and of the cosmos represent the transition of Greek thought from myth to rationality, and whose ideas posed fundamental questions which modern science and philosophy are still attempting to resolve.

The archaic city of Miletos was totally destroyed by the Persians in 494 BC, during the Ionian Revolt, and those of its inhabitants who survived the massacre were enslaved and resettled on the Persian

Gulf. (A play entitled *The Fall of Miletos* was later performed in Athens and caused the entire audience to burst into tears; afterwards the authorities fined the playwright 1000 drachmae.) Although the city was rebuilt and repopulated after the Greek victory over the Persians it never regained its former greatness. Nevertheless, in Hellenistic times Miletos was a prosperous and populous commercial centre, as can be seen from the extent of the ruins from that period which remain today. And the city continued to produce men of genius down to the very end of antiquity, most notably the great physicist Isidorus of Miletos, one of the architects of Haghia Sophia.

The **theatre** at Miletos is by far the most impressive of the town's surviving monuments. In its present form it dates from the beginning of the second century AD, replacing an earlier Hellenistic theatre on the same site. Although there are larger and more famous theatres elsewhere in western Asia Minor none is more magnificent than this.

If you climb to the top tier of the theatre you can survey the whole site of ancient Miletos. Looking backwards from the theatre, you see on the hill directly behind the ruins of a Byzantine fortress. Off to the right are the extensive remains of a large number of structures from the Hellenistic and Roman periods: the council-chamber, the senate, market-places, temples and baths. I have tried to picture Miletos as it was in the days of its greatness, but the effort of evocation is more difficult here than elsewhere in Ionia, for the Maeander has silted up the port, leaving the melancholy ruins completely isolated in a marsh far from the sea. If you stroll out behind the theatre you come to what was once the Porto Leonas, named for the marble statues of the two lions who guarded the entrance to the inner port. They remain in place to this day, though half-buried in silt, reminding one that from here the ships of Miletos sailed all over the ancient world, carrying not only goods but the ideas which would give rise to Western civilization.

There is one Islamic monument of note in Balat, the village near Miletos. This is **Ilyas Bey Camii**, founded by a prince of the Menteşe, the Turcoman clan which ruled this corner of Anatolia before the Ottomans gained the upper hand. Ilyas Bey built this handsome mosque in 1404 to celebrate his return to freedom after having been a hostage in the court of Tamerlane.

You should now return to Akköy and continue straight ahead past the crossroads to the road which leads to the **site of ancient Didyma**. The countryside becomes much prettier and more cheerful and the road passes a number of fine sand beaches. The best swimming along this coast is at Altínkum, out on the end of the peninsula beyond

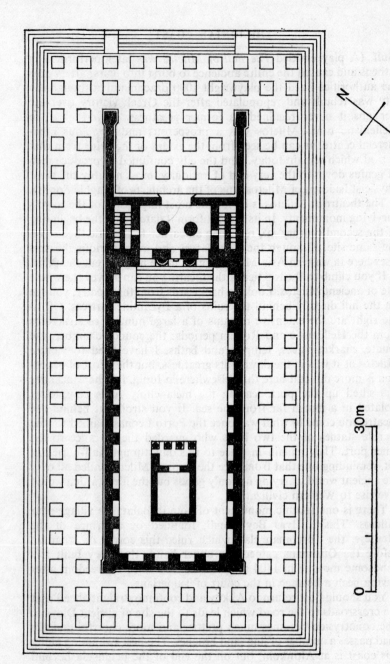

Temple of Apollo, Didyma

Didyma. Altínkum also has a number of good restaurants and hotels, and it is worth spending the night there after visiting Didyma.

Didyma, like Claros, was never a city in its own right, but a Miletian sanctuary of Apollo inhabited only by priests and the suppliants who came to consult the famous oracle there. The oracle at Didyma was the oldest known to the Greeks in Asia Minor, and Pausanias says that it existed even before the arrival of the Ionians. The archaic Temple of Apollo was destroyed at the time of the Persian sack in 494 BC, and for nearly two centuries afterwards the sanctuary remained in ruins. Around 300 BC Seleucus began the immense temple which you can see today; it took five centuries to build and was never completed.

The temple is of the Ionic order and its plan is 'dipteral decastyle'; that is, a sanctuary surrounded by a double row of columns, numbering ten each at the front and back, and with a double row of twenty-one each along the sides. There were twelve more columns in the pronaos, the forecourt of the cella, making a total of 120. Between the pronaos and the cella there is an antechamber with two Corinthian columns; from here three doors open on to a flight of steps leading down to the cella, while from the pronaos it is reached by two sloping tunnels. The cella is unroofed and is like a great open courtyard, with walls over seventy feet in height. At the rear end of the cella you see the foundations of a small Ionic sanctuary which probably housed the sacred cult-statue of Apollo.

Unlike Miletos, these ruins are not melancholy, for the splendid edifice stands proudly in the midst of a cheerful village constructed partly from its remnants. Somehow one always arrives in Didyma late in the day, exhausted after having visited half of the archaeological sites in ancient Ionia. The temple is most beautiful then, with the massive ruins washed with the pale pastels of approaching sunset, the great column drums casting deep purple shadows across the ancient sanctuary. It is not hard to picture this place as it was in ancient times at the celebration of the Didymeia, the quincentennial festival of Apollo. As Homer writes:

. . . there the long-robed Ionians gather with their children and shy wives; mindful, they delight you with boxing and dancing and song, so often as they hold their gathering. A man would say that they are deathless and unaging if he would come upon the Ionians so met together. For he would see the graces of them all, and would be pleased in heart gazing at the men and the well-girded women with their swift ships and great wealth . . .

CHAPTER THIRTEEN

Caria

❧

Heracleia – Euromos – Milas – Bodrum – Cnidos – Stratoniceia – Alabanda – Alinda – Aydín

After leaving Didyma return to the main highway and continue driving south, as the road now leaves the Maeander valley and winds up into the hills beyond. You are now entering ancient Caria, a land which rivals Ionia in its natural beauty and historic interest.

In antiquity Caria comprised the south-west corner of Anatolia, a mountainous region which even today is isolated from the rest of the country. The ethnic origin of the Carians was long a matter of dispute, but modern scholars are generally agreed that they were an indigenous Anatolian people who had lived there long before the Aeolian and Ionian migrations at the beginning of the first millennium BC. Like most of the other native peoples of western Anatolia the Carians were more or less Hellenized in the century or so after Alexander's appearance, and thenceforth the history of that region is much the same as that of the rest of Asia Minor.

Soon after driving into the hills you will see **Lake Bafa**, which in antiquity formed the inner end of the Latmian Gulf. The silting-up of the Maeander valley long ago closed the entrance to the Gulf, and in the centuries since then it has become a fresh-water lake. This is surely one of the most beautiful sights in Turkey, with the sky-blue waters of the lake mirroring the lunar slopes and peaks of Mount Latmos. Halfway along the lake shore you come to a very pleasant camping-ground in an olive grove; here there are two simple but excellent restaurants where you can dine well while resting your eyes on this spectacular lake and the mountain which rises sheer at its far shore.

At the far end of Lake Bafa is one of the most fascinating ruins in all of Turkey, that of **Heracleia-under-Latmos**. It can be reached either by hiring a boat at the camp site or by driving around the far end of the lake. Perhaps it is better to go by boat, for the slow and dramatic approach to Mount Latmos across the lake adds to the

166

romance of arriving at this ancient place.

Heracleia was never an important city, and at the height of its fortunes it was no more than a fortified outpost on the northern borders of Caria. Nevertheless, the ruins are quite extensive and extremely picturesque, with the cella of a temple to Athena perched on a promontory above a beach littered with ancient columns and sarcophagi, and a mighty line of Hellenistic defence-walls and towers marching up the side of this magic mountain.

The legends associated with Heracleia are as romantic as the site, for this is where the moon goddess Selene fell in love with the handsome shepherd Endymion when she saw him sleeping one night on Mount Latmos. Zeus therefore decided that Endymion should never wake but should slumber on in perpetual youth, and while he dreamed Selene lay with him and in time bore him fifty daughters. Apparently the myth lingered on into Christian times, when Endymion was venerated locally as a mystic saint. According to tradition, the Christian anchorites who took refuge on Mount Latmos in early Byzantine times discovered an ancient tomb which they took to be Endymion's and made it into a sanctuary. Each year the anchorites would open the lid of the sarcophagus inside the tomb, whereupon the skeleton within invariably emitted a strange humming sound. This they interpreted as Endymion's attempt to communicate to man the name of God, which he had learned from Selene while they slept together on Latmos. And indeed a very interesting and unique tomb-sanctuary has been found in Heracleia, about three hundred metres to the south-east of the Temple of Athena; it has been tentatively identified as Endymion's sanctuary, though no sepulchral humming has been heard from the sarcophagus within.

The ruins which lie scattered about on the lower slopes of Latmos date principally from the early Hellenistic period, when Heracleia was undergoing a transition from Carian to Greek culture. There are also a number of structures dating from the Byzantine period, the most interesting of which are the churches and monasteries which stand on the several islets in the lake, some of them half-submerged. Altogether Heracleia is an unforgettable and haunting place, particularly if one sees it as we first did with a full moon rising over the serrated peak of Latmos, silvering the columns and sarcophagi on the lake shore, and evoking visions of the shepherd who was enchanted here in ancient times.

Some twenty kilometres past Lake Bafa you see on your left the **ruins of Euromos**, another ancient Carian city. The only monument of any size which has survived from this once important town is the

Temple of Zeus, which stands in an olive grove a few hundred metres from the road. This Corinthian temple, which dates from the first half of the second century AD, is one of the best preserved in Asia Minor, with sixteen of its columns still standing along with their architrave. In recent years a dirt road has been built so that one can drive directly to the temple; this is a pity, since it greatly detracts from the natural beauty of the setting. When we first saw it many years ago the temple stood alone and serene in the midst of the grove, with a gnarled old olive tree entwined around one of the mottled columns as if embracing it. We sat there gazing at the temple in the shade of an olive tree, our evocation of the classic past aided by a large bottle of red wine from Bodrum. Two old Turkish shepherdesses joined us and generously shared their lunch of bread, goat's cheese and olives, though they politely declined our wine. My friend Jim Lovett turned to one of the women and asked her if she knew how old the temple was. She shook her head in wonderment and replied, 'It is old: very, very old.' 'Yes,' added the other, 'it was standing here when we were little children.'

A short way past Euromos a dirt road leads off to the right to the **site of ancient Iasus**. Iasus has been thoroughly excavated in recent years and now the site is one of the most interesting in Caria. But, unfortunately, those on a first trip to Turkey usually pass Iasus by on the way to Bodrum, for there are so many other places to see along the Aegean coast.

Some four kilometres past the turn-off for Iasus is a quaint hump-backed bridge and a stretch of Roman road still in use beside the modern one. You then come to **Milas**, a busy town which since antiquity has been the most populous city in this region. As Mylasa it was the capital of Caria for a time in the middle of the fourth century BC, when the satrap Mausolus created a semi-autonomous principality for himself in the south-western corner of Asia Minor. Mausolus later built a new capital at the more defensible site of Halicarnassus, the modern Bodrum, although Mylasa still remained the principal city of Caria.

There is little left today of ancient Mylasa, for the modern city is built directly on its site and has literally used the ruins as a quarry for building material, as is so often the case in Anatolia. All that remains of the city walls is an impressive Roman gateway locally called **Baltalí Kapí**, the **Gate of the Axe**. It takes its name from the relief of a double axe on the keystone of the arch on the outer side. This double axe was the symbol of the temple-city of Labraynda, which was centred on the great Carian sanctuary of Zeus Stratius.

During the reign of Mausolus a Sacred Way was built from this gate to the shrine, which stood in a mountain grove fourteen kilometres to the north. Labraynda has also been excavated in recent years and is now an impressive and interesting site, but here again the hurried traveller may have to postpone a visit there.

Besides the Baltalí Kapí there are two other ancient monuments in Milas. One of these is the fragmentary ruin of the **Temple of Zeus Carius**, of which only a single column remains standing, with a stork's nest perched on top of its Corinthian capital. On the western edge of the town is a handsome Roman tomb known locally as **Gümüşkesen**. It was built in the first century BC and was designed as a miniature replica of the famous Mausoleum in Halicarnassus; today it is used by a local farmer as a cowshed.

Milas did not suffer the fate of so many other ancient sites in Asia Minor, for it continued to be an important town throughout the Byzantine and Turkish periods. It became capital of a principality again in 1291, when the Menteşe emirs controlled south-western Anatolia before the rise of the Ottomans. The Menteşe were Turcoman tribesmen who swarmed into Anatolia in the thirteenth century, one of many nomadic clans from central Asia who occupied lands that had formerly belonged to the Byzantine Empire. Three fine old mosques remain in Milas from the period of the Menteşe emirate: the **Ulu Cami** and **Orhan Bey Camii** were built in the first half of the fourteenth century and the handsome **Firuz Bey Camii** was completed in 1392.

Five kilometres south of Milas is an enormous flat-topped rock that rises dramatically from the plain to a height of nearly 250 metres. This is **Peçin Kale**, which in the fourteenth century was the principal stronghold of the Menteşe Turks. The most important monument on Peçin Kale is the Menteşe fortress, but there are also remains dating back through classical times to the Early Bronze Age.

At the base of Peçin Kale the road forks, the left branch leading to Muğla and the right to Bodrum. Here you take the Bodrum road, which leads up into a range of hills covered with olive groves. Here and there in the hills are curious domed structures which look rather like Turkish tombs; actually they are cisterns built to store rain water for irrigation.

After driving westwards for fifteen kilometres you come to a turn-off for **Güllük**, where the main Bodrum highway turns south. Güllük is a pretty seaside village which has so far escaped the ravages of tourism. One can hire a boat there to explore the surrounding shores of the Güllük Gulf, one of the most unspoiled regions along the Aegean coast.

The main highway continues south for a while and then veers westwards along the Myndus peninsula. The ride is long and tortuous, as the road winds around the innumerable foothills of Kaplan Daği, the Tiger's Mountain. But at the end you are rewarded with one of the most magnificent sights in Turkey, the beautiful port and town of **Bodrum**, the **ancient Halicarnassus**, with its mighty Castle of St Peter towering on a promontory above the Aegean.

Herodotus was born in Halicarnassus in about 485 BC, and from there travelled widely before finally retiring in Thuri, in southern Italy. There he completed his great *Histories*, beginning with these lines: 'In this book, the result of my enquiries into history, I hope to do two things: to preserve the memory of the past by putting on record the astonishing achievements both of our own and of the Asiatic peoples, and more particularly, to show how the two races came into conflict.'

The most illustrious period in the history of Halicarnassus began in the second quarter of the fourth century BC, when Mausolus rebuilt and fortified the town and made it the capital of Caria. Mausolus reigned from 377 BC until his death in 353, and under his vigorous rule Caria became a powerful and virtually independent state. Mausolus was succeeded by Artemisia, his wife and eldest sister, who began the construction of the monumental tomb which has immortalized his name. (After the death of her brother-husband Artemisia daily drank her wine mixed with some of the ashes from his funerary urn, a practice which she continued until her own death two years later.) Philo of Byzantium listed the **Mausoleum of Halicarnassus** among his Seven Wonders of the World. The Mausoleum was not only the most gigantic tomb ever built in the Greek world, but it must have been the most beautiful, for its four sides were each adorned with friezes created by four of the best sculptors of the age, including Scopas. The Mausoleum survived the siege of Halicarnassus by Alexander the Great, in which much of the ancient city was destroyed, and it remained standing for more than seventeen centuries afterwards. But when the Knights of St John arrived in 1415 they found the Mausoleum in ruins, and used it as a quarry for the construction of the Castle of St Peter. A first attempt at excavation was made in the middle of the nineteenth century by Sir Charles Newton, who carried off to the British Museum in London most of the surviving reliefs and the statues of Mausolus and Artemisia. More scientific excavations have been made in recent years and most of the foundations have now been unearthed; from their vast extent one can well see why this was one of the wonders of the world.

Little else now remains of the city of Mausolus. Parts of the defence wall and a single gate can be seen, as well as remnants of the theatre, but the rest lies buried beneath modern Bodrum. Much of the charm of Bodrum is that it is an architectural palimpsest, with ancient marble fragments embedded in walls, capitals serving as well-heads and columns as door-stops, the present constructed out of the ruins of the past.

The magnificent **Castle of St Peter** dominates Bodrum and adds greatly to its beauty and historic interest. Construction of the castle was begun some time after 1402, when Tamerlane took the city of Smyrna and the Knights of St John consequently lost their fortress there. The Tower of France was the first to be built, and the other walls and towers were added in the course of the next century. The conquest of Rhodes by Süleyman the Magnificent in 1522 deprived the Hospitallers of their main base, and in the following year the Knights evacuated their castle in Bodrum and set sail for Malta.

Passing through the outer gate of the fortress you enter the north fosse, where Ottoman cannons and ancient architectural and sculptural fragments are displayed. From here you pass through a courtyard and into the west fosse, with the wall of the citadel on the left and the counterscarp on the right. From the top of the counterscarp you cross the scarp by a footbridge and make your way into the outer bayle, or citadel. Set into the walls and over the gateways are a large number of architectural fragments and reliefs from the Mausoleum, as well as Christian reliefs and escutcheons bearing the arms of the various Grand Masters of the Hospitallers and commanders of the fortress.

Immediately to the right as you enter the outer bayle is the Chapel of the Knights. This now houses part of the Bodrum Museum's collection of antiquities, including some interesting Mycenaean pottery and a portion of the frieze from the Mausoleum. A stairway beside the chapel leads up to the two buildings which house the remainder of the museum's collection, the Carian Hall and the Hall of Underwater Archaeology. The Carian Hall, as its name implies, houses antiquities from excavations in Bodrum and elsewhere in Caria. The fascinating exhibits in the second hall are the finds made in the pioneering work in underwater archaeology by Professor George Bass and his team from the University of Pennsylvania.

You are now in the inner bayle of the citadel, surrounded by the towers of the various nations of the Hospitallers: the French and

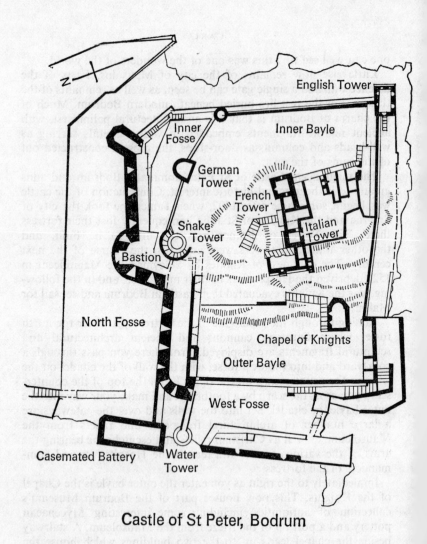

Castle of St Peter, Bodrum

Italian towers on the uppermost level of the citadel, the English at the far corner of the lower level, the German Tower and the Snake Tower along the north wall of the citadel, beyond which are the great bastions of the outer wall. On the west wall of the English Tower there is the relief of a marble lion surmounted by the arms of Edward Plantagenet, and inside the window frames are inscribed with the names of various English knights who were confined to this beautiful castle so far from home.

The upper towers of the citadel command a panoramic view of the whole town and its surroundings. Below to the east are the renowned boatyards of Bodrum, where beautiful caiques are made according to designs which have hardly changed for centuries. Below the castle to the west is the main harbour, lined with the caiques of local fishermen and sponge-divers, as well as the luxurious sailboats of the travellers who in recent years have made Bodrum the principal yachting port in Turkey. The seafront beyond the port is lined with pleasant cafés and restaurants, the best of which are the Korfez and the Han, the latter housed in a beautifully restored eighteenth-century caravansarai.

A few years ago one could look forward to meeting along the waterfront here the dean of Turkish writers, Cevat Şakir Kabaağaç, better known as the Fisherman of Halicarnassus. Cevat was exiled to Bodrum in 1908 and remained there for most of the rest of his life, making the town famous by his books and stories about the local fishermen and their way of life. But now the Fisherman is dead and gone to whatever paradise scribblers are allowed to enter. For his epitaph I would like to choose these lines written twenty-two centuries ago by Kallimachos of Kyrene, as his last farewell to a poet of Halicarnassus:

They brought me news of your death, Herakleitos, and I wept for you, remembering how often we watched the sun setting as we talked. Dear Halicarnassian friend, you lie elsewhere now and are mere ashes; yet your songs – your nightingales – will live forever. And never will the underworld, destroying everything, touch them with its ugly hand.

Those with time to spare might drive out past Bodrum to the far end of the peninsula, particularly to the lovely beach at Gümüşlük. There are other superb beaches which can be reached only by caique from Bodrum, the most beautiful of which is a deserted sandy cove appropriately called Cennet, or Paradise. After an afternoon spent there swimming and picnicking one might well wonder, as the Fisherman of Halicarnassus once did, whether the paradise beyond the grave could ever be more pleasurable than this sybaritic peninsula.

From Bodrum there is a regular ferry service to the Greek island of Cos (the political situation permitting). One can also charter a caique to visit some of the interesting archaeological sites along the southern coast of Caria, many of which are difficult of access by land. The most famous is **Cnidos**, which is at the end of the long dragon-like peninsula across the Ceramus Gulf from Bodrum, and which can be visited on a long day's outing.

Cnidos was renowned in antiquity for a statue and for a scientist. The statue was that of Aphrodite by Praxiteles, the greatest of all Greek sculptors; it was modelled on the fair Phryne, the most famous Athenian courtesan, and in antiquity it was considered to represent the archetype of feminine beauty. The statue stood in the Temple of Aphrodite Euploia (of Fair Sailing) at Cnidos, and apparently it was designed more as an adornment to the city than as a cult-figure; certainly it was a great tourist attraction and visitors came from afar to see it. (According to tradition, one admirer was so overcome by the beauty of Aphrodite, that he sneaked into the sanctuary at night and embraced the statue, which ever afterwards bore a dark stain on its inner thigh where he had kissed it passionately.) A team led by Professor Iris Love has recently unearthed the circular base of the Temple of Aphrodite and has even found a marble fragment inscribed with the first letters of the names of Praxiteles and the goddess, making the identification certain. Less certain by far is Professor Love's claim to have discovered Aphrodite's head in the basement of the British Museum, included among the loot which Newton brought back to London in 1859. The authorities at the British Museum insist that the rather battered head is that of Persephone from the Temple of Demeter at Cnidos.

The scientist was Eudoxos of Cnidos, who flourished in Athens at the same time as Praxiteles, in the first half of the fourth century BC. Eudoxos was a student of Plato's and together with Theaetetus is considered to be the founder of Greek geometry. Eudoxos was also the first to apply mathematics to the study of astronomy. He returned to Cnidos in his later years and built an astronomical observatory there, the first such institution in the Greek world.

After leaving Bodrum there is no alternative but to drive back as far as the crossroads south of Milas, below Peçin Kale. Here you continue straight on and head east along the Muğla highway, going deeper into the interior of ancient Caria.

The first village of any size is Eskihisar, recently rebuilt after having been destroyed in an earthquake. The village stands on the **site of Stratoniceia**, a Hellenistic city founded in about 280 BC by Seleucus I of Syria on the site of an ancient Carian town. Stratoniceia was important in ancient times because it had on its territory the Temple of Zeus Chrysaoreus, the central sanctuary and meeting-place of the confederation of Carian towns. The city was rich and populous in Hellenistic and Roman times, but today very little remains standing. The most prominent ruins are those of the Temple of Serapis and a city gate with a lone Corinthian column standing beside it.

A short way beyond Eskihisar the highway comes to a major inter-section near the town of Yatağan, with one branch leading north to Aydín and the other south to Muğla and thence to Marmaris and the Lycian shore. Here the traveller is faced with two alternatives. Some may prefer to drive down to Marmaris and from there travel along the Lycian coast to Antalya. Others will want to drive north to Aydín, and from there go up the Maeander valley and across the Taurus Mountains to Antalya. The present itinerary will follow the latter route, completing the tour through Caria at Aydín, while the two following chapters will describe the two routes from Caria to Antalya.

Turning north at Yatağan, you drive up the valley of the **Çine Çayí**, the **ancient Marsyas**, through a gorge of savage beauty. The river is named after the satyr Marsyas, a devotee of the goddess Cybele. Marsyas one day found a double flute which had been made by Athena from the bones of a stag, and when he put it to his lips it played by itself, inspired by the memory of those melodies that Athena had played upon it at a banquet of the gods. Marsyas travelled through Caria in Cybele's entourage, playing upon his flute and delighting the peasants, who exclaimed that his music was sweeter than that of Apollo's lyre. This angered Apollo, who challenged Marsyas to a contest before the Muses, with the winner entitled to inflict whatever punishment he pleased upon the loser. When Apollo was eventually declared the winner he wreaked a most savage revenge on Marsyas, flaying him alive and nailing him to a pine tree, near the source of the Carian river which thereafter bore his name.

Some ten kilometres past Yatağan the gorge is spanned by an ancient bridge, and two kilometres beyond that you cross the Gökbel Pass, some four hundred metres above sea-level. From there the road descends into a fertile highland plain, the heart of ancient Caria. Eventually you arrive in the busy farming town of **Çine**, the richest and most populous community in the region.

Çine is a good base for visiting two very interesting cities of ancient Caria, Alabanda and Alinda. **Alabanda** is seven kilometres to the west of Çine, approached by a dirt road leading off to the left from the main street of the town. To reach **Alinda** you continue for another seven kilometres along the Aydín highway and then turn left; the site is twenty-five kilometres to the west. In their time these were two of the most important cities in Caria, and each served for a time as the capital. Their great days, like those of all other cities in Caria, came in the middle of the fourth century, during the reign of Mausolus. At the time of Alexander's campaign the two cities were ruled by Queen Ada, a younger sister of Mausolus and Artemisia. Before Alexander began his siege of Halicarnassus in 334 BC he travelled to Alinda, which was voluntarily surrendered to him by Ada. Alexander lingered in Alinda for a while to make preparations for the siege. During this time he and Ada became very close friends; he addressed the middle-aged Queen as 'Mama' and she even offered to adopt him as her son. Ada commanded the Carian contingent of Alexander's army during the siege, and it was she who captured the last two strongholds after Alexander's capture of the main fortress. Before he departed Alexander appointed Ada satrap of Caria, and after she had put down the last Persian resistance in Halicarnassus she returned to Alinda, which she then made her capital. After her death a few years later Alabanda was made the capital, but with the end of the extraordinary family of Mausolus the great days of Caria had come to an end.

The sites at Alabanda and Alinda have never been properly excavated, a fact which undoubtedly adds to the considerable charm of their ruins. In both places the remains of ancient structures are found in the local village and in the fields around: sheep grazing in the agora, a kitchen garden in the cavea of the theatre, children playing in the ruins of the market hall, a farmer living in a mausoleum, with bits and pieces of sculptures, inscriptions, columns and capitals built into the houses, a scene reminiscent of the prints which illustrate the accounts of early travellers to the Ottoman Empire.

After seeing Alabanda and Alinda you return to the main road and continue driving towards Aydín. Some twenty-seven kilometres past the Alinda turning you cross over the brown alluvial waters of the Büyük Menderes, the main stream of the ancient Maeander, and seven kilometres beyond that you arrive in the large town of Aydín.

The theatre in Miletos.

The Street of the Curetes in Ephesus. The arched portal halfway along is the entrance to the Temple of Hadrian.

CHAPTER FOURTEEN

The Lycian Shore

Marmaris – Fethiye – Xanthus – The Letoon – Patara – Kaş – Myra –
Finike – Limyra – Phaselis – Antalya

The road to Marmaris continues from Yatağan to Muğla, a charming old town with a picturesque bazaar and some of the most handsome Ottoman houses surviving in Turkey. After passing through
Muğla the road goes south across heavily wooded hills and through
wild gorges, until you are finally rewarded with a spectacular view
of the Ceramus Gulf. Then you drive around the plain at the head of
the Gulf and across the neck of the Loryma peninsula to arrive at
Marmaris.

Marmaris must once have been a beautiful town, but it has never
fully recovered from the earthquake which wrecked it in 1958, and
now it is merely picturesque in a broken-down way. But its situation
is magnificent, the white and ochre town with its ruined medieval
fortress standing on a promontory at the end of an immense green
fiord. (Nelson anchored his entire fleet here in 1798.) Across the way
from Marmaris is the Greek island of Rhodes, to which ferries sail
regularly in untroubled times. Off to the west is a huge dragon-
headed peninsula with Cnidos at the tip of the northern jaw, ancient
Loryma at the end of the southern one, and the Greek island of
Syme literally between the dragon's teeth. In antiquity this region
was known as the Rhodian Peraea, since at various times in its
history the Anatolian foreshore here was controlled by Rhodes. As
Pindar wrote of this lovely coast and its offshore islands: 'Sea-girt
Rhodes, child of Aphrodite and bride of Helios . . . nigh to a promontory of spacious Asia.'

Antalya, looking across the gulf towards the Lycian coast. In the
foreground is Yivli Minare, the Fluted Minaret.

The harbour of Marmaris.

Marmaris stands near the boundary between the coast of ancient Caria and that of Lycia, which forms an enormous sea-bound bulge at the south-western corner of Anatolia. Lycia is even more remote and inaccessible than Caria, and today as in antiquity its principal means of communication with the outside world is by sea. One can travel along the coast as far as Fethiye on a passable highway (with some bad stretches), but beyond that the road is for the most part very poor and in places downright perilous. And so, if one has time to spare, the best way to see this coast is by hiring a caique in Marmaris; they come complete with captain and crew who will catch fish for your evening meal and help drink your wine and *raki*. There is no more pleasurable way to spend a holiday in Turkey than to sail along the Lycian shore in an old caique with a merry company, stopping here and there to swim or wander through an ancient ruin, and then dining under the stars in a deserted cove.

The first town of any size east of Marmaris is **Fethiye, ancient Telmessus**, which since antiquity has been the principal harbour of Lycia. One can see why this is so on entering the great roadstead, with its string of pine-clad islets forming a natural breakwater for the port, the ancient Bay of Glaucus. The bay takes its name from one of the two leaders of the Lycian contingent who fought as allies of the Trojans, as Homer describes them at the end of Book II of the *Iliad*: 'Last, Sarpedon and the peerless Glaucus lead the Lycians, from distant Lycia and the swirling streams of Xanthus.' The Sarpedon whom Homer mentions here was the legendary founder of Miletos. He was the younger brother of Minos of Crete, and after being expelled by the King he led his followers to Ionia, from whence centuries later they made their way to Lycia and founded the first cities there. Although such a migration may have taken place, it is now generally believed that here as elsewhere along the coast of Asia Minor the original inhabitants were indigenous Anatolian people, who in later centuries were Hellenized by contact with Greek colonists.

The modern town of Fethiye is pleasant but nondescript, for whatever distinction it might once have had was destroyed in the same earthquake that levelled Marmaris. All that remains of ancient Telmessus is its **necropolis**, but what a fascinating sight that is, with its unique Lycian sarcophagi and its extraordinary rock-hewn tombs. One of the sarcophagi is displayed beside the Town Hall. It is mounted on a high stone pediment and its sculptured lid is curved like a Lycian cottage or tent with a pitched roof, the eternal home of the deceased thus resembling the one in which he resided in life. The more elaborate tombs are cut into the cliff face behind the town; some of these have their façades carved so as to resemble that of a mansion or temple. The grandest of these is the **Tomb of Amyntas**, dating from the fourth century BC, a huge rock-hewn chamber with a façade in the form of an Ionic temple with two columns *in antis*, that is, a pair of columns standing between the projecting corner posts that terminate the lateral walls of the temple. Altogether these strange Lycian tombs have an eerie and haunting effect, particularly when viewed in the sombre shadows of twilight, at which time the necropolis does indeed seem to be a city of the dead.

From Fethiye the road turns inland as far as Kemer, after which it winds back towards the sea along the valley of the Koca Çayí, the River Xanthus of antiquity. About twenty kilometres past Kemer a track (not signposted at present) leads off to the right to the ancient Lycian city of **Pinara**, whose ruins stand on top of a dramatic butte in the foothills of the Anticragus Mountains. (The site is near the village of Minare Köy, which can be reached from the main road in a Land-Rover.)

Some forty kilometres past Kemer you come to Kíník, a village on the Koca Çayí near the **site of Xanthus**, once the greatest city of ancient Lycia. According to Homer, Xanthus was the oldest of the Lycian cities, and throughout most of antiquity it was the capital of that region. The Xanthians were renowned for the fierce resistance they offered to invading armies in order to preserve their independence, and on two occasions they literally fought to the last man and burned down their city rather than surrender. The first of these heroic defences occurred in the middle of the sixth century BC, when the Persian general Harpagus, commanding the army of Cyrus the Great, advanced into Lycia. As Herodotus tells the tale:

> When Harpagus advanced into the plain of the Xanthus, they met him in battle, though greatly outnumbered, and fought with much gallantry; at length, however, they were defeated and forced to retire within their walls, whereupon they collected their women, children, slaves and other property and shut them up in the citadel of the city, set fire to the place and burned it to the ground. Then having sworn to do or die, they marched out to meet the enemy and were killed to a man.

The Xanthians fought just as valiantly to resist the Romans, when in 42 BC Brutus besieged their city. Once again they fought to the bitter end, and when they saw that there was no hope of victory

179

they burned the city down. As Plutarch completes the story in his life of Brutus:

> It was so tragical a sight that Brutus could not bear to see it, but wept at the very mention of the scene . . . Thus the Xanthians, after a long space of years, repeated by their desperate deed the calamity of their forefathers, who after the very same manner in the Persian Wars had fired their city and destroyed themselves.

The ruins at Xanthus were first excavated in 1838 by Sir Charles Fellows, who carried off to London all of the reliefs which were then visible; these are now on exhibit in the Lycian Room of the British Museum. More scientific excavations began in 1950; this work has unearthed structures covering the entire span of the city's history, from the original Lycian town of the eighth century BC through the classical, Hellenistic, Roman and Byzantine periods up to the twelfth century AD, a total of two thousand years. Here, as elsewhere in Lycia, the most interesting remains are the funerary monuments, but unfortunately all of these are now devoid of their original sculptural decoration.

The two most important funerary monuments stand side by side next to the Roman theatre. One of them is a **Lycian pillar-tomb**, a handsome sarcophagus of the fourth century BC standing on a tall platform. Beside this is the famous **Tomb of the Harpies**, a tall monolith supporting a sarcophagus in the form of a chest decorated with sculptures in low relief. (The relief *in situ* is a plaster copy of the original, which is now in the British Museum.) The so-called harpies from which the tomb takes its name are actually sirens, half-birds and half-women, who are shown conducting the souls of the dead to the underworld.

Beside the road near the Roman agora you find the so-called **Inscribed Pillar**. This is part of a funerary monument which once held the remains of the Lycian King Kherei. The inscription is in Lycian, which has not yet been completely deciphered, but a Greek epigram on one face tells us that the monument was erected to commemorate King Kherei's victory over the Athenians. This is probably a reference to the battle which took place in Lycia in 430 BC, the second year of the Peloponnesian War, an incident which is thus described by Thucydides:

> Six ships, under the command of Melisander, were sent to Caria and Lycia to collect tribute from that area and also to prevent

Peloponnesian privateers from using it as a base . . . Melisander, after marching inland from Lycia with a force of Athenians from the ships and some allies, was killed and defeated in battle, losing a number of his men.

The theatre is built against the north face of the **acropolis**, the site of Lycian Xanthus. The oldest ruins are those of the palace of the Lycian kings, destroyed at the time of the Persian conquest of the city. All of the Lycian monuments on the acropolis, including a Temple of Artemis, were eventually replaced by the Byzantine structures which one sees there today.

Looking to the north-east from the Lycian acropolis one sees a second eminence which was the centre of Xanthus during the Hellenistic, Roman and Byzantine periods. The south-eastern slope of this acropolis was apparently the principal necropolis of Lycian Xanthus, as evidenced by the number of sarcophagi and rock-hewn tombs one sees there. The most splendid of these is an almost perfectly preserved **pillar-tomb** of the fourth century BC; this stands just above the ruins of the famous **Payuva Tomb**, whose reliefs are now in the Lycian Room of the British Museum. The ascent of the acropolis is rather difficult because of the dense undergrowth, but it is well worth the effort because of the superb view which it affords of the ruins and their surroundings, with the great massif of Ak Dağı to the north-east and to the south the River Xanthus winding its way to the sea. This is the river of which Alcman of Sparta wrote in the fifth century BC: 'She sings like a swan, beside the yellow stream of Xanthus.'

The road from Fethiye passes to the left of the only surviving gate of the Hellenistic city. The gate bears an inscription honouring Antiochus III (223–187 BC), the greatest of all the Seleucid kings of Syria. The inscription probably dates from 197 BC, the year when Antiochus sailed along the coast of Asia Minor accepting the surrender of the towns which had previously been held by Ptolemy V Epiphanes of Egypt. Just outside the gate there is an honorific archway dedicated to Vespasian, probably erected soon after he was proclaimed Emperor by his legions in Caesarea (the modern Kayseri) on 1 July AD 69.

Continuing past Xanthus and turning right after about two kilometres, one soon comes within sight of the **Letoon**, the central meeting-place and sanctuary of Lycia. The Letoon has been excavated in recent years, resulting in the discovery of the remains of three temples, a Roman nymphaion, and an early Byzantine church with a fine mosaic floor. The Roman nymphaion appears to have replaced an earlier sanctuary of similar type, whose fountain had as its source the sacred spring of which Ovid writes in Book VI of his *Metamorphoses*. According to Ovid's version of the myth, Leto stopped here on her flight from the wrath of Hera after bearing Apollo and Artemis. Leto was exhausted and parched, and she paused to rest and drink at the spring with her two divine infants. But the local peasants tried to drive her away, jumping into the pool and dancing there to foul the water, whereupon Leto took her revenge by turning them all into frogs.

Some ten kilometres farther along is the village of Kelemiş; from here you can hire a jeep to visit the **ruins of Patara**, the ancient port of Xanthus. Patara's greatest days were during the Roman period, when it was the principal harbour in Lycia, and most of the surviving ruins are from that period. This was the birthplace of Bishop Nicholas of Myra, the almost legendary Lycian saint. Among the famous personages who stopped here when Patara was a great port were Hannibal, St Paul, and the Emperor Hadrian, who constructed the huge granary which is one of Patara's principal surviving monuments. Patara's fate was the same as that of many of the ancient harbours along the coast of Asia Minor: it was silted up by the alluvial deposits carried by the Xanthus. Today huge sand dunes have drifted into the theatre, the ancient harbour is a vast marsh, and the ghostly silence is broken only by the sighing of the sea-breeze in the holm oaks which grow among the ruins.

The main road descends to the sea at Kalkan, which is the next port of call along the coast east of Fethiye. From there the road continues along the coast to **Kaş**, the **ancient Antiphellus**. This pretty town has a superb setting, encircling a crescent bay at the end of a verdant fiord, which is enclosed to the north by a long lizard-like peninsula and on its seaward side is sheltered by the lovely Greek islet of Castelorizzo. In and around the village are more of the characteristic Lycian sarcophagi and rock-cut tombs which make this whole coast seem one vast necropolis, where the ancient cities of the dead are grander than the modern cities of the living. The only major monument surviving from ancient Antiphellus is the **Hellenistic theatre**, which is a short distance west of the town. The theatre is well-preserved and its setting is beautiful, looking out across an olive grove to the blue Mediterranean, with the green isle of Castelorizzo floating in the background.

After leaving Kaş the road takes you inland once more, coming down towards the sea again at **Demre**, a village some three kilometres from the coast. Demre stands near the site of ancient Myra, famed as the episcopal seat of St Nicholas, patron saint of pawn-brokers and sailors and known to children as Father Christmas. Within the village of Demre you find a now disused church dedicated to the saint; it is a heavily restored eleventh-century structure built on the site of an earlier sanctuary of the same name. Nicholas suffered martyrdom here in 655 and his grave soon became a famous place of pilgrimage, but in 1072 his bones were stolen by merchants from Bari, where they rest today in a church dedicated to his name. The **site of ancient Myra** is about one and a half kilometres outside Demre. The most notable surviving monument there is a splendid late Roman theatre; this stands below a dramatic cliff in whose face are hewn some of the most remarkable rock tombs in Lycia, many of them still decorated with beautifully carved figures in low relief, usually depicting funerary scenes.

From Demre one can make an excursion down to the coast to see the **ruins of Andriake and Aperlae**, the latter of which is now a hamlet clustered around the remains of a medieval castle. Offshore between these two sites is the lizard-shaped isle of Kekova, the Greek Asthene. The island and the adjacent coast are hauntingly beautiful, with Lycian sarcophagi scattered along the shore and lying half-submerged in lonely coves.

A drive of thirty kilometres past Demre takes one to **Finike**, the ancient Phoenicus. Finike itself has little of interest for the traveller, but it is a base for visiting some of the archaeological sites in eastern Lycia.

From Finike there are two alternative routes to Antalya. One route takes you north over the mountains via Elmalí to Korkuteli, where there is a good asphalt highway leading down to Antalya. The other road, which is very poor in places and in others is still under construction, takes you right around the eastern Lycian shore, directly under the spectacular peaks which form the western rim of the Gulf of Antalya. Most enterprising travellers choose this latter route, for although it is more difficult and hazardous the scenery is more beautiful, though the inland route has much to recommend it also.

The ancient Lycian city of **Limyra** stands six kilometres to the north of Finike, approached by the Elmalí road. During the first half of the fourth century BC Limyra was for a time the dominant city of Lycia, particularly during the reign of King Perikles, the last of the local dynasts. The **necropolis** at Limyra is the most extensive in all of Lycia and contains the most beautiful tombs and sarcophagi of their type in existence. The most magnificent of these has recently been excavated at the very top of the acropolis, just above the Roman theatre. This is in the form of an Ionic temple modelled on that of Athena Nike on the Athenian acropolis, and it is believed to have been the tomb of King Perikles himself. The view from the acropolis is spectacular, for one can see the whole coastline from Cape Finike to Cape Chelidonia, the south-eastern extremity of Lycia.

The coastal road curves round the Gulf of Finike and turns inland across the base of the peninsula which terminates in Cape Chelidonia, after which it veers north to run along the eastern Lycian shore. This is the most remote and inaccessible region along the whole of the Turkish coast, with sheer rocky cliffs plunging into the sea and the great crags of the Lycian mountains looming in the background.

The road reaches the Gulf of Antalya at Porto Genovese, a little cove whose foreshore is covered with shapeless ruins heavily overgrown with trees and bushes. Just to the north is the **site of Olympus**, which in antiquity was one of the two important cities on the eastern shore of Lycia. The ruins here are in a poor state of preservation but the site is picturesque.

One of the most extraordinary natural phenomena in Turkey is to be seen in the mountains to the north-west of Olympus. This is a fire issuing from the earth, hardly noticeable by day but visible at night far out to sea, appearing almost as if it were an active volcano. Its cause is as yet unknown, but it is probably due to the subterranean combustion of coal gas or methane. This is undoubtedly the origin of the Greek myth of the Chimaera, the fire-breathing monster which was thought to dwell in Lycia. As Homer described it in the *Iliad*: 'Chimaera the unconquerable . . . of divine birth was she and not of men, in front a lion, and behind a serpent, and in the midst a goat, and she breathed dread fierceness of blazing fire.'

About twenty-five kilometres north of Olympus you come to the **site of Phaselis**, which in antiquity was the greatest city in eastern Lycia. According to tradition, Phaselis was founded in 690 BC by settlers from Rhodes. It soon became a member of the Lycian League, and during the thousand years of its existence it shared the history and culture of that region. Along with the other Lycian cities, Phaselis fought valiantly for its freedom, but in 333 BC its citizens had the good sense to surrender their city to Alexander the Great, greeting him at the gate with a golden crown. After Alexander's death Phaselis and the other Lycian cities were fought over by his successors, but none of them ever succeeded in establishing a foothold among these fiercely independent people. So strong was their love of freedom that in 167 BC the Roman Senate was actually persuaded to declare that Lycia was an independent state, a status which it retained longer than any other part of Asia Minor.

Phaselis has never been systematically excavated and its remains are completely overgrown; nevertheless it is one of the most picturesque sites along the Mediterranean coast of Turkey. The ruins stand in lonely grandeur on the shore beneath the great massif of Tahtalí Daği, the ancient Mount Solymnus. This was the peak on which Poseidon stood when he watched Odysseus sail off from Calypso's isle, a scene which Homer thus describes: 'From the mountains of the Solymni, even thence he saw Odysseus as he sailed over the deep.'

A short drive beyond Phaselis brings one to Kemer, a pleasant seaside village which is now becoming a popular summer resort, reached by a good road from Antalya. Here one has left behind the tomb-haunted Lycian shore, to reach what sailors in medieval times called the pirate coast of Pamphylia.

CHAPTER FIFTEEN

The Maeander and the Taurus

✣

Aydín – Nysa – Aphrodisias – Pamukkale – Burdur – Isparta – Termessus – Antalya

The valley of the Büyük Menderes, the Greek Maeander, is the most fertile region in Turkey, and the whole alluvial plain is rich with farms, orchards, vineyards and olive groves. This valley was one of the main avenues from the Aegean into Anatolia in ancient times, and along it Greek culture made a deep and lasting penetration, as cities were established right up to the headwaters of the river in the Taurus and even beyond. The ruins of many of these ancient sites can still be seen along the valley, including some that in their beauty and interest rival those along the Aegean coast.

The principal town in the region is **Aydín**, where one usually begins the journey up the Maeander valley and across the Taurus Mountains to Antalya. There is little of interest to see in Aydín itself, for most of the town is of relatively recent origin. Tralles, its ancient ancestor, is a short distance to the north-east of the modern town, on the plateau known as Güzel Hisar, the Beautiful Castle. The ruins are not particularly impressive and are hardly worth a visit, particularly since they are in a military zone and special permission is required to enter. But before passing Tralles one might recall that the last great mathematical physicist of antiquity was born here about AD 500. This was Anthemius of Tralles, one of the architects of Haghia Sophia and the most gifted scientist of his time.

After leaving Aydín you take the main road which leads east along the Menderes valley. Some thirty kilometres along you come to the village of Sultanhisar, where a road to the left brings you in one kilometre to the **site of ancient Nysa**. The setting of Nysa is very romantic, with the overgrown ruins standing astride a wild gorge running down from the slopes of Mount Messogis. Strabo was a student here in the latter half of the first century BC, and described Nysa as a double city, bisected by the torrential stream which in winter and spring flows down the gorge from Mount Messogis. He

186

described three structures which were built on or over the gorge: a bridge, a long tunnel to canalize the stream, and an amphitheatre which was constructed above the gorge, an ingenious engineering feat which thus joined the two halves of the city. Remains of all these structures can still be seen, along with the considerable remnants of the usual public buildings of a Roman town in Asia Minor. The **theatre** is prominent and particularly picturesque because of the grove of olive trees which has taken root among its tiers of seats. The **library** is the best-preserved in Asia Minor after that of Celsus in Ephesus. All of the ruins date from the Roman period.

Twelve kilometres past Sultanhisar you come to Nazili, where a road leads off to the right for Karacasu and the **site of ancient Aphrodisias**, about an hour's drive to the south. The scenery along this road is lovely, as you drive along a highland plateau past rich farms and orchards, with the snow-capped peaks of Baba Daği, the Father's Mountain, looming majestically in the distance.

The ruins of Aphrodisias are scattered in and around the village of Geyre, which was itself ruined in an earthquake and rebuilt a short distance away. (The name Geyre is a Turkish corruption of Caria, the name which Aphrodisias bore in early Byzantine times when it was capital of the Carian province.) The area has been under intensive study since 1961 by Professor Kenan Erim of New York University, whose excavations have transformed Aphrodisias from an attractive ruin into one of the most important and interesting archaeological sites in Anatolia. Besides unearthing and restoring the monuments of ancient Aphrodisias, Professor Erim and his team have discovered a large number of superb works of art on the site; these will soon be on exhibit in the local museum, which is now nearing completion. The signatures of local artists have also been found on statues in Greece, Italy and elsewhere, and it is now apparent that Aphrodisias was the Florence of the Graeco-Roman world, not only adorning its own city with the work of its native sculptors, but shipping their masterpieces to other places around the Mediterranean.

A road leads off to the right from the town square of Geyre to the archaeological site; this takes you past the newly re-erected propylon, the monumental gateway to the city, a handsome structure built in the second century AD. The road then bends left and soon brings you to the **Temple of Aphrodite**, the most important monument on the site.

The original sanctuary of Aphrodite is thought to date back to the sixth or fifth century BC, though only scant evidence of this earlier building has been found as yet. The sanctuary and its associated settlement seem to have developed into a proper city by about the second century BC; at about that time men began to call it Aphrodite after its leading deity, 'golden Aphrodite . . . who stirs up sweet passions in the gods and subdues the tribes of mortal men'. The present Temple of Aphrodite is thought to date from about 100 BC. It was designed in the Ionic order with a peristyle of thirteen columns along the sides and eight at the ends, surrounding a cella preceded by a pronaos. The peristyle is in the 'pseudo-dipteral' style, in which the single colonnade is placed at twice the usual distance from the walls of the inner sanctuary. Fourteen of the columns are still standing, all but one of them complete with their Ionic capitals, and with two groups still supporting fragments of the architrave. The apsidal structure at the east dates from the fifth century AD, when the temple was converted into a Byzantine church. A hundred metres or so to the east of the temple are two spiral-fluted columns supporting an architrave; this appears to have been part of a monumental gateway, but since it is not aligned with the temple its purpose is obscure.

Most of the other monuments are in the area south of the temple. Opposite the east end of the temple you see the recently-discovered **odeion**; this dates from the second century AD and is one of the best-preserved structures of its type in Asia Minor. The floor of the auditorium was covered with a mosaic pavement and the stage was adorned with sculptured reliefs and statuary, while a backstage corridor opened on to a porticoed square lined with portrait statues of prominent Aphrodisians; many of these works of art have survived and will soon be on exhibition in the local museum. Adjoining the odeion to the west is a circular **heroon**, a shrine dedicated to some deified dead person; in the centre of this stood an ornate altar and a sarcophagus decorated with sculptures in low relief, both of which have survived. Beyond the odeion to the west is a complex of ruins centring on a courtyard with a peristyle of blue marble columns; this is thought to have been the residence of the Bishop of Aphrodisias in early Byzantine times.

Just to the south of the odeion are the remains of the vast **agora**, which has not yet been excavated. A splendid colonnade complete with capitals and architrave can be seen in a poplar grove, giving one some idea of the vanished grandeur of Roman Aphrodisias. Beyond the agora to the south is the Portico of Tiberius, which opened on its west to the monumental Baths of Hadrian. Still farther to the south is the **theatre**, which is now under excavation.

The theatre is built into the eastern slope of a mound which was apparently formed by the debris of Early Bronze Age settlements going back as far as the third millennium BC. To the east of the theatre, in the village itself, is a second mound which has also revealed considerable evidence of Bronze Age occupation.

The **stadium** stands in the fields about half a kilometre to the north of the Temple of Aphrodite. This is one of the largest and best-preserved stadia surviving from the Graeco-Roman world, with a seating capacity of about thirty thousand. The eastern end of the arena is enclosed by a low wall so as to create a circular area for gladiatorial combats and similar barbarous Roman entertainments. The stadium was also the scene of athletic events, games, contests of various kinds (including one in sculpture), musical performances, theatrical productions, as well as civic and religious festivals, the full colourful panoply of life in the good old days of Roman Asia Minor. Several olive trees have taken root along the top tier of the theatre, providing shady spots where one can enjoy a pleasant picnic while looking out over the ruins of this once great city.

One should not leave Aphrodisias without sitting for a while in the picturesque village square of Geyre. It was our good fortune to do so once in late afternoon, when the villagers were returning from working in the surrounding fields, the men mounted proudly on horseback, the shy women dressed in the colourful local costume, some carrying their babies in bundles on their backs, young girls waiting at the village fountain with amphorae poised gracefully on their shoulders, looking like figures on an Attic frieze.

After leaving Aphrodisias you return to the main highway and continue on to Denizli, a large and pleasant town near the head of the Menderes valley. Denizli itself is of little interest, but it is a good base for visiting Pamukkale, one of the major tourist attractions in Turkey.

You leave Denizli on the Burdur-Isparta highway, turning left three kilometres outside town for Pamukkale. As soon as you start down this road you see on the left a sign indicating the way to **Laodiceia**, about four kilometres along a rough dirt road. Only a small part of the ruins of Laodiceia has been excavated, and what there is to see is not of very great interest. Those who visit the site generally do so because Laodiceia was one of the Seven Churches of the Apocalypse, the one which Ramsey called the City of Compromise. The Letter to the Church in Laodiceia begins: 'I know thy works, that thou art neither cold nor hot. So because thou art lukewarm and neither cold nor hot I will spew thee out of my mouth.'

Some fourteen kilometres south of the turning you get your first view of **Pamukkale**, the **Cotton Castle**, one of the most extraordinary sights in Turkey. As you approach you see a plateau more than a hundred metres high rising abruptly out of the plain, its cliff-face a dazzling chalk-white array of fantastically shaped stalactites. Vaporous water flows down the face through a widening succession of scallop-shell basins and petal-like elfin pools surfaced in glistening limestone. These remarkable effects are caused by lime-bearing thermal springs issuing from the lower slopes of Çal Daği; as they flow out across the plateau and pour over the cliff they form calcareous deposits which each year add to the size of the plateau and create ever more spectacular shapes – hence the name Cotton Castle.

On the top of this fairyland plateau are the ruins of **ancient Hierapolis**, the Holy City, supposedly so named because of the many temples which once stood there. But unfortunately the Holy City has been profaned by tourism in recent years, with luxury hotels enclosing most of its unique thermal pools, and with shoddy souvenir shops and annoying postcard pedlars lining the approaches to the ruins, spoiling what was once an enchanting scene.

Hierapolis was founded in the second century BC by the Pergamene kings, probably by Eumenes II, and was bequeathed to Rome in 133 BC by Attalus III along with the rest of his realm. Apart from the tombs in the necropolis, there is hardly anything left of the Hellenistic city, and virtually all of the surviving monuments are from the Roman period. Indeed, during the days of imperial Rome Hierapolis must have been as popular a resort as it is today, and at least three emperors came here to bathe in the thermal springs and to look upon the extraordinary natural phenomena. The first buildings one sees on arriving are the huge **Roman baths** which line the right side of the parking area; these date from the second century AD. One of the chambers in the baths is now used to store the sculptures and other antiquities which have been discovered in recent excavations, and it is hoped that this will soon be open to the public as a museum.

Walking on beyond the baths you come to the Turizm Hotel, which is built around what was once the **Sacred Pool**, now a swimming-pool for the hotel's guests. This must be the most unusual and delightful swimming-pool in the world, and not even the bad taste of modern tourism can completely spoil it. The pool winds around the hotel courtyard, bounded by a delightful garden of rose bushes, hibiscus, oleanders, mulberry trees, cedars and cypresses, and on its bottom one sees fluted columns and Corinthian capitals from the Roman portico which once stood nearby, looking like the submerged ruins of an enchanted kingdom. The calcinated water is just slightly above body temperature, so that one can swim here comfortably even in mid-winter, when in the absence of tourists the Holy City regains something of its magic.

Just behind the Sacred Pool and the Turizm Hotel there are the ruins of a monumental fountain of the fourth century AD, and behind that the remains of a **Temple of Apollo**, the only one of the city's many sanctuaries which has survived. The upper parts of the building have been dated to the third century AD at the earliest, though the foundations go back to the Pergamene period. On the south side of the temple recent excavations have revealed a grotto which has been identified as the Plutonium, which in antiquity was sacred to the memory of Pluto and one of the famous sights which brought travellers to Hierapolis; today it is known locally as the Place of Evil Spirits.

On the hillside behind the Turizm Hotel is the **Roman theatre**, a splendid structure which has recently been restored. Some of the fine statues and reliefs with which it was adorned are now stored in the Roman baths; one relief shows a scene representing the Emperor Septimius Severus, and the theatre is dated to the period of his reign, AD 193–211.

Behind the theatre you see the Roman defence wall, which extends in an irregular semi-circle around the city as far as the edge of the plateau. Outside the defence wall, to the north-east of the theatre, an impressive tomb has recently been discovered; it has been identified as the **Martyrium of St Philip the Apostle**, who is known to have lived out his last years in Hierapolis.

The main thoroughfare of ancient Hierapolis was a colonnaded street which began just south of the Sacred Pool, extending for a distance of about two kilometres parallel to the edge of the plateau. The street terminated at both ends some two hundred metres outside the walls at monumental portals; only the northern one remains largely intact, consisting of a triple arch flanked by two round towers. An inscription on the gateway records that it was erected in honour of the Emperor Domitian in AD 84–5. The extensive necropolis of Hierapolis lies outside the city walls to the north, where scores of tombs and sarcophagi flank a path leading off from the Gate of Hadrian.

After leaving Pamukkale you return to the main highway and drive westwards towards Burdur and Isparta. You are now just past the confluence of the Maeander and the Lycus, a spot which in antiquity marked the common boundary of Caria, Phrygia and Pisidia. The present route will take you along the valley of the upper Lycus as far as the Pisidian Lakes, where you turn south to cross the Taurus Mountains for the Mediterranean shore.

Just beyond the turning to Pamukkale you pass on the left a handsome Selcuk caravansarai, the **Ak Han**. An inscription over the outer doorway records that the caravansarai was completed on 19 July 1254, during the reign of the Selcuk Sultan Izzeddin Key-kâvus II. There are more than fifty of these Selcuk caravansarais still standing along the highways of central Anatolia, all of them built during the thirteenth century. That was the period when the Selcuk Turks were the dominant power in Anatolia, adorning their cities and the land around with magnificent mosques, *medreses*, tombs, bridges and these wayside *hans* for travellers.

You are now on a lower level of the great Anatolian plateau, with the massive peaks of Honaz Daği dominating the landscape to the south. About an hour's drive past the Ak Han you pass Çardak, a pretty town set in a pine grove at the tip of Acı Göl, the Bitter Lake. The highway skirts the slime-covered northern shallows of Acı Göl, with a striking view across the lake towards the precipitous cliffs which form its forbidding northern boundary.

An hour's drive past Acı Göl brings you to the vicinity of Dinar, where you turn south for **Burdur** and **Isparta**. After another half-hour's drive you come to an intersection, the right fork leading to Burdur and the left to Isparta. The two branches join again an hour's drive to the south of both towns, so that one inevitably agonizes over the map trying to decide which route to take. Both Burdur and Isparta are interesting and lively mountain towns, and the scenery along each route is equally grand. The Isparta road passes through Ağlasun, from which one can visit the ruins of **Sagalassus**. Or one can take an excursion out of Isparta north-east to **Eğrídír**, a lovely old Turkish town at the southern tip of the most beautiful of all the Pisidian lakes. From Burdur a road runs south-west along the shore of Burdur Gölü to the site of **Hacílar**, one of the most important Bronze Age sites in Turkey.

After the Burdur and Isparta roads rejoin one heads south through some of the most beautiful mountain country in western Anatolia,

---

Pamukkale, the Cotton Castle.

The Temple of Apollo at Didyma.

passing emerald green valleys and mountain meadows, with the snow-capped peaks and buttresses of the Taurus rising majestically on all sides. At the hamlet of Dağ (which means simply Mountain) you enter the deep gorge which leads to the Çubuk Boğazí, the principal pass on this route over the Taurus. You then descend quite rapidly along the gorge on the other side of the pass. Soon you find yourself looking down on to the series of descending plains which form the Pamphylian shore, a thin fringe of sub-tropical coast between the Taurus Mountains and the Mediterranean.

Soon after you emerge from the gorge, if you look carefully, you see to the left another Selcuk caravansarai, the Kírkgöz Han, built by Sultan Giyaseddin Keyhûsrev (1236–46). Some distance after this a signpost to the right indicates a turning that leads to the Karain Cave, the most important Stone Age site in Turkey.

Some ten kilometres before you reach the coast a highway leads off to the right for Korkuteli. Eighteen kilometres along this highway a dirt road leads off to the left and steeply uphill to the site of ancient Termessus. The ruins here have never been thoroughly excavated and cleared, which makes this ancient mountain stronghold all the more romantic in its appearance. The setting is superb: this mighty Lycian fortress-town perched on a peak of Güllül Dağ, the Roseate Mountain, the impressive ruins of the ancient city overgrown with trees and bushes, and the whole wild landscape littered with broken sarcophagi and violated tombs. In antiquity this was one of the most impregnable fortresses in Asia Minor, and even Alexander the Great was turned back by its defences when he marched this way over the Taurus in 333 BC. For those who have time to make the detour a visit to Termessus is extremely rewarding, for this is one of the most impressive ancient sites along the whole southern coast of Turkey.

Once past the Korkuteli road you are soon down on the last of the descending plains below the Taurus. After a short drive through the increasingly tropical landscape you find yourself in the outskirts of Antalya, the principal city and port along the Pamphylian coast.

Interior of the Mevlana shrine. The large catafalque in the rear covers the tomb of Celaleddin Rumi, the founder of the Mevlevi order of dervishes.

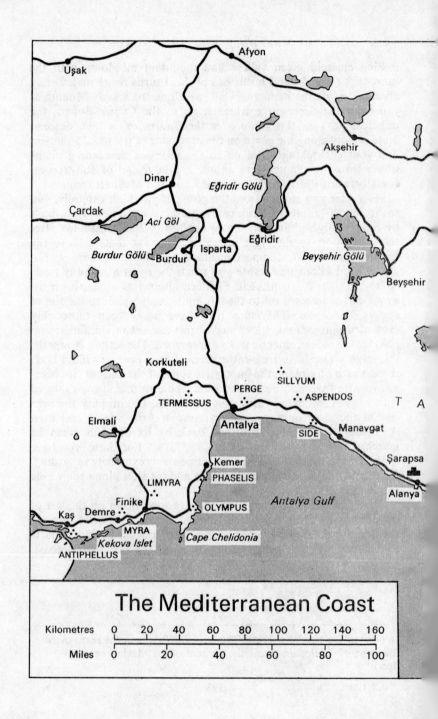

The Mediterranean Coast

Kilometres	0	20	40	60	80	100	120	140	160
Miles	0		20		40		60	80	100

Afyon

Uşak

Akşehir

Dinar

Eğridir Gölü

Çardak

Acı Göl

Burdur Gölü

Burdur

Isparta

Eğridir

Beyşehir Gölü

Beyşehir

Korkuteli

SILLYUM

PERGE

TERMESSUS

ASPENDOS

T A

Elmalı

Antalya

SIDE

Manavgat

Kemer

PHASELIS

Şarapsa

LIMYRA

Antalya Gulf

Alanya

Finike

OLYMPUS

Kaş

Demre

MYRA

Kekova Islet

Cape Chelidonia

ANTIPHELLUS

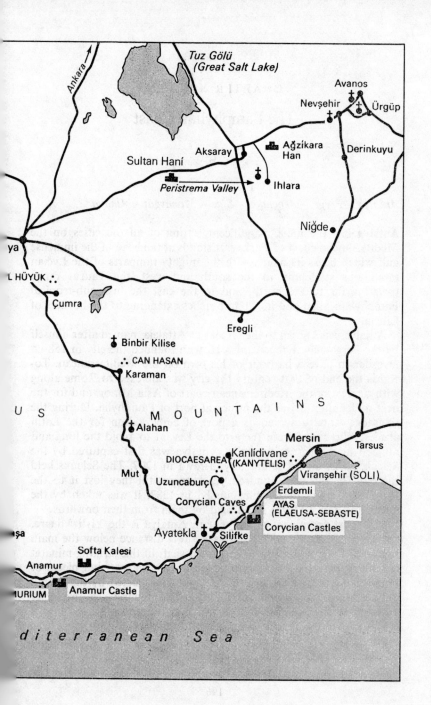

Tuz Gölü
(Great Salt Lake)

Ankara

Avanos

Nevşehir
Ürgüp

Derinkuyu

Aksaray
Ağzíkara
Han

Sultan Haní

Peristrema Valley
Ihlara

Niğde

ya

L HÜYÜK

Çumra

Eregli

Binbir Kilise

CAN HASAN

Karaman

U S

M O U N T A I N S

Alahan

Mersin

Tarsus

Kanlídivane
(KANYTELIS)

DIOCAESAREA

Viranşehir (SOLI)

Mut

Uzuncaburç

Erdemli

Corycian Caves

AYAS
(ELAEUSA-SEBASTE)

Ayatekla
Silifke

Corycian Castles

şa

Softa Kalesi

Anamur

URIUM
Anamur Castle

diterranean   Sea

CHAPTER SIXTEEN

The Pamphylian Coast

✤

Antalya – Perge – Aspendos – Side – Manavgat – Alanya

Antalya has the most magnificent setting of all the cities on the Mediterranean coast of Turkey. It stands at the head of the immense gulf which bears its name, with the mighty ramparts of the Lycian mountains stretching to the south and west, the Taurus range towering far to the north, and to the east the lush sub-tropical Pamphylian plain and its white beaches extending to the borders of Cilicia.

Antalya was known to the Greeks as Attaleia, named after himself by the Pergamene King Attalus II, who founded the city in 158 BC in order to have a harbour of his own on the Mediterranean. Towards the end of that century the city was annexed to Rome along with the rest of the Mediterranean coast of Asia Minor, and for the next millennium it was the principal port of Pamphylia. During the Crusades Antalya served as a port of embarkation for the Latin armies, who sailed from there to the Levant to avoid the long and difficult march across Anatolia. Antalya was first captured by the Selcuk Turks under Sultan Keyhûsrev I in 1207. The Selcuks held the city for the next hundred years or so, till they lost it to the Hamitoğlu emirs of Eğrídír; finally, in 1387, it was taken by the Ottomans under Murat I and held by them from then onwards.

The most prominent monument in Antalya is the **Yivli Minare**, the **Fluted Minaret**, which stands a short distance below the main square of the modern town. The fluted shaft of this striking minaret is built of pink-red bricks into which have been set small pieces of blue-green Selcuk tiles. The minaret was constructed by the Selcuk Sultan Alâeddin I Keykûbad in 1219. The minaret was originally attached to a Byzantine church which had been converted into a mosque after the Selcuk conquest of Antalya. This structure was replaced in 1373 by the present one, which is covered by three pairs of domes supported by a dozen columns in three rows, some of them capped with ancient Ionic and Corinthian capitals. The founder of the mosque was Mehmet Bey, the Hamitoğlu emir who ruled Antalya in the years before its conquest by the Ottomans. Mehmet Bey is also responsible for the *türbe* with the pyramidal roof which stands in the courtyard above the mosque. This was built in 1377 for Mehmet Bey's eldest son, who died before he could succeed his father. The other building in the upper courtyard is an eighteenth-century *tekke* which once housed a community of Mevlevi dervishes.

The Yivli Minare mosque now houses the **Antalya Ethnological Museum**, one of the most interesting of its type in Turkey. Most of the exhibits are connected with the *yürük*, the nomadic tribes which have for centuries wandered across the map of Anatolia, camping down on the coastal plain in winter, and then when warm weather comes returning to their *yayla*, mountain encampments and pasturages. These proud and independent people have been little influenced by modern life, and their ways have hardly changed since they migrated into Anatolia on the heels of the first Turkish *gazi* warriors nearly a thousand years ago. The museum has a fascinating collection of their belongings, including their goat-hair tents, their finely-carved wooden household articles (including wooden locks and keys for the tents), their hand-made musical instruments, and their colourful *kilims* and native costumes.

In the courtyard before the museum there are the ruins of two Selcuk *medreses*. The isolated gateway to the right as one leaves is all that remains of a *medrese* built in 1239 by Sultan Keyhûsrev II, and across from that are the more substantial ruins of a *medrese* built about two decades earlier by his father, Sultan Alâeddin I Keykûbad.

Only fragments now remain of the ancient walls which once enclosed the city on its landward side. These walls were originally built during Hellenistic times, and one or two of the surviving towers are certainly of that period, but much of the structure dates from a tenth-century reconstruction by the Byzantines. The best preserved stretch of the wall can be seen along Atatürk Bulvarí, where stands the **Gate of Hadrian**. This was built to honour Hadrian on the occasion of his visit to the city in AD 130. The gateway is flanked by two defence towers of the Hellenistic wall; it consists of two coffered arches of equal height, with Corinthian columns standing on detached pedestals in front of the pier of each gate. The gateway has been restored in recent years and now gives one some idea of the grandeur of Roman Attaleia.

Another impressive monument remaining from the Roman town is the **Hídírlík Kulesi**, a huge tower which stands on top of the cliff beside Karaali Park. This Roman building, which is thought to date from the second century AD, consists of a massive square base on the lower level and a cylindrical drum on the upper, topped by a poorly built parapet of more recent construction. Various theories have been proposed as to the purpose of the tower, but the most likely one is that it was built as the mausoleum of some important Roman citizen of Attaleia. And indeed it does bear a strong resemblance to Hadrian's own mausoleum in Rome.

The promenade of the pleasant Karaali Park commands a magnificent view of the Gulf of Antalya and the Lycian shore beyond, with the snow-capped peaks of Mounts Solymnos and Climax towering regally in the distance.

From the park one can stroll into the **old town** of Antalya, whose winding streets are lined with some of the most picturesque Ottoman houses in Turkey, many of them just on the point of falling into ruins. One of these, now used as the local primary school, dates back to the late eighteenth century. There are also a number of Selcuk and Ottoman mosques and *medreses* in this quarter. The most ancient of these is the Karatay Medresesi, founded in 1250 by the Vezir Celaleddin Karatay, one of the great builders in Selcuk history. The most ancient structure remaining from the Byzantine period is Kesik Minare Camii, formerly the Church of the Panaghia. This once splendid building, now a dismal ruin, was originally constructed in the fifth century and was apparently converted into a mosque early in the Turkish period.

The winding lanes of the old town invariably lead one down to the port, a tiny haven tucked in under the cliff, with the ancient Roman walls towering above. But a scene which should be wildly romantic is instead melancholy and depressing, for this once beautiful port quarter is rapidly falling into ruins, devoid of the spirited life which once made it one of the liveliest harbours along the Mediterranean coast of Turkey.

Antalya's new **Archaeological Museum** is located outside the town to the west, just above the beginning of the Konyaaltí Beach. The museum complex is not completely finished at the time of writing, but when it is it should be the finest institution of its kind in the provinces. For this will be the central museum for exhibiting antiquities unearthed all over the south-western part of Anatolia, covering the whole range of the ancient cultures which existed in this area.

You now leave Antalya and drive eastwards along the Pamphylian plain. Some fifteen kilometres along you come to the village of Aksu, where a road to the left brings you to the **site of Perge**, one of the most interesting archaeological sites along the Mediterranean coast of Turkey.

According to tradition, Perge was founded soon after the Trojan War by a 'mixed multitude' of people led by the legendary seers Mopsus and Calchas. The original settlers were probably Greeks who immigrated from the mainland about 1100 BC under the pressure of Dorian invaders from the north. Perge shared the same general history as the other Greek settlements in Asia Minor, being subjected at various times by the Lydians, Persians and mainland Greeks, before its peaceful surrender to Alexander the Great in 333 BC. Afterwards Perge and the other cities of Pamphylia were fought over by his successors and were subsequently absorbed, in turn, into the empires of the Romans, Byzantines, and the Selcuk and Ottoman Turks.

Unlike the Ionian cities on the Aegean coast, Pamphylia produced almost no thinkers, artists or poets of renown, perhaps because of its remoteness from the centres of Greek culture. But the single exception to that statement is a very great one, namely Apollonius of Perge, whom historians of science rank second only to Archimedes among the giants of Greek mathematics. Apollonius was born in Perge about 260 BC, some twenty-five years before Archimedes. As a youth he went off to school in Alexandria, where he may have studied with Euclid. Apollonius was later invited to Pergamum as a guest of King Attalus I, to whom he dedicated several of his books on mathematics. Among these the most important was his work on conic sections, which when rediscovered in the Renaissance enabled Kepler to formulate his laws of planetary motion.

The road to the archaeological site at Perge brings one first to the **theatre**. This was originally built in the Hellenistic period and redesigned in Roman times, with a seating capacity of fifteen thousand. The stage building is still largely intact, and at its southern end, near the present entrance, one sees some of the fine sculptures in relief with which it was adorned; these are principally scenes from the life of Dionysus, god of wine and of the theatre.

The road winds around the curved northern end of the **stadium**, the best-preserved in Anatolia after that at Aphrodisias, with a seating capacity of about twelve thousand. We then come to the outer gate of Perge, which was built in the fourth century AD, when the city was extended to the south.

Passing through the gate, one sees on the right the remains of a Byzantine church. Then one comes to the older gate in the **Hellen-**

istic walls; these enclosed the city to the east, west and south, while the northern side was protected by the acropolis hill. This early gate is the most impressive monument in Perge; together with the defence walls it is the only surviving remnant of the Hellenistic city, for the rest of the ruins date from Roman times. The gate is flanked by two huge round towers and gives entrance to a semi-elliptical courtyard, built in AD 120–2.

Beyond the courtyard you come to the beginning of a **colonnaded street**; this was the main thoroughfare of Perge, and its marble paving still shows the ruts of wagon wheels. The street is divided in two by a water channel, which was fed by a cistern at the base of the acropolis and passed down through a series of pools. This monumental way is flanked by column bases and pediments which once supported statues of prominent citizens of Perge, and behind these stood the usual porticoed shops of a Roman town in Asia Minor.

To the right of the first stretch of the colonnaded street is a large open area now under excavation; this was the agora of the Roman city. Farther on the main thoroughfare is crossed by a second street; its left branch passes a well-preserved palaestra, an open courtyard used for gymnastics. Beyond that the road leads off to the necropolis, where it becomes a street of tombs.

The colonnaded street finally ends at a monumental nymphaion at the base of the acropolis hill. From here water issued from behind a reclining figure of the river-god Kestros, to pour down along the watercourse through the main street of ancient Perge.

Seated on top of the nymphaion recently, we recalled the scene as we had looked upon it in the winter of 1960, on the occasion of our first trip through Anatolia. A mountain stream served as the source of the fountain, and its water had trickled down the marble street and frozen there in a thin sheet of ice, through whose crystalline glaze we could see the toppled columns and capitals of the arcade. We watched our three small children playing among the ruins, and noticed that there was not a single other soul in sight. The only sounds we could hear were their excited cries and the resonant tinkling of goat-bells in the surrounding hills, for the once great city of Perge was shrouded in the profound silence of the graveyard.

After leaving Perge you return to the main road and continue eastwards. Soon you see off to the left a very prominent table-topped acropolis rising up out of the plain, about five kilometres inland from the highway. This is the **site of Sillyum**, once one of the most important cities of Pamphylia. The site is approached by a dirt road leading to the village of Kocayatak, where one can engage a guide.

For those who have the time, this is an excursion well worth the effort, for the ruins of Sillyum are extensive and quite well-preserved, and its situation is splendid, surveying the whole of the Pamphylian coast.

Some twenty kilometres past the Perge road you reach the turning for **Aspendos**. This is a pleasant drive of five kilometres up the valley of the Köprü Çay, the ancient River Eurymedon, passing on the way a quaint hump-backed bridge built by the Selcuks in the thirteenth century.

According to tradition, Aspendos was one of the original Pamphylian cities founded by Mopsus and his 'mixed multitudes'. Throughout antiquity it was one of the wealthiest and most important cities along the Pamphylian coast. Aspendos had much the same history as Perge, except that its citizens were emboldened to resist Alexander on his eastward campaign, but when his army besieged the city it quickly surrendered, paying dearly in increased tribute for its folly.

Those who visit Aspendos almost invariably do so because of its magnificent **theatre**, the finest of those which have survived from the ancient Graeco-Roman world. The remainder of the city has never been properly excavated, and the ruins are heavily overgrown and difficult of access. This makes the superb state of preservation of the theatre all the more remarkable; except for some minor restoration it looks exactly as it did when it was originally built in the second century AD.

The most striking difference between the classic Greek theatre and that of the Romans is the massive stage building erected before the latter. The finest extant example of such a structure is that at Aspendos, with its imposing exterior façade 80 feet in height and 360 in length. Compare this, for example, with the classical Greek theatre at Epidauros, where the audience faced out across the surrounding countryside, whereas here at Aspendos the theatre is self-contained, with the background provided by the interior wall of the stage building, the *scaenae frons*. The difference grew out of the development of theatrical performances during the Hellenistic period. The earlier classical dramas were acted out on the floor of the circular orchestra itself, while in Hellenistic times the action was transferred to the top of the elevated proscenium, much as on a modern stage, with the *scaenae frons* acting as a backdrop and the stage building itself filling the role of the present backstage area.

The present entrance to the theatre at Aspendos is through the middle door of the stage building, but in Roman times the audience

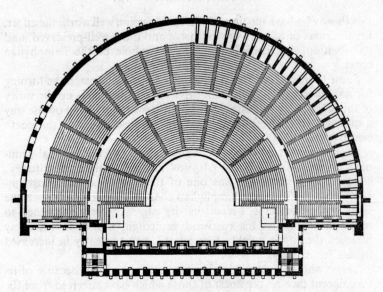

Aspendos: the Theatre

passed through two paradoi, or stage entrances, which are unique here in being vaulted passageways parallel to the proscenium. The auditorium itself has two ranges of seats separated by a diazoma, with twenty-one rows in the lower and nineteen in the upper, seating an estimated twenty thousand spectators. The stage itself extended some twenty-five feet from the *scaenae frons* and was four and a half feet high. At the rear of the proscenium there were two rows of columns, each pair of which framed niches in the *scaenae frons* containing statues. These have all disappeared, and the only decoration which now remains is the relief in the pediment above the upper colonnade; this represents Bacchus, who is shown flanked with scrolls of flowers, presiding over the theatre of which he was the divine patron. An inscription records that the theatre was erected during the reign of Marcus Aurelius (161–80).

The stadium of Aspendos is a short distance to the right of the theatre, as one faces the entrance; this has not been excavated and is in a poor state of preservation. The other surviving buildings stand on top of the hill behind the one into which the theatre is built. The most impressive structures there are the market-hall and a basilica which was once used as a business exchange; both of these are still standing up to a height of fifty feet. Off to the north are the remains of the splendid **Roman aqueduct** which brought water to the city from the foothills of the Taurus; it is the finest still standing in Anatolia.

Returning once again to the coastal highway you continue eastwards, crossing the **Eurymedon**. This otherwise insignificant stream was the site of one of the most momentous battles in antiquity. In about 467 BC Cimon of Athens mustered a fleet at Cnidos and sailed along the Mediterranean coast of Asia Minor, regaining the maritime cities from the Persians. The Persian fleet withdrew into the basin of the Eurymedon upon his approach, but Cimon sailed shoreward and boldly attacked them at the mouth of the river. After totally routing the Persian fleet, Cimon's troops pursued the survivors on to the shore and then attacked and defeated the Persian army which was based there. This remarkable double victory on land and sea virtually ended the Persian dream of conquering the Greek world, and within a year the long war came to its end. A monument was afterwards erected on the shore to commemorate those who had given their lives there for the cause of Greek independence, and this epitaph was inscribed upon it:

These are the men who laid down the splendour of their manhood beside the Eurymedon; on land and on the swift-sailing ships alike they fought with their spears against the foremost of the bow-bearing Medes. They are no more, but they have left the fairest memorial of their valour.

Five kilometres beyond the Eurymedon a road leads inland to the village of Beşkonak, where one can hire a jeep to visit the **ruins of ancient Selge**, an important city in Hellenistic times. The ruins are interesting and impressive, but the trip would require the better part of a day, so that most travellers on a first trip to Turkey pass it by and drive on to Side.

Some twenty-five kilometres past the Eurymedon you turn off to the right for **Side**. As you approach the site you see stretches of the Roman aqueduct which carried water nearly twenty-five kilometres from the lower slopes of the Taurus to the city. This and the profusion of ruins in the fields around are a testimony to the importance of Side in its time.

Ancient historians were in agreement that Side was established in the seventh century BC as a colony of the Aeolian city of Cyme. A legend associated with the colony held that the Cymeans soon lost their Greek on settling here and began speaking the barbarous language of the local people, indicating that there was already an indigenous Anatolian settlement on the site when they arrived. Along with the other Pamphylian cities, Side became completely Hellenized soon after Alexander's conquest of the region, and from about 300 BC onwards all of its inscriptions are in Greek. The city really began to flourish in the second century BC, when it derived most of its income from the slave trade. The Pamphylian and Cilician coasts were notorious in antiquity for their piracy, and Side was the principal port in the region for the landing and sale of slaves taken by the corsairs. The pirates were finally crushed by Pompey in 67 BC and with that the slave trade ceased for centuries, thus ending Side's first period of prosperity.

The city began to flourish again in the second century AD under the mantle of the Pax Romana, and during the next century and a half it reached the height of its wealth and importance. Much of this wealth seems to have been used in adorning the city, for the major part of Side's surviving antiquities date from that period. But as Rome's power declined Side fell victim to invading barbarians from the north, and in the middle of the fourth century the city was forced to wall itself in at the end of the peninsula on which it stood, thus reducing its area by about one half. It revived once again in early Byzantine times, but its final decline set in with the Arab invasions beginning in the middle of the seventh century. Although the Byzantines eventually repelled the Arabs and regained their lost territory, Side and many other coastal towns along the Mediterranean never fully recovered from the disastrous effects of the invasions. The city was finally destroyed by fire in the tenth century, and for the next thousand years it was utterly deserted, as sand driven in by the south wind piled up in dunes over the ruins. At the end of the nineteenth century Greek-speaking Moslem refugees from Crete were settled on the site, founding the fishing village of Selimiye, and they and their descendants still live there among the ruins. In recent years the site has been excavated by Turkish archaeologists, who have unearthed most of the surviving monuments without unduly displacing the villagers.

The approach road leads up to what was once Side's main gate, beside which are the remains of a nymphaion of the second century BC. From here one can see the best-preserved stretch of the outer city walls and defence towers; these were originally erected in the second century BC and were rebuilt in the Roman and Byzantine periods.

Inside the gate the road continues along what was once a colon-naded street, approaching the inner gate. Towards the end of the street on the left are the remains of two Hellenistic houses, and beyond them the ruins of an immense **Roman agora** of the second century BC which consists of the usual porticoed court lined with vaulted shops. The ruins of a round structure at the centre of the agora are believed to be those of a temple of Tyche, the goddess of Fortune.

Directly across from the agora are the **Roman baths**; these have been superbly restored and the building is now in use as a museum. Exhibited here are some of the finest Roman statues in Asia Minor, all of them discovered on the site in recent years.

Just beyond the agora is the **Roman theatre**, by far the most im-pressive monument in Side. This was built in the second century AD and was designed along the same general lines as that at Aspendos. The only difference between the two is that here the auditorium has been extended beyond the exact semi-circle of the classic Roman theatre, and so the vaulted paradoi are oblique to the proscenium. The stage building must have been splendidly adorned, as one sees from the fragments of reliefs among the ruins which have tumbled into the orchestra. In later Roman times, as elsewhere in Asia Minor, the orchestra was used for the performance of gladiatorial combats, and in the fifth century two open-air Christian sanctuaries were constructed there, with the congregation seated in the audi-torium. Traces of the frescoes still remain in one of these chapels.

The view from the upper tier of the theatre is superb, for you can see the whole of the ancient city and its surroundings, with golden-yellow sand beaches stretching away on either side into the distance. The scene is particularly romantic at sunset, when the white marble of the ruins in the orchestra below takes on a pink and then a roseate glow.

The stage building of the theatre formed part of the inner wall of the city, erected in the fourth century AD when the citizens of Side retreated to the far end of the peninsula. The main gate through this inner wall is just inside the theatre, where one now enters the village of Selimiye. This monumental gateway was once much grander than the remains one sees today; in Roman times it was surmounted by a quadriga, a four-horse chariot, which bore a statue of the deified Emperor. Just to the left of the gate on the outside are the remains of an elegant fountain. This was built as a monument to the deified Trajan, whose statue stood in the central niche.

Once inside the gate the road curves around the theatre, next to

which are the ruins of a late Roman temple of Dionysus. From there
the road goes straight out towards the end of the peninsula, following the course of an ancient colonnaded street. This part of the site
has not been systematically excavated, since it is occupied by the
modern village, the most attractive one along the Mediterranean
coast of Turkey.

The road ends just before the end of the peninsula, and a short
walk to the right takes you out to the ancient **harbour**, now almost
completely sanded up. At the south side of the harbour are the
remains of two adjoining temples; the one on the left, as you face
them from the seashore, was dedicated to Athena, and that on the
right to Apollo. This spot must have been a sacred one, for behind
the two sanctuaries stands a Byzantine basilica, and a short distance
away along the shore is a temple of Man, the Anatolian God of the
Moon. All three of the temples are dated to the second century AD.

Continuing along the shore in the same direction you pass a
number of Roman and Byzantine ruins, and at the neck of the peninsula you come to the point where the sea walls meet the defence walls
of the inner city. Just inland from here are the ruins of the **State
Agora**, at the east end of which was a hall dedicated to the deified
Emperor. Along the back and side walls of this hall there were niches
for statues, some of which are now in the Side museum. One of these
remains in place in a niche at the south-east corner of the hall, a
headless statue of Nemesis, one of the relentless goddesses who
eventually spelled out the doom of this beautiful city.

One always leaves Side reluctantly, for despite the ravages of
tourism it is still an enchanting place. Soon after regaining the main
road and continuing eastwards one crosses the Manavgat Çayí, the
Greek Melas, and then passes through the town of the same name.
It is tempting to linger for a while in Manavgat, for the restaurants
along the riverside serve freshly-caught trout. Afterwards one might
take a short excursion upstream to the **Manavgat Falls** at Şelale, a
famous beauty spot.

Soon after passing Manavgat the road approaches the shore,
passing a succession of sandy beaches and deserted coves, many of
them still untouched by tourism. Farther along you begin to see
orange groves and banana plantations along the road, with the
snow-capped peaks of the Taurus looming on the northern horizon
and the blue Mediterranean sparkling to the south.

About an hour's drive beyond Manavgat you pass on the left the
Şarapsa Haní, constructed by the Selcuk Sultan Giyaseddin
Keyhûsrev II (1236–46). This fortified caravansarai was one of

several built along the high road between the Selcuk capital at Konya and their principal port at Alanya.

Soon after passing the caravansarai you come within view of Alanya, one of the grandest sights along the whole Mediterranean coast of Turkey, with the serrated line of the rose-pink Selcuk fortress crowning the great peninsular rock. In Greek times this was known as Kalonoros, the Beautiful Mountain, and it marked the boundary between Pamphylia and Cilicia.

CHAPTER SEVENTEEN

The Cilician Coast

❧

*Alanya – Anamur – Silifke – The Caves of Heaven and Hell – Corycius
– Ayaş – Kanlídivane – Viranşehir – Mersin – Tarsus*

Alanya, the port town at the foot of the peninsular rock of Kalonoros, was known in antiquity as **Coracesium.** Coracesium was of only minor importance in classical times, and served as a haven for the pirates who plagued the Cilician and Pamphylian coasts. The most famous of the local rulers was Diadotus Tryphon, the Voluptuary, who at one point became so powerful that he tried to seize the Seleucid throne in Syria; but he was eventually put down and killed by Antiochus VII (139–29 BC). The Romans put an end to piracy when they assumed control of the Mediterranean coast of Asia Minor. In a lightning three-month campaign in 67 BC Pompey completely cleared the corsairs from the coast, destroying their fleet in a final battle off Coracesium. Coracesium literally disappeared from history for more than a thousand years after that, occupied in turn by the Romans and the Byzantines. When Byzantine power in Asia Minor was weakened after their defeat by the Selcuks at Manzikert, the Armenian kings in Cilicia extended their domains westward and controlled Coracesium for a century and a half. The Selcuks finally took over the town in 1221, when Sultan Alâeddin Keykûbad I ejected the last Armenian lord of Coracesium. Alâeddin then renamed the city after himself, Alaiyya, which through linguistic change became the Alanya of modern times. The city remained in Selcuk hands until about 1300, when after the collapse of the Sultanate of Rum it fell to the Karamanid emirs. The Karamanids held Alanya until 1471, when the city was taken by an Ottoman army led by Gedik Ahmet Pasha, Grand Vezir of Sultan Mehmet the Conqueror.

The modern town of Alanya clusters around the harbour and clambers up the lower southern slope of the peninsula. The most conspicuous monument in the lower town is **Kízíl Kule,** the **Red Tower,** an octagonal fortress more than a hundred feet high and nearly as much in diameter. This was undoubtedly the first structure Alâeddin built when he began to fortify the city; it served not only to defend the harbour but also to anchor the land walls to those which extended along the southern shore of the peninsula.

Across the harbour from the Red Tower stands the Selcuk **tershane**, or **dockyard**, the only one of its type still extant in Turkey. It is a long building with five vaulted galleries opening directly on to the sea; within these the ships of the Selcuk fleet were built, repaired, and kept safe from the elements when not at sea. Just beside the *tershane* is the Tophane, an ammunition storehouse and fortress designed to protect the arsenal and that side of the harbour; it is also known as Şeytan Kalesi, the Devil's Castle.

The main line of the land walls climbs steeply uphill from the Red Tower; since this was the most vulnerable side of the rock the walls and towers in this section are the strongest in the whole system of fortifications. The motor road from the lower town winds uphill and passes through **Kale Kapísí**, the main gate in the outer wall. This is a handsome double portal with two entrances at right angles to one another; a Persian inscription above the outer gate dates it to 1226, and the one above the outer one reads 1230–1.

Inside the Kale Kapísí the motor road runs out towards the tip of the peninsula, after which it cuts back sharply and winds uphill to the gate of **Iç Kale**, the **Inner Fortress**. Although this is the quickest and easiest way to get to the top of the rock, it is far less interesting than walking. Those with time to spare would be well advised to leave their car at the first turn inside Iç Kale, and from there proceed on foot up through the picturesque upper town. The path leads into the castellated enceinte known as the **Ehmediye**, where the main town was located in Selcuk and early Ottoman times. From these periods there still remains an ancient caravansarai, a *bedesten*, a mosque, and the tomb of a holy man beside which there is a magical well which is the object of pilgrimages. The Ehmediye is occupied by a felicitous community which by its remoteness from the modern town has been relatively preserved from change, giving the appearance of an old Ottoman village.

The Iç Kale stands on the flat top of the peninsular rock, a rectangular area bounded on three sides by vaulted galleries and on the fourth by a defence wall running along the sheer edge of the cliff. Inside the fortress is a pretty little Byzantine chapel which somehow survived the centuries of Turkish rule in Alanya. At the far end of the Iç Kale one can climb up on to the patrol wall of the fortress and walk out on to a platform at the very edge of the cliff.

The platform was once called **Adam Atacağí**, the **Place from Which Men Are Thrown**; so named, according to tradition, because condemned prisoners were hurled down from here on to the rocks below. The view from the platform is stupendous.

From the other outer corner of the İç Kale one looks down upon Cílvarda Burnu, the rocky promontory which juts out four hundred metres into the sea at the south-western tip of the promontory. Part of the way along this almost inaccessible tongue of craggy rock there is a Selcuk structure which has been identified as the Darphane, or Mint, and farther out are the ruins of a Byzantine chapel and some remnants of a monastery.

If time permits, one should hire a small boat and explore the peninsular rock on its seaward sides, which are honeycombed with marvellous grottoes. At the western end of the rock, approached from the superb beach on that side, there is an immense subterranean cave called Damlataş. The cave is always hot and extremely humid, which makes it a favourite haunt of rheumatics and arthritics, who journey here from all over Turkey to ease their aching joints.

After leaving Alanya you continue eastward along the coastal highway. You are now entering the land which in ancient times was called Cilicia, a region which extended from Pamphylia to the borders of modern Syria. Cilicia itself was composed of two distinct parts, each very different in character. The western section was known as Cilicia Tracheia, or Rugged Cilicia, for there the Taurus Mountains march right down to the sea, leaving hardly any level land for roads or cultivation. The eastern part was called Cilicia Campestris, or the Plain, where the Taurus retreat far inland, leaving an immense fertile plain along the coast.

Rugged Cilicia is the poorest and least populous region along the southern coast of Turkey, and only in recent years has it been opened up for convenient travel by the new coastal highway. There are only a very few towns of any size along the whole stretch of coast between Alanya and Mersin, the large city at the eastern end of Plain Cilicia. The other settlements are poor fishing villages, formerly pirate havens, that eke out a living from the sea and from the export of timber from the Taurus, just as they did in antiquity. But the scenery is superb, as the road winds *en corniche* around a succession of heavily wooded headlands and deep fiords, with wild cliffs plunging sheer into the sea.

The Cilician coast is littered with the ruins of ancient fortress-towns, most of them of the Hellenistic or Roman periods and none of any great importance. Some are on remote and inaccessible hill-

tops, rarely visited except by archaeologists; but others stand right
beside the coastal road or in direct view on the shore below. Their
very number and extent are a testimony to how much more populous
this coast was in ancient times than it is today.

The first of these sites lies some thirty-five kilometres east of
Alanya. This is Iotape, one of three fortress-cities established in this
region by the Seleucid King Antiochus IV (175–63 BC), who named
the town after his wife, Iotape Philadelphus. All that is now visible
are some huge column drums scattered beside the roadway and the
ruins of defence walls and towers on a promontory above the sea.

Soon afterwards you come to the fishing village of Gazipaşa, the
first settlement of any size east of Alanya. Until recent years the
name of the village was Selinty, a corruption of the ancient Selinus,
whose ruins lie about half an hour's walk towards the sea. Selinus
was founded by Antiochus IV at about the same time as Iotape. The
Emperor Trajan died here in the first week of August AD 117, and
the town was thereafter called Trajanopolis in his honour.

The road now leaves the sea for about twenty kilometres, but
when it returns it is to a scene even more spectacular than before,
as one drives high above the sea under towering vertical cliffs, with
the magnificent ramparts of the Taurus looming on the northern
horizon. Off to the right, on a sea-girt promontory, one sees some
of the ruins of Antiochia ad Cragum (literally 'on a crag'), the third
of the three towns founded by Antiochus IV as bastions along this
inhospitable and pirate-infested coast.

The highway descends to cross a river valley at the end of a
magnificent fiord. Here is the little hamlet of Kaladiran, guarded by
the ruins of an ancient fortress brooding on a hilltop. This is all that
remains of ancient Charadrus, a place which Strabo describes as
a fortified port on the rugged coast called Platanistes.

The road climbs up into the hills once more and then comes down
to a broad valley, on the far side of which one can see Anamur, one
of the two towns of any size in Rugged Cilicia. Here a dirt road leads
off seaward to the **site of ancient Anemurium**, which stands on a
promontory at the southernmost point of Asia Minor. This is by far
the most impressive site in Rugged Cilicia, a vast ghost city still
guarded by the splendid ruins of its massive walls and towers, looking
as if it had been sacked and abandoned only yesterday.

The highway then leads around the head of the valley and through
modern Anamur, the descendant of ancient Anemurium. Six kilometres beyond the town you pass **Mamure Kalesi**, the **Castle of
Anamur**, the largest and best-preserved medieval fortress on the

Mediterranean coast of Turkey, with all of its walls and thirty-six towers still standing. It is believed to have been built in the twelfth century by the kings of Lesser Armenia, the realm that flourished in Cilicia during the twelfth and thirteenth centuries. After the fall of the Armenian kingdom in the mid-fourteenth century the castle was held for a time by the Frankish kings of Cyprus, but subsequently it fell in turn to the Selcuks, the Karamanid Turks, and finally to the Ottomans. The castle was restored in 1840 by the Ottomans and was used by them as a fortress right up to the last days of the Empire.

Some twelve kilometres farther on the impressive towers and curtain walls of a medieval fortress appear on top of a precipice to the left of the road. This is Softa Kalesi, an Armenian fortress which is thought to have been built in the same period as the Castle of Anamur.

The road once again winds along so high above the sea that on a clear day one can see Cyprus, only some sixty kilometres distant. You then return to sea level at Aydíncík, a pretty little village on a sandy cove at the head of a deep bay. The former name of this place was Gilindere, a corruption of the Greek Celendris, whose ruins stand on a promontory above the village. This was one of the very oldest towns in Rugged Cilicia, founded in the late fifth century BC as a colony of Samos.

Once again the road climbs up into the hills and out on to the last stretch of the mountainside road above the sea. You are now approaching the eastern limit of Rugged Cilicia, as the Taurus sends down its last spur to the sea to form Cape Cavalierè, as it was known to sailors in Ottoman days. The first traveller to describe this dramatic coast in modern times was Sir Francis Beaufort, who made a survey of the Mediterranean shore of Asia Minor in 1811–12. As Beaufort wrote in his *Karamania*:

> The peninsula of Cape Cavalierè is the last and highest of the series of noble promontories that project from this coast, its white marble cliffs rising perpendicularly from the sea to an altitude of six or seven hundred feet . . . To the eastward of Cape Cavalierè the higher mountains recede from the coast; a succession of low points takes place of the rude outline we had so long pursued; and the general aspect of the country materially changes.

Just beyond Cape Cavalierè the road comes down to the sea at a crescent bay called Boğsak, where there is an excellent motel on a fine sandy beach, a place where one might be tempted to break one's journey before continuing into Plain Cilicia. Just offshore from the beach there is a strange islet that seems to have escaped the notice of modern travellers, though it was known to Beaufort. It is like a haunted isle of the dead, for every square foot of the place is littered with broken sarcophagi, tombstones, and the ruins of medieval buildings, the most striking of which is a small Crusader church. We learn from Beaufort that in Crusading times this was known as Provençal Isle, for in the thirteenth century it was occupied by the Provençal order of the Knights Hospitallers of St John.

The promontory which forms the eastern arm of the bay at Boğsak is occupied by a fourteenth-century Turkish fortress called Liman Kalesi. Some seven kilometres beyond this, after passing the ruins of two medieval chapels, you reach the seaside village of Taşucu, the port of Silifke. Taşucu stands at the head of a small bay called Ağa Limaní, which in times long past was a pirate haven. Knolles, the old English traveller, has a stirring account of what this lair of corsairs was like in its day:

> From this haven, in former times, has come forward a powerful army of pyrats with a thousand sayle, so proudly rigged, as many of them had their sayles of purple, the tackling of golden thread, and the oars garnished with silver; marks of the spoyles of above four hundred cities ruined by these pyrats.

A few kilometres past Ağa Limaní an archaeological sign directs one left to Ayatekla, the site of the Byzantine church of St Thecla. This huge basilica, of which only part of the apse remains standing, was built by the Emperor Zeno the Isaurian (474–91). Before becoming Emperor, Zeno had been chieftain of the wild Isaurian tribesmen who dwelt in the Taurus Mountains above the Cilician plain, and who became relatively civilized only in early Byzantine times.

Moments after leaving Ayatekla one comes within sight of Silifke, a medium-sized town on the banks of the Gök Su, the Greek Calycadnus. This town was founded by Seleucus I Nicator at the beginning of the third century BC, when it was called Seleucia ad Calycadnum. In antiquity it was the most important city in Rugged Cilicia, for then, as now, it stood at the junction of the coastal highroad and the road which led up through the Taurus into the central Anatolian plateau. Despite its antiquity it has little of interest apart from the fragmentary ruins of a Roman temple and its impressive medieval citadel. The original fortress was built by the Byzantines in the seventh century as a defence against the invading Arabs. In 1098 it was taken by the Crusaders but six years later it was re-captured by the Byzantines, at which time the present fortress was built. Subsequently the castle was fought over and taken in turn by the Armenians, Byzantines, Crusaders, Selcuks, Karamanids and Ottomans, who finally captured the fortress permanently in 1471.

A short way past the river a road to the left leads into Silifke. From near the town another road continues north to Uzuncaburç, the site of ancient Diocaesarea. Those with time to spare would be well advised to make the detour to Uzuncaburç, for the ruins of Diocaesarea are far and away the most impressive to be seen along the Cilician coast, particularly the great Temple of Zeus Olbius. This sanctuary is believed to have been built by Seleucus I at the beginning of the third century BC; it has the distinction of being the oldest known temple to have been built in the Corinthian order.

After crossing the marshy delta of the Gök Su the road reaches the sea again near Susanoğlu, where there is a good motel on a sandy beach. Some five kilometres further on is the tiny fishing village of Narlí Kuyu, the Pomegranate Well, where there are a couple of simple restaurants suspended on stilts above the sea. A small shed beside the village square houses the remains of a Roman bath from the fourth century AD. The place is known locally as Kízlar Hamamí, the Bath of the Maidens, from the three female figures depicted in the mosaic pavement. These are thought to represent the Three Graces, the beautiful daughters which Zeus begat on Eurynome. As Hesiod wrote of them in the *Theogony*:

And Eurynome, the daughter of Ocean, beautiful in form, bare him three fair-cheeked Graces: Aglaea, Euphrosyne and lovely Thaleia, from whose eyes as they danced flowed love and un-nerves the limbs; and beautiful is their glance beneath their brows.

Outside the bath a modern sign asserts that this is the legendary Fountain of Knowledge (*Nus*, in Turkish), which Beaufort sought for in vain, along with the nearby Corycian Cave described by Strabo. Beaufort must have sailed by the cove at Narlí Kuyu without landing, for Strabo's Corycian Cave is just two kilometres inland. A road leads off directly opposite the village, bringing one to the brink of a huge chasm called Cennet Deresi, or Vale of Paradise. An easy pathway leads down to the bottom of the chasm, 228 feet deep from the edge of the sheer cliff which overlooks it on the far side. A medieval Armenian chapel stands at the mouth of a vast cave. You follow a slippery path down another 200 feet into this immense subterranean cathedral, till at the far end you hear the roaring of a great underground river. According to tradition, this is the Stream of Paradise, which emerges at the Fountain of Knowledge on the shore below.

A pathway off to the right from the parking space leads to **Cehennem Deresi**, or **Vale of Hell**, a forbidding pit which is almost impossible of access except for experienced rock-climbers. According to both Christian and Moslem tradition, this is one of the entrances to Hell, and superstitious locals have tied little rag pennants to the branches of the surrounding trees as talismans to ward off the evil spirits who dwell below. This is undoubtedly the spot where Greek mythology places the birthplace of the monster Typhon, one of the pre-Olympic deities of primitive Greek religion. Another road leads off to the left from the parking space to Dilek Magarasí, the Cavern of Wishes, another part of the Corycian Cave complex. Here again the trees around the mouth of the cave have rags tied to their branches, but in this case they are not talismans but petitions to the benevolent spirits who dwell below.

Five kilometres past Narlí Kuyu one comes to the famous **Kíz Kalesi**, the **Maiden's Castle**. Kíz Kalesi is actually made up of two castles, one of them crowning a promontory at the end of a superb beach of white sand, and the other apparently floating on an islet about a hundred metres out to sea, looking like the setting for a medieval romance. The two fortresses were originally connected by a causeway, so as to create a fortified port for the town of Corycius. An inscription in Armenian on the sea castle records its construction in 1151, and the other fortress was presumably built at the same time, thus dating them to the early years of the Armenian kingdom of Cilicia.

The story of this medieval Cilician kingdom is one of the most interesting episodes in the history of the medieval Levant, and one of the few bright chapters in the otherwise unhappy history of the Armenian people. After the Turkish invasions had forced the Armenians from their ancient lands in north-eastern Anatolia, many of them settled in Cilicia as subjects of the Byzantine Emperor. During the first half of the twelfth century the Rubenid dynasty succeeded in creating an Armenian principality in Cilicia, and by the middle of that century they had effectively established their independence from Byzantium, as evidenced by their construction of the Corycian castles. The Rubenid kings maintained their independence largely through their close alliances with the various Crusader kingdoms in the Levant, cementing their ties by marriages

215

between Armenian princesses and Frankish rulers. As a result, the Kingdom of Cilicia came to combine the finest elements of Armenian culture with those from Latin Europe of the early Renaissance, bringing about a curious flowering of western chivalry in south-eastern Asia Minor. A contemporary description of the palace of these medieval Armenian kings gives one a glimpse of that vanished age, as the chronicler describes the 'gilt throne on which the King is seated in elegant majesty, surrounded by brilliant-faced young men, attendants of his rejoicings, also by groups of musicians and young girls dancing in an admirable manner'.

But at the beginning of the fourteenth century the advance of the Mongol hordes into south-eastern Anatolia brought about the collapse of the Crusader kingdoms there, and the Armenians found themselves alone facing numerous enemies far stronger than themselves, including Mongols, Turks, Mamelukes, and Saracen pirates. As a chronicler of the time wrote:

> The King of Armenia is under the fangs of four ferocious beasts: the lion, or the Tartars, to whom he pays a heavy tribute; the leopard, or the Sultan, who daily ravages his frontiers; the wolf, or the Turks, who destroy his power; and the serpent, or the pirates of the sea, who worry the very bones of the Christians of Armenia.

Under these overwhelming pressures the Armenians retreated to their castles and mountain strongholds, just as they had earlier in their history, but time was fast running out on them. In 1361 the Corycian castles were taken by King Peter I of Cyprus and fourteen years later their capital fell to the Mamelukes, thus bringing to an end the Armenian kingdom of Cilicia. The Armenians continued to live on in Cilicia under Turkish rule until the first quarter of the present century, but then the massacres and mass deportations in the last years of the Ottoman Empire removed nearly all traces of their race from Anatolia, leaving only these castles to remind one of their vanished medieval kingdom.

The extensive ruins of the town of Corycius are scattered over the countryside beyond the land castle, including the remains of several medieval churches and an enormous number of rock tombs and sarcophagi. As Beaufort described the scene along the coast past Corycius:

> From Korghos [Corycius] to Ayash, and for several miles beyond it, the shore presents a continued scene of ruins, all of which being

white, and relieved by the dark wooded hills behind them, give to the country an appearance of splendour and populousness, that serves only, on a nearer approach, to heighten the contrast with its real poverty and degradation.

The Cilician shore is far more prosperous now than it was in Beaufort's time, though it still lags well behind the more fortunate Aegean coast. But the landscape beyond Corycius is just as ruin-haunted today as it was when Beaufort first saw it, and during the drive from there to Tarsus one passes a succession of ancient cities, each with a vast necropolis representing centuries of human occupation.

The first of these sites is Ayaş, a village three kilometres east of the Corycian castles. Ayaş is built on the **site of ancient Elaeusa**, which in the Augustan Age was renamed Sebaste (Greek for Augustus) in the Emperor's honour. The original settlement was an islet, now connected to the shore, and the Roman town was built on the mainland just opposite. The most interesting monument here is a ruined temple of the Roman period; the only one, besides that at Uzuncaburç, which has survived to some extent.

For some distance beyond Ayaş the road is lined with tombs and sarcophagi which were once part of the necropolis of Elaeusa-Sebaste. About four kilometres past Ayaş a road to the left leads to Kanlídivane, a village near the **site of ancient Kanytelis**. The ruins of Kanytelis are quite extensive and more impressive than those of Elaeusa-Sebaste, with which it may have been administratively associated in antiquity.

Just beyond the turning the road crosses the Lamas Çayí. Strabo considered this to be the natural boundary between Rugged Cilicia and Cilicia the Plain, for here the rocky coast finally ends and gives way to the flatlands which extend inland to the foothills of the Taurus, now receding into the distance.

Beyond the river on the left you see a Roman aqueduct with two rows of arches; this is part of the water system which brought water from the Taurus to Kanytelis, Elaeusa-Sebaste and Corycius. Five kilometres farther along the road passes the beach resort of Limonlu, with the ruins of a medieval fortress standing on the heights to the left. The road continues through Erdemli, the largest town between Silifke and Tarsus. The next village of any size is Mezitli, where a road to the right leads to Viranşehir, a village near the **site of ancient Soli**. Soli was one of the oldest cities in Cilicia Campestris, founded as a Rhodian colony in about 700 BC. In 83 BC Soli was taken by the Armenian King Tigranes the Great, and its entire population was resettled in the Armenian capital of Tigranocerta. Two decades later the city was repopulated by Pompey after his victory over the Cilician pirates, at which time he renamed it Pompeiopolis. The principal remnant of ancient Soli-Pompeiopolis is a splendid colonnaded street nearly half a kilometre in length; this once led down to the harbour, which is now almost completely filled in with sand. Only a score of columns remain standing, about a tenth of those which once flanked this very Roman avenue.

Soon after returning to the main road you reach the outskirts of Mersin, the largest port-city on the Mediterranean coast of Turkey. Although Mersin itself is of very great antiquity, with origins going back to the Old Hittite Empire, the modern city has nothing of interest to offer. So most travellers merely use Mersin as a base for seeing the Cilician coast, or stop there briefly before going on through Adana to eastern Anatolia.

About half an hour's drive past Mersin on the Adana highway a road turns off left for **Tarsus**, renowned as the birthplace of St Paul the Apostle. The origins of Tarsus go back as far as those of Mersin, but here again there are few evidences of the great antiquity of the city. The principal monument of ancient Tarsus is Kancík Kapísí, the Gate of the Bitch, once one of the main entrances to the Roman city. This is sometimes called St Paul's Gate, though it has no known connection with the Apostle.

Despite its lack of ancient monuments, you feel in Tarsus that you are in a very ancient and historic place. For its strategic position on the coast below the Cilician Gates has made it one of the great crossroads of history, and it has seen some of the world's most famous conquerors pass through its gates: Sennacherib, Alexander the Great, Seleucus I Nicator, Tigranes the Great, Pompey, Hadrian, the Caliph El Maymum, Bohemund, Sultan Selim the Grim . . .

But the entry into Tarsus of all these great men is eclipsed by that of an extraordinary woman, Cleopatra, who arrived here one autumn day in 41 BC for her first meeting with Marc Antony. As Plutarch described the scene:

She came sailing up the Cydnus on a galley whose stern was golden; the sails were purple, and the oars were silver. These, in their motion, kept tune to the music of flutes and pipes and harps. The Queen, in the dress and character of Aphrodite, lay on a couch of gold brocade, as though in a picture, while about her were pretty boys, bedight like cupids, who fanned her, and

218

maidens habited as nereids and graces, and some made as though they were rowing, while others busied them about the sails. All manner of sweet perfumes were wafted ashore from the ship, and on the shore thousands were gathered to behold her.

CHAPTER EIGHTEEN

Karamania

❧

Silifke – Mut – Alahan Monastery – Karaman – Konya

At Tarsus the traveller can choose from a number of alternative itineraries. This chapter describes the journey from the coast of Cilicia up over the Taurus Mountains to Konya on the Anatolian plateau. You could drive north and cross the Taurus at the historic Cilician Gates, and then at Pozantí head west across the barren steppes to Konya. But I would recommend going back along the Cilician coast to Silifke and from there going directly over the Taurus to Konya: this drive passes through some of the most beautiful mountain country in southern Turkey, and there are several historic sites to see along the way.

As the road heads inland there is a striking view of the medieval citadel of Silifke dominating the modern town. The road then winds up into the pine-clad hills above the coastal plain, after which it follows the gorge of the Göksu up into the heart of the Taurus Mountains.

Some seven kilometres past Silifke there is a car park to the right of the road where one can stop to take in a dramatic view of the **Göksu gorge**. Beside the gorge there is a sign in Turkish commemorating the historic event which took place there eight centuries ago at the beginning of the Third Crusade: 'The Emperor Frederick Barbarossa, having agreed with the Selcuk Sultan Kílíç Arslan II to cross his lands freely in peace, was drowned in the Göksu in this region on 10 June 1190 on his way to Palestine at the head of his army.' The Emperor's untimely death was a severe blow to the morale of the German knights, many of whom turned back at this point, with only part of the once powerful army continuing on to Antioch under the Duke of Swabia. The Duke carried the Emperor's corpse along, pickled in a cask of vinegar, so that he might be buried in the cathedral in Antioch. Some of the Emperor's bones were set aside at the burial and taken on the campaign to the Holy Land by the remnants of his army, 'in the vain hope,' as Runciman put it, 'that at least a portion of Frederick Barbarossa should await the Judgement Day in Jerusalem.'

The highway now continues up the gorge, with spectacular cliffs, towers, and spires of rock rising hundreds of metres sheer above the road. Then the valley begins to broaden out into a long highland corridor flanked by rows of hills covered with wild olive trees. In the distance villages of sand-coloured stone houses blend in with the tawny hills around them, as if they were a natural part of the landscape in which they stand.

The first town of any size is **Mut**, the ancient **Claudiopolis**, which is situated deep down in the valley of a tributary river of the Göksu. Claudiopolis was founded in the middle of the first century BC by Marcus Aurelius Polemo, high priest of the temple-city of Olba, who organized the wild Isaurian tribes of the Taurus into an independent kingdom. The most prominent monument in the town is the medieval citadel, a Byzantine fortress which was rebuilt in the fourteenth century by the Karamanid Turks.

Just beyond Mut a road leads off to the left for Ermenek, the ancient Germanicopolis, founded in the first century BC by King Antiochus IV of Commagene (see pages 356–9).

Twenty kilometres farther along you see on the right an archaeological sign pointing the way to **Alahan**, two kilometres uphill along an extremely rough dirty road. The ascent is well worth the effort, for the monastery at Alahan is the most interesting example of Byzantine architecture in Cilicia. The monastery was founded in the middle of the fifth century, and the oldest buildings date from that period. Its site is spectacular, perched on a platform looking out over the Göksu gorge and its surrounding mountains.

Some twenty kilometres beyond Alahan the road goes over the Sertavul Pass at an altitude of 1610 metres, and then descends into a broad valley flanked by khaki-coloured hills. The valley soon merges into a barren highland plain dotted here and there with camel caravans and grazing flocks; the only humans one sees are occasional herdsmen clad in the stiff sheepskin cloaks whose style does not seem to have changed since ancient times. This is the great barren plateau which comprises nearly all of central Anatolia, where the harsh landscape is so entirely different from that of the felicitous coasts of the Aegean and the Mediterranean.

The first town of any size is **Karaman**, the ancient **Larende**, which stands in a surprisingly green oasis off to the right of the highway. As far back as the fourth century BC Larende was the principal city of Lycaonia, the province within the Taurus north of Cilicia. The town takes its Turkish name from the Karamanids, a Turcoman tribe who took it from the Selcuks in 1261 and for a time made it the capital of their emirate.

The most prominent monument in Karaman is its medieval citadel, originally constructed in the twelfth century by the Selcuks and rebuilt by the Karamanids. In the quaint old quarter around the citadel there are a number of mosques and pious foundations from the Karamanid period. One of the most interesting of these is the **Ak Tekke**, a former monastery of Mevlevi dervishes. The *tekke* was founded in 1371 and remained in constant use until the dissolution of the dervish orders in 1925. Within the precincts of the *tekke* are the tombs of several members of the family of Mevlana Celaleddin Rumi, the founder of the Mevlevi order of dervishes and one of the great poet-philosophers of Islam (see pages 228–9). Mevlana was born in Balkh (in modern-day Afghanistan) about 1200 and moved to Karaman with his family in 1221, remaining there for seven years before finally settling in Konya.

The oldest Karamanid structure in Karaman is the **Yunus Emre Camii**, built in 1349 and heavily restored in the present century. The mosque is named for the medieval Turkish poet, Yunus Emre, whose reputed tomb is within its precincts. (There are half a dozen other towns in Turkey which also claim to possess his tomb.) Yunus Emre (*c.* 1280–1320) was the first Turkish poet to write in the ordinary language of his people, rather than in the courtly Persian used by most other Turkish poets until modern times. For that reason he was long neglected in anthologies of Turkish poetry, and only in recent years has his work received the attention it deserves. Today he is recognized as the greatest poet in Turkish literature, and the common people of Anatolia can recite his poems by heart, for they feel very deeply that he wrote for and about them. Little is known of the man himself, except for a tradition that he was a poor peasant who spent his life as a wood carrier in the service of Hací Bektaş Veli, the founder of the Bektaşi order of dervishes. But one need only read his work to discover that he was as much a Renaissance poet as his contemporary, Petrarch, with a consuming love of mankind and of the world around him. One poem in particular reveals the character of Yunus Emre; it consists of but a single line which might well serve as his epitaph: 'I love you, so the hand of death can never touch me.'

There are two interesting sites in the vicinity of Karaman: the first is **Canhasan**, twelve kilometres to the north-east. The earliest levels

here date back as far as the sixth millennium BC. But, like other
Neolithic and Bronze Age sites in Anatolia, the place itself has little
visual interest for the ordinary traveller, and one can far better
appreciate the culture discovered there by looking at the fascinating
artifacts from Canhasan which are on exhibit in the Museum of
Anatolian Cultures in Ankara.

The other site is **Binbir Kilise**, or **Thousand-and-One-Churches,**
some forty kilometres north of Karaman in the foothills of Kara
Dağ, the Black Mountain. The modern village of Maden Şehir
occupies the site of what was an important monastic centre in
medieval times, and in the surrounding countryside there are the
ruins of a number (though not 1001) of Byzantine churches and
monasteries. These structures were first studied in 1905 by Sir
William Ramsey and Gertrude Bell, and they have been dated
variously from the middle of the ninth century to the last half of the
eleventh.

About an hour's drive beyond Karaman a turning to the right
leads to Çumra, and from here a drive of ten kilometres takes
one to **Çatal Hüyük**, probably the most important archaeological site
in Turkey. It was discovered in 1958 by James Mellaart, whose
excavation of the site in the 1960s led to an enormous increase in the
knowledge of Neolithic and Bronze Age cultures in Anatolia. The
deepest levels in one of the two mounds excavated there have given
radiocarbon dates as early as 6800 BC, which makes this the most
ancient Neolithic site yet discovered in Anatolia. Mellaart's investigations have revealed that this ancient Anatolian culture was
remarkably advanced, as evidenced by their sophisticated tools,
jewellery, sculptured figurines, and particularly by the brilliant
wall-paintings which decorated their religious shrines. But again the
site is unimpressive, for many of the mud-walled structures discovered
in the original excavations have been worn away by the elements,
so one must wait till one gets to the museum in Ankara to appreciate
the culture which was discovered here.

Returning to the main road, you now cross the flat and treeless
Lycaonian plain on the last stretch of the journey to Konya, with
the snow-streaked peak of Alacadağ rising to the west. The road
comes into town along Karaman Caddesi, which finally leads to
Hükümet Meydaní, the main square of Konya.

Konya, the Roman **Iconium**, is one of the most ancient cities in
Anatolia. During the Roman period it was capital of the province
of Karamania, which comprised much the same region as that of the

emirate of the Karamanids. Then, as now, the city owed its importance to the fact that it stood astride the junction of several important trade and communication routes. These ancient Roman roads continued to be used by the Selcuks and the Ottomans, and the modern highways in central Anatolia follow approximately the same course.

The most illustrious period in the city's history began in the early years of the twelfth century, when it became capital of the Selcuk Sultanate of Rum. The Selcuk Empire at that time comprised the greater part of Anatolia, which under the enlightened rule of sultans such as Keykâvus I (1210–19) and Keykûbad I (1219–36) reached an unprecedented level of prosperity. The Selcuk power was broken after their defeat by the Mongols at the battle of Kösedağ in 1242, and though their sultans continued to rule in Konya for another half-century, they were little more than pawns in the hands of those who contended for their former empire. Konya was finally captured by Sultan Mehmet II in 1467, and twenty years later all of Karamania was annexed to the Ottoman Empire, with Konya serving as its provincial capital. Today Konya is one of the most attractive and interesting cities in Anatolia, adorned by many splendid monuments from Selcuk times. As Bernard Berenson once wrote, reminiscing on a visit to Konya:

> What a miracle is this Selcuk architecture! It has an elegance, a distinction of design and a subtle delicacy of ornamentation surpassing any other known to me since French Gothic at its best . . . Konya was the residence of the Selcuk sultans and is still an unrivalled monument to their taste and love of beauty and magnificence.

The ancient city of Iconium stood on the acropolis in what is now Alâeddin Parkí. In Selcuk times the inner city on the acropolis was surrounded by a defence wall, of which only a single ruined fragment remains standing at the north end of the park. This is the Alâeddin Köşkü, a defence tower which was converted into an imperial residence in the first half of the thirteenth century.

On the hilltop above the kiosk is **Alâeddin Camii**, the largest Selcuk mosque in Konya. The mosque took some seventy years to build and later underwent several periods of construction and modification; thus its design and layout are unusual and irregular. To the north there is a monumental façade behind which you see the tops of two *türbe*. The present entrance to the mosque is on the east side; there one passes into a large hall with a flat timbered roof

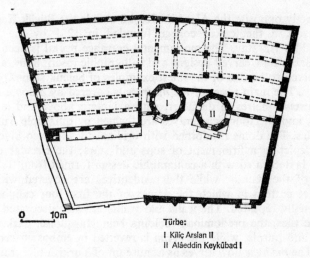

Türbe:

I Kílíç Arslan II
II Alâeddin Keykûbad I

Alâeddin Camii, Konya

supported by a colonnade of forty-two ancient columns forming
seven aisles. Beyond the east hall one comes to a domed area in the
south wall of which is the *mihrab* and beside it a magnificent *mimber*
(pulpit) of carved ebony. The *mimber*, which dates from 1155, is
the oldest inscribed and dated Selcuk work of art in existence, and
also one of the most beautiful. To the west of the domed area there
is a smaller hall divided into four somewhat crooked aisles, while
beyond the *eyvan* to the north stand the two *türbe*. The eastern *türbe*
is decagonal with a conical turret, while the western one, only partially
completed, is octagonal with a dome.

There has been much debate about the sequence of construction
of the various parts of the mosque. The prevailing opinion is that the
domed area was the core of the original mosque, begun by Sultan
Mesud I (1116–56) and completed by his son, Kílíç Arslan II
(1156–88), who also built the decagonal *türbe*. The second period of
building began during the reign of Keykâvus I (1210–19), who is
perhaps responsible for the west hall, while the large eastern hall
and the octagonal *türbe* were built by Alâeddin Keykûbad I (1219–
36), with construction completed by about 1220. Within the decagonal
türbe are the simple sarcophagi of eight Selcuk sultans; the oldest of
these is that of Kílíç Arslan II and the latest that of Keyhûsrev III
(1264–83), the last Selcuk sultan to rule supreme in Konya before
the city was taken by the Mamelukes in 1277.

Directly opposite the Alâeddin Köşkü stands the **Büyük Karatay Medresesi**, a theological college founded in 1251 by the Emir Celaleddin Karatay. The monumental entrance portal is decorated with elaborately carved designs and calligraphic inscriptions, and is considered to be one of the finest examples of Selcuk stonework in Turkey. The main room of the *medrese* is covered by a dome more than twelve metres in diameter, with a lantern above and a pool below, and the four pendentives are formed by quintuple Turkish triangles. The dome is adorned with brilliant tiles in deep blue and gold depicting a firmament of suns and stars; the circular drum below is decorated with a calligraphic design formed from the first verse of the Kuran; while the pendentives are covered with an abstract pattern in which the names of the first four caliphs are continually repeated. The walls and vaults are also decorated with faience tiles, the predominant colours being turquoise, dark blue, green and purple, while the *eyvan* is revetted in embossed ceramic tiles. The *medrese* now serves as a museum of Turkish tiles, ranging in date from Selcuk work of the thirteenth century to Ottoman ceramics of the eighteenth century. Especially interesting are the early Selcuk tiles with figures of humans, animals, birds and fabulous beasts.

To one side of the main room is the *türbe* of the founder, one of the most distinguished men in the history of the Selcuks. Celaleddin Karatay, a freedman of Greek origin, was the trusted adviser of Keykûbad I, served as vezir under his son, Keyhûsrev II, and acted as regent during the triumvirate of Keyhûsrev's three sons: Keykâvus II, Kílíç Arslan IV, and Keykûbad II. Those were difficult times for the Selcuks, for the Mongols were threatening to sweep all before them after their victory at Kösedağ, but Celaleddin managed to hold the Sultanate together and to govern and administer its affairs wisely until his death in 1253.

Walking around Alâeddin Parkí on its western side, you come to the **Ince Minare Medresesi**, or **Medrese with the Slender Minaret**. (The minaret was struck by lightning in 1901 and is now less than half its former height.) The *medrese* and its adjoining mosque, now in ruins, were founded in 1258 by the Emir Sahip Ata Fahrettin Ali. The entrance portal is one of the grandest and most elaborately decorated in Turkey, and is an outstanding example of the baroque period in Selcuk architecture. The main room of the *medrese* is now a museum of Selcuk stonework, including some fascinating sculptural reliefs from the citadels at Konya and Karaman.

Continuing around the park in the same direction you come to the

French Church just beyond the southern end of the square. The first turn to the right past the church takes you on to Ressam Sami Sokaği, and on the third corner to the right you find the Sírçalí (Glazed) **Medrese**. This *medrese*, now partially ruined, was built in 1242 by Badr al-Din Muslih, tutor of Alâeddin Keykûbad II. This was the first large-scale structure in Anatolia to be decorated throughout with ceramic tiles, some fine examples of which still survive in the *eyvan*. The *medrese* is now used to exhibit a collection of tombstones from the Selcuk, Karamanid and Ottoman periods, most of them decorated with superb calligraphic stone carvings.

The first alley to the left beyond the *medrese* leads to the handsome Hasbey Darülhafízí, a school for the memorization of the Kuran. Built in 1421, this is one of the very few examples of Karamanid architecture which have survived in Konya.

Continuing along Ressam Sami Sokaği, you soon come to the **Sahip Ata complex**, consisting of a mosque, *türbe* and *hanikâh*, or oratory. The complex was founded in 1258 by the Emir Sahip Ata Fahrettin Ali, the same who founded the Ince Minare Medresesi. Fahrettin Ali was the greatest builder of his time, for in addition to the two *medreses* in Konya he founded two others in Sivas as well as a mosque in his home town of Kara Hisar. Fahrettin Ali succeeded Calaleddin Karatay as vezir during the triumvirate of the three sons of Keyhûsrev II. He continued in that post under Keyhûsrev III until he was executed in 1277 after the Mongol capture of Konya. He and Celaleddin Karatay were the two greatest vezirs in Selcuk history, and between them they directed the affairs of the Sultanate of Rum for the last half-century of its independent existence.

To the west of Sahip Ata Camii is the **Archaeological Museum**, which houses antiquities from the Phrygian, Greek, Roman and Byzantine periods, all of them discovered in and around Konya.

Returning along Ressam Sami Sokaği, you complete the circuit of the park at Alâeddin Bulvarí, the main thoroughfare of Konya. A few hundred metres along on the right is **Iplikçi Camii**, a mosque originally founded in the twelfth century, rebuilt in 1332, and restored in the present century. Mevlana Celaleddin Rumi taught in the *medrese* of this mosque in his early years in Konya, and there is a small domed room to the south of the mosque which is believed to have been his place of meditation.

You now come to Hükümet Meydaní, the north side of which is dominated by the huge Şerefettin Camii. It was originally founded in Selcuk times but was rebuilt in 1636 and restored in the mid-nineteenth century.

Continuing in the same direction along Mevlana Caddesi, you soon come to Selimiye Camii, a monumental Ottoman mosque. Its date is uncertain, but it is thought to have been begun during the reign of Süleyman the Magnificent and completed by Selim II, whose name it bears.

Behind the Selimiye mosque is the **Mevlana Tekke**, the most famous monument in Konya and the object of pilgrimages from all over Turkey. For the *tekke* is not only a museum and national monument, but one of the most sacred Islamic shrines in the country.

Mevlana Celaleddin Rumi, the founder of the Mevlevi order of dervishes, first came to Konya in 1228 with his father, Bahaeddin Veled, who had been invited there by Alâeddin Keykûbad I. After the death of Bahaeddin in 1231 Mevlana gathered his father's disciples around him and began lecturing and preaching to an ever-increasing audience. At the same time he engaged in meditation and began a spiritual dialogue with a succession of dervish philosopher-poets, most notably Çelebi Husamettin. It was to Husamettin that he dedicated his greatest work, the *Masnawi*, a collection of several thousand odes in which he sings of his mystical beliefs and his doctrine of ecstatic universal love. Mevlana's other major work is the *Divani Kebir*, a collection of poems and prose works, including sermons and letters. As one of his translators wrote of him:

> In Rumi we encounter one of the world's greatest poets. In profundity of thought, inventiveness of image, and triumphant mastery of language, he stands out as the supreme genius of Islamic mysticism . . . Future generations, as his poetry becomes wider known and more perfectly understood, will enjoy and applaud the poems of this wisest, most penetrating, and saintliest of men.

When Mevlana died in 1273 he was buried beside his father, and in the following year a mausoleum was built to house their sarcophagi. The original tomb was a typical Selcuk *türbe* in the form of a domed chamber and an *eyvan*; then in 1397 the Karamanid Emir Alâeddin Ali added the fluted drum and conical turret revetted in green tiles. The other parts of the building were added in Ottoman times, and a number of sultans rebuilt and restored the *tekke* and adorned it with precious furnishings and works of art.

After Mevlana's death Çelebi Husamettin assumed the leadership of the Mevlevi order, and he in turn was succeeded by Mevlana's son, Sultan Veled. The Mevlevi order subsequently established *tekkes* all over Anatolia and even beyond, as Mevlana's mystical thought came to influence the whole Islamic world. The *tekke* in Konya flourished for more than six centuries as a centre of art, music, literature and religion, until the dervish orders were finally banned and dissolved in 1925. The following year the *tekke* was opened as a museum, but though tens of thousands of tourists visit it each year it remains essentially, though unofficially, a religious shrine of profound importance in the religion of the Turkish people.

On entering the museum you come into a pleasant flower-filled courtyard with a large *şadirvan*. The rooms to the left house a fine collection of Selcuk, Karamanid and Ottoman fabrics and carpets dating from the thirteenth to the eighteenth century. Some of the cells have been refurbished to show what they were like in the days of the dervishes.

To the right of the entrance there is a fountain called Şebi Arus, the Pool of Nuptial Night, named after the night on which Mevlana died. On the anniversary of that occasion the dervishes commemorated Mevlana's death by partaking of their evening meal around the pool, and then performing the *sema*, the ethereal whirling dance that made the Mevlevis famous throughout Europe as the Whirling Dervishes.

At the far right-hand side of the courtyard are four Ottoman *türbe*, all dating from the sixteenth century. There is a fifth Ottoman *türbe* in the dervish graveyard to the south of the *tekke*, a place known in Turkish as the Garden of Spirits.

The door to the *tekke* opens on to a small chamber once used as a reading-room by the dervishes; this now houses an exhibit of Turkish calligraphy. From here you enter the *tekke* proper through the Silver Door, made in 1599 and presented to the *tekke* by Hasan Pasha, son of the famous Sokollu Mehmet Pasha.

The central hall of the *tekke* is called Huzurí Pir, the Presence of the Saint. On a raised platform on the left side of the hall are the sarcophagi of the Men from Horosan, six dervishes who accompanied the family of Mevlana on their journey from Balkh to Konya. At the foot of the first pair of sarcophagi is a superb bronze urn known as the April Bowl, so called because it was used to collect the rain water of that month, which was reputed to have miraculous healing powers. According to an inscription, the April Bowl was presented to the Mevlana Tekke in 1333 by Ebu Said Bahadír, Khan of the Ilkhanid Mongols.

On the right side of the central hall are the sarcophagi of the

Çelebi, Mevlana's successors as head of the *tekke*, as well as the sarcophagi of certain members of Mevlana's family. Farther along, directly under the Green Dome, are the marble sarcophagi of Mevlana and his son, Sultan Veled; and beyond are those of Mevlana's father and other members of his immediate family. This is the most sacred part of the shrine, and the area before Mevlana's tomb is always crowded with Anatolian peasants, many of whom weep unashamedly in a fervour of religious feeling as they pray before the grave of the man who for them transcends sainthood and approaches the divine. An inscription in the *türbe* quotes Mevlana's own words:

Do not search for our graves in the earth
Our graves are in the hearts of the enlightened.

Two glass showcases in the central hall exhibit masterpieces of Selcuk calligraphy, as well as the oldest extant manuscripts of the *Masnawi* and the *Divani Kebir*, the former dating to 1278, just five years after the death of Mevlana.

The northern end of the *tekke* is made up of two large domed chambers; the one to the west was used as a mosque and that to the east served as the *semahane*, or dancing-room. The mosque is now used as an exhibition hall for ancient books, calligraphy and prayer-rugs. The *semahane* has a fascinating collection of musical instruments used by the dervishes in their ceremonies. Also exhibited here is one of the most precious treasures of Selcuk art, a beautifully carved Kuran lectern in walnut dated 1278. The inner face of the lectern is decorated with a fabulous scene depicting lions and two-headed eagles, the only surviving example of Selcuk painting.

At the north end of the *semahane* are the musicians' quarters, while the visitors' gallery is to the east. We once sat there many years ago on a winter afternoon when the *tekke* was empty save for a few pilgrims praying before Mevlana's tomb, and the only sounds were the murmur of their prayers and the haunting sound of a Mevlevi melody played softly on a speaker in the *semahane*. This inevitably evoked the scene which so fascinated visitors to Turkey in times past, the dervishes in their white gowns and turret caps whirling ecstatically around the room to the ethereal music of the *ney*, or Turkish flute. Now this enchanting ceremony is held in Konya only during the annual Mevlana festival in December, when it seems more of a theatrical production than a religious ceremony. So one must turn to the accounts of the old travellers to recall the vanished scene. The oldest known account is that of Samuel Purchas, an

Englishman who witnessed a performance at the Mevlevi *tekke* in Pera in 1613, giving this description of the *sema*:

... some five and twenty of the two and fifty Darvises suddainly rose up bare-legged and bare-footed, and casting aside their upper Garment, some of them having their brests all uncovered, they began little by little to turne about the Interpreter of the Law turning gently in the midst of them all, afterwards they redoubled their force and turned with such incredible swiftnesse, that I could not chuse but admire it. The forme of their dancing is as strange as the continuance of their swiftness, for sometimes they stretch out their Armes as farre as they can in length, sometimes they contract them in a lesser compasse, sometimes they hold them about their Heads, sometimes againe they performe certaine merry gestures, as if they were drawing a Bow and shooting forth an Arrow. Likewise some of them did continue turning during the whole time in one and the selfe same place, and others move forward from one corner to another.

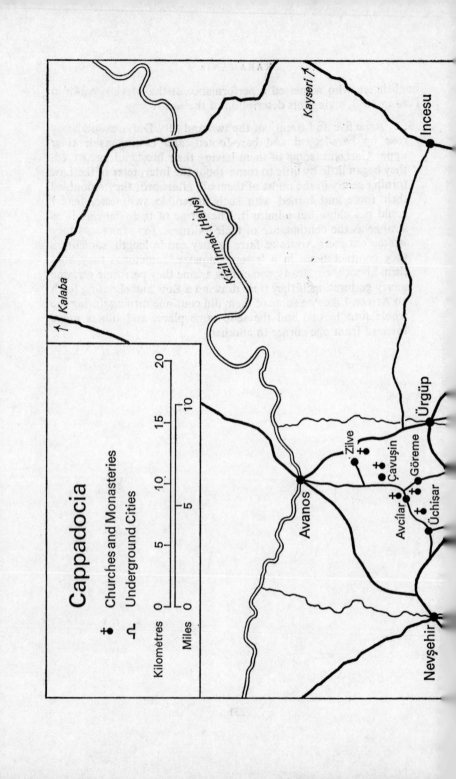

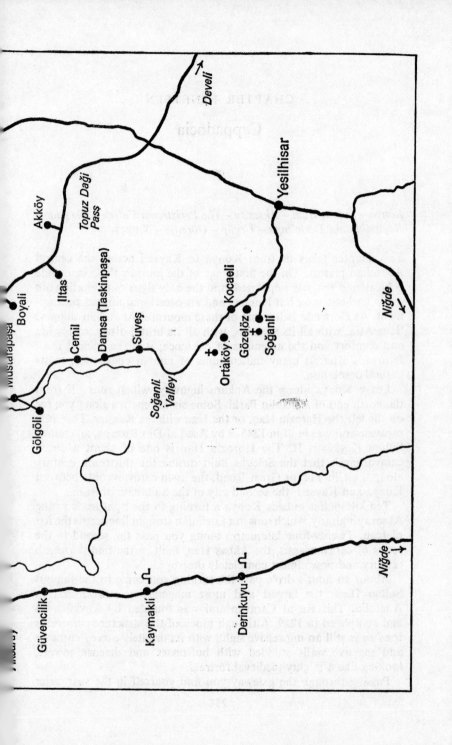

CHAPTER NINETEEN

Cappadocia

❧

Konya – Sultan Hani – Aksaray – The Peristrema Valley – Nevşehir – Kaymaklí and Derinkuyu – Ürgüp – Göreme – Kayseri

This chapter takes us from Konya to Kayseri across the central Anatolian plateau. On the first stage of the journey the countryside is bleak and sparsely populated, and the only signs of habitation are a few pathetic mud hut hamlets and an occasional nomad encampment. As Gertrude Bell wrote of these mournful Anatolian steppes: 'It is Asia, with all its vastness, with all its brutal disregard for life and comfort and the amenities of existence; it is the ancient East, returned, after so many millenniums of human endeavour, to its natural desolation.'

Leave Konya along the Ankara highway, which runs off from the north end of Alâeddin Parkí. Some six kilometres along you see on the left the **Horozlu Han,** or the **Han with the Rooster.** This little caravansarai was built in 1246–9 by Asad al-Din Ruzapa, an emir of Sultan Keykâvus II. The Horozlu Han is one of about a dozen caravansarais that the Selcuks built during the thirteenth century along the Ulu Yol, or Great Road, the main caravan route between Konya and Kayseri, the second city of the Sultanate of Rum.

Ten kilometres outside Konya a turning to the right leads to the Aksaray highway, which runs in a Euclidian straight line across the flat plateau. Twenty-four kilometres along you pass the second in the series of caravansarais, the **Akbaş Han,** built in the mid-thirteenth century and now almost completely destroyed.

About an hour's drive past the turning you come to the famous **Sultan Haní,** the largest and most magnificent caravansarai in Anatolia. This Royal Caravansarai was founded by Keykûbad I and completed in 1229. Although much of the structure is in ruins the *han* is still an impressive sight, with its ornately carved entrance and massive walls studded with buttresses and defence towers, looking like a mighty medieval fortress.

Passing through the gateway you find yourself in the vast outer courtyard, in the centre of which is the ruined *mescit,* or chapel. The *mescit* is in the form of a kiosk carried on four open arches and reached by corner staircases, with the space below serving as a *şadirvan.* The courtyard is flanked by two arcades whose vaults have mostly collapsed. The first chamber on the left side of the courtyard served as the kitchen. The next two rooms were dormitories, while the chambers on the right side were shops, storerooms, workrooms and baths.

You then pass through a second monumental porch into the covered inner hall, which served as a stable for the horses and camels of the caravans. This section consists of a wide central aisle with nine aisles running perpendicular to it on either side; the central vault was roofed with a dome which had an open oculus to provide light and ventilation. Part of the dome and much of the vault of the central dome have collapsed, nevertheless the hall is still grand and impressive.

These Selcuk *hans* were virtually self-sufficient. In addition to providing food and lodging for merchants, drivers and animals, they were staffed with physicians, veterinary surgeons, cooks and bakers, as well as the various workers and artisans needed to service and maintain the caravans. Caravansarais also served as military stations in time of war, and were used to feed and supply the Selcuk armies when they were on the march. During Selcuk times all merchants in their domains paid a yearly tax to the Sultan, and in return they and their animals were allowed to use the caravansarais free of charge while travelling from town to town.

Forty kilometres past the Sultan Hani the road crosses the Adana-Ankara highway, which you follow north for three kilometres before turning right for Aksaray. In a few minutes you reach **Aksaray** itself, a large town in the midst of a green oasis of pines, cypresses and fruit trees, a welcome sight after miles of driving across the barren and monotonous plateau.

Aksaray is a very ancient town, founded in Hittite times. However, there are only a few ancient monuments to be seen here, and most have been so heavily restored that they have lost their original character. The Ulu Cami, built by the Karamanids in 1433, has a beautifully-carved *mimber* of Selcuk workmanship which was removed from the ruined mosque of Kílíç Arslan II. There are also two medieval *medreses* of some interest: the Zinciriye Medresesi, built by the Karamanids in 1336, and the Ibrahim Kadiroğlu Medresesi, a Selcuk structure restored by the Karamanids in the middle of the fifteenth century.

Aksaray is near the natural boundary between the Lycaonian plain and the eroded hill country of south-western Cappadocia. During medieval times Cappadocia was one of the principal monastic centres of the Byzantine Empire, and an enormous number of churches and monasteries were built here. One of the leaders of this movement was St Basil the Great (329–79), Bishop of Caesarea, the modern Kayseri. St Basil formulated the Rule which governed monasticism in the Eastern churches and which later spread to Europe, profoundly influencing the thought of St Benedict and through him the whole course of the monastic movement in Europe. Monasticism flourished in this region for a full thousand years, until it was finally brought to an end by the Turcoman-Mongol invasions and the subsequent occupation of Cappadocia by the Turks. Nevertheless, many of the churches continued in use until 1923, when the Greek Christians of Anatolia were deported in the exchange of minority populations following the Greek-Turkish War. The rupestrine churches and monasteries of Cappadocia and their fascinating wall paintings remained virtually unknown to the outside world, save for the accounts of occasional travellers, until Father Guillaume de Jerphanion made his first pioneering visit in 1907. Father Jerphanion devoted the remainder of his life to exploring Cappadocia and studying these rock-hewn churches and their works of art, finally publishing his findings in his magisterial work, *Une nouvelle province de l'art Byzantine: les églises rupestres de Cappadoce* (Paris, 1925–42). Since then other scholars have continued and extended Jerphanion's work. As a result, Cappadocia is now internationally famous and is visited by tens of thousands of tourists annually, an invasion that has only slightly spoiled its natural beauty.

The most famous rupestrine churches are in the region around Ürgüp and Göreme, a short distance to the east of Nevşehir. But before proceeding there one might want to explore the **Peristrema valley**, a region south-east of Aksaray in the foothills of Hasan Daği where there are more than a score of Byzantine churches and monasteries. These churches and their frescoes were first studied in the 1950s by Nicole and Michele Thierry, whose *Nouvelles églises rupestres de Cappadoce* (Paris, 1963) is a worthy successor to Father Jerphanion's work.

The easiest approach to the Peristrema valley is to take the main road from Aksaray to Nevşehir and after twelve kilometres turn right along the Ihlara road; a drive of about twenty kilometres brings one to Ihlara, a village at the head of the Peristrema valley.

This is really a gorge some twelve kilometres in length between Ihlara and Selimiye, gouged through the volcanic rock and earth by the sinuous Melendiz River rushing down from the foothills of Hasan Dağí. The yellow walls of the canyon drop vertically for several hundred feet down to the rocky stream bed, which is bordered by groves of poplars, willows and cypresses. Almost all of the churches are in the upper half of the gorge, between Ihlara and the village of Belisirama, and one can hire a guide from either place. The path is quite rough and crosses the stream several times, either over home-made suspension bridges or at fords, altogether an exciting and very interesting expedition.

The main road now continues on towards Nevşehir, and soon one sees on the right the **Ağzíkara Han**, one of the best-preserved and most impressive Selcuk caravansarais in Anatolia. It is built to the same general plan as the Sultan Haní: a monumental gateway leading to an arcaded courtyard with a kiosk-*mescit* in the centre and a second portal opening into the inner hall. In this case the hall has six aisles running off perpendicular to the main aisle, with the open dome over the centre of the fourth aisle in from the entrance. According to an inscription, the inner hall was completed in 1231 during the reign of Alâeddin Keykûbad I, and the courtyard and inner porch were finished about a decade later.

Some seven kilometres farther along you see on the left the very ruined **Öresin Haní**, a small Selcuk caravansarai of the late thirteenth century. About thirteen kilometres past that you pass the **Alay Han**, of which only the entrance porch and front wall remain standing. This was the first royal Selcuk caravansarai to be built in Anatolia; it has been tentatively dated on stylistic grounds to 1192, the last year in the reign of Kílíç Arslan II.

The road then passes Acígöl, a village in a green oasis at the foot of eroded hills. Soon after that you arrive in **Nevşehir**, a characterless modern town under an acropolis crowned with the ruins of a Selcuk fortress. In the main square there is a statue of the famous Nevşehirli Damat Ibrahim Pasha, who was born here in about 1670. Ibrahim Pasha was a son-in-law (*damat*) of Ahmet III and served the Sultan as Grand Vezir from 1718 until 1730, during the gay years of the Tulip Period. He was one of the most enlightened men of his time, and during his term in office the Ottomans for the first time made cultural contacts with Europe, particularly in France. But his progressive attitude aroused the conservative factions in the Empire, eventually leading to Ibrahim's downfall and execution by the Janissaries in 1730.

Some amazing troglodyte settlements have been discovered south of Nevşehir in recent years. The two most important are the underground complexes at **Kaymaklí** and **Derinkuyu**, on the Nevşehir-Niğde road. There are more than a score of others in the area, but so far only these two have been opened to the public. The subterranean towns at Kaymaklí and Derinkuyu were hewn from the tufa to a depth of eight to ten storeys, with the upper levels apparently designed for living quarters and the lower ones for storerooms and places of refuge. Labyrinthian tunnels run off in all directions, leading to rooms of various sizes, here and there opening out to form large areas of regular shape, like squares at street junctions. These underground towns were provided with numerous ventilation shafts and wells, and at strategic locations the passages could be sealed off from inside by large round slabs like millstones, so as to block entry by invaders. It is not known when these troglodyte towns were founded, but they probably date back, at least in part, to pre-Christian times. They have been used as places of refuge as recently as 1839, when the local population went underground to escape the invading Egyptian army led by Ibrahim Pasha.

As soon as one leaves Nevşehir and begins driving eastward the scenery changes suddenly and dramatically, for one is now entering the heart of the lunar Cappadocian countryside. Perhaps the best approach is to drive on to **Ürgüp**, a picturesque village at the foot of a pinnacle riddled with the doors and windows of rock-hewn dwellings. There are several good hotels in the village, and it is an ideal centre for exploring the surrounding countryside.

Most of this part of Cappadocia is covered with a deep layer of tufa, a soft stone of solidified mud, ash and lava which once poured down from the now extinct volcanoes on Hasan Daği and Erciyes Daği, the two great mountain peaks of Cappadocia. In the eons since then the rivers of the region have scoured canyons, gorges, valleys and gulleys through the soft and porous stone, and the elements have eroded it into fantastic crags, folds, turrets, pyramids, spires, needles, stalagmites, and cones, creating a vast outdoor display of stone sculptures in an incredible variety of shapes and colours. The cone is the most frequent form in Cappadocia's lunar rockscape: many of them stand more than a hundred feet tall, some in groups and others standing alone like eccentric obelisks or sand castles fashioned by a giant child. Many of them are topped by a fragment of the basalt strata which once lay above the tufa; these huge rocks protected the tufa directly beneath them while the surroundings were eroded away. These black basalt capitals, balanced precariously on the fantastic phallic cones, are known by the locals as *peri bacalarí*, or fairy chimneys. The predominant colour in some areas is brick-red, rust, ochre, or umber, while in others it may be ashen or even salt-white; but the sensuous rock surfaces subtly change their hues with the shifting patterns of sunlight and shadow, here and there deepening into pools of midnight blue, deep violet, or even an ephemeral green, and then at twilight the whole countryside is pervaded with an evanescent pink and golden glow, fading into a palette of pale pastels as night falls on this enchanted landscape.

What nature has left undone in the way of phantasmagoric architecture has been completed by the restless ingenuity of man; for since time immemorial the Cappadocians have been cutting into the cones and walls of rock, excavating and carving rupestrine houses, storerooms, churches and monasteries, many of them elaborately sculptured and adorned with vivid and imaginative frescoes capturing the religious visions of medieval Byzantine Christianity.

Ürgüp and most other villages in this part of Cappadocia are either perched on spires of rock or hollowed out of precipices or gigantic cones, with the doors and windows of their dwellings giving the appearance of a huge honeycomb or dovecote. Even the free-standing houses have been built of volcanic rock, and many of them have handsome arcades with façades and portals decorated with carved and sculptured designs; while some Cappadocians burrow into the hillsides and live like modern cavemen, but far more comfortably. For the apparently arid soil is incredibly fertile, and the local residents live very well on the abundant produce of their vegetable gardens, orchards and vineyards. The wine of the region is deservedly famous, with a heady aroma like a whiff of brimstone. One of the local hotels serves it on tap in every room, so that you can brush your teeth with wine instead of water.

One authority estimates that there are about one hundred and fifty **rupestrine churches and monastic establishments** in this part of Cappadocia, about half of which are decorated with medieval wall paintings. Most travellers with limited time visit only the better known and more easily accessible churches, which are mostly in the region north of the Nevşehir-Ürgüp highway, a more or less triangular area with its vertices at the villages of Göreme, Üçhisar and Avanos. There is a second group of churches south of the main road in the general vicinity of Ortahisar. South of Ürgüp is a third group in the region around Mustafapaşa, and still farther south there is a fourth group in the Soganlí valley. Those wishing to see these regions and their churches in some detail would be advised to hire a guide in Ürgüp or one of the other villages mentioned above.

The basic plan of the majority of Cappadocian churches is simple, just a barrel-vaulted nave culminating in an apse with a horse-shoe arch. Often two churches stand side by side, perhaps separated by an arcade of piers, with one serving as a funerary chapel. There are also three-aisled basilicas, churches with transverse naves, churches with the ground plan of a free-standing cross, and inscribed Greek-cross churches, not to mention variations on these themes or eccentricities introduced because of the irregular shapes of the rock masses out of which they were cut. The monasteries range from primitive hermitages and simple oratories, often dug out of cones or cut high in an inaccessible cliff face, to elaborate monastic establishments with attached church, funerary chapel, dormitory, refectory and storerooms, with all of the liturgical fixtures and household furniture carved out of the living rock. The local architects have tried to recreate the forms of free-standing structures as they hollowed out the rock, and the churches have what at first sight appear to be conventional columns, capitals, arches, vaults, pendentives and domes. But often the lower parts of the 'supporting' structures have worn away, leaving columns hanging like stalactites, arches and vaults suspended in mid-air, and gravity-defying domes hovering aloft as if held there by a magical magnet.

The paintings in the Cappadocian churches constitute the world's most extensive museum of Byzantine painting, covering almost the whole span of medieval Christian art in Anatolia. A number of examples survive from the Early Christian or Pre-Iconoclastic Period (c. 550–725), where the designs are principally from the symbols of the early Church: the cross, the palm tree of paradise, the pomegranate symbolizing eternal life, and the fish, which owed its popularity to the fact that the first four Greek letters in the phrase 'Jesus Christ, Son of God, Saviour', spell out the word in that language. During the Iconoclastic Period, which lasted from 726 until 843, except for a brief respite during the reign of the Empress Eirene (797–802), portraits were forbidden as idolatrous, and those which existed at that time were mostly destroyed and replaced by large crosses and aniconic ornamentation such as vine-scrolls, trees, or geometric designs. This was followed by what Father Jerphanion called the Archaic Period (c. 850–950), in which Cappadocian artists returned to figurative wall-painting, principally narrative cycles of the life of Christ from the apocryphal Gospels. (One art historian has likened these narrative cycles to strip

CAPPADOCIA

cartoons.) After a transitional phase, *c.* 950–1020, Cappadocian art began to develop rapidly and reached its peak in the eleventh and twelfth centuries. This was a period of resurgence for monasticism, and a large number of churches and monasteries were built in Cappadocia by wealthy Byzantine officials, who commissioned some of the best artists in the Empire to adorn them. For that reason the Cappadocian art of this period is almost wholly Byzantine in the traditional sense. The Christological scenes with which the churches were principally decorated were now taken from the canonical rather than the apocryphal Gospels, with a tendency towards individual scenes or portraits rather than the cinematic narratives of the Archaic Period. But after this brilliant flowering the development of Cappadocian art came to an abrupt end, except for a brief revival under the Selcuks in the thirteenth century. The paintings of the latter period are usually quite crude, as the provincial schools of art died out and the craft traditions were forgotten, for Cappadocia was now permanently occupied by the Turks and was cut off from the main centres of Christian art in Byzantium and the West.

Those with limited time at their disposal should probably begin their itinerary at **Göreme**, for this has the greatest concentration of accessible rock churches. The main group is found in a large natural amphitheatre bounded by nearly vertical cliffs and opening into a steep-sided green valley. Just under the cliffs is a central group of impressive rock-hewn chambers, their two-storeyed porticoes and arcades decorated with geometrical designs. Some of the chambers in the cliff face, designed either as refuges or hermit retreats, are accessible only by perilous flights of steps or narrow passages which could be blocked by stones similar to those at Kaymaklí and Derinkuyu. On either side of this central group are scattered churches and monastic buildings of various types, including refectories, kitchens and storerooms, all hewn out of the rock. In the enclosure below the car park there are about twenty of these, including the Barbara Kilise (Church of St Barbara), Elmalí Kilise (Church of the Apple), Çaríklí Kilise (Church of the Sandal), and Karanlík Kilise (The Dark Church), along with the refectory connected with the latter church, all of them decorated with wall paintings of the eleventh century.

Continuing past the car park one sees on the right the New Church of Tokalí, dating from the middle of the tenth century, when it was hewn from the rock behind an earlier sanctuary of the same name. The New Church of Tokalí is the archetype of the transverse-nave churches in Cappadocia and is decorated with some of the

C.G.T. 241 Q

finest wall paintings from the Archaic Period. Clustered around it are several other churches and chapels from the same period, with half a dozen more in the valley behind.

Beyond Göreme is the rock village of **Avcílar**, where one branch of the road goes left to Üçhisar and the other right to Avanos. In the village you can see the façade of a Roman tomb cut high in the face of a gigantic cone, one of the few rupestrine works in Cappadocia dating from pre-Christian times.

If you take the Avanos road you soon come to **Çavuşin**, a troglodyte village partly built into a pock-marked cliff face. On top of the cliff is the impressive colonnaded façade of the Church of St John the Baptist. This three-aisled basilica is thought to have been built as early as the fifth century, which would make it the oldest known Christian sanctuary in Cappadocia, and it is decorated with wall paintings from the Pre-Iconoclastic Period. A short way beyond Çavuşin you see the so-called 'Pigeon House', a tenth-century church built into an imposing rock tower. Among the frescoes here is a portrait of the Byzantine Emperor Nicephorus II Phocas (963–9) and his wife, the faithless Empress Theophano. This portrait undoubtedly commemorates the Emperor's visit to his native Cappadocia in 964, at the beginning of his campaign against the Arabs. (He was called 'the Pale Death of the Saracens'.) For a time it was hoped that Nicephorus would drive the Arabs completely out of Asia Minor and the Holy Land, but in 969 he was murdered by his wife and her Armenian lover, John Tzimisces, who usurped the throne and dismissed Theophano to a nunnery.

For those with time to explore the area on foot there are a number of rock churches in two valleys south-east of Çavuşin: Güllü Dere and Kízíl Çukur. The churches are decorated with wall paintings ranging in date from the seventh to the tenth century.

Beyond Çavuşin a road turns off right to **Zilve**, where there is a concentration of about a dozen churches; most of these date from the ninth and tenth centuries, but there are three earlier chapels decorated with Pre-Iconoclastic paintings. This is one of the most spectacular landscapes in Cappadocia, a natural amphitheatre at the junction of a valley and three canyons, the cliff faces riddled with the openings of churches and houses. The troglodyte village of Zilve was abandoned some years ago because of the danger of rock falls, but one can still see the rock-hewn mosque, the only rupestrine Islamic sanctuary in Cappadocia.

Returning to the main road you soon reach **Avanos**, a large village on the banks of the Kízíl Irmak, the Red River. This is the ancient

Halys, the longest river in Asia Minor; it originates in the Pontic Alps and flows in a great circular arc encompassing the whole of western Cappadocia; then it turns north and forms the boundary between ancient Paphlagonia and the Pontus as it flows through mountain gorges to the Black Sea, the ancient Euxine. The Turkish name for the river comes from the rust-red colour it takes on when flowing through the red clay deposits of Cappadocia. In antiquity this clay was highly regarded for the making of pottery and was exported all over the eastern Mediterranean. Even today it is the principal source of income for the people of Avanos, where there are scores of small kilns where the local potters turn out the rather crude Avanos ware.

From Avanos one can drive back past Avcílar to **Üçhisar**, the most picturesque village in Cappadocia, perched on a veritable Gibraltar pitted with cave dwellings and crowned with the ruins of a medieval fortress. The upper village commands a sweeping view of this most spectacular part of the Cappadocian countryside.

After leaving Üçhisar one can return to the main Nevşehir-Ürgüp road, perhaps stopping off at **Ortahisar** on the way back to Ürgüp. Ortahisar is a smaller version of Üçhisar, a castellated village clustering around a rocky eminence honeycombed with cave dwellings. South of Ortahisar there are about a dozen rock churches with wall paintings dating from the tenth and eleventh centuries.

From Ürgüp another road leads south to Damsa and the **Soğanlí valley**, where there are more than thirty rupestrine churches and monasteries, with frescoes ranging in date from the ninth century to the latter part of the thirteenth. But most travellers will probably postpone this excursion for a subsequent visit, for it would take the better part of a lifetime to see all of Cappadocia in the detail that it deserves.

Instead, those with limited time will probably want to push on to Kayseri. The road from Ürgüp leads up into the eroded hills and along a green valley, and at the village of Akköy one sees the last of the tufa cones and troglodyte dwellings. As the road goes over the pass at Topuz Daği (1524 metres) the landscape changes dramatically once again. One is now back on the Anatolian steppes, which appear more bleak and mournful than ever after the dramatic beauty of rocky Cappadocia. Ahead to the north looms the snow-capped massif of Erciyes Daği, the highest peak in central Anatolia (3194 metres), and around it winds the road to Kayseri.

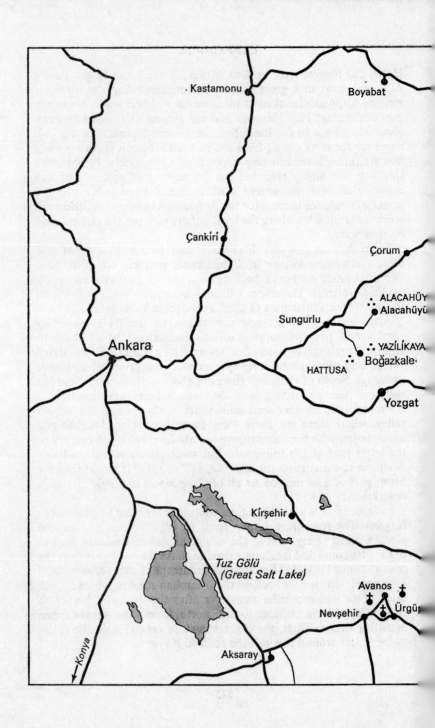

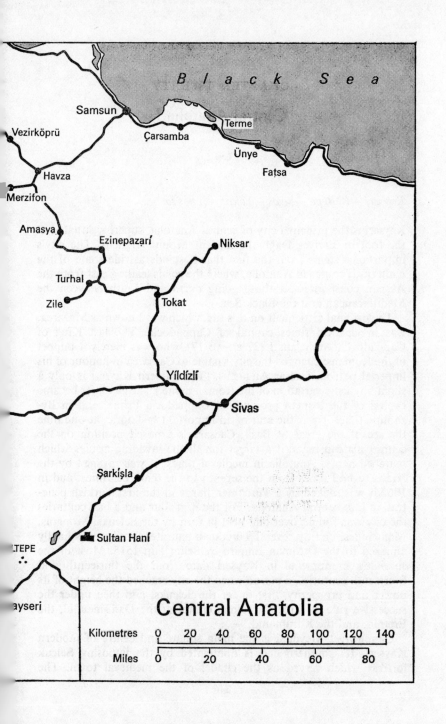

Central Anatolia

Kilometres	0	20	40	60	80	100	120	140
Miles	0		20		40		60	80

CHAPTER TWENTY

Central Anatolia I

❧

Kayseri – Kültepe – Sivas – Tokat – Amasya

Kayseri is the principal city of central Anatolia, superbly situated at the foot of Erciyes Daği, the ancient Mount Argaeus. The city's importance stems from the fact that it stands astride some of the main trade routes in Anatolia, where the roads leading east from the Aegean coast intersect those going north and south between the Mediterranean and the Black Sea.

The original settlement on this site, which was known as Mazarca, was in classical times capital of Cappadocia. The last King of Cappadocia, Archelaus I (37 BC–AD 17), who was merely a puppet of the Romans, changed the city's name to Caesarea in honour of his imperial patron, Caesar Augustus. (The modern Kayseri is only a slight linguistic variation of the Roman name.) The city later became capital of the Roman province of Cappadocia Prima, and in Byzantine times it was the seat of an important bishopric, at one time the see of the great St Basil. Caesarea's exposed position on the central plateau made it a target for all the invading armies which marched across Anatolia in medieval times: it was ravaged by the Arabs several times from the seventh to the tenth centuries, and in 1067 it was sacked by a Turcoman horde in the first Turkish penetration into central Anatolia. For the next four and a half centuries the city was fought over and held in turn by the Selcuks, Mongols, Mamelukes, and by several Turcoman emirates, until it was finally annexed to the Ottoman Empire by Selim I in 1515. Most of the surviving monuments in Kayseri date from the thirteenth and fourteenth centuries, a period when the city reached the height of its power and prosperity, first under the Selcuks, and then under the successive rule of three Turcoman emirates; the Danişmendid, the Eretnid, and the Karamanid.

Cumhuriyet Meydaní is the main square and centre of modern Kayseri. Its southern end is dominated by the imposing **Selcuk fortress** which served as the citadel of the medieval town. The citadel is remarkably well-preserved, with all nineteen of its black basalt towers still standing, one of the finest extant examples of Selcuk military architecture. Construction of the citadel was begun by Keykâvus I in 1210, the first year of his reign, and was completed in 1226 by Alâeddin Keykûbad I. The fortress was extensively repaired by Sultan Mehmet II when he took Kayseri in 1466. At that time he also built inside the citadel the mosque which bears his name.

The medieval town of Kayseri was bounded by a defence wall erected by Justinian in the first half of the sixth century. This wall followed the course of two of the main thoroughfares which radiate out from Cumhuriyet Meydaní: Istanbul Caddesi, which leads south-west to the Ankara highway, and Talas Caddesi, which runs off to the south-east. A short length of the Byzantine defence wall can still be seen near Talas Caddesi on the street which extends in a semi-circular arc between the two avenues.

Most of the important monuments in Kayseri are within the bounds of the medieval city or just outside its periphery. The most colourful part of this old quarter is the bazaar area, near the south-west gate of the citadel. The oldest of the market buildings here are the **Bedesten** and the **Vezir Haní**, Ottoman structures of the late eighteenth century. Just south of them is the **Ulu Cami**, which is thought to date to about 1140; this mosque was probably built by the Danişmendid Emir Yaghibasan, a grandson of Danişmend, the eponymous founder of the Danişmendid clan. The Danişmendid dominated Cappadocia from about 1070 till 1177, usually as allies of the Selcuks, and several cities of central Anatolia are still adorned with the fine buildings they erected.

Just south of the Ulu Cami are two monuments from the period when the Karamanid held Kayseri; these are the **Melek Gazi Medresesi** and the **Hatuniye Medresesi**, both of which were constructed in 1432.

The only important Ottoman building in Kayseri is the **Kurşunlu Cami**, which stands in Atatürk Parkí at the west side of Cumhuriyet Meydaní. This mosque was built in 1585 for Kízíl Ahmet Pasha, a brother of the famous Şemsi Pasha, two members of an old Selcuk family which retained power under the Ottomans.

The narrow streets which wind to the north from behind the Kurşunlu Cami soon bring you to the **Çifte** (Double) **Medrese**. This was founded in 1206 by Keyhûsrev I and his sister Gevher Nesibe Hatun, and is the oldest Selcuk *medrese* in Kayseri. The *medrese* consisted of a hospital and an associated medical school, the first

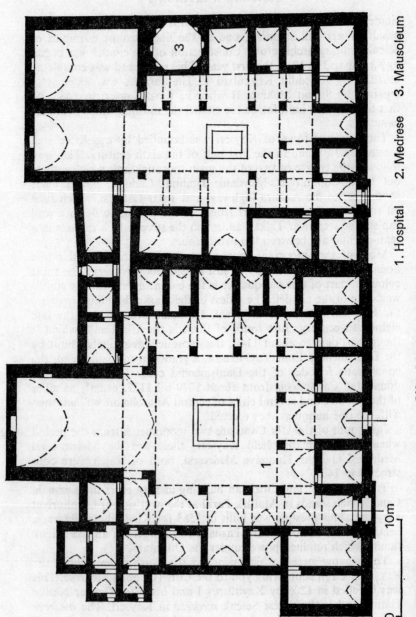

Çifte Medrese Kayseri

1. Hospital   2. Medrese   3. Mausoleum

such institution to be founded in Anatolia. The hospital occupied the building to the left as you enter, while the medical school was housed in the building to the right. The mausoleum at the far side of the medical school is undoubtedly that of the foundress, Gevher Hatun.

Turning left after leaving the *medrese* you soon come to Istasyon Caddesi, where you turn right to return to Cumhuriyet Meydaní. At the far side of the street where it reaches the square there is another fine Selcuk structure, the **Sahibiye Medresesi**. This was founded in 1268 by Sahip Ata Fahrettin Ali, the great Selcuk vezir. The *medrese* has recently been restored and there are plans to convert it into a medical clinic or student residence.

Crossing the square to its south-eastern corner and starting down Talas Caddesi you come to the **Huant** foundation, just opposite the citadel. This was the first mosque complex to be built in Anatolia by the Selcuks; it includes the mosque itself and its associated *medrese*, *türbe*, *hamam* and *çeşme*, or fountain, the last two having now almost completely vanished. The complex was founded in 1238 by Mahperi Huant Hatun, a Greek woman who became the wife of Alâeddin Keykûbad I and mother of Keyhûsrev II. The large structure set back to the right is the great mosque, whose massive outer façade gives it the appearance of a medieval fortress, and the smaller building to the left is the *medrese*. In the far right-hand corner of the *medrese* you see the *türbe* of the foundress, who is buried in a marble sarcophagus on top of a high pedestal. Until recent years the *medrese* served as an archaeological museum, but now it is used for occasional art exhibits and displays of local arts and crafts.

To reach the new archaeological museum you go about one kilometre down Talas Caddesi and turn left at the signpost. On the way you pass a number of *kümbet*, or Selcuk tombs, with distinctive conical or pyramidal roofs. Their shape is believed to be modelled on the royal tents of the Great Selcuks of Iran, though they do bear a striking resemblance to the medieval Armenian churches in the east of Turkey. The most splendid of these tombs in Kayseri is the **Döner Kümbet**, which stands on the right side of Talas Caddesi just opposite the turning to the museum. According to an inscription, the mausoleum was built for the Selcuk princess Şah Cihan Hatun; no date is given, but on stylistic grounds it has been dated to 1276. It is a twelve-sided structure built entirely of cut stone and surmounted by a conical roof resting on stalactite cornices. The *türbe* is decorated with a remarkable number of figural reliefs, including a pair of winged leopards, a griffin, and a two-headed eagle, the Selcuk symbol of royalty.

There is another *kümbet* just across the way, on the right side of the road which leads from Talas Caddesi to the museum. This is the **Sirçali Kümbet**, constructed in the middle of the fourteenth century, at a time when Kayseri was held by the Eretnid Turks. This dynasty was founded by an Uyghur Turk named Eretna, who was governor of Anatolia under the Ilkhanid Mongols. When the Ilkhanid empire was beginning to disintegrate Eretna seized the opportunity and in 1335 proclaimed an independent state in central Anatolia. The Eretnid dynasty controlled this region for only half a century, but it left as its legacy a number of fine buildings in Kayseri, Sivas, and other towns of central Anatolia. Among other buildings in Kayseri, Eretna also erected the unusual **Köşk Medrese**, which stands a little to the east of the museum, looking like a miniature fortress with its crenellated outer walls of cut stone. Eretna built this *medrese* in 1339 in memory of his wife Suli Pasha; he is believed to be buried beside her in the *türbe* that stands in the centre of the courtyard.

The attractive new **archaeological museum** is surrounded by a garden in which an impressive collection of ancient sculptures, principally monumental Hittite works, is exhibited. The most fascinating objects inside the museum are the pottery, cylinder seals, and sacred figurines from Kültepe, an archaeological site some twenty kilometres north-east of Kayseri.

At Kayseri the great Selcuk caravan route divided into two branches: one headed east to Malatya and the other north-east to Sivas, from whence it turned north-west to Amasya. The present itinerary will follow the latter route, describing a great arc through central Anatolia.

Sivas Caddesi leads off north-east from Cumhuriyet Meydaní and out on to the main Sivas road. A short distance along on the right you see the **Çifte Kümbet**, a Selcuk mausoleum consisting of an octagonal structure on a cubical plinth. Its pyramidal roof has collapsed to reveal the inner dome. According to an inscription, the tomb was built in 1243–4 for the Princess al-Malika al-Adilyya, another wife of Keykûbad I.

Some twenty kilometres out of Kayseri a turning to the left leads to **Karahüyük**, a village near the site of Kültepe. The large mound there has been identified as the **ancient Kaneş**, one of the most important settlements in Anatolia during the Bronze Age. Several palatial structures have been discovered inside the mound, along with a hoard of beautiful pottery and other artifacts, much of it dating to the period 2000–1800 BC. Even more interesting finds have been made in the lower town, which was inhabited by a colony of Assyrian traders during the same period. Apparently the Assyrians had a number of these trading colonies, or *karum*, scattered throughout central Anatolia, where they were taxed and lived under the protection of local potentates such as the King of Kaneş. The most important discoveries made at Kaneş are the cylinder seals on which these Assyrian merchants recorded the details of their commercial transactions. This is the first appearance of writing in Anatolia, and indicates that Kaneş was a centre for the spread of Mesopotamian culture among the indigenous people of the central plateau, first the Hatti and then the Hittites.

About half an hour's drive past the turn-off to Kültepe you come to the **Sultan Hanı**, the second of the two royal Selcuk caravansarais of that name. According to an inscription this was built by Alâeddin Keykûbad I during the period 1232–6, the last four years of his reign. The Sultan Hanı repeats the plan of the earlier royal caravansarai on a slightly smaller scale.

The first village of any size on the Kayseri-Sivas road, about an hour's drive beyond the Sultan Hanı, is **Şarkışla**, renowned as the birthplace and lifelong home of Aşík Veysel, the greatest folk-poet in modern Turkey. Veysel was born of a poor peasant family near Şarkışla in 1894 and lost his sight in early childhood. Nevertheless, he learned to play the *saz*, the stringed instrument which is used almost exclusively by musicians throughout Anatolia. Soon he began to compose the naive and homespun songs which make up the repertoire of the Turkish bard, the *aşík*, a tradition that goes back to the wandering folk minstrels of medieval Anatolia. The songs of Aşík Veysel were concerned with the world of the humble peasants among whom he lived, sharing their labours, their sorrows and occasional joys. And when he sang of the first nightingale in April, his cracked and wavering old voice produced that ache of joy and sadness which the song of the nightingale itself evokes, particularly in the brief beauty of an Anatolian spring. Aşík Veysel died in the spring of 1971 and was buried in the same field where his mother had given birth to him seventy-seven years before. In one of his last songs, *Kara Toprak*, the Black Earth, he sang of his devotion to the farmland which had nourished him through all his days: 'My faithful sweetheart is the black earth, for though I wounded her with my hoe and shovel, she smiled and gave me red roses; my only true love is the black earth . . .'

Beyond Şarkışla the road climbs over the passes at Yassíbel and Saylar. They are both more than 1500 metres above sea-level

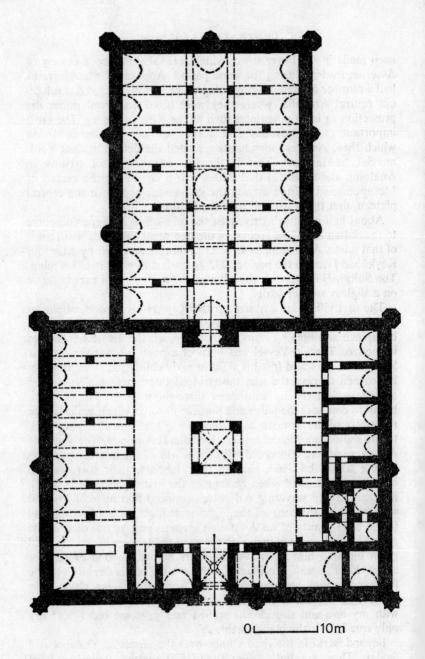

Sultan Hanî, near Kayseri

0 ⌐————————10m

but the great plateau itself is so high that you hardly notice them. The road descends and crosses the Kízíl Irmak at Kesik Köprü, after which it crosses the main highway from Ankara to Sivas. Finally you arrive in **Sivas**, the **ancient Sebasteia** of Cappadocia.

Sivas first appears in history in about 65 BC when Pompey consolidated several settlements on the Cappadocian frontier and established the Roman city of Megalopolis on this site. In the following century it was renamed Sebasteia, which in Turkish speech has been transformed to Sivas. Sivas had much the same history in medieval times as Kayseri and the other towns of Cappadocia, and during the Selcuk period it was one of the principal cities of the Sultanate of Rum, occasionally serving as the capital. Most of the important monuments in Sivas date from Selcuk times, or from the period immediately following, when the city was controlled by the Mongols or by various Turcoman emirates.

Konak Meydaní is the main square of the modern city. A monument at its western end commemorates the Sivas Congress of 1919, when Atatürk rallied his countrymen to begin what Turks proudly call the War of Independence. Most of the medieval Turkish monuments are located in the area just south of Konak Meydaní, between the square and the prominent mound known as Toprak Kale.

Taking the street which leads south from the middle of the square, you come first to the **Muzaffer Bürücirde Medresesi**. This school was founded in 1271 by the Ilkhanid Emir Muzaffer, a Persian from the town of Bürücird near Hamadan. It is a two-storeyed structure with four *eyvans*, the square tomb of the founder standing to the left of the entrance *eyvan*. On the façade of the tomb there is a frieze in faience mosaic bearing the inscription: 'This is the tomb of Muzaffer of Bürücird, the humble servant and homeless stranger. May God forgive him for his sins.'

Just to the south of this you find the **Darüşşifa of Keykâvus I**, the largest and most elaborate medical institution ever constructed by the Selcuks. Founded by Keykâvus I in 1218, it is a four-*eyvan* structure with an arcaded courtyard. The tomb of the Sultan is behind the *eyvan* to the right; it is ten-sided and was originally covered with a pyramidal brick dome, now replaced by a wooden replica. The tomb and the left-hand *eyvan* are adorned with superb brick and faience decorations.

Like the Çifte Medrese in Kayseri, the Darüşşifa of Keykâvus I was a combined hospital and medical school, and it also cared for mental patients. The Sultan's deed of foundation, which was recently discovered and published, records that music and hypnosis were among the methods used to treat the mental patients.

Directly across the street from the Darüşşifa stands the **Çifte Minare Medrese**, of which only the façade remains. The *medrese* takes its name from the pair of brick minarets which flank the monumental porch. The *medrese* was founded in 1271 by Şemsettin Cuwaymi, a vezir of the Ilkhanid Mongols.

A short walk to the south-east brings you to the **Ulu Cami**, the oldest Turkish structure in Sivas. This has little architectural distinction, just the usual vast pillared hall which the Selcuks built as the principal mosque in their large towns. According to a recently-discovered inscription, the mosque was built in 1197, at a time when Sivas was ruled by Kethuddin Melek Şah, eldest of the eleven sons of Sultan Kílíç Arslan II.

Still farther south, just to the east of Toprak Kale, is the **Gök Medrese**, the most important monument in Sivas. This was completed in 1271, one of three *medreses* built in Sivas that year, a testimony to the importance of the town in late Selcuk times. The founder was the famous Sahip Ata Fahrettin Ali, whose fine buildings have already been seen in Konya and Kayseri. Fahrettin Ali was known in his time as Abdül Khayrat, the Father of Good Works, because of the many splendid buildings with which he adorned central Anatolia. And of all these the Gök Medrese is the most magnificent. Like the other two *medreses* built in Sivas in 1271, this is a two-storeyed structure with four *eyvans*. It has the most magnificent façade in Selcuk architecture, with a monumental entrance porch flanked by twin minarets, and a pair of buttress towers at the corners decorated with reliefs. To the left of the entrance is a *çeşme*, the first in Selcuk architecture. Within there is a domed *mescit* on the right side of the entrance and a *dershane* on the left, and around the arcade two dozen rooms were arrayed in two storeys. The *mescit* and the two side *eyvans* are decorated with mixed brick and tile mosaics that constitute one of the highest achievements of Selcuk art. The harmonious design of the building, the delicate stonework on the porch and façade, and these lovely mosaics, altogether make this the most beautiful *medrese* ever built by the Selcuks.

From Sivas you drive back along the main Ankara road for about an hour, and then at Yíldízlí head north for Tokat. The road goes over the pass at Çamlíbel (1646 metres) and descends from the barren central plateau into the lush tree-clad valleys of the Pontus.

Just before the village of **Çamlíbel** there is a ruined Selcuk caravansarai to the left of the road, and about ten kilometres past the village there is another, the Çiftlik Han, also on the left. These are two of a series of caravansarais built along the Sivas-Amasya road in 1238–9 by Mahperi Hatun, mother of Keyhûsrev II. The Selcuk caravan route bypassed Tokat and headed north-west at this point, whereas the modern road makes a great loop to pass through Tokat before turning westward towards Amasya.

After Çamlíbel the road runs along the gorge of the Ak Su, a tributary of the Yeşil Irmak, the River Iris of antiquity. About ten kilometres before Tokat you see a steep eminence called Horoz Tepesi, on top of which are the ruins of an ancient fortress. This has been tentatively identified as the site of ancient Dadasa, one of the seventy-five strongholds which the Pontic kings are known to have built to protect their domains.

The modern town of **Tokat** is clustered below another of these Pontic fortresses, the **ancient Dazimon**. Dazimon guarded the southern approach to the temple-city of Comana Pontica, whose site is about ten kilometres to the north of the modern town. Comana Pontica was a sanctuary of the Great Anatolian Earth Mother, who was worshipped in the Pontus under the name of Ma. The high priests of Comana Pontica and the other Pontic temple-cities were veritable princes, ruling over a subservient community of sacred serfs, with the female votaries of the goddess serving as temple prostitutes. This undoubtedly accounted for the widespread popularity of the biennial feast of the Mother Goddess at Comana Pontica, which was a combination of market-fair and orgiastic religious festival. On these occasions the statue of the goddess – said to have been the image of Artemis brought by Orestes from the Taurians – was carried about in procession, escorted by priests, temple prostitutes and frenzied worshippers, some of whom practised flagellation and slashed themselves with knives or thrust spears into their bodies.

With the coming of Christianity the worship of the Earth Mother died out, her shrine at Comana Pontica was abandoned, and around the fortress at Dazimon there grew up the Byzantine town of Tokat. Tokat was occupied by the Danişmendid Turks in the second half of the eleventh century, and then was held in turn by the Selcuks, Mongols and Eretnid Turks before it was finally annexed to the Ottoman Empire in the latter part of the fifteenth century.

The monuments of Tokat are clustered below the southern and eastern slopes of the spectacular twin-peaked rock on which stand the ruins of the fortress of Dazimon, rebuilt in Byzantine and Ottoman times. A number of these old buildings are on Sulu Sokağí, which leads left off the main road at the town square.

Turning down Sulu Sokağí, you see on the left the **Pasha Hamamí**, founded in 1425 by Yürgüç Pasha, a vezir of Sultan Mehmet I. At the next corner on the left stands the **Ali Pasha Camii**, an Ottoman mosque built in 1573. The *türbe* of Ali Pasha is in the garden to the east of his mosque; he is believed to have been a descendant of Eretna, the eponymous founder of the Eretnid clan.

Farther on down Sulu Sokağí you see on the right a *türbe* built in 1234 by Abdül Kasim bin Ali al-Tuşi, a vezir in the reign of Alâeddin Keykûbad I. Beyond the *türbe* there are a number of old *hans* clustered around the *bedesten*, all of them dating from Ottoman times. This old market quarter is the best place to shop for the fine copper ware for which Tokat has been famous for centuries. Farther on down Sulu Sokağí and along the alleys on either side there are a number of old *hans, mescits, hamams* and tombs, ranging in date from Selcuk to Ottoman times.

Another group of monuments stands around the large square just below the steep east end of the fortress hill. On entering the square you see immediately on the left the **Voyvoda Haní**, a large market building constructed in 1631, principally for the Armenian merchants who traded here since the early days of the city. Tokat, Sivas and Kayseri all had large Armenian communities until half a century ago, but now only very few Armenians remain.

Next to the *han* stands the **Gök Medrese**, built in about 1270 by the famous Selcuk emir, Mu'in al-Din Süleyman. Its two-storeyed courtyard has two *eyvans*, with an arcade of slender columns below and sturdy piers above. Only a few patches remain of the turquoise tiles which gave the *medrese* its name ('Gök' means 'sky'). The Gök Medrese is now used as an archaeological museum for antiquities found in the surrounding area, particularly from Comana Pontica.

In the south-east corner of the *medrese* there is a funerary chamber with several cenotaphs. One of these covers the grave of the founder, who was known in his time as Pervane, or the Butterfly. This strange and exotic title was occasionally used by the Selcuks to describe the Sultan's principal adviser and minister of state, and since Mu'in al-Din Süleyman was the most powerful ever to hold that office he is better known by that name than by his own. The Pervane held that post under Ruknuddin Kílíç Arslan IV, and since the Sultan was merely a puppet of the Ilkhanid Mongols the real power remained in the hands of his chief minister. Ruknuddin bitterly resented this and the two of them finally had a violent confrontation in 1264 at a royal banquet, at the climax of which the Sultan was strangled to death, some say at the command of the Pervane. The Pervane then became regent for Ruknuddin's infant son, whom he raised to the throne as Keyhûsrev III. For the next decade the Pervane was the virtual ruler of the Selcuk Empire, trying to maintain some degree of independence under the suzerainty of the powerful Mongols. Then in 1276 the Pervane entered into a plot with Baibars, the Mameluke Sultan of Egypt, and the two of them concocted a scheme to evict the Mongols from Asia Minor and make the Pervane himself Sultan of Rum. The plan went well at first and in 1277 the Mamelukes defeated the Mongols at Elbistan, after which Baibars's troops occupied Kayseri. But then as the Mongols marched westward Baibars lost his nerve and hurriedly withdrew his army to Egypt. This left the Pervane isolated and helpless in his family seat in Tokat, where he was executed the following year by Abagha, the Ilkhan of the Mongols. Though the Pervane's possessions were confiscated by the Mongols after his death, his descendants later recovered much of the territory over which he had ruled, and reigned for a time as feudal lords of the Pontus.

Directly across the square is the **Hatuniye mosque and medrese**. This complex was founded in 1485 by Sultan Beyazit II, who dedicated it to the memory of his mother, Gülbahar Hatun. The handsome outer portal is considered to be the finest work of its type created in the fifteenth century, with a frame of alternating white and black marble and an intricate stalactite niche above.

The street at the far end of the square leads to the Amasya highway. A block beyond the square you see on the left the Sümbül Baba Zaviyesi, a small dervish oratory dating from 1291–2, and farther along on the same side is the ruined *türbe* of the Mongol Emir Nureddin Şen Timur, built in 1313. Just beyond the *türbe* the road crosses the Yeşil Irmak over a handsome Selcuk bridge built in 1250.

On the far side of the bridge a road turns right for **Niksar,** an interesting detour for those with time to spare. After about ten kilometres the road passes on the left the village of Gümenek, near which are the scanty ruins of Comana Pontica. Finally, after an hour's drive through scenic mountain country, you come to Niksar, a town on the banks of the Kelkit Çayí, the River Lycus of antiquity.

The name Niksar is a corruption of Neocaesarea, the name which in the Roman era was given to the old Pontic town of Cabeira. Cabeira was one of the principal strongholds of the Pontic kings, and the greatest of them all, Mithradates VI Eupator, had a palace and hunting park here. Some of the most important battles in the fabulous career of Mithradates (see page 259) were fought in this part of the Pontus, and he was several times besieged in the fortress of Cabeira, whose ruins still stand on a crag above the town.

Shortly after the turning to Niksar the road turns westward and runs along the valley of the Yeşil Irmak, the fertile region known in antiquity as the Dazimonitis. Twenty-six kilometres out of Tokat a left turn leads to the village of **Pazar**, where there is a particularly fine Selcuk caravansarai, the Hatun Haní. It was built in 1238–9 by Mahperi Hatun, the mother of Keyhûsrev II, and is by far the grandest of the caravansarais which she built along the road from Sivas to Amasya.

Another twenty kilometres brings one to **Turhal,** which has been identified as the ancient Pontic fortress-town of **Gaziura**. The dramatic ruins of the citadel still perch upon the rocky peak above the town; like the fortresses at Tokat and Niksar it was rebuilt by the Byzantines and the Turks in turn.

In the centre of Turhal there is a left turn leading to **Zile**, some twenty kilometres to the south. This is the site of **ancient Zela,** another fortress-town and sanctuary of the Pontic kings, with the ruins of the citadel here too brooding above the modern town.

The plain north of Zela was the scene of two great battles between the Romans and the Pontic kings. Here in 67 BC Mithradates VI Eupator annihilated an army led by Triarious, a lieutenant of Lucullus, and twenty years later on the same field Mithradates's son Pharnaces was defeated by Julius Caesar, thus ending the long and bloody Mithradatic Wars which troubled Asia Minor for half a century. Caesar's victory was won on the fifth day after he led his army into the Pontus, and was achieved after only four hours of fighting. The rapidity of Caesar's great victory was advertised in his triumphal procession in Rome, where his attendants displayed signs with the laconic legend: '*Veni, vidi, vici*!' 'I came, I saw, I conquered!'

After passing through Turhal the road goes north as far as Ezinepazar and then turns west towards Amasya. In **Ezinepazar** there are the ruins of yet another Selcuk caravansarai, founded in about 1238 by Mahperi Hatun. This was the last caravan-stop on the road from Sivas to Amasya. In those days Ezinepazar was a day's journey from Amasya by camel, whereas today it is only half an hour by car.

CHAPTER TWENTY-ONE

Central Anatolia II

❧

Amasya – Boğazkale – Yazílíkaya – Alacahüyük – Ankara

Amasya, the **ancient Amaseia**, has the most superb setting of any town in central Anatolia. Strabo, the renowned geographer of the ancient world, was born in Amaseia in 64 BC, when it was capital of the Pontic kingdom, and his description of his birthplace does justice to the grandeur of its situation:

> My native town is situated in a deep and large valley through which flows the river Iris. It has been provided in a surprising manner by art and nature for answering the purpose of a city and a fortress. For there is a lofty and perpendicular rock which overhangs the river, having on one side a wall erected close to the bank where the town has been built, while on the other it runs up on either hand to the summits of the hill. These two are connected to each other and well fortified with towers. Within this enclosure are the royal residence and the tombs of the kings.

The foundation of the Pontic Kingdom was laid early in the third century BC by an adventurer named Mithradates, a nephew of the last of the Greek tyrants of the city of Cius on the Propontis. In 302, when his uncle was executed by Antigonus, he made his escape with a few followers to the Pontic mountains and eventually established himself in the fortress of Amaseia. In the course of time he assumed the title of King, thus beginning a dynasty which was to endure for more than two centuries, ending with the death of Mithradates VI Eupator. In 70 BC, during the third and last Mithradatic War, Amaseia and Sinope surrendered to an army led by Lucullus, and before the end of the year the whole of the Pontic kingdom was in Roman hands. Some two decades later Pharnaces, a son of Mithradates VI, made an attempt to regain his father's kingdom, but his defeat by Julius Caesar at Zela in 47 BC finally ended the long and turbulent history of the Pontic kingdom.

Today Amasya is one of the loveliest of all Anatolian towns, adorned with mosques, mausolea and pious foundations built by the Danişmendid Turks, Selcuks, Mongols and Ottomans, and with old wooden houses lining the banks of the Yeşil Irmak. Most of the town lies on the right bank of the river, which is spanned by five bridges, with some of the old houses lining the left bank and clustering at the base of the steep citadel hill. The ruins of the ancient fortress still stand on the crags above, and in the cliff face below are the rupestrine tombs which Strabo describes.

The road from Tokat comes in along the right bank of the Yeşil Irmak. At the very edge of the town you see on the right the **Gök Medrese Cami**, built in 1266–7 by the Selcuk governor Turumtay. A lane leading left from the main road opposite Turumtay's *türbe* takes you to a small mosque complex on the river bank, founded in 1428 by Yürgüç Pasha, the vezir who built the Pasha Hamamí in Tokat.

On the street which runs parallel to the main road on its right there are a number of old Turkish tombs. The most ancient is the **türbe of Halifat Gazi**, which is dated to 1145–6. Halifat Gazi was vezir under Melek Gazi, the Danişmendid ruler of Amasya at the time. The founder is buried in a splendid marble sarcophagus decorated with the heads of rams and Medusas bedecked with garlands, probably taken from a necropolis of the early Christian period. There are two Ottoman tombs farther on down the main street on the left; the first of these, the Şehzadeler Türbesi, was built in 1410 and buried within it are sons of Sultans Mehmet I, Beyazit I and Beyazit II.

You now come to the **külliye of Sultan Beyazit II**, an impressive mosque complex in a large walled garden beside the river. It was built by Beyazit in fulfilment of a vow he made while governor of Amasya, when he was heir to the throne. He began the mosque when he became Sultan in 1481 and it was completed in 1486 by his son Şehzade Ahmet, who had succeeded his father as governor of Amasya.

There are a number of old Ottoman and Selcuk buildings farther on down the main street, but none is of particularly great interest. So you might be advised to continue along the right bank of the river on the embankment road, perhaps crossing to the other side on one of the five bridges.

Across the river there is a rock terrace supported by ancient walls and known locally as **Kízlar Sarayí**, or **Palace of the Maidens**; this was once the palace of the Pontic kings and it was used as a royal residence in both Byzantine and Ottoman times. Above the terrace there are three rock-cut tombs, and the entrance to a tunnel, one of three which led down from the citadel to the water supply below. Paths lead from Kízlar Sarayí to the tombs and on up to the citadel itself. Most of the present citadel walls are of Byzantine or Turkish construction, but there are the remains of two fine Hellenistic towers, probably from the Mithradatic era.

There are a number of interesting Ottoman and Selcuk monuments farther on down the river, which here makes a great S-bend first north and then north-east. Going along the right bank you first come to the **Timarhane**, or **Asylum for the Insane**, which was founded in 1308–9 by Sultan Ölceytü, Ilkhan of the Mongols, and his wife Yíldíz Hatun. During Ölceytü's reign, 1306–13, the last of the Selcuk sultans was murdered by the Mongols and the long history of the Sultanate of Rum came to an end. Nevertheless the traditional forms of Selcuk architecture continued under their successors, as in this Ilkhanid building. Just beyond the Timarhane is the Mehmet Pasha Camii, built in 1486. Its founder was regent for Şehzade Ahmet, son of Beyazit II.

Continuing on around the bend you pass the last of the five spans across the Yeşil Irmak, Kuş Köprüsü, the Bird's Bridge. Just beyond it is the handsome **Beyazit Camii**, built between 1414 and 1419 by a Grand Vezir of Mehmet I.

Across the river stands the **Kapí Ağasí Medresesi**, which was founded in 1488 by Hüseyin Ağa, Chief White Eunuch in the reign of Beyazit II. Hüseyin Ağa founded several other institutions in Amasya and elsewhere in the Ottoman Empire, and it was he who converted the church of SS Sergius and Bacchus in Istanbul into the mosque of Küçük Aya Sofya.

At Amasya you must inevitably make a choice about the itinerary for the remainder of your journey through Anatolia. Those with plenty of time at their disposal can continue north from Amasya to Samsun, and from there follow the Black Sea coast out to Trabzon or Rize. From the coast one can then drive right across the east of Anatolia to Lake Van, and then head back across the Arab border-lands of Turkey to the Mediterranean. Alternatively, those with more limited time can drive from Amasya to Ankara and thence to Istanbul. The remainder of the present chapter and the subsequent one will follow the latter itinerary, while the last five chapters in the book describe the long journey along the Black Sea coast and around the eastern and southern borders of Turkey.

The first leg of the journey to Ankara is an hour's drive westward to Çorum, a large industrial town of no interest to the traveller.

From there you take highway 41 south-west to **Sungurlu**, a good base for seeing the archaeological sites at Boğazkale, Yazílíkaya and Alacahüyük. All three sites are approached by the road which turns off towards Yozgat just before Sungurlu. Driving down this road you see on the left a turn-off for Alacahüyük; Boğazkale is thirteen kilometres farther on down the Yozgat road; while to reach Yazílíkaya you drive a kilometre or so past Boğazkale and then turn left on to a dirt road and drive another four kilometres. One should plan the itinerary so as to be in Yazílíkaya some time between 11 a.m. and 1 p.m., for then the reliefs on the walls of the rock sanctuary can be seen to best advantage. If you start from Sungurlu quite early you can see Boğazkale and Yazílíkaya in the morning and early afternoon, and perhaps in the late afternoon have time to stop at Alacahüyük on the way back.

The modern village of **Boğazkale** (formerly Boğazköy) stands near the **site of Hattusa**, the capital of the ancient realm of the Hittites. The story of the discovery of this city and the great empire of which it was capital is one of the most remarkable chapters in the history of archaeology. A century ago the Hittites were virtually unknown, save for some references in the Old Testament; there they were described as one of the tribes that the Israelites found inhabiting Palestine when they entered the Promised Land. Later, when the historical records of the Egyptians were deciphered, it was revealed that the pharaohs of the eighteenth dynasty had been in contact with a country called Kheta, and it was established that the people of Kheta and the Hittites of the Old Testament were one and the same. Further support to this view was given when the cuneiform inscriptions of Assyria began to be deciphered, and it was found that the region inhabited by these people was known as 'The Land of Hatti', the indigenous Bronze Age Anatolians from whom the Hittites took their name.

The ruins at Boğazköy (as it was then known) were discovered in 1834 by Charles Texier, whose text and drawings provided the first description of the distinctive monumental rock sculptures which have since become the hallmark of the Hittites. As Texier wrote at that time: 'The grandeur and the peculiar nature of the ruins perplexed me extraordinarily when I attempted to give the city its historical name.' Later in that century other travellers discovered similar sculptures all over Anatolia and northern Syria, along with peculiar hieroglyphs which were eventually identified as Hittite, the earliest Indo-European language then known in Anatolia. Excavations at Boğazköy began in 1906 under Hugo Winckler and soon after resulted in the discovery of about ten thousand cuneiform tablets. During the subsequent half-century these and the hieroglyphic inscriptions were deciphered, and today the history and culture of the Hittites are known almost as well as those of the other great civilizations of the ancient Near East.

The first evidence of permanent human occupation on the site dates to about 2500 BC, when a settlement was established on and below Büyükkale, the rocky plateau south-east of Boğazkale. The first settlers were a very advanced Bronze Age people whom the Akkadians called Hatti, and the whole of the Anatolian plateau was known to them as 'The Land of Hatti'. Assyrian merchants established a trading colony there in about 1900 BC, at about the same time as they set up their *karum* in Kültepe. In the middle of the seventeenth century BC the lands of Hatti were conquered by a warlike people from southern Europe or the Caucasus. These invaders, who in time came to be known as the Hittites, established themselves in Hattusa and adopted much of the culture of their predecessors.

The later Hittite rulers liked to trace their lineage back to the first king at Hattusa, Labarnas, and with him therefore Hittite history may be said to have begun. Labarnas died in about 1650 BC and was succeeded by his son, Labarnas II, who changed his name to Hattusili, 'the Man from Hattusa'. Thus began the period which historians call that of the Old Kingdom, when the Hittites expanded to the south and east, capturing Aleppo and Babylon early in the sixteenth century BC. Later in that century an outbreak of civil war and anarchy caused the Hittites to lose much of their conquered territory. In 1525 Telipinus came to the throne and restored stability to the kingdom, recovering the lost domains of his ancestors. When he died in 1500 BC, an event which historians mark as the end of the Old Kingdom, the Hittites were the dominant power in Anatolia.

The death of Telipinus was followed by nearly half a century of unrest and anarchy, but this came to an end when Tudhaliyas II came to the throne in 1460 BC, beginning the dynasty which created the Hittite Empire. The Hittite Empire reached its greatest extent during the reign of Mursilis II (1353–20 BC), when it extended from the Aegean to beyond the Tigris and from northern Anatolia to Palestine. But in the middle of the following century the fortunes of the Empire declined, as new and aggressive nations began to rise in Anatolia and the East, challenging the supremacy of the Hittites. Then around 1200 BC there took place the great migration of warlike peoples from the north which was to destroy the old regimes of the late Bronze Age, the Hittites among them. In Anatolia, to judge from archaeology and legend, the Phrygians soon replaced the Hittites as the dominant power, settling in the charred ruins of Hattusa and making it one of their principal cities.

Although after 1200 BC the great Hittite Empire was no more, a ghost of Hittite civilization lingered on for another five centuries in Syria and in south-eastern Anatolia. The Hittite language and culture survived there in the dozen or so petty kingdoms whose inhabitants were called Hittites by their neighbours, though it is unlikely that they were ethnic Hittites at all. Their principal cultural contributions were their monumental stone sculptures in what has come to be called the Neo-Hittite style, outstanding examples of which are on display in Ankara, in the Museum of Anatolian Cultures.

These Neo-Hittite kingdoms were eventually absorbed by the Assyrians, and gradually the old language and culture of the Hittites disappeared. By the sixth century BC, when the Greeks first began to travel in the ancient lands of Hatti, the very existence of the Hittites was unknown in the region which they had ruled for half a millennium. And by the beginning of the Christian era Hattusa was little more than a remote village clustering around the ancient fortress, to be totally forgotten until its rediscovery in the nineteenth century.

The ruins of Hattusa are about three hundred metres east of Boğazkale, a vast assemblage of limestone blocks laid out in a regular but asymmetrical grid pattern. This has been identified as the Great Temple, a sanctuary dedicated to the Weather God Teshub of Hatti and his consort the Sun Goddess Hebut of Arinna. The temple was started in the fourteenth century BC, perhaps during the reign of Suppiluliumas I, and was completed in about 1250, just half a century or so before the collapse of the Hittite Empire. The main entrance to the temple was near its southern end, where some huge blocks remain of the propylon and the sentry rooms which stood on either side. During religious festivals the Hittite king and queen led their subjects in procession through this gate, passing into the vestibule and then the hall which surrounds the sanctuary proper. Around this hall there is an array of more than eighty rooms. Because of the downward slope of the ground from south to north there were two floors on the west, south and east sides and three at the northern end, making this perhaps the largest sanctuary ever constructed in Bronze Age Anatolia. These chambers seem to have served mainly as storerooms and archives, as evidenced by the discovery there of thousands of cuneiform tablets and a large number of *pithoi*, huge storage jars similar to those found at Knossos and Mycenae.

The king and queen entered the inner temple through a monumental gate building at its southern end, passing from there into a large inner courtyard ending in a portico. At the far right-hand corner of the courtyard there are the remains of a small pavilion which is believed to have housed a sacred font where the royal pair paused to perform their ritual ablutions before entering the holy of holies. The inner sanctum consisted of twelve chambers in an annexe at the northern end of the central building, with the two largest rooms dedicated to the worship of the two deities. The sanctuary of the Weather God Teshub is thought to have been in the room to the left and that of the Sun Goddess Hebut on the right, where you see a stone base which probably supported her golden cult statue.

More recent excavations on the south-western side of the main temple have revealed a second temple complex, separated from the main temple by a wide street. This consists of a congeries of nearly a hundred rooms around a central courtyard. It is known as the House of Services and is believed to have been used by the various functionaries of the temple and by the artisans and workers of the household staff.

The Hittite kings resided in the fortified acropolis on **Büyükkale**, the site of one of the original Hatti settlements. The modern road leads up from the temple to the south-western corner of the citadel, where the city walls merged into the massive fortifications of the acropolis. The walls of the citadel and the structures on the acropolis date from the fourteenth and thirteenth centuries BC, the height of the Hittite Empire. The main gate to the citadel was here at the south-western corner, where one passed into a forecourt at the lowest level of the acropolis. This part of the citadel was the centre of the administrative and household services of the palace, while the upper part of the acropolis was normally reserved for the private residence of the royal family.

From the citadel on Büyükkale the road leads up to what was once the upper city on the slope of the hill. A short way along you see on your left the scanty remains of the **Southern Citadel**, a Hittite fortress of the fourteenth century BC, and on your right a rocky spur known as **Nişantepe**. On the east face of Nişantepe is a ten-line hieroglyphic inscription eight and a half metres in length, the longest Hittite inscription ever discovered. Unfortunately most of the inscription is badly weathered and only the beginning of the first line has been deciphered, revealing the name of King Suppiluliumas.

Some two hundred metres south-west of Nişantepe there is another fortress-rock called **Sari Kale**, and three hundred metres beyond that in the same direction still another called **Yenice Kale**. Both of these have remains of well-built Hittite walls of the thirteenth century BC.

Beyond Nişantepe the road climbs up to the **King's Gate**, one of the three principal portals in the defence walls which formed a great arc around the southern part of the upper city. The gate takes its name from the imperious figure on the left jamb of the inner gate; it is a concrete cast of the original, which is now in the Museum of Anatolian Cultures in Ankara. The figure was once thought to represent a Hittite warrior-king but now it is known to be the Weather God Teshub. He is shown here wearing a short kilt and a conical helmet, holding a battle axe in one hand and with a scimitar stuck in his belt, a formidable warrior who is obviously here to guard the gate to Hattusa. The double gate itself is an impressive structure, particularly the enormous stone monoliths which make up its paraboloidal door jambs, still standing to about half their original height.

South-east of the King's Gate are the remains of four temples of the fourth century BC. All are variants of the same basic plan of the Great Temple, a congeries of outer rooms surrounding a central courtyard and with the inner sanctuary or cult-room in the back. It is not known to whom the temples were dedicated.

The second of the three gateways is the **Sphinx Gate**, at the southern extremity of the walls. It receives its name from the figures of sphinxes which flanked the inner portal; one of these is now in the Archaeological Museum in Istanbul, a second is in Berlin, and the fragments of a third are still visible *in situ*. The door jambs of the gate are also made of large stone blocks forming a paraboloidal arch standing to about half the original height. One remarkable element of the fortifications here is the perfectly-preserved tunnel which has been dug under the gate in a straight descending line through the slope of the hill; it is seventy-one metres long and is twelve metres below the ground where it passes under the walls, an impressive engineering feat for the thirteenth century BC. It was used by the Hittites as a sally-port, enabling them to make surprise forays outside the walls in time of siege, and allowing them to attack the enemy at the gates from the rear.

The third gate is near the western extremity of the walls; like the other two it is a double gate with paraboloidal archways. This is the **Lion Gate**, so called because of the talismanic lions on the outer door jambs, sculptured with their head and forequarters emerging from the stone. These ferocious beasts were designed to frighten away invaders and ward off evil spirits from the city. They are very striking figures indeed, and evoke something of the atmosphere of the wondrous Bronze Age world of war and magic.

The sanctuary of **Yazílíkaya** is two kilometres north-east of Boğazkale, far outside the area of ancient Hattusa; nevertheless it was one of the most important shrines of the city in the latter days of the Hittite Empire. This is a natural rock sanctuary in front of which a temple complex was built at various times in the thirteenth century BC. The sanctuary consists of two natural clefts in a cluster of rocky spurs; these are the Large Gallery on the left and the Small Gallery on the right. Both are decorated with nearly a hundred figures in low relief, mostly depicting the multitudinous gods of the Hittite pantheon.

The left wall in the **Large Gallery** shows a procession of gods and the right wall depicts a similar procession of goddesses, sixty-three deities in all. The two lines meet at the junction of the side walls with the north end of the gallery. The gods wear pointed conical helmets, are dressed in kilts or sometimes in long cloaks, and wear the characteristic Hittite boots with turned-up toes; many of them are armed with a scimitar or a mace or a simple club. The celestial rank of the various gods can be determined by the number of horns attached to their helmets, ranging from a single horn for a minor godling up to six for such powerful heavenly monarchs as the Storm God or the Weather God. The goddesses have long braided hair and wear trailing robes with belted cloaks. Their distinctive head-dress is that which the Greeks would call the *polos*, a cylindrical turban-like crown with crenellated edges. At the meeting place of the gods on the north wall you see on the left the Weather God Teshub standing on the crowned peaks of the deified mountains Nanni and Hazzi, while behind him in similar posture is the Storm God of Hattusa. On the right the procession is led by the Sun Goddess Hebut of Arinna, who is shown standing on a panther and greeting her husband. Behind her on another panther is her son, the god Sharruma, the only male deity in the procession of goddesses, and behind him are two deities presumed to be daughters of Hebut, standing lightly on the wing tips of a double-headed eagle.

The most outstanding relief in the Large Gallery is a large and well-preserved portrait of an imperial figure, located just behind the procession of goddesses on the right-hand wall. This robed figure wears a round cap, the costume of a Hittite king when acting as a high priest. He is standing on the peaks of two pomegranate-like mountains, holding in his left hand an inverted shepherd's crook

and with his right hand holding aloft the winged sun-disc, symbol of
the divine Hittite kingship. He has been identified as King Tudhaliyas
IV (1250–20 BC), and it is thought that the magnificent reliefs in this
gallery were commissioned either by him or by his father, Hattusili
III (1275–50 BC).

A recently discovered text has now strengthened the belief that
this sanctuary was where the Hittites celebrated their principal
religious festival, that of the New Year, which coincided with the
beginning of spring and the return of the sun.

> In honour of the Weather God at the beginning of the New Year a
> great festival of heaven and earth was celebrated. All the gods
> assembled and entered into the house of the Weather God.
> Whichever god harbours anger in his soul shall chase the evil
> anger from his soul. Now eat at this feast, drink! Satisfy your
> hunger and quench your thirst. Hail to the King and Queen!
> Hail to the Heaven and Earth and the grain!

The **Small Gallery** is also adorned with a number of well-preserved
reliefs. At the entrance there are the reliefs of two talismanic figures
guarding the sanctuary, winged lion-daemons straight from a
Hittite nightmare. On the left wall there is a line of twelve gods
armed with raised scimitars, quaint figures looking as if they were
marching quick-step into battle. On the right wall there is a strange
figure with the head and shoulders of a god and a body made up of a
composite of four lions, while the lower part of the figure tapers into
a double-edged blade with a distinct midrib – the so-called Dagger-
God.

Behind the Dagger-God there is a relief showing the god Sharruma
holding in close embrace a Hittite king who has been identified as
Tudhaliyas IV. The dominant position of this superb relief suggests
that Tudhaliyas IV was the founder of this sanctuary, which is
believed to have been a shrine dedicated to deified Hittite kings.
Tudhaliyas, the last but one of the Hittite kings, is thought to have
been elevated to the status of a god in his own lifetime, which ended
just a few years before the fall of Hattusa and the final collapse of
the Empire.

If there is time you should stop at **Alacahüyük** on the way back to
Sungurlu or Ankara, for although the site is far less impressive than
Boğazkale it has a special place in the history of Anatolian art.

As you come into the hamlet of Alacahüyük you will see on your
left the Sphinx Gate, which was the principal entrance to the ancient
city. The sphinxes themselves are original, as is the relief on the

base of the one on the right showing a goddess supported by a double-headed eagle with a brace of hares in his claws. The interesting orthostat reliefs on either side are all from the period of the Hittite Empire (1450–1200 BC), although the origins of the city go back to the Late Chalcolithic Age, that is, to about 3000 BC. The city seems to have reached its peak in the Early Bronze Age (*c.* 2500–2000 BC), as evidenced by the magnificent works of art which have been found there from that period. Some of these are exhibited in the museum on the site, but the most important are housed in the Ankara Museum: the extraordinary and mysterious standards with stags, bulls and sun-discs, the golden banquet ware, jewellery and ornaments, the haunting silver statuettes of slender goddesses – veritable Bronze Age Madonnas – together give the picture of an extraordinarily advanced civilization with superb taste and artistic sense, a culture which had flourished on this site for more than a thousand years before the Hittites ever set foot in the land of Hatti.

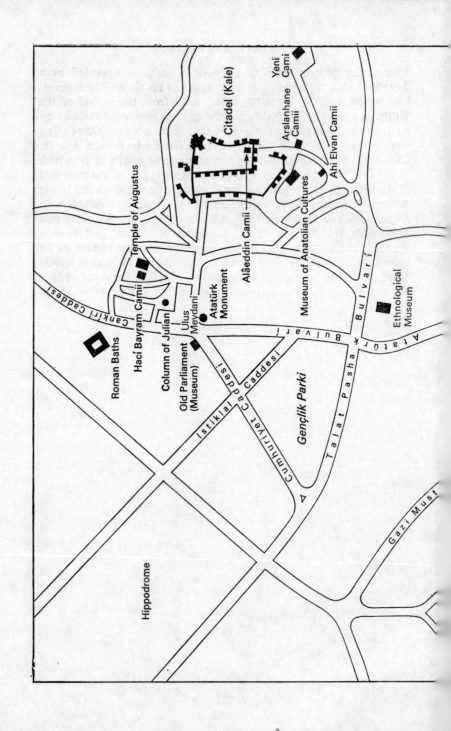

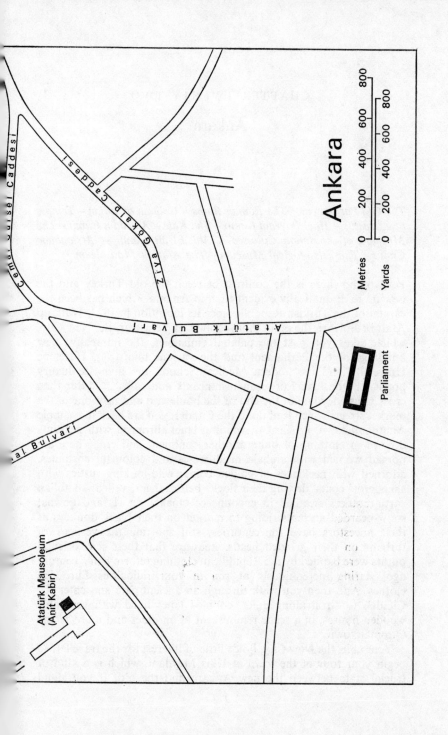

Ankara

Metres 0   200   400   600   800
Yards   0   200   400   600   800

Cemal Gürsel Caddesi

Ziya Gökalp Caddesi

Atatürk Bulvarı

...al Bulvarı

Parliament

Atatürk Mausoleum
(Anıt Kabir)

CHAPTER TWENTY-TWO

Ankara

❧

The Old Parliament – The Roman Baths – Column of Julian – Temple of Augustus – Hacı Bayram Camii – The Kale – Alâeddin Camii – The Museum of Anatolian Cultures – Ahi Elvan Camii – Arslanhane Camii – The Ethnological Museum – The Atatürk Mausoleum

Perhaps nowhere is the contrast between the old Turkey and the new more dramatically evident than in Ankara, which has been the capital of the Turkish Republic since its inception in 1923. Walk up Atatürk Bulvarí, the main thoroughfare of Yenişehir, the New City, which takes you past the palatial embassies, the impressive new buildings of the Parliament and the various ministries, Hacetepe University and its modern Medical School, the high-rise luxury hotels, the de luxe European restaurants and cafés . . . But then cross Ulus Meydaní at the end of the boulevard and take one of the market streets which lead up to the Citadel: you are back in a simple Anatolian town, its narrow, winding lanes thronged with peasants dressed in clothing of quite another continent and era. There are nomad women with archaic headdresses and colourful costumes, adorned with necklaces of golden coins; wild-looking rustics with shepherds' coats, driving their flocks before them; veiled Anatolian earth-mothers swathed in cocoons of cloaks, shawls and gowns; snow-bearded ancients riding to market on their black donkeys as their ancestors have for centuries, still sporting the vestiges of turbans on their grizzled heads, unaware that their semi-oriental outfits were banned by the Republican clothing reform half a century ago, staring incredulously at *you* in your ridiculous European clothes. And then you walk through an ancient gate and enter the Citadel, to stroll along quiet, cobbled lanes lined with venerable wooden houses, in a scene reminiscent of an older and more serene Ottoman town.

Yenişehir, the New City, holds little of interest for the traveller, so begin your tour of the town at Ulus Meydaní, which is a kind of trucial state between the new Ankara and the old. If you stand

facing north along the boulevard you will see on your right a large
equestrian statue of Atatürk, and on the corner at the left the **Old
Parliament**, now a museum. Most foreign visitors ignore the Old
Parliament, if indeed they are even aware of its existence, but it is
more interesting than some of Ankara's more famous monuments.
For in this dowdy little building the modern Turkish state was
formed, beginning with the first meeting of the Grand National
Assembly there on 23 April 1920. Over the next three and a half
years this was the scene of some of the most important events in
modern Turkish history, culminating on 29 October 1923 when the
Turkish Republic was founded with Atatürk as its first President
and Ismet Inönü as Prime Minister. The Grand National Assembly
met here until 1925, when it moved to a larger and grander edifice
(now the headquarters of CENTO, the Central Treaty Organization)
a little way down Cumhuriyet Caddesi. Across the street from the
second Parliament Building is the **Ankara Palas**, the city's oldest
hotel and still its grandest, although one wag claims that it looks
like the palace of a Kurdish general. This is where Atatürk and his
associates talked and drank through the night in those turbulent
early years of the Republic, the legends of which are still passed
on in the sumptuous bar room.

Begin your tour of old Ankara by walking north up Çankírí
Caddesi, the continuation of Atatürk Bulvarí. A five-minute walk
along the left side of the avenue brings you to the ancient **Roman
baths**. The entrance opens on to a large field lined with fragments of
marble columns, pedestals, and an occasional piece of statuary.
This was the palaestra or exercise-ground, a colonnaded portico
which enclosed a large area just to the north of the baths themselves.
Only the lower walls and a few shattered arches remain from the
baths, nevertheless you can easily make out their general structure.
From the palaestra one entered the *frigidaria*, or cold rooms, which
consisted of a swimming pool on the left and dressing rooms to the
right. Then one passed into a series of *tepidaria*, or warm rooms,
which occupied most of the central area of the baths, and finally on
to the *caldarium*, or steam room, which was probably at the far left
corner. The low brick columns you see in this area supported the
floor of the baths and allowed hot air to circulate from the furnace
and heat the *tepidaria* and *caldarium* from below. Coins found on the
site indicate that the baths were built in the reign of Caracalla
(AD 212–17) and remained in use for three centuries thereafter.
There are also a number of ancient funerary stelae scattered around
behind the baths. One of them bears the proud name of Deiotarius,

King of the Gauls, who ruled over the combined Galatian tribes before the region was annexed as a province by Rome in 25 BC.

The other monuments of Roman Ankara are only a short distance away; to find them you walk back down Çankírí Caddesi and take the second left on to Armutlu Sokak. At the end of this street you come to a square in whose centre stands a brick column surmounted by a Roman capital on which sits a stork's nest. It is thought, though without definite evidence, that this column was built in honour of the Emperor Julian the Apostate, who passed through Ankara in the summer of 362, in the last year of his brief but memorable life. Perhaps the Galatians of Ankara, whom St Paul in earlier times had criticized as unfaithful Christians, were celebrating Julian's restoration of pagan practices in the Roman Empire. As Libianus of Antioch wrote, rejoicing under the rule of Julian, his former pupil: 'The blood flows once more across the deserted altars, and the gods honoured with practices which old men scarcely remembered . . . and the Romans could again attempt great things.' Julian would probably be amused to know that his column is known locally as the **Minaret of Belkis, the Queen of Sheba**.

Leaving the square at its upper end you turn right and then left on to Bayram Sokak; this soon brings you to the ruins of the **Temple of Augustus**, the most impressive of Ankara's ancient monuments. The temple was built during the years 25–20 BC, just after Augustus had made Ancyra (as it was then called) the provincial capital of Galatia, and it was dedicated to the newly formed cult of *Roma et Augustus*. On the walls of the temple you can still see an inscription in both Greek and Latin; this is the famous *Res Gestae Divi Augusti*, literally *The Achievements of the Deified Augustus*. The *Res Gestae* is a political autobiography of the Emperor and was completed by him on 11 May AD 14. The record was deposited with the vestal virgins until his death one hundred days later; then, by direction of the Roman Senate, it was carved on bronze tablets outside the Emperor's mausoleum and inscribed on the walls of every temple of Augustus throughout the Empire. The copy on the temple in Ankara is the only one which has survived more or less completely, and is a primary source of information about the Augustan Age. The *Res Gestae* begins with this preamble: 'Subjoined is a copy made of the exploits of the deified Augustus, by which he brought the whole world under the empire of the Roman people . . .' Among the many imperial exploits recorded in the inscription is listed a census which Augustus ordered in the year 8 BC. This is the very census of which Luke writes in his Gospel, causing Joseph to journey to Bethlehem with Mary for the enrolment.

The Temple of Augustus was converted into a Christian church in about the fifth century AD, at which time the apse of alternating courses of brick and stone was built at the far end of the structure. Then in the first half of the fifteenth century it was converted into a *medrese* attached to the adjacent Hací Bayram Camii. Today its ruins are inhabited only by a tramp and his dog, who live in a cave in what was once the crypt of the Byzantine church.

The **Mosque of Hací Bayram** was originally built in 1427 but was heavily restored in the eighteenth century. It is named after Hací Bayram Veli, who is buried in a *türbe* just in front of the mosque. This holy man was the founder in Ankara of the Bayrami order of dervishes, and for more than five centuries he has been venerated as Ankara's favourite Moslem saint. Evliya Efendi made a pilgrimage to Hací Bayram's *türbe* on his return from a campaign in Persia in 1647, and tells this fabulous story about the saint:

> In his youth he was once invited by a cunning woman, who in order to seduce the Saint, with whom she was in love, began to praise his hair, beard, brows and eyelashes. The Saint retired into a corner and prayed to God that he might be delivered of these four inducements to lust, and become of an ugly form; he then returned without a hair into the woman's presence, who was so shocked at his ugliness that she had him turned out of doors by her maidens. Hence the descendants of the Saint by his daughter actually wear short beards.

After leaving the mosque walk back along Bayram Sokak and turn left on Hisar Parkí Caddesi, the next main thoroughfare. This brings you to a flight of steps which leads up between the outer and inner walls of the **Kale**, the medieval **Citadel**. The main body of the defence walls dates to the Byzantine period, although there has been substantial reconstruction in Turkish times. Inscriptions on the walls commemorate their construction by Michael the Sot in 859, but it is thought that the original fortifications may have been built by the Emperor Heraclius, perhaps after he recaptured the city from the Persians in 630. And indeed the acropolis must have been fortified since the beginning of the city's history, since Ancyra stood astride one of the main east-west highways of Asia Minor, and many great generals and emperors have marched their armies past this place: Croesus and Cyrus in 546 BC, Xerxes in 481 BC, Alexander the Great in 333 BC, to be followed in turn by Gauls, Romans, Persians, Arabs, Turks, Crusaders and Mongols. A few miles to the north-east of the city one can still see the battlefield where Pompey defeated Mithradates the Great in 63 BC, effectively eliminating Rome's last rival power. And on the same field, on 28 July 1402, Tamerlane and his Mongol hordes crushed the armies of Sultan Beyazit the Thunderbolt, temporarily halting the advance of the Ottoman Turks into Europe and prolonging the life of the Byzantine Empire for another half-century. Today the Kale is the quietest and most peaceful quarter of old Ankara, its labyrinthian alleyways lined with Ottoman houses of the last century. Here and there fragments of ancient columns and capitals serve as doorsteps, well-heads, window-frames or parts of a retaining wall.

The main gate from the inner Citadel is at its southern end. As you approach it you see on your right **Alâeddin Camii**, one of the three surviving Selcuk mosques in the city. It was built in 1178, during the reign of Sultan Izzeddin Kílíç Arslan II, but was much restored during Ottoman times. The elaborately carved *mimber* remains from the original mosque, and is a fine example of the Selcuk wood-work of that period.

You now pass through the South Gate, a double portal guarded by two huge towers connected by a high curtain wall. Embedded in this wall are an astonishing variety of re-used marble fragments, including a row of garlanded Roman altars resting on four recumbent statues of Priapus, the Roman god of male procreation. A short distance farther on you leave the outer Citadel through the Hisar Gate. Turning right, you head downhill along Gözcü Sokaǧí, and soon you see below the domes of the **Bedesten**, one of the landmarks of old Ankara.

The Bedesten was built in the years 1464–71 by Mahmut Pasha, the greatest of Fatih's Grand Vezirs; it has been beautifully restored in recent years and now serves as the **Museum of Anatolian Cultures**. This is certainly one of the most interesting museums of antiquities in the world, and a visit here must be considered one of the high points in any trip to Turkey. The Museum houses a quite extraordinary collection of antiquities and works of art, all superbly displayed in an unusual setting, covering virtually the entire span of time from the classical period back as far as the dawn of human culture. All of these antiquities have been unearthed in Turkey itself, many of them in recent times, and represent discoveries which have immensely extended our knowledge of the beginnings and development of civilization in the Near East.

One should begin a tour of the Museum by turning right at the entrance, for the exhibits are arranged chronologically, beginning at the far end of the north hall. The first exhibit you see, on the left, contains a collection from the **Palaeolithic Period** (i.e. prior to about 7000 BC); these include the skull of a Neanderthal man and some primitive stone implements and weapons. Most of these objects were found in a cave at Karain, some twenty-seven kilometres north-west of Antalya, where the earliest known wall paintings in Anatolia were also discovered.

You now enter the long west hall, the first section of which is devoted to finds from the **Neolithic Period** (*c.* 7000–5500 BC). The most interesting exhibit here is a reconstructed sanctuary house from Çatal Hüyük; here you see the earliest known examples of hand-made pottery, as well as frescoes whose designs have been likened to those on modern Anatolian *kilims.* Notice too the fresco of the kissing leopards and the ritual bull horns suspended on the walls of this adobe-like house. On the wall just beyond the sanctuary are displayed other frescoes discovered at Çatal Hüyük, the most striking of which shows tiny, naked hunters stalking a huge red bull. Apparently these frescoes were part of an early Anatolian rite of hunting magic. Also displayed in this section are several clay figurines of the Anatolian Earth Mother, with her enormous breasts, thighs and buttocks, the steatopygous type of which peasant exemplars can still be seen in the market streets of modern Ankara. One statuette of the goddess shows her seated between a pair of guardian lions, the earliest representation of the female procreative deity as Mistress of Animals, forerunner of the Anatolian Cybele, the Phrygian Kubaba, the Greek Artemis, the Roman Diana, and, ultimately, the Christian Virgin Mary.

Walking down the west hall you go forward in time into the **Chalcolithic Period** (*c.* 5500–3000 BC). Here again you see numerous figurines of the Mother Goddess, as well as painted pottery, stone tools and weapons. Most of these objects are from the sites at Hacílar, Canhasan, Alíşar and Alacahüyük.

Continuing into the second half of the west hall you come upon the splendours of the early **Bronze Age** (*c.* 3000–2000 BC). Most of the objects here are from the royal tombs at Alacahüyük, including golden pitchers, goblets and jewellery, the most beautiful of which is a golden headband in openwork design – perhaps once the diadem of an Anatolian queen. But the most extraordinary objects here are those which are thought to have been used as ritual standards in funerary rites. Some of them are in the form of bronze 'sun-discs', others are topped with the bronze figurines of stags with designs inlaid in silver. Figurines of the Mother Goddess appear here too, but now she has become as slim as a nymphette, particularly in the Hasanoğlan statuette, where her body is made of electrum, her face is encased in a golden mask, and her tiny breasts are covered with golden sheaths. And in another figurine from Alacahüyük she has taken on the stylized violin-form by which she was represented in the Aegean Isles during the Bronze Age. The Mother Goddess, if indeed it is really she, takes on even more stylized and unrealistic forms in the idols found in Alişar and exhibited at the far end of the west hall. The marble statuettes there represent her with a flat, flask-like body with one, two, or even three snake-like heads set on long necks – altogether weird and unbelievable, but evoking a feeling for the primitive origins of this ancient fertility symbol.

You now turn into the south hall, the first half of which is devoted to objects found in the **Assyrian** *karum* at Kültepe, all dating to the period 1950–1750 BC. Among the interesting exhibits here are tablets written in old Assyrian cuneiform, the earliest writings ever discovered in Anatolia. The pottery from Kültepe is the most unusual in the Museum, particularly the rhytons, or libation vases, which are made in the form of fantastic animals and birds. They include the oldest known examples of wheel-made pottery, dating to about 2000 BC. Here too you see a dirk inscribed with the name of Anitta, King of Kussara, from whom the rulers of the Old Hittite Kingdom were descended. Anitta was the author of the oldest known Hittite inscription, a *res gestae* of his reign beginning with this preface: 'Anitta, son of Pithana, King of Kussara; he was beloved of the Weather God of the Sky . . .' And with that phrase one comes to the beginning of recorded history in Anatolia.

The far end of the south hall contains antiquities from the **Old Hittite Kingdom** (*c*. 1700–1450 BC). The first object one notices is the large Inandík vase, discovered in 1967 by Raci Temizer, director of the Museum. The figures in painted relief around the vase depict what appears to be a wedding procession, showing priests, singers, musicians and celebrants, as well as a rather interesting act of sodomy. Farther along the hall are two large rhytons in the form of red bulls; these were discovered in recent years at Boğazkale and represent Seris and Hurris, the divine bulls who pulled the celestial chariot of the Weather God. At the end of the south hall there is a stele inscribed in Hittite hieroglyphics, also from Boğazkale. The history of the Old Hittite Kingdom has been derived almost entirely from such inscriptions, principally the Text of Telipinus. This was the *res gestae* of Labarnas, the first Hittite king, beginning with this preamble: 'Thus speaks Labarnas Telipinus, the Great King!' And after a long and often exciting account of his exploits and his tribulations the old king concludes with these mournful words, a last will and testament addressed to his son Mursilis: 'Thou shalt wash my dead body according to the custom. Hold me to your heart, and embracing me, lay me in the earth.'

From here you turn back and enter the central hall, which is almost completely devoted to an exhibition of monumental Hittite sculpture. This is mostly in the form of orthostatic reliefs which were carved on the lower blocks of palaces, temples and city walls. There are also several free-standing statues, usually monstrous representations of lions or sphinxes which guarded the city gates to frighten away enemies. These sculptures cover a span of more than eight centuries, beginning with the period of the Hittite Empire (*c*. 1450–1200 BC) and extending through the Late Hittite Period (*c*. 1200–700 BC).

The most interesting works from the **Empire Period** are reliefs from Alacahüyük: a king and queen offering libations to a sacred bull, three priests in adoration, and a scene showing a juggler, a musician and an acrobat performing at a court festival. The huge pair of sphinxes in this section are copies of those which flank the Sphinx Gate at Alacahüyük. Another sculpture from this period stands just outside the portal leading to the west hall, a figure in high relief of a kilted warrior with a plumed helmet. This figure stood outside the King's Gate at Hattusa and is undoubtedly a representation of the Weather God Teshub. It is probably the finest work surviving from the Hittite Empire.

Elsewhere in the central hall you find statues and orthostatic reliefs from the **Late Hittite Period**, principally from the sites at Eski Malatya and Carchemish. The most notable works from Malatya are the statues of a bearded king and of a guardian lion, as well as some charming reliefs showing King Shulmeli in devotional scenes with members of his family. The reliefs from Carchemish represent fabulous monsters from Hittite mythology: a sphinx with two heads, one human and one leonine; two dancers with the heads of hawks, and cloven-hoofed daemons with the heads of lions and bulls. There is also a dramatic battle scene with archers firing from a chariot drawn by a prancing war-horse with a crested headdress – altogether an astonishing display of the art of this great nation of warriors, who ruled Anatolia through the first millennium of its recorded history.

You now return to the south-east corner of the Museum to see the exhibits in the east hall. The first section here is devoted to the

Phrygians, the people who ruled central Anatolia after the collapse of the Hittite Empire. Most of these antiquities come from the royal tombs at Gordion, and they are particularly interesting because many of them foreshadow later artistic and architectural developments in classical Greece. Notice in particular the handsome bronze cauldron with affixed heads of Sirens; the glazed polychrome rhyton in the form of a toy duck, found in a child's grave; the bronze situla, or ceremonial bucket, with its lower end fashioned into the head of a snarling lion; and one of the oldest known examples of glasswork, a translucent bowl with moulded ornamentation – all dating from the eighth century BC.

The next section of the east hall houses **Urartian** antiquities. These almost forgotten people ruled in north-eastern Anatolia from the ninth to the seventh centuries BC, but then they disappeared from history until they were rediscovered by archaeologists during the last century. Their ruined fortresses still stand on mountain tops in eastern Turkey, particularly in the region around Lake Van, from whence come most of the Urartian antiquities in the Museum. The most outstanding of these is a huge bronze cauldron with affixed bulls' heads, resting on a tripod with cloven feet. It is very similar to the Phrygian cauldron farther up the hall – such is the continuity of Anatolian culture.

The last section of the east hall is used mostly to exhibit antiquities from the **Classical Greek and Roman Periods**. Along the right side of this section five of the original shops from Mahmut Pasha's bazaar have been preserved and are now used to exhibit Phrygian antiquities. In one of the booths is a life-sized statue of Kubaba, the patron goddess of the Phrygians; she is shown holding a bird in her hand to symbolize her role as Mistress of Animals, and her pleasant face is lighted by an archaic smile as she is serenaded by two musicians. We have come a long way from the gross and primitive Earth Mother seen at the beginning of the tour of the Museum – in fact we have passed through more than six millennia of Anatolian culture.

At this point you will undoubtedly be suffering from museum feet, and there is no more pleasant place to sit and rest than in the attractive cocktail lounge at the end of the east hall. Here one can relax and have a drink at a table supported by a Roman capital, serenaded by the tropical birds which are caged among the Hittite statues in the main hall of the *bedesten* – a delightful experience with which to end a visit to this incomparable museum.

Leaving the Museum by the main entrance, you turn left and then left again at the next through street, Saraçlar Sokağí. This is one of the main arteries of the market quarter and it is lined with shops selling every conceivable type of merchandise. Turn left at the first main crossroads and walk uphill along Can Sokaği. A short way along you pass **Ahi Elvan Camii**, one of several ancient mosques in this quarter. Founded in the late thirteenth century, it was restored and took its present form in 1413. It is typical of the so-called 'forest mosques' of Anatolia, where the flat wooden ceiling is supported by a veritable copse of wooden columns, in this case three rows of four each. The founder of the mosque was a member of the Ahi sect – medieval guilds of merchants and craftsmen closely connected with the various dervish orders, who apparently were very merry and hospitable fellows. The Ahi sect was a powerful political force in Ankara in the thirteenth century, and many of the city's finest mosques were built during that period by members of the group.

Farther up Can Sokaği you see on the right another foundation of the Ahi sect: **Arslanhane Camii**, or **Mosque of the Lion-House**. Built in 1289, this is the only Selcuk period mosque in Ankara which still retains its original form. It too is a 'forest mosque', with four rows of six columns each, most of them topped with Roman capitals. Notice the superb *mimber*, one of the last brilliant examples of Selcuk carved woodwork, and the *mihrab*, a fine work of tile and stucco in the rococo style. In the outer façade of the mosque are embedded a number of architectural fragments re-used from ancient buildings.

Across the narrow street beside the mosque is the mausoleum of its founder, Ahi Şerafettin, who died in about 1292. This is the only surviving example in Ankara of a Selcuk-style *türbe*, with its octagonal body and conical roof. At the moment of writing it is undergoing a thorough restoration.

You now walk downhill from Arslanhane Camii and soon come to Samanpazari Meydani, the main square of the market quarter. There you bear right along Talat Pasha Bulvari and soon you see on your left the domed building which houses the **Ethnological Museum**. This contains some very interesting collections of things Turkish, including fine embroidery, rugs, folk costumes, antique armaments, old books and calligraphy, dervish costumes, and old-fashioned household articles and furnishings. Some of these latter objects have been used to recreate the salon of an Ottoman house in old Ankara, a room that looks far more gracious and comfortable than the living rooms one sees today in modern Turkish apartments.

The pride of the Museum's collection is its exhibit of carved Selcuk woodwork from mosques in Ankara and elsewhere in Anatolia.

Perhaps the most beautiful of these are the sarcophagus of Ahi Şerafettin, whose mosque and *türbe* you have just seen, and the throne of the Selcuk Sultan Keyhûsrev III (1264–83); this originally stood in Kízíl Bey Camii, another of Ankara's ancient mosques.

A large marble slab in the entrance hall of the Ethnological Museum marks the place where Atatürk was originally interred after his body was brought to Ankara from Istanbul after his death in 1938. In 1953 his body was removed to the magnificent mausoleum which was built for him on a hilltop in the south-western part of the city.

The **Atatürk Mausoleum** is known in Turkish as Anít Kabir and is about three kilometres from Ulus. It is now a national shrine, honouring the great leader who was known to his countrymen as the Father of modern Turkey. A museum on the site preserves some photographs and personal memorabilia of Atatürk, evoking something of the human being behind the pages of the history books.

Atatürk, whose name was originally Mustafa Kemal, was born in Salonica in 1881. He chose the Army as a career when he was only twelve, and after attending a number of military academies he graduated from the Harbiye War College in Istanbul in 1905 with the rank of staff captain. He served with distinction in the Balkan Wars in 1911 and 1912. In 1915 he led the Turkish forces in their defence of the Gallipoli peninsula, and it was his courageous leadership that was principally responsible for the repulse of the British landings and their subsequent evacuation. He later distinguished himself on the Russian front and again in Palestine, where he led the Turkish forces in a fighting retreat into northern Syria, keeping his army intact until the end of the war. He was the one authentic Turkish hero to emerge from the debacle of World War I, and the Turkish people rallied behind him in the period immediately afterwards, when the victorious Allies tried to carve up Turkey and divide it among themselves. He led the Turkish Nationalist forces in their victorious war against Greece in 1919–22, and Turkish sovereignty was guaranteed in the Treaty of Versailles the following year. Even before the War of Independence Atatürk and his followers had laid the foundation of the new republic that would arise out of the ashes of the Ottoman Empire. The Sultanate was abolished in 1922 and on 29 October 1923 the Republic of Turkey was formally established, with Kemal Atatürk as its first President. During the remaining fifteen years of his life Atatürk guided his countrymen to a more modern and enlightened way of life. He died in Dolmabahçe Palace in Istanbul on 10 November 1938, profoundly mourned by his people then and revered by them still.

CHAPTER TWENTY-THREE

Western Anatolia

✢

Ankara – Gordion – Pessinus – Seyitgazi – Midas Şehri – Kütahya – Çavdarhisar – Söğüt – Bilecik – Istanbul

There are two main roads connecting Ankara and Istanbul. The quickest and most direct route is via Bolu, but this is a heavily travelled road with a very high accident rate, and those who drive that way will need to focus all their attention on the lethal traffic. A somewhat longer but far more pleasant route goes via Eskişehir, passing farther to the south through the land which in antiquity was known as Phrygia. Those who take this route and have time to spare can make a number of detours to interesting places in western Anatolia before returning to Istanbul.

The first sizable town you come to is Polatlí, seventy-six kilometres from Ankara. Seventeen kilometres past Polatlí a signposted road leads off to the right for **Gordion**, one of the most important archaeological sites in western Anatolia. Twelve kilometres from the turning the road crosses the Sakarya River and then immediately to the right you see a large mound; this is the site of Gordion, the capital of ancient Phrygia.

Gordion's importance in Phrygia arose from the fact that it was on the principal east-west route through western Anatolia. It stands on the banks of the Sakarya, the Greek Sangarius, just above its junction with the Porsuk, the ancient Tembris. The easiest route from the north-east Aegean and Marmara coasts into central Anatolia followed the lower valley of the Sangarius to reach the plateau near Dorylaeum, the modern Eskişehir. From there it ran eastward along the valley of the Tembris to its junction with the Sangarius near Gordion, thence eastward again along the valley of a tributary of the Sangarius to Ancyra. This is the route followed by the railway and the road on which you will be travelling for most of this itinerary, on the track of one branch of the Royal Persian Road.

Archaeological evidence shows that the original settlement at Gordion dates back to the Early Bronze Age, i.e., to the latter part

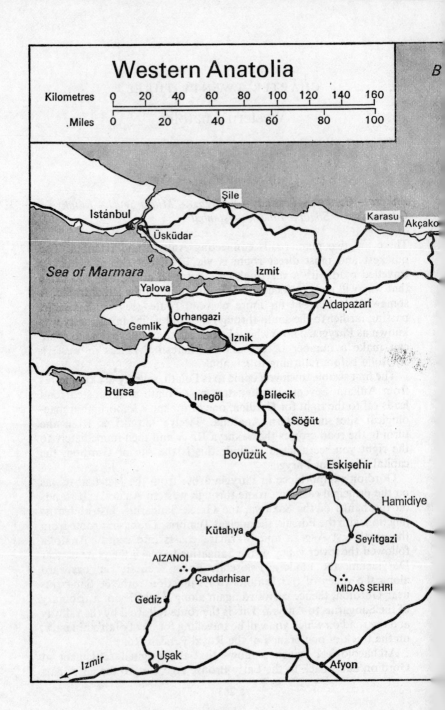

Western Anatolia

| Kilometres | 0 | 20 | 40 | 60 | 80 | 100 | 120 | 140 | 160 |

| Miles | 0 | 20 | 40 | 60 | 80 | 100 |

B

İstanbul
Şile
Üsküdar
Karasu
Akçako

Sea of Marmara
Yalova
İzmit
Adapazarı

Gemlik
Orhangazi
İznik

Bursa
İnegöl
Bilecik
Söğüt

Boyüzük
Eskişehir
Hamidiye

Kütahya
Seyitgazi
AIZANOI
Çavdarhisar
MIDAS ŞEHRİ
Gediz

Uşak
Afyon

Izmir

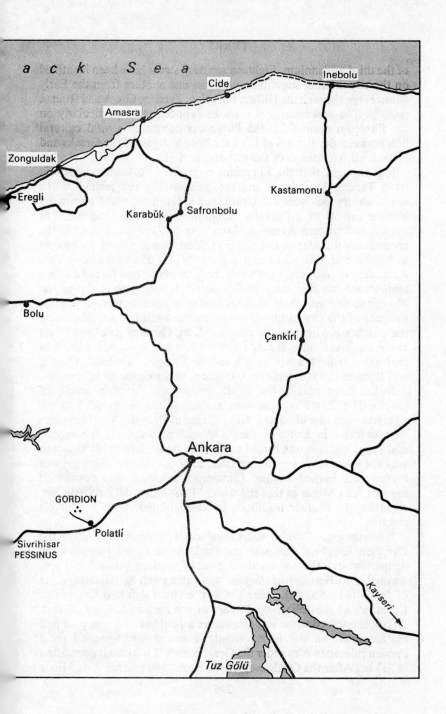

of the third millennium. Eighteen separate strata have been identified on the city mound, superimposed upon one another from the Early Bronze Age through the Hittite, Phrygian, Persian, Greek and Roman periods. The archaeological work has concentrated particularly on the Phrygian period, for the Phrygians constitute a vital cultural link between the Hittites of the Late Bronze Age and the Greeks and Hellenized Anatolians of the classical period.

It is thought that the Phrygians migrated into western Anatolia from Thrace, Macedonia and the Balkans. By the middle of the ninth century they were well established at Gordion, which eventually became capital of a Phrygian kingdom which embraced most of central and western Anatolia. According to Phrygian tradition, the eponymous founder of the city was King Gordios, and the second to hold the throne was the legendary Midas of the golden touch. According to one version of the legend, an oracle had foretold that a man would one day come to Gordion in a wagon to rule over the Phrygians and end their discord. Midas, a poor farmer, arrived at the gate of the city in his wagon when the assembly was discussing the oracle's prediction: the childless King Gordios recognized him as the city's saviour and made him his heir and successor. Midas, in gratitude, dedicated his wagon to the Phrygian Goddess Cybele, and it stood in her temple on the acropolis for centuries afterwards.

In the latter part of the eighth century the Assyrian annals of Sargon II (722–05 BC) mention a ruler called Mitas of Mushki, who has been identified as a King Midas of Phrygia. The Phrygians were defeated in battle by the Assyrians, according to the annals, and though Midas was forced to pay tribute to Sargon his kingdom was not invaded. A generation later, in about 690 BC, Gordion was sacked and burned by the Cimmerian invaders who devastated most of Asia Minor at that time, and Midas either died in battle, or, according to another tradition, he killed himself shortly after his city fell.

Nevertheless, Gordion soon regained its prosperity, though the Phrygian kingdom was now confined to the upper valley of the Sangarius and the surrounding area of western Anatolia. Then, according to Herodotus, Phrygia was subjugated by Alyattes, King of Lydia (615–560 BC). After Cyrus the Great defeated Croesus of Lydia, all of Anatolia became part of the Persian Empire, though Gordion retained some importance as a fortified garrison post and market town on the Royal Road. It was finally liberated from Persian rule when Alexander the Great occupied it without opposition in 333 BC. After the Gauls crossed the straits and entered Asia Minor in 278 BC, they ravaged all of western Asia Minor, Phrygia included, and the people of Gordion fled from their city to take refuge elsewhere. When a Roman army under Manlius Volso arrived at Gordion in a campaign against the Gauls in 189 BC they found the city completely deserted. Apparently the Gordions never returned, for over most of the area of the city mound little or nothing has been found which dates from after 200 BC. Writers in the Augustan Age remark that in their time the once-great city of Gordion was no more than a hamlet clustering around the city mound and the tumuli of the Phrygian kings of former times.

The city mound is a low, flat hill whose diameter ranges from 350 to 500 metres, an accumulation of more than two millennia of human existence on the site. In Phrygian times the city was encircled by a defence wall, which was rebuilt at a higher level in the Persian period. The population of this rather limited enclosure was probably quite small, as capitals go, and the citadel was undoubtedly limited to the use of the king and his administrative and household staff. The common people, for the most part, must have lived outside the city walls, and come to the city only to market or to seek refuge in times of war.

The most prominent structure surviving from the Phrygian town is the great **gateway** at the south-eastern side of the mound. Nine metres wide and twenty-three deep, the gateway was closed at its inner end by a cross wall (now vanished) with a central doorway that opened on to an open rectangular court. The gateway was flanked by two tall towers, from which the defenders could pour down a deadly fire on the attackers confined to the narrow space before the gate. These towers also looked down on two courtyards that flanked the doorway to north and south, both of them backed against the inner face of the city wall and opening inward to the town. The north court has been excavated, but the one on the south has been left uncleared so as to preserve the massive south wall of the Persian gateway. Apparently these courts were used as storage areas, for large *pithoi* for wine and grain were unearthed in the north court.

The central part of the acropolis was a walled citadel enclosing the palace area; this was oriented at an angle of forty-five degrees to the gateway. The palace square was bordered by large buildings of the megaron type; that is, a front vestibule opening on to a larger inner room with a round hearth near the centre. **Megaron 2** (numbering inward from the gate) was paved entirely with mosaics, the most ancient floor of this type ever discovered. It is in a good state of preservation and consists of dark red, white and deep blue pebbles in a variety of geometrical designs.

Megaron 2 must have been the largest and most impressive building on the acropolis, and there is every reason to believe that it was the palace of the Phrygian king. It was divided by two rows of posts into a central nave with aisles on either side, with three posts on either side in the inner room and a single pair in the vestibule. A series of holes left by smaller poles in the side and back walls indicate that there was a wooden gallery running around those three sides of the inner room. Among the debris found on the floor of the megaron when it was excavated were charred fragments of what must once have been very elegant palace furniture with elaborately decorated ivory inlays.

Megaron 4, which is almost as large, is thought to have been the Temple of Cybele, where the legendary wagon of King Midas was stored. This would have been the place where Alexander the Great severed the Gordion Knot at the time when he occupied the town in 333 BC. The tale is told by his biographer Arrian, who first recounts one version of the Midas legend and then describes how Alexander coped with the difficult knot (which was apparently what sailors call a 'Turk's head', with the ends of the rope tucked inside the knot):

There was also another traditional belief about the wagon: According to this, the man who untied the knot which fixed its yoke was destined to be lord of Asia. The cord was made from the bark of the cornel tree, and so cunningly was the knot tied that no one could see where it began or where it ended. For Alexander, then, how to undo it was indeed a puzzle, though he was none the less unwilling to leave it as it was, and his failure might possibly lead to public disturbance. Accounts of what followed differ: some say that Alexander cut the knot with a stroke of his sword and exclaimed, 'I have done it!', but Aristobulus thinks he took out the pin – a sort of wooden peg which was driven right through the shaft of the wagon and held the knot together – and this pulled the yoke away from the shaft . . . In any case, when he and his attendants left the place where the wagon stood the general feeling was that the oracle about the untying of the knot had been ful-

A Laz from Trabzon in his native costume.
Mevlevi dervishes performing the *sema*, their sacred dance.

filled. Moreover, that very night there was lightning and thunder – a further sign from heaven; so Alexander, on the strength of this, offered sacrifice the next day to the gods who had sent this sign from heaven and proclaimed the Loosing of the Knot.

Behind and above the palace buildings, abutting them to the south-east, stood a vast structure which has been called the **Terrace Building**. This was more than a hundred metres in length and consisted of eight large megarons, each measuring about eleven by fourteen metres and arrayed in a long row facing south-east. Across the road which the front of the Terrace Building faced there was another structure of identical design, of which only two rooms have been excavated as yet. These rooms were undoubtedly used by the household services of the palace, and they were destroyed in the same fire which ruined the palace itself in about 690 BC.

The tumulus to the south-east of the city mound is called **Küçük Hüyük**; it consists of a huge clay mound higher than the acropolis itself. Apparently this was a suburb of Gordion in Phrygian times, and during the Lydian period it seems to have been used as a fortified garrison post by their army of occupation. The outer spurs of the mound were formed by the disintegration of an outer defence wall of crude brick. But the central citadel of the fortification was buried beneath the tumulus and consequently is in a good state of preservation. Excavation has revealed that the citadel was destroyed by fire some time in the middle of the sixth century BC. Large numbers of arrowheads were found in the building and embedded in the walls, indicating that the fire had been preceded by a siege. This leads one to believe that the destruction occurred in 547–6 BC, when the army of Cyrus the Great marched through this region to attack King Croesus at Sardis. The tumulus which was piled over the citadel was undoubtedly intended to cover the tomb of the King of Gordion and those who died with him in the siege.

A number of other tumuli have been explored in the area to the east of the village of Yassí Hüyük, in the vicinity of the Gordion museum. The grandest of these is the **Royal Tumulus**; this was originally some 70–80 metres high and 250 metres in diameter, but erosion has diminished its height to 53 metres and broadened its girth to 300 metres. It is the second largest tumulus in Anatolia,

---

Karanlík Kilise, the Dark Church, one of the rock-hewn churches of Cappadocia.

exceeded in size only by the one at Bintepe, north-west of Salihli, the tumulus which Herodotus called that of King Alyattes. These tumuli were built to cover the graves of royal personages or wealthy nobles, protecting their tombs from grave robbers and at the same time serving as conspicuous funerary monuments. In the Royal Tumulus at Gordion the tomb was in the form of a wooden cabin. When the corpse had been placed in the tomb along with the grave offerings, a double gabled roof was placed over the cabin; this was covered with a large heap of stones and then the tumulus of earth or clay was heaped over it. Since the Royal Tumulus is a monument in itself, the archaeologists have preserved it by boring a tunnel through to the tomb at ground level. Inside the wooden tomb they found a large bed on which lay the skeleton of what was presumed to be a Phrygian king, a very short man who was about sixty years old at the time of his death. The tomb was furnished with two elaborately decorated wooden screens and with ten tables loaded with grave offerings; a representative collection of these objects is now on display in the museums at Gordion and Ankara. Since such a grandiose tomb would hardly have been constructed after the catastrophic sack of Gordion by the Cimmerians in 690 BC, it must have been built at an earlier time. The Assyrian annals say that the King Midas who died in the Cimmerian raid was alive in 717 BC, so the tomb must belong to one of his predecessors; this and the pottery found in the tomb suggest that it dates from 750–25 BC.

The most interesting of the other tumuli in the vicinity is the so-called **Princely Tomb**, a short distance to the south-east of the museum. This tumulus, dated to about 700 BC, proved to contain the skeleton of a boy about four or five years old. The body had been laid in a large bed in one corner of the room, and on the floor beneath it were a large number of bowls containing food. The other grave offerings were toys of various kinds – small animals carved in wood and a number of pottery vessels shaped and painted like animals, including a charming goose and gander with spouts for beaks.

The next town beyond Polatlí is **Sivrihisar**, the Byzantine **Justinian-opolis**. As its name implies, the town was founded by Justinian the Great, as a fortified garrison on the western approach to Ancyra. The remains of the Byzantine fortress which was built at that time can still be seen on a crag above the town.

Just beyond Sivrihisar there is a turn-off to the left for **Balíhisar**, the **site of ancient Pessinus**. Pessinus was a Phrygian temple-city whose high priest, a eunuch called the *gallos*, was the absolute ruler of this independent city-state. Pessinus was the principal sanctuary of the Phrygian goddess Cybele, the Great Earth Mother, the mistress of wild animals, the protector of mankind, the guardian of the dead, and the recipient of orgiastic worship which sometimes involved self-emasculation by her votaries. These horrible rites were a re-enactment of the drama connected with Cybele's youthful lover Attis, the god of vegetation, a weird tale best told by Pausanias:

At Pessinus they have a local legend of how Zeus dropped his seed on the soil in his sleep, and in the course of time the soil sent up a daemonic creature with both female and male parts, whom they called Agdistis. The gods were frightened of Agdistis and chopped off his male organs, and an almond tree grew out of them with the nuts already ripe. They say a daughter of the river Sangarius took some of the nuts and put them in a fold of her dress; at once the almonds disappeared and she was pregnant, and, when she abandoned the son she bore [Attis], a he-goat looked after him. The boy grew up more beautiful than the form of man is capable of being, and Agdistis fell in love with his son. When the boy was fully grown his family sent him away to Pessinus to marry the king's daughter; the wedding song was being sung when Agdistis appeared and Attis chopped off his private parts and his bride's father did the same. Agdistis was obsessed by remorse for what he had done to Attis, and got Zeus to grant that the body of Attis should never corrupt or wither in any degree.

The site of Pessinus has been excavated in recent years; the most notable monument which has been unearthed is the **Temple of Cybele**, dating to the Hellenistic Period. The cult object in this temple was a black meteorite called the Baitylos, the symbol of the Great Earth Mother, which figured in an interesting bit of Hellenistic diplomacy. During the latter part of the third century BC the kings of Pergamum had formed a close alliance with the high priests of Pessinus. This friendship enabled Attalus I in 205 BC to persuade the high priest to send the Baitylos to Rome after the Sybilline Books had ordered that it be brought there, and it was duly enshrined on the Capitoline Hill a few years later. This cemented Pergamum's alliance with Rome and in turn created a bond of friendship between Rome and Pessinus. When Manlius Volso invaded Galatia in 189 BC, the priests of Cybele met him in procession outside Pessinus and announced that the Great Earth Mother had predicted victory for the Romans.

Fifty-seven kilometres past Sivrihisar a turning to the left at Hamidiye offers an interesting detour for those who have the time to spare. After two kilometres you come to Mahmudiye; here you take the right fork to **Seyitgazi**, which is twenty-six kilometres to the south-west. The town is named after Seyit Battal Gazi, commander of one of the Arab armies that raided Asia Minor in the eighth century, and its principal monument is a mosque complex surrounding his supposed tomb. According to the legend, Seyit Battal had fallen during the Arab siege of Akoenos, the modern Afyon, and he was buried with the Byzantine princess who had died for love of him. The location of the hero's last resting-place was revealed in a dream to the mother of Sultan Alâeddin Keykûbad I, and the following day she found the remains of Battal and the princess enshrined in a Christian convent. Immediately afterwards she built a grand *türbe* for Battal that subsequently became one of the most popular Islamic shrines in Anatolia, and Hacî Bektaş himself established a Bektaşi *tekke* there. During the reign of Selim I (1512–20) the *türbe* and *tekke* were restored and a mosque and *imaret* added, creating the impressive complex that one sees today. When you visit the tomb you will immediately recognize the cenotaph of Seyit Battal Gazi, for it is fully twenty-five feet long, symbolic of the greatness of the warrior-saint who is buried there. Beside the Gazi's cenotaph lies one of normal size which is said to cover the grave of the Byzantine princess who died for love of her slain hero, evoking memories of a medieval Anatolian romance.

Seyitgazi is a good starting-place for exploring the fascinating Phrygian rock-monuments to the south, most notably the ones at **Yazílíkaya**. Take the road from Seyitgazi to Çukurca, thirty kilometres to the south. From there a road leads south-east along the valley of the Doğanlí towards Yazílíkaya, in the heart of the Phrygian highlands. Yazílíkaya is a village of Circassians huddling at the base of the extraordinary acropolis hill which the Turks call **Midas Şehri**, or the **City of Midas**.

The City of Midas was discovered in 1800 by a party of European travellers. Among them was Captain Leake, who wrote an account of the expedition in 1824. Leake and all subsequent travellers were most profoundly impressed by an enormous and beautifully decorated façade carved out of a projecting spur of the acropolis at its north-eastern corner, just above the village of Yazílíkaya. As Leake described it:

The rock which has been shaped into this singular monument

rises to a height of upwards of one hundred feet above the plain; and at the back, and on one of the sides, remains in its natural state. The ornamented part is about sixty feet square, surmounted by a kind of pediment, above which are two volutes. The figures cut upon the rock are nowhere more than an inch deep below the surface, except towards the bottom, where the excavation is much deeper, and resembles an altar. It is not impossible, however, that it may conceal the entrance into the sepulchral chamber, where lie the remains of the person in whose honour this magnificent monument was formed.

Leake attempted to decipher the inscription in Phrygian on the monument, and interpreted one phrase to read 'to King Midas'. He therefore presumed that the monument had been erected as a sepulchre for a King Midas of the Gordion dynasty. Subsequent investigations have shown conclusively that it was not a tomb but a sanctuary of the Phrygian goddess Cybele, whose cult statue stood in the doorlike niche of the monument. The Monument of Midas, as it is still called nevertheless, has been dated to the last third of the eighth century BC, contemporary with the Royal Tumulus at Gordion. Explorations and excavations at the City of Midas and elsewhere in the highlands have revealed a large number of rock-hewn sanctuaries, altars, tombs and hilltop fortresses from that period, a time when the old Phrygian kingdom reached the heights of its power and prosperity. Other rock-hewn monuments in the region date from the first half of the sixth century BC, when Phrygia enjoyed a revival of good times under Lydian rule. Besides those at Midas Şehri, the most famous monuments in the region are **Arslan Kaya** and **Arslan Taşí**; both of which are in the Köhnüş valley, in the general area south-west of Yazílíkaya. Those with time to spare might hire a guide in the village to explore the Phrygian highlands to find these and other extraordinary monuments of a vanished kingdom.

From Seyitgazi one can drive directly to Eskişehir without returning to the main road. Eskişehir is a large industrial city, with nothing of interest for travellers except its fine meerschaum, fashioned into elaborately shaped pipes and other ware by the local craftsmen.

A side trip to **Kütahya** is well worth while if time permits. Kütahya has been renowned since the sixteenth century for its fine ceramic tiles, which in their time were second only to those of Iznik. The modern Kütahya tiles cannot compare in quality with those of Ottoman times, but they are the best made in modern Turkey and some pieces are certainly worth purchasing.

Most of the interesting monuments in Kütahya date from the period when it was ruled by the Germiyanid, a Kurdo-Turkish tribe resettled in western Anatolia by the Selcuks in about 1275. The Germiyanid succeeded in gaining control of Kütahya in 1302 and made it the capital of an emirate which included much of Phrygia. Although they lost the city for brief periods to the Ottomans and the Mongols, the Germiyanid regained control of Kütahya and held it until its final annexation by the Ottomans in 1428. The oldest Germiyanid structure here is the Vacidiye Medrese, built in 1414 by the Emir Umar bin Savcí as an astronomical observatory and school of science and mathematics. The *medrese* now serves as the local museum, which is principally given over to displays of old Turkish arts and crafts, including examples of Kütahya ceramics from all periods.

The most important monument in the vicinity of Kütahya is the Temple of Zeus at Çavdarhisar. The easiest way to get there from Kütahya is to drive south-west along the Izmir highway for forty-seven kilometres and then turn right for Emet. This will take you across the Orhaneli Çayí, the Rhyndicus of antiquity, which is here spanned by two Roman bridges that are still used by the locals. The village of Çavdarhisar is just to the left, and beside it is the magnificent Temple of Zeus and other remains of the Roman town of Aizanoi.

The **Temple of Zeus at Aizanoi** is the best-preserved Roman sanctuary in Asia Minor and is an extremely impressive sight, standing majestically alone on the barren Anatolian plateau, dwarfing the modern village which huddles in its shadow. The temple is believed to have been built in the reign of Hadrian and was probably completed around AD 125. It stands on a stylobate measuring approximately thirty-three by thirty-seven metres, which in turn is raised on a podium over a vast rectangular terrace, approached by a stairway on the east side. The peripteral colonnade of eight by fifteen columns is arranged in the pseudo-dipteral manner; that is, with the distance between the inside of the colonnade and the side walls of the sanctuary equal to twice the intercolumnar spacing. The naos of the sanctuary is preceded by a pronaos and behind there is an opisthodomus. The pronaos is fronted by four prostyle columns; that is, arranged so that the two end columns are directly in front of the antae, the pilasters that terminate the side walls of the open porch; while the opisthodomus has two columns between the antae, or *distyle in antis*. In addition, there is a vaulted chamber under the naos, reached by a staircase from the opisthodomus. This subterranean sanctuary was dedicated to the worship of Phrygian Cybele, whose orgiastic cult seems to have survived well into Christian times in her ancient homeland.

From Eskişehir the main road runs north-west as far as Bozüyük, after which the left branch continues on to Bursa and the right turns north for Istanbul via Bilecik and Adapazarí, the route which will be followed in the present itinerary. Here at last one leaves behind the barren and monotonous steppes, as the road winds inexorably down towards the coast through the verdant hills and valleys of ancient Bithynia, the fairest landscape in all of Anatolia.

There are several rustic cafés beside the road on this stretch, and a number of garden restaurants serve trout freshly caught from the Sakarya. Just before Bilecik the road passes through **Küplü**, one of the loveliest villages in western Anatolia, with old-fashioned Ottoman houses of pastel stone and weathered wood perched serenely on the green slopes of this beautiful river valley.

Just past Küplü a right turn leads to **Söğüt**, a small town in the Bithynian hills which was the first capital of the Osmanlí Turks. The Osmanlí – or Ottomans, as they came to be known in Europe – descended from a small tribe of Oğuz Turks who were settled as vassals in the region around Söğüt by the Selcuk Sultan Alâeddin Keykûbad I in about 1275. Their leader in the great migration from central Asia to western Anatolia was Ertuğrul Gazi; he died in Söğüt in 1281 and was succeeded by his son, Osman Gazi (1281–1324), from whom the Osmanlí dynasty subsequently took its name.

There are only two very minor monuments in Söğüt to remind one that the history of the Ottoman Empire started there. One of these is the little mosque called the Ertuğrul Gazi Mescidi. There is a tradition that this stands on the site of a mosque built by Ertuğrul himself, but the present structure was founded by Sultan Abdül Aziz (1861–76), who in the last stages of his own decline and that of the Ottoman Empire seems to have cherished this link with his warrior ancestor. The other monument is the *türbe* of Ertuğrul Gazi, but this too has been restored and altered, though it is reasonably certain that the catafalque within covers the tomb of the Gazi. According to one tradition, Osman Gazi was also buried here, but in accordance with his dying wish he was later reburied in the citadel at Bursa after its capture by his son Orhan.

Returning to the main road, one soon comes to the lovely old town of **Bilecik**, adorned with more of the gracious Ottoman houses of the same type as those seen in Küplü, half stone and half timber, each with its own flower garden. Down a ravine to the right as you approach the town you see the Orhan Gazi Camii, one of the most ancient Ottoman mosques in existence. The actual date of construction is not known, but it was probably built in the first half of the thirteenth century. The twin minarets of the mosque are late nineteenth-century additions; the stump of the original minaret can be seen jutting out from a rock some distance away.

After passing Bilecik the road continues to wend its way downhill and then runs along the valley of the Sakarya, passing one pretty village after another in felicitous surroundings. Just past Osmaneli a road to the left leads to Iznik; those who wish to return to Istanbul by the Yalova ferry should turn off here. You are strongly advised to take this route rather than continue on to the main Ankara-Istanbul highway, for the last stage from Adapazarí is the most unpleasant and murderous stretch of road in Turkey. Instead one can drive through the lovely Bithynian countryside past Iznik and its lake, turning right at Orhangazi for Yalova. In spring this bucolic region is at its most beautiful, as all of ancient Bithynia becomes one vast garden of flowering fruit trees and wild flowers. Seeing it at that season, one wonders why the Osmanlí did not sheathe their swords and remain here content in this Anatolian arcadia, where for at least a time they lived happily at peace with their neighbours. As Richard Knolles wrote in his *Lives of the Othoman Kings and Emperors* (London, 1609):

> Thus is Ertogrul, the Oguzian Turk, with his homely heardsmen, becoome a petty lord of a countrey village, and in good favour with the Sultan; whose followers, as sturdie heardsmen with their families, lived in Winter with him in Sogut; but in Summer in tents with their cattle upon the mountains. Having thus lived certain yeares, and brought great peace with his neighbours, as well the Christians as the Turks . . . Ertogrul kept himself close in his house in Sogut, as well contented there as with a kingdom . . .

CHAPTER TWENTY-FOUR

The Black Sea Coast

❧

Amasya – Sinop – Samsun – Ordu – Giresun – Trabzon – Rize – Hopa

As mentioned earlier, the last five chapters of this book will guide you on an immensely long journey around the eastern regions of Turkey. The first part of the itinerary takes you over the Pontic mountains to Sinop and Samsun on the Black Sea, and then eastward along the coast to Trabzon and the Russian border.

Take the main road leading north from Amasya towards Samsun as far as Havza, forty-six kilometres along. Those wishing to go directly to Samsun should take the right fork on to highway 45, while those who will start the tour of the Black Sea coast at Sinop should take the left fork on to highway 40. The present itinerary will follow the latter route, which is longer and more difficult but more scenic.

From Havza highway 40 heads north-west through the land which in antiquity was known as Paphylagonia. After passing through Vezirköprü it follows the Kízíl Irmak to its confluence with the Gök Irmak, the River Amnias of antiquity. The road then follows the Gök Irmak and soon comes to the town of Duruğan, where there is a ruined Selcuk caravansarai, the **Durak Han**. According to an inscription, it was built in 1226, during the reign of Sultan Giyaseddin Keyhûsrev III, and the founder was the famous Pervane (see page 256). At that time the Pervane was the virtual ruler of this part of the Sultanate of Rum, and even after his execution by the Mongols in 1278 his sons and their descendants continued to rule in Paphylagonia for a time, with their capital in Sinop.

The road continues along the Gök Irmak for another thirty kilometres past Duruğan, till a turning on the right takes one to the Sinop highway. Just off to the south-west is the picturesque citadel rock and ruined Byzantine fortress at **Boyabat**, which dominates the rice-growing plain called Kaz Dere, or Goose Valley. On this plain in 88 BC Mithradates Eupator won a great victory over King Nicomedes of Bithynia and the Romans under Marius, in the opening

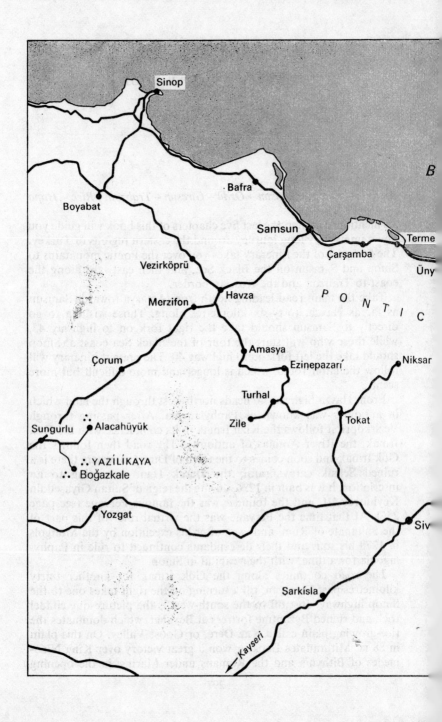

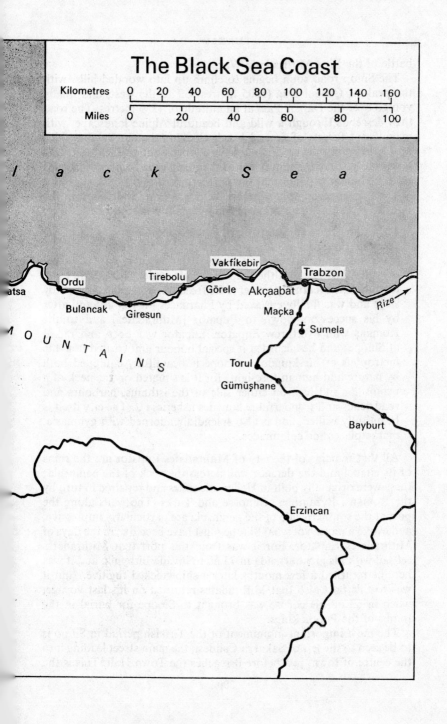

The Black Sea Coast

| Kilometres | 0 | | 20 | | 40 | | 60 | | 80 | | 100 | | 120 | | 140 | | 160 |
| Miles | 0 | | | 20 | | | 40 | | | 60 | | | 80 | | | 100 |

Black Sea

atsa

Ordu

Bulancak   Giresun

MOUNTAINS

Tirebolu

Görele

Vakfíkebir

Akçaabat

Trabzon

Maçka

Rize →

✝ Sumela

Torul

Gümüşhane

Bayburt

Erzincan

battle of the First Mithradatic War.

The Sinop road soon begins to climb up into wooded hills, with the peak of Çangal Dağ (1605 metres) off to the west, and finally you go over the Damaz Pass at an altitude of 1280 metres. The road then descends through a wild and beautiful Alpine landscape, with magnificent forests of fir and beech cloaking the surrounding hills up to their very peaks. Finally a view opens out to the coast, and far ahead you see the thin finger of the **Sinop cape** pointing eastward from its immense peninsula, the northernmost point in Anatolia.

The ancient geographer Strabo, who was born and raised in the Pontus, gives this description of Sinope, as it was called in his day:

> Then one comes to Sinope itself . . . the most noteworthy of the cities in that part of the world. The city was founded by the Milesians; and, having built a naval station, it reigned supreme over the Euxine . . . Although it was independent for a long time, it could not eventually preserve its freedom, but was captured by siege and was finally enslaved by Pharnaces [in 183 BC] and after by his successors down to Eupator [Mithradates] and to the Romans who overthrew Eupator. Eupator was born and raised at Sinope; and he accorded it special honour and treated it as the metropolis of his kingdom. Sinope is beautifully equipped both by nature and human foresight; for it is situated on the neck of a peninsula, and has, on either side of the isthmus, harbours and roadsteads and wonderful palamydes fisheries . . . The city itself is beautifully walled, and is also splendidly adorned with gymnasia, marketplaces and colonnades.

All that remains of the city of Mithradates Eupator are the ruins of its citadel and the defence wall across the neck of the peninsula; these were originally built in Hellenistic times and repaired in turn by the Romans, Byzantines, Genoese and Turks. The walls along the port at the southern side of the peninsula are particularly impressive, and evoke a picture of what Sinope must have been like in the days of Mithradates Eupator. For it was from this port that Mithradates set sail with his great armada in 73 BC to invade Bithynia, and it was here he returned a few months later a shipwrecked fugitive. And it was to this port also that Mithradates returned on his last voyage, when in 63 BC his corpse was brought to Sinope for burial in the tombs of the Pontic kings.

The most important monument of the Turkish period in Sinop is to be seen to the left of Sakarya Caddesi, the main street leading into the centre of town, just before it reaches the Town Hall. This is the

Ulu Cami, also called the Alâeddin Camii, built in 1267–8 by the Pervane Mu'in al-Din Süleyman and since twice restored. The most notable feature of the mosque is its *mimber*, beautifully carved in geometrical designs.

The drive from Sinop to Samsun is a pleasant trip of about two hours. Most of the drive is along or above the seashore, except where the coast curves outwards in a broad peninsula formed by the delta of the Kízíl Irmak, the ancient Halys. The Pontic Riviera is a more or less narrow strip walled in on the south by mountains, widening out only at the deltas of the Kízíl Irmak and the Yeşil Irmak, the Greek Iris, which flows into the Black Sea on the other side of Samsun. The mist-shrouded mountains form the background to every inland view, their heavily-wooded spurs occasionally thrusting right down to the sea, at which points the road either runs *en corniche* or winds around a succession of promontories and coves, many of which are carpeted in fine sand as black as basalt.

Amisus, the modern **Samsun**, was founded in the middle of the eighth century BC by Ionian settlers, about the same time as Sinope. But Amisus soon surpassed Sinope as a port and commercial centre. For it stood at the head of the main route from central Anatolia to the Euxine, and landborne commerce came to it more easily and directly than to Sinope. Along with Sinope, Amisus was one of the principal cities of the Pontic kings, and it too was adorned by Mithradates Eupator with splendid public buildings, temples, palaces and defence walls. But of these not a trace remains, and the only monuments in Samsun are a few relatively unimportant mosques of the early Turkish period.

From Samsun the highway cuts across the delta of the Yeşil Irmak, returning to the sea once again just beyond **Terme**, a little port on the banks of the Terme Çayí. Because of the similarity of their names, Terme has been identified as the **site of ancient Themiscyra**, and the Terme Çayí as the River Thermodon. The delta land between the Iris and the Thermodon was also known as the Themiscyra, a region which has always been the most fertile and productive along the whole coast of the Euxine.

Themiscyra was fabled in antiquity as the home of the Amazons, as Strabo says in his description of this region:

Themiscyra and the plains above Thermodon and the mountains that lie above them are by all writers mentioned as having belonged to the Amazons... The Amazons spend ten months of the year off to themselves performing their individual tasks, such as ploughing, planting, pasturing cattle, or particularly in training horses, though the bravest engage in hunting on horseback and practise warlike exercises. The right breasts of all are seared when they are infants, so that they can easily use their right hands for any purpose, and especially that of throwing the javelin. They also use bows and arrows and light shields, and make the skins of wild animals serve as helmets, clothing and girdles. They have two months in spring when they go up into the neighbouring mountain which separates them from the Gagarians. The Gagarians, also in accordance with an ancient custom, go thither to offer sacrifice with the Amazons and also to have intercourse with them for the sake of begetting children, doing this in secrecy and darkness, any Gagarian at random with any Amazon; and after making them pregnant they send them away; and the females that are born are retained by the Amazons, but the males are taken to the Gagarians to be brought up; and each Gagarian to whom a child is brought adopts the child as his own, regarding the child as his son because of the uncertainty . . .

After passing through Terme the road runs along the sea for some twenty kilometres to **Ünye**, a small port on the site of ancient Oenoe. Another twenty kilometres brings you to **Fatsa**, a picturesque little harbour on the site of Phadisama, and then six kilometres farther along is **Bolamon**, the former Polemonium, all three places having retained something like their ancient Greek names. The road now rounds a great peninsula, passing first Yasun Burnu, the ancient Jasonium Promontorium, then Cam Burnu, the Greek Cape Vona, after which it runs along the shore of the great bay called Genetes Liman, known in antiquity as the Port of Genetaean Zeus. This brings you to the large and beautifully situated port town of **Ordu**, on the site of ancient Cotyora. These places, too, retain the names by which Greek sailors and travellers knew them in former times, going back as far as the legendary days of Jason and the Argonauts.

The next large port along the coast is **Giresun**, a pretty town stretching out along the flanks of a rocky promontory on which stand the ruins of a Byzantine-Genoese fortress. This is often called the site of ancient Cerasus, but it is more probably to be identified with Pharnacia, one of the towns founded by Pharnaces I (185–57 BC), the first of the great Pontic kings.

This region is famous for its *fındık*, or hazel nuts, which are exported in enormous quantities from Giresun and the other nearby ports along the coast. The wild cherry grows in great abundance along the coast as well, and indeed it was from here that the Roman general Lucullus first brought back the cherry tree to Europe.

About six kilometres past Giresun you catch sight of the islet called **Giresun Adasí**. This has been identified as the Insula Aretias, which was celebrated in antiquity for a temple of Ares erected by the Amazon queens Otrere and Entiope.

The next sizable town is **Tirebolu**, the ancient Tripolis, some fifty kilometres farther east along the coast. Tripolis is a typical Pontic sea port, with its crescent bay guarded by a ruined fortress built by the Genoese in late Byzantine times.

Five kilometres past Tirebolu the road crosses the **Harşit Çayí**, a turbulent river that rises far up in the Pontic mountains. The view of the river valley from the coast is wild and picturesque, with a succession of heavily forested mountain chains rising above one another far into the interior, their foothills covered with dense growths of mulberry and cherry trees. This is perhaps the most beautiful stretch of the Black Sea coast: the road winds around heavily wooded hills intersected by numerous ravines, and the blue sea glitters through the verdant screen of tall trees and dense shrubbery.

Sixty-four kilometres past Tirebolu you come to **Görele**, the ancient Philocalea, and fifteen kilometres farther along to **Eynesil**, a village near the **site of ancient Coralla**. The ruined castle of Coralla can be seen on a rocky promontory known as Görele Burnu, whose modern name is a linguistic variation of the original one. In Büyük Liman, the bay between this headland and the next, you come to the village of Vakfíkebir, which is near the site of ancient Cerasus. The headland which forms the eastern horn of Büyük Liman is Fener Burnu, the ancient Hieron Oros, the Sacred Mountain, a landmark for sailors along the Euxine since the days of Jason and the Argonauts.

After rounding the cape you pass **Akçakale**, the **ancient Cordyle**, where there is a ruined fortress built in the thirteenth century by the emperors of Trebizond. Then you come to **Akçaabat**, known to Greeks in modern times as Platana and in antiquity as Hermonassa.

You now approach **Trabzon, ancient Trapezus**, known to travellers of an earlier age as the fabled Trebizond. Trapezus was founded in the eighth century BC as a colony of Sinope, and was already a flourishing city when Xenophon and the Ten Thousand stopped there on their memorable journey. We learn from Arrian that Trapezus was the most considerable place along the Euxine when he visited it as governor of Pontus in the reign of Hadrian. Hadrian endowed the city with an artificial harbour and it soon rivalled Sinope and Amisus as a port and commercial centre, for it was strategically located at the terminus of the long overland route from Asia through the Pontic mountains. This prosperity continued through the early Byzantine period, and Justinian strengthened the defence walls which had been built there in Hellenistic times, constructing a palace within the inner citadel.

The most illustrious period in the city's history began in 1204, when Alexius Comnenus founded what would become the Byzantine Empire of Trebizond. Alexius was a son of Manuel Comnenus and a grandson of the Emperor Andronicus I, who was deposed and brutally murdered by the mob in Constantinople in 1185. His oldest son Manuel was so badly blinded that he died, and his sons Alexius and David eventually took refuge with their paternal aunt, Queen Thamar of Georgia. After the Latin occupation of Constantinople in 1204 Alexius and his Georgian supporters occupied Trebizond, Oenoe and Sinope, while his brother David, the Grand Comnenus, occupied all of Paphylagonia and extended the bounds of the new empires as far west as Heracleia Pontica, the modern Ereğli. Thus began a dynasty which was to endure for more than two and a half centuries, outliving the Byzantine Empire in Constantinople by eight years. In the latter days of the Comneni the Turkish conquests had reduced their empire to little more than Trebizond and what is now the eastern Black Sea coast of modern Turkey. The end came in the spring of 1461, when Sultan Mehmet II besieged Trebizond with an enormous fleet and army. The Emperor David Comnenus was persuaded that resistance was hopeless, and he surrendered the city to the Conqueror, thus ending the last Greek empire of the medieval world.

Trabzon, as it came to be called, continued to be an important city under the Ottomans, and in the century after the Conquest it rivalled Edirne as a second capital of the Empire. Selim the Grim set up his princely court in Trabzon while governor of Anatolia before his accession to the throne in 1512, and his son Süleyman the Magnificent was born and dwelt there until his own accession in 1520. The city suffered severely during the First World War, when it was bombarded and occupied by the Russians, and in 1923 it lost all of its considerable Christian population in the exchange of minorities. Nevertheless, Trabzon has revived markedly in recent

The Church of St Gregory in Ani, the former capital of the medieval kingdom of Armenia.
The Castle of Ishak Pasha in Doğubayazít.

years and is now the leading city on the Black Sea coast of Turkey.

Trabzon's most renowned monument is the magnificent **Church of Haghia Sophia**, which stands on a high terrace overlooking the Black Sea some three kilometres west of the town centre. Until two decades ago the church was in a very bad state of repair and was beginning to fall into ruins, but then in 1957 Professor Talbot Rice and his associates began the painstaking process of uncovering and cleaning the surviving paintings and restoring them and the building as much as was humanly possible. The restoration of Haghia Sophia and its priceless works of art is now complete and it is open to the public as a national monument, recreating something of the past grandeur of the Empire of Trebizond.

The basic plan of the church is approximately a cross-in-square: four columns support the central dome on a high drum, the east bays of the aisle are barrel-vaulted and the longer west bays cross-vaulted. At the eastern end of the church there are three apses; the central one is five-sided externally and those on either side are rounded. The northern side apse serves as the prothesis and the one on the south as the diaconicon. At the western end there is a narthex of the same width as the church with a chapel above it; and at the north, south and west ends there are great barrel-vaulted porches. There is a battered but once fine *opus Alexandrinium* pavement in the dome bay, containing nine different types of marble, and a magnificent set of capitals, columns and bases made from Proconnesian marble. The capitals and columns of the porches are all re-used and are of various dates from the fifth century onwards. The south porch is one of the most remarkable features of the church, principally because of its superb sculptured frieze. The figures in relief that make up the frieze are all on separate stones and represent the story of Genesis, with a single-headed heraldic eagle – the symbol of the Comneni – on the keystone of the arch above.

The paintings that once decorated the inner walls of the south porch have now almost completely vanished. In the north porch the paintings on the north wall are still well preserved, with eight

---

The Lion Gate in the citadel of Boğazkale, the former capital of the Hittite Empire.

Relief on the façade of the Armenian church of the Redeemer on the isle of Akhtamar, Lake Van. The tall figure on the right is Goliath;
David is in the centre; and the smaller one on the left is King Gagik I, who founded this church in about AD 915.

Nemrut Daği: the Hierotheseion of King Antiochus I of Commagene.

complete scenes from the Old Testament. In the western porch one complete scene from the Old Testament survives along with two portraits of saints.

The narthex contained portions of a very full cycle of scenes from the New Testament, all of them concerned with the Miracles of Christ. It is roofed by a vault which springs from the sides at a low level, and is divided into three sections by wide ribs. Both the northern and southern sectors contain five scenes, separated near the middle by a decorative band. The central sector is in the form of a quadripartite groined vault decorated along the junction with geometric patterns and with two pairs each of seraphim and tetramorphs in the four quarters. The south wall of the narthex is decorated with three more scenes and the fragmentary figures of Christ and of SS Sergius and Bacchus.

In the naos all or part of twenty-five scenes and forty-eight portraits survive. The vault of the central apse displays *The Ascension* and the conch *The Virgin Enthroned* between archangels. The dome is decorated with the awesome figure of *Christ Pantocrator*, of which only the head and shoulders remain. Below this there is a long inscription containing the text of Psalm ci, 19, 20: 'Out of the heavens did the Lord behold the earth, that He might hear the mournings of such as are in captivity and deliver the children appointed unto death that they may declare the name of the Lord in Sion and His worship in Jerusalem.' Below the inscription there is a frieze of angels of surpassing beauty.

In the south apse, just outside the diaconicon, is an unpaved area which was clearly the site of a tomb; it is thought that this may have been the burial-place of the Emperor Manuel Comnenus, the man to whom we owe this magnificent church and its beautiful works of art.

There are also wall paintings in the bell tower to the west of Haghia Sophia, but these are far inferior to those in the church itself. The bell tower was built in 1443, just eighteen years before the fall of the Empire, and the fading culture of Trebizond in its latter years is reflected in the declining quality of its art, which at its prime rivalled that of Constantinople in the last great Byzantine renaissance.

As you approach the old quarter of Trabzon you come to a handsome Ottoman mosque in a square shaded by giant plane trees. This is the **Gülbahar Hatun Camii**, built in 1514 by Sultan Selim the Grim in honour of his mother, Ayşe Hatun, wife of Sultan Beyazit II. In her latter years she was called Gülbahar, the Rose of Spring, a name which Beyazit's mother also bore. The latter Gülbahar was born in Trebizond as the Princess Maria, a relative of the imperial Comneni, and she met and married Beyazit while he was on campaign in the Pontus. When her son Selim later became governor in Trebizond, Gülbahar accompanied him to her birth-place and distinguished herself by her charity and good works. When she died there in 1512 Selim, then in the first year of his reign, endowed this mosque for her and buried her in a grand *türbe* beside it.

Before proceeding farther you might pause to look upon the famous **walls of Trebizond**, beneath which you now stand. The fortified inner town of Trebizond consisted of three separate enceintes. The lowest of these was a large rectangular area bounded on the north by the sea. Just to the south of this, separated from the lower section by a wall, stood the second section on high ground flanked to east and west by deep ravines. From here the ground rises in a series of terraces, so that the third and highest section is protected on either side by steep precipices, and on the north and south by massive defence walls. The upper citadel was thus almost im-pregnable, and hence within its walls were located the royal palace and the principal administrative offices of the Empire of Trebizond. The ivy-covered ruins of these ancient walls are still grand and impressive, with ramparts and arches towering over the rooftops of the modern town.

You cross the ravine over an old Ottoman viaduct and then pass through the walls into the **old quarter** of Trabzon. A short way along on the left you see Fatih Camii, the former church of the Panaghia Chrysokephalos, the Golden-Headed Virgin. According to tradition, the original sanctuary on this site was founded by Constantine the Great, though the present structure is thought to date from the tenth or eleventh century. During the last two centuries of the Empire it served as a funerary chapel for the imperial Comneni family.

A little farther along you come to the Town Hall, where you turn right on to Kale Sokaği; this brings you through an ancient gate and up into the **citadel**. After entering the upper citadel turn sharply to the right and make your way out to the walls on the western side, where there is a breathtaking view of the city below. This south-western corner of the upper citadel is thought to have been the site of the 'Golden Palace of the Comneni', of which there now remain only a few fragmentary walls and arches.

From the other side of the upper citadel you can see on the hill across the eastern ravine the former church of St Eugenios, the patron saint of Trebizond. This was one of the first Christian sanctuaries in Trebizond, but the present structure probably dates from the second half of the thirteenth century. It is now known as the **Yeni Cuma Cami**, the New Friday Mosque, because Sultan Mehmet II converted it into a mosque on the first Friday after the conquest of Trebizond, and there offered up his first prayers in the city. Immediately afterwards, as recorded by his Greek biographer Kritoboulos: 'He ascended to the citadel and the palace, and saw and admired the security of the one and splendour of the other, and in every way he judged the city worthy of note.'

There are a number of other Byzantine churches in Trabzon, but most of them are in such poor condition that they are of little interest except to the specialist. Most travellers will at this point probably just be content to wander around the old town, which still retains some haunting remnants of its romantic past. As Rose Macaulay wrote at the end of her novel, *The Towers of Trebizond*:

> Still the towers of Trebizond, the fabled city, shimmer on a far horizon, gated and walled and held in a luminous enchantment. It seems that for me, and however much I stand outside them, this must forever be. But at the city's heart lie the pattern and the hard core, and this I can never make my own: they are too far outside my range.

The scenery changes subtly as one drives east of Trabzon; the Pontic mountains in the background are loftier and more rugged and heavily wooded, the coastal plain narrower and more humid and verdant. The people are different too, for the eastern coast of the Black Sea is largely populated by Laz, the fiercely independent Caucasians who are undoubtedly the descendants of the savage tribesmen whom the ancient Greeks wrote of as inhabiting this region. They are alert, hard-working, intelligent, and highly aggressive, generous friends but deadly enemies. Occasionally one sees them dressed in their elegant folk costumes on national holidays, the men wearing their distinctive black head scarf with pendent folds framing their haughty faces, arms clasped on one another's shoulders as they perform their lively regional dance, the *horon*, to the wild and primitive music of a home-made bagpipe. As Evliya Efendi wrote of these indigenous Pontic people: 'The climate and air being favourable, the inhabitants are all jolly, merry fellows, who think of nothing but eating and drinking, of amusement and pleasure. Being all idle, amorous fellows, their colour is red, and the women fair, every one a moon or a portion of the sun.'

The drive from Trabzon to Rize is an easy one of about an hour, passing en route a number of pleasant towns and fishing villages. After forty-six kilometres you come to the village of **Sürmen Kastil**, where there is an exceptionally handsome old Ottoman mansion by the side of the road. This was built around 1800 by the Yakupoğlu family, who at that time were the local Derebeyler, literally Lords of the Valley.

Rize is an attractive port town pleasantly situated on wooded hills, whose spurs reach down to the sea on both sides of the town to form a great crescent bay. The riviera around Rize is one vast tea plantation, the principal export crop and source of income for this entire region. Much of the tea growing is done by the local Laz, whose villages in the hinterland are utterly unlike those in other less favoured parts of Anatolia. Their well-made timber and stone houses are always surrounded by gardens, the dwellings of each community often stretching out for miles along ridges and mountain meadows, for these independent people do not care to be confined in a squalid village but need breathing-space in which to be free. The most notable of these mountain Laz communities is Çamlîhemşin, which is reached by driving east from Rize along the coast past Pazar, and then climbing some twenty kilometres up a mountain road. The road is rough and difficult, but in the end one is rewarded by the discovery of what life is like in a Pontic town.

The last port on the Black Sea coast of Turkey is **Hopa**, where there is a road leading up over the mountains to Artvin and thence to either Kars or Erzurum. This is inevitably the end of the line in any journey along the Black Sea coast, for the remaining thirty kilometres to the Russian border are largely in a military area and travel is usually restricted.

Hopa was known in antiquity as Apsyrtis, named after Medea's brother, whose supposed tomb was still shown to travellers in classical times. This is a reminder that you are now in the legendary land of Colchis, of which Strabo has this to say in concluding his own description of the southern coast of the Euxine:

> The great fame this country had in early times is disclosed by the myths, which refer in an obscure way to the expedition of Jason as having proceeded as far as Media . . . It is said that in their country gold is carried down by the mountain-torrents, and that the barbarians obtain it by means of perforated troughs and fleecy skins, and that this is the origin of the myth of the golden fleece . . .

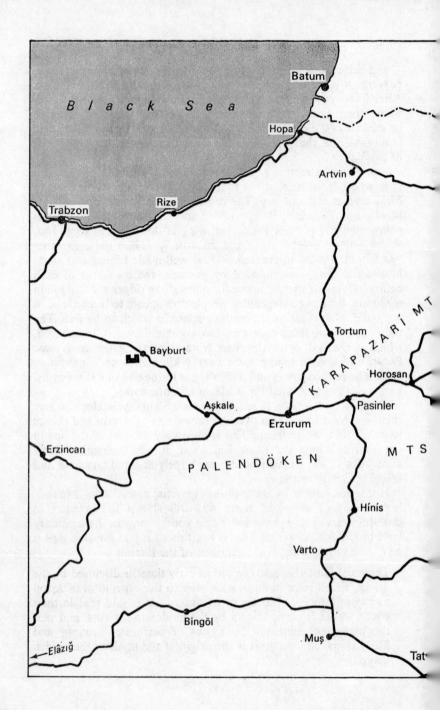

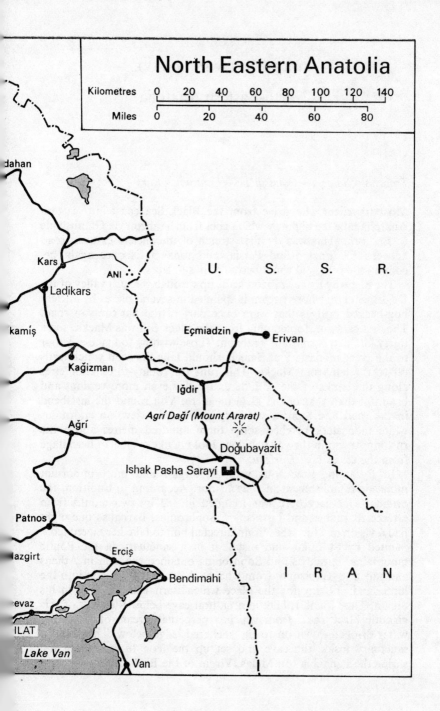

CHAPTER TWENTY-FIVE

North Eastern Anatolia

Kilometres 0 20 40 60 80 100 120 140

Miles 0 20 40 60 80

...dahan

Kars

ANI

Ladikars

...kamiş

Kağizman

Eçmiadzin

Erivan

U. S. S. R.

Iğdir

Agrí Dağí (Mount Ararat)

Ağrí

Doğubayazít

Ishak Pasha Sarayí

Patnos

...azgirt

Erciş

Bendimahi

I R A N

...evaz

ILAT

Lake Van

Van

North-Eastern Anatolia

❧

Trabzon – Sumela – Gümüşhane – Erzurum – Kars – Ani

Most travellers who drive from the Black Sea coast into eastern Anatolia take the highway which goes from Trabzon via Gümüşhane to Erzurum. This was the first stretch of the ancient caravan road between the Euxine and Persia, and today it is once again becoming the principal route between those places.

The highway from Trabzon leads up through the lush valley of the Değirmendere, whose stream is spanned in several places by ancient hog-backed bridges that were once part of the old caravan road. The first caravan stop coming from the Black Sea was Maçka, some thirty kilometres south of Trabzon. Those wishing to make a detour to the great monastery at Sumela should take the road which leads off to the left from Maçka. This runs for twenty-three kilometres along the banks of the Altíndere, a valley even more verdant and beautiful than that of the Değirmendere. You round the last bend in the road and Sumela suddenly comes into view, an enormous white monastery perched some three hundred metres above the rushing stream in the valley below, looking like a Tibetan hermitage from the set of *Lost Horizon*.

In Byzantine times this was the largest and most important monastic establishment in Asia Minor. According to tradition, the original sanctuary here was founded in 385 by two monks from Greece, Barnabas and his nephew Sophronius. Barnabas one night had a vision in which the Virgin directed him to take her sacred icon, painted by St Luke, and install it in a sanctuary in the Pontic mountains. Barnabas and Sophronius obtained the icon in Athens and sailed to Trebizond, from whence they carried the icon into the hinterland, looking for the place which Barnabas had seen in his dream. They found it here in a natural cave below the peak of this gigantic black rock, from which a perpetual stream of life-giving water dripped down on to the sheltered ledge below. They built a sanctuary inside the cave and set up the icon there, calling the shrine the Panaghia tou Melas, Virgin of the Black Rock, which in the Pontic dialect subsequently became Soumelas, or more simply, Sumela. Tradition goes on to say that a monastery was established there during the reign of Justinian, but not a trace remains of this foundation. In any event the importance of the monastery must have been well established by the fourteenth century, for in 1349 Alexius III Comnenus chose it as the most suitable site for his coronation as Emperor of Trebizond.

The monastery buildings are laid out along one side of a long, narrow rectangle, the back of which is formed by the sheer cliff of the mountain. The only entrance is at the south end, where a long and narrow stone stairway leads up past the arches of an Ottoman aqueduct. Inside the entrance are the quarters once used by the monastery porter, who in times past would receive the visitor with a glass of *ouzo* and a plate of cheese and olives, as in the monasteries of Athos today. There is a small court some two metres below to the north. The main court lies some fifteen metres below this, at much the same level as the platform outside the monastery; it is reached by a long stairway, bordered on the eastern side by the main living and guest rooms. These continue along the east side of the main court, on the west of which is the cave church, a few minor buildings and a library. There are additional dormitories to the north-east, within which are three more chapels. The innermost part of this complex is the oldest; one of the chapels contains remnants of frescoes of the fourteenth century, perhaps from the reign of Alexius III. To the north of the main court the outside buildings continue for some thirty-five metres along a narrower part of the ledge, their rear walls separated from the edge of the precipice by nothing more than a narrow verandah.

The main church is built in two sections, a large cave closed at the eastern end by a wall, and a small sanctuary built out of the wall in the form of an elongated apse. The church and the frescoes that originally decorated its walls date from 1710, at which time the monastery was almost completely restored and rebuilt; the present frescoes date from a redecoration in about 1740. The cave church itself is far older, probably dating from the reign of Alexius III.

The monastery today is in an appalling state of ruin and decay. Much of this was caused by a disastrous fire which took place just after the abandonment of the monastery in 1923, when the Pontic Greeks were expelled from Asia Minor, but a great deal of deliberate damage has since been done by visitors to the monastery. Nevertheless, this does not spoil the magnificence of the site of this ancient sanctuary.

Returning to Maçka, you continue on towards Erzurum, as the road enters the dense forests which cover the northern slopes of the Pontic Alps, with the lordly peak of Zigana Dağ (3063 metres) looming to the south. Some forty kilometres beyond Maçka you go over the Zigana Pass at 2025 metres, and the lush Pontic forests suddenly disappear, to give way to the bare uplands of the eastern Anatolian plateau, enlivened here and there by patches of evergreens.

It was somewhere in this vicinity that the Ten Thousand caught their first glimpse of the Euxine after their long march back from Persia. As one reads in the *Anabasis*:

So Xenophon mounted on his horse and, taking Lycus and the cavalry with him, rode forward to give support, and, quite soon, they heard the soldiers shouting out 'The sea! The sea!' and passing the word down the column. Then suddenly they all began to run, the rear guard and all, and drove on the baggage animals and the horses at full speed, and when they had all got to the top, the soldiers, with tears in their eyes, embraced each other and their generals and captives.

The first sizable town after the Zigana Pass is **Torul**. To the left of the road here are the remains of an ancient fortress, Ardasa Kale, standing dramatically on a spire-like peak. The road then enters the gorge of the Harşit Çayí, which extends to the south-east, and soon you come to the large town of **Gümüşhane**. Its name means literally Silver House, or Mint, a reminder of the silver mines which existed here in former times, and which Marco Polo remarked upon in his description of the region.

The road continues along the valley of the Harşit Çayí, and at **Kale**, some twenty kilometres farther along, you see on the right the ruins of another ancient fortress, Kovkalesi; this too is perched romantically on a slender crag. The road then enters a defile with cliffs some seventy metres high on either side, and scends the Dumadek Dere, going over the Vavuk Pass at 1910 metres.

Sixty kilometres beyond the pass you come to **Bayburt**, a garrison town on the banks of the Çoruh, the ancient River Lycus of Armenia. The town is dominated by one of the most impressive and best-preserved fortresses in Anatolia. It was originally built by the Bagtarids, the dynasty which ruled Armenia from the ninth century to the eleventh, but an inscription on the walls says that it was completely reconstructed between 1200 and 1230 by Mugis al-Din Tuğrul Şah, ruler of the Saltukid Turks at the time.

The road now runs along the valley of the Çoruh, following one of its branches to its source on the slopes of Dümlü Dağ (2600 metres), the great barrier separating the waters of the Black Sea from those of the Persian Gulf. Then the road climbs over the Kopdağí Pass at 2390 metres, an infamous crossing in earlier times when whole caravans would be snowed in and frozen to death.

A magnificent alpine view opens out beyond the pass, with the Karapazarí Mountains to the east and the Palendöken range to the south-east, both with peaks over three thousand metres high. The road then descends into the valley of the Karasu, the northernmost branch of the Euphrates, and soon you come to Aşkale, a large village dominated by a ruined Byzantine fortress. The road continues along the Karasu valley, which eventually widens out into the Erzurum Ovasí, a great highland plain bounded on the south by the Dumanlí range, on the east by the Palendöken Mountains, and on the north by Gavur Dağlarí, the Mountains of the Infidel. One sees quite a different kind of life here than in western Anatolia, particularly in summer, when the tribal Kurds and Yürüks spread out over the plain in their *yayla*, or summer encampments. The settled Kurds live in primitive stone houses with their inner rooms burrowed into the earth for warmth, exactly as Xenophon described them when he passed through this region in about 400 BC. This is one of the few areas in Turkey where the peasants still wear their colourful native costumes, far more attractive than the drab 'modern' clothes worn elsewhere in Anatolia.

At the eastern end of the plain you come to Erzurum, the largest and most important city in eastern Anatolia. The ancient settlement on this site was called Camacha, but in the latter part of the fourth century it was renamed Theodosiopolis in honour of Theodosius the Great, who refounded it as a fortress-city. The name Erzurum dates from around the time of the first Turkish occupation of the city early in the twelfth century. The name probably derives from Arz er Rum, or Land of Rome, as the Selcuks called the domains of the Byzantine Empire. Erzurum was always the principal city on the marchlands of eastern Anatolia, and because of its strategic position it was fought over and held in turn by the Armenians, Persians, Romans, Byzantines, Turks, Mongols, and most recently, the Russians, who captured the town twice in the nineteenth century and once again in 1916. For that reason Erzurum has always had the rough and ready appearance of a frontier garrison town, a sombre and colourless place isolated on the harsh and barren high plateau of eastern Anatolia, some two thousand metres in altitude and ringed by three-thousand-metre mountains.

The highway brings you into Erzurum along Cumhuriyet Caddesi. Continuing along the avenue, you see to the left the truncated minaret of the Yakutiye Medresesi. This was built in 1310 by Kwaca Yakut, Emir of Erzurum and Bayburt in the reign of the Ilkhanid Mongol ruler Ölceytü (1306–13), and dedicated to the Sultan and his wife, Bulgan Hatun. The conical-topped *türbe* behind the *medrese* was intended as the Emir's tomb, but he seems to have died elsewhere, for no evidence of a burial has been found within it.

Just before the end of the avenue you see on the left the principal monuments of Erzurum, first the Ulu Cami and beyond that the Çifte Minare Medrese, sometimes called the Hatuniye Medrese.

The Ulu Cami is a huge but very simple building of cut stone without the usual courtyard, and within it is the forest of columns characteristic of the great mosques of the early Selcuk period. The Ulu Cami was built in 1179 by Abdül-Fath Muhammed, grandson of Ali ibn Saltuk, the eponymous founder of the Saltukid clan of Turks who conquered Erzurum in 1103, thus beginning a dynasty which ruled there for more than a century.

The Çifte Minare Medrese takes its name from the pair of elaborately-tiled minarets which frame its façade. It is architecturally and artistically related to the Gök Medrese in Sivas, and there has been considerable discussion as to which was built first. Recent studies indicate that this may have been built as late as 1291, some twenty years after the Gök Medrese, and that its foundress may have been the Mongol princess Hüdavend Padişah Hatun. She is known to have lived in Erzurum from 1285 till 1291, leaving in that year when her husband, Prince Keyhato, became ruler of the Ilkhanid Mongols and moved to the capital at Tabriz.

On the heights directly across from Çifte Minare and Ulu Cami is the medieval citadel of Erzurum; a number of Greek inscriptions attest to its Byzantine origins but obviously it has been restored in Ottoman times. At the western end of the citadel is the conspicuous clock tower, a famous landmark in Erzurum. The tower is actually a reconstructed minaret, the Tepsi Minare. Next to the clock tower is the Kale Mescidi, an unusual little mosque in the form of a domed mausoleum whose *mihrab* is actually set into one of the towers of the citadel. Both the minaret and the *mescit* were built in the middle of the twelfth century, during the period when Erzurum was controlled by the Saltukid.

About a hundred and fifty metres behind the Ulu Cami there is a group of three tombs, the Üç Kümbet. The largest and most interesting of these is the so-called **Tomb of the Emir Saltuk**. Its lower part is in the form of an octagon, each side of which terminates in a triangular lunette, while the upper part is a cylinder topped by a low conical roof somewhat resembling a dome. No inscription remains on the tomb, but according to local tradition its founder was one of the Saltukid emirs. It is thought that the *türbe* was built at about the same time as the *mescit* in the citadel, that is, in the middle of the twelfth century. The other two *türbe* probably date from the late twelfth or early thirteenth century.

There are also a number of Ottoman monuments in Erzurum. The most important of these is the **Lala Mustafa Pasha Camii**, founded in 1563 by the Grand Vezir who eight years later was to conquer Cyprus.

From Erzurum you take the highway which leads eastward to Kars and the Russian frontier. The first sizable town you pass is **Pasinler**, some forty kilometres beyond Erzurum. Close by is the village of **Hasankale**, named after the once-mighty fortress which stands on a rocky eminence dominating the vast plain to the south. The fortress, originally built by the Bagtarid Armenians, was one of the strongholds of the formidable Uzun Hasan, who in the middle of the fifteenth century was chief of the Akkoyunlu, or White Sheep, a powerful Turcoman tribe who then ruled most of eastern Anatolia. Throughout the fifteenth century the Akkoyunlu were in continual conflict with the Karakoyunlu, or Black Sheep, the Turcoman tribe that ruled the region just to the south of theirs.

Eighteen kilometres beyond Pasinler, at **Çobandede**, you cross a tributary of the Aras River over an old Ottoman bridge which is sometimes attributed to Sinan. This handsome structure is 220 metres long, with six graceful arches, and is the finest ancient bridge still in use in Turkey.

Once past Çobandede the road follows the left bank of the Aras, the ancient Araxes, which rises in the Bingöl Mountains south of Erzurum, flowing from there more than a thousand kilometres to the east until it finally empties into the Caspian Sea.

Just after Horosan, twenty-seven kilometres past Çobandede, you turn left off the Iran highway and take the road which follows the river as far as Karakurt. At Karakurt the road at last leaves the Aras, turning north to Sarıkamış and thence north-east towards Kars. Some ten kilometres before reaching Kars you see on the right the Kümbet Kilise, a ruined Armenian church of the tenth century, a reminder that you are now approaching what was a thousand years ago the Kingdom of Armenia.

TURKEY

The road approaches **Kars** across an undulating highland plain
nearly two thousand metres above sea-level, one of the best pasture-
lands in eastern Anatolia. Finally you enter the town, a nondescript
settlement spread out along the banks of the winding Kars
Çayí, dominated by the medieval citadel standing on an eminence
to the north. This was originally built by the Bagtarid King Abas I
(928–52), who established the Armenian capital at Kars during his
regime. Later in that century the capital was transferred to Ani,
after which Kars took second place for the remainder of that chapter
of Armenian history. During the millennium since then Kars has
been besieged by all the armies that have marched along this historic
invasion route between Anatolia and the Transcaucasus: the
Selcuks, Byzantines, Georgians, Mongols, Turks and Russians. The
most memorable siege in recent history took place here during the
Crimean War, when a Turkish and British garrison under the British
General Sir Fenwick Williams held out valiantly for more than five
months against a superior Russian army, before finally surrendering
on 28 November 1855. Kars was again taken by the Russians in
1877 and held by them until 1920, when the town was captured by a
Turkish Nationalist army led by General Kâzim Karabekir. When
the Russo-Armenian army retreated from Kars it was accompanied
by most of the Armenian population of the region, leaving, apparently for ever, the lands in which they had dwelt since antiquity.

The only ancient monuments remaining in Kars are the citadel
and the former church of the Holy Apostles. The church was built
by King Abas I in the early years of his reign and served as the
cathedral of Kars until Ottoman times, after which it became a
mosque. During the Russian occupation it once more became a
church, then a mosque again in 1920, before finally being secularized
as a museum in recent years.

Almost all travellers who come to Kars do so in order to visit
the **ruins of Ani**, some fifty kilometres to the east on a dirt road. The
site of Ani is right on the Russian border, so those wishing to go
there must obtain permission at the Emniyet Müdürlüğü, the
Security Headquarters, and must proceed with a police escort. The
Tourism Bureau is very helpful in obtaining permission and also
arranges for group transport to the site.

As you cross the undulating Kars plateau and approach the
Russian border, you see the massive walls and towers of Ani looming
ahead, looking like the mirage of a ghost medieval city. A ghost city
it is indeed, uninhabited now for more than six centuries, with only
its ruined walls and the shells of half a dozen churches remaining

318

from a royal capital where once dwelt a hundred thousand souls.

Although it had long been an Armenian fortress-town, the history of Ani really began in the second half of the tenth century BC, when the Bagtarid kings transferred their capital there from Kars. The Bagtarids, who claimed descent from Kings David and Solomon of Israel, had been one of the leading princely families of the Arascid dynasty, who succeeded the earlier Artaxiad and Orontid dynasties which had ruled Armenia in ancient times. The Arascid dynasty came to an end in AD 428, not long after Armenia had been divided up between the Byzantines and the Persians. Later the whole of eastern Anatolia was overrun by the Arabs, and Armenian nationhood was preserved only by the semi-autonomous *nakharars*, princely families such as the Bagtarids. The Bagtarids eventually came to the fore, establishing themselves in the region of Mount Ararat and the Araxes valley, and in 862 their ruler, Ashot the Great, was granted by the Caliph of Baghdad the title of 'Prince of Princes of Armenia, of Georgia, and of the Lands of the Caucasus'. Urged on by the Catholicus of Armenia, the Armenian nobles ultimately forgot their differences and appointed Ashot their king, after which both the Arabs and Byzantines recognized his royal title and sent him golden crowns. A grandson of Ashot the Great, Ashot II the Iron (914–28), rid the country of Moslem invaders and established Armenian authority throughout eastern Anatolia and Transcaucasia. Armenia reached the pinnacle of its greatness under his successors: Ashot's brother Abas I (928–52), who set up his capital at Kars; the son of Abas, Ashot III the Merciful (952–77), who transferred the capital to Ani; and then the sons of Ashot III, Sembat II the Conqueror (977–89), and Gagik I (989–1020), who strengthened Ani's fortifications and adorned it with palaces, public buildings and sanctuaries, so that chroniclers of the time called it the 'city of a thousand and one churches'.

The long reign of Gagik I marked the apogee of Bagtarid rule, but his death in 1020 was followed by a rapid decline. The rivalry between his two sons, John-Sembat III and Ashot IV the Valiant, ended in the partition of a kingdom which had already been much reduced by Moslem and Byzantine invasions. John-Sembat III finally willed his inheritance, which included Ani, to the Emperor Basil II, and after his death in 1040 the Byzantine Empire annexed much of what remained of Armenia. Nevertheless, the Armenians fought on for another two decades, as Prince Vahram Pahlavuni rallied the nobility and army to the cause of John-Sembat's nephew and successor, Gagik II; but in 1045 Gagik abdicated in favour of

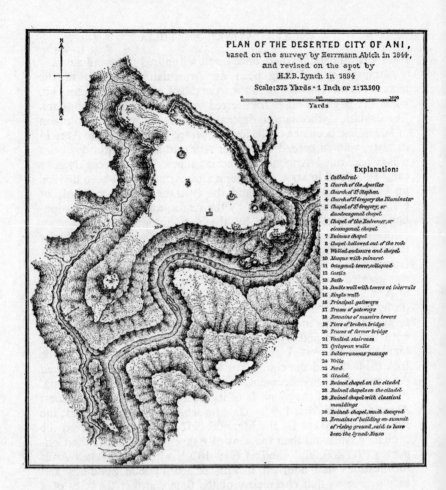

PLAN OF THE DESERTED CITY OF ANI,
based on the survey by Herrmann Abich in 1844,
and revised on the spot by
H.F.B. Lynch in 1894
Scale: 375 Yards = 1 Inch or 1:13,500

Yards

Explanation:
1 Cathedral
2 Church of the Apostles
3 Church of St Stephen
4 Church of St Gregory the Illuminator
5 Chapel of St Gregory, or duodecagonal chapel
6 Chapel of the Redeemer, or eicosagonal chapel
7 Ruinous chapel
8 Chapel hollowed out of the rock
9 Walled enclosure and chapel
10 Mosque with minaret
11 Octagonal tower, collapsed
12 Castle
13 Bath
14 Double wall with towers at intervals
15 Single wall
16 Principal gateways
17 Traces of gateways
18 Remains of massive towers
19 Piers of broken bridge
20 Traces of former bridge
21 Vaulted staircase
22 Cyclopean walls
23 Subterraneous passage
24 Wells
25 Ford
26 Citadel
27 Ruined chapel on the citadel
28 Ruined chapels on the citadel
29 Ruined chapel with classical mouldings
30 Ruined chapel, much decayed
31 Remains of building on summit of rising ground, said to have been the Synod House

the Byzantine Emperor Constantine IX Monomachus, and all resistance ceased when Prince Vahram died heroically in battle against the Emir of Dvin in 1047. But Byzantium did not long benefit by its annexation of Armenia, for, beginning in 1045, its eastern borders were subjected to repeated attacks by the Selcuk Turks. Ani was captured in 1064 by the Selcuk Sultan Alparslan, who seven years later defeated the Byzantines at Manzikert and ended for ever their rule in eastern Anatolia.

The Armenians enjoyed a brief revival with the rise of Georgian power, beginning under King David IV (1089–1125) and culminating in the reign of Queen Thamar (1184–1213). After freeing their own

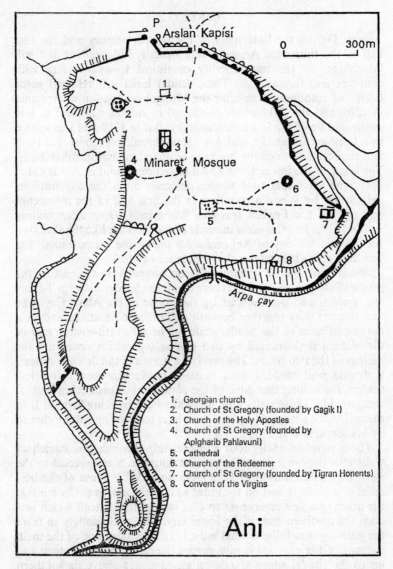

P

Arslan Kapísí

0   300m

1

2

3

4   Minaret   Mosque

6

5

7

8

Arpa çay

1. Georgian church
2. Church of St Gregory (founded by Gagik I)
3. Church of the Holy Apostles
4. Church of St Gregory (founded by Aplgharib Pahlavuni)
5. Cathedral
6. Church of the Redeemer
7. Church of St Gregory (founded by Tigran Honents)
8. Convent of the Virgins

Ani

land from the Selcuks, the Georgians advanced into Armenia, liberating the northern, central and eastern provinces of the kingdom, including Kars and Ani. These provinces were then ruled by Armenian-Georgian feudal lords, the most powerful of whom were the Zakhariads, whose fiefdom included Ani and the region around Mount

Ararat. During the latter part of the twelfth century and the first half of the thirteenth Armenia was virtually independent and still flourishing, as the new nobility continued to endow Ani with churches and monasteries. These feudal lords still retained some degree of autonomy even after the Mongol occupation of Armenia in 1236, and the Zakhariads continued to rule in Ani until as late as the middle of the fourteenth century. But in 1319 Ani was visited by a terrible earthquake, and Armenian chroniclers report that from that time on the ruined city began to be abandoned by its inhabitants. The latest of the inscriptions which have been found in Ani is dated 1348, and after that time silence descends upon the city until its rediscovery by Western travellers in the first half of the nineteenth century. As the English traveller Wilbraham wrote after visiting Ani in 1837: 'The shapeless mounds of Babylon are like the skeleton, yet the deserted city of Ani resembles the corpse whose breath has fled, but which still retains the semblance of life.'

Ani is built upon a spacious plateau bounded on the east by the ravine of the Arpa Çay, which here forms the border between Turkey and Russia, and on the west by the ravine of the Alaca Çay. The two streams flow together beneath a fortified crag at the end of a narrow isthmus to the south, while the broad north-eastern end of the plateau is delineated by two side valleys which open into the ravines of the two rivers. The surviving stretch of the defence system, a double wall studded with massive rectangular and cylindrical towers, runs along that edge of the plateau, thus protecting it at its weakest side. These walls were originally built by King Sembat II at the end of the tenth century and were later restored and strengthened by his son Gagik I.

There were originally four gates leading through this stretch of walls into the inner city. The present entrance is the second to the west, the **Arslan Kapísí**, or **Lion Gate**, so called because of the bas-relief of a running lion on the inner wall of the gateway. Once inside the inner gate you emerge on to that part of the plateau which was once the northern end of the lower city. The track leading in from the gateway here follows what must once have been one of the main avenues of the city, for it runs across the centre of the plateau and up to the citadel which stands on an eminence above its southern end. The citadel was probably the fortress which guarded this strategic site before the establishment of the Armenian capital at Ani in 961.

About a hundred and fifty metres from the gate you come to the ruins of a Georgian church built in 1218, adorned with some fine reliefs of biblical scenes. About a hundred metres to the west are the foundations of what is believed to be the **Church of St Gregory the Illuminator**, built in 998 by Gagik I. This is one of three churches of that name still standing in Ani, all of them dedicated to the sainted Armenian prince who converted his people to Christianity at the beginning of the fourth century.

About four hundred metres beyond the Lion Gate are the ruins of the **Church of the Holy Apostles**, now in an advanced state of decay. Inscriptions indicate that the church was built in 1031 and that it was endowed by the noble Pahlavuni and Zakhariad families.

A little farther along you come to the **Cami Minaresi**, an isolated minaret whose parent mosque has now vanished. From here a path to the right takes you to the second **Church of St Gregory**, an attractive building which overlooks the ravine of the Alaca. This was built in about 1040 by Prince Aplgharib Pahlavuni.

Returning to the minaret, you see to the right a mosque with a hexagonal minaret standing at the edge of the ravine above the Arpa. According to the Cufic inscription on the minaret, the mosque was founded in 1074 by the first Moselm ruler of Ani, Menüçahir, son of the Selcuk Emir Abulsevar.

A short distance south-east of the minaret is the **Cathedral of Ani**, the largest and most impressive building remaining from the medieval city. It was begun by Sembat II in 989, the last year of his life, and completed in 1001 by King Gagik I and Queen Katramide. The church was designed by the famous architect Trdat, who repaired the dome of Haghia Sophia after it collapsed in an earthquake in 989. Trdat's plan is a variation of the cross-in-a-rectangle. Externally the apse is indicated only by two deep niches which recess back from the eastern wall; there are also two similar niches on the north and south sides, where they mark the articulation of the design and set off the elegance of the slender columns of the blind arcade. On the north, south and west sides there are low doorways each surmounted by a narrow window with a rectangular frame of chiselled stone. The dome, now vanished, was supported by four massive piers of coupled pillars from which rise pointed and stepped arches, giving a Gothic appearance to the nave.

About three hundred metres east of the Cathedral is the **Church of the Redeemer**, yet another foundation of the pious Pahlavuni family. An inscription records that in 1034 Prince Aplgharib Pahlavuni, having journeyed to Constantinople on the orders of King John-Sembat III, obtained there a fragment of the True Cross; upon his return to Ani he built this church and directed that nocturnal devotions be held within it until the second coming of Christ.

The third church dedicated to **St Gregory the Illuminator**, about two hundred and fifty metres east of the Church of the Redeemer, stands dramatically on a headland at the edge of a cliff high above the Arpa. It is on a much smaller scale than the Cathedral, but similar in style and plan; what is more, it retains its high drum and part of its conical roof, giving one a good idea of how the Cathedral must once have appeared. The interior of the church is quite well-preserved, with the walls and ceilings still adorned with frescoes. The figure of *Christ Enthroned* appears in the conch of the central apse and *The Communion of the Apostles* is represented on the semi-circular wall below, while *The Ascension* covers the dome, with a circlet of Prophets on the drum below. The north and south zones of the church are decorated with scenes from the life of Christ and the Virgin, while the west zone is given over to a cycle of the life of St Gregory the Illuminator. The commemorative inscriptions on the exterior record that the church was built in 1215 and that the founder was a nobleman named Tigran Honents, who hoped that his benefaction would bring long life to his house and that of the Zakhariads, the rulers of Ani at that time.

The inscription goes on to say that when Tigran Honents bought the land on which he built his church a chapel dedicated to the Virgin already stood upon it. This is undoubtedly the little ruined chapel which is situated a short way down the Arpa ravine, standing on a projecting mass of rock that forms an almost vertical cliff above the stream. The chapel and its situation are wildly romantic, a tiny medieval sanctuary of pink stone perched on barren cliffs. But for all its beauty the scene is somehow mournful, with the ghost of this once great city on one side of the gorge and on the other the forbidding no-man's land along the Russian border. Looking upon this stark landscape one might recall the lines with which Aristakes of Lastivert ended his threnody nine centuries ago, mourning the fall of Ani:

Where are the thrones of our kings? They are seen nowhere. Where are the legions of soldiers that massed before them like dense cloud formations, colourful as the flowers of spring, and resplendent in their uniforms? They are nowhere to be seen. Where is our great and marvellous pontifical throne? Today it is vacant, deprived of its occupant, denuded of its ornaments, filled with dust and spider-webs, and the heir to the throne removed to a foreign land as a captive and a prisoner. The voices and the sermons of the priests are silent now. The chandeliers are extinguished now and the lamps dimmed, the sweet fragrance of incense is gone, the altar of Our Lord is covered with dust and ashes . . . Now if all that we have related has befallen us because of our wickedness, then tell heaven and all that abide in it, tell the mountains and the hills, the trees of the dense woodlands, that they too may weep over our destruction.

CHAPTER TWENTY-SIX

The Eastern Borderlands

❧

Kars – Doğubayazít – Mount Ararat – Ishak Pasha Sarayí – Lake Van – Van – Toprakkale – The Hakkâri – Akhtamar – Tatvan – Ahlat

After returning to Kars you must retrace your way back along the Erzurum road as far as Ladikars, where there is a turning to the left for Iğdír and Doğubayazít. This takes you southward to the valley of the Aras and then eastward again towards the Russian border. The scenery along this part of the drive is splendid, for the Aras runs in a canyon whose northern wall forms the termination of the north-eastern Anatolian plateau, with an immensely long line of cliffs towering over the river valley below.

The road continues along the canyon as far as the Russian border, where the Aras is joined by the Arpa. A few miles to the north of the confluence of the two rivers is the village of **Pakran**, site of the ancient Armenian city of **Bagaran**, which served as the capital of the Bagtarid kingdom during the reign of Ashot I the Great (856–90). A thousand years before that it was a temple city of the Orontids, the dynasty which ruled Armenia during the Hellenistic period. Unfortunately the site is presently inaccessible because of its proximity to the Russian border.

The road continues along the Aras valley, which is here flanked by the two great peaks that form part of the mountain wall between north-eastern Anatolia and the Transcaucasus: to the north in Russia is **Alagöz Dağí** (4094 metres), and to the south is **Ağrí Dağí** (5165 metres), better known as **Mount Ararat**. Their peaks are fully one hundred kilometres apart as the eagle flies, but so high do they tower above the surrounding landscape that one can see both of them in a single panoramic view.

At Iğdír you turn right and leave the valley of the Aras, which from there flows south-east to form the border between Russia and Iran, as it earlier marked the boundary between Turkey and Russia. You then drive past the western flank of Ararat, going over the Çengel Pass at 2138 metres, and finally come to the Kurdish village of **Doğubayazít**. This is the best base for ascending Ararat, or, for the ordinary traveller, a place where one can stop and rest while contemplating the splendours of this fabled mountain.

From Doğubayazít the massif of Ağrí Dağí dominates the whole horizon to the north-west, with the perpetually snow-capped dome of Great Ararat to the left, some three hundred and fifty metres higher than Mont Blanc, and across the saddle to the right the pyramidal peak of Little Ararat, 3925 metres in altitude. The extraordinary elevation of Ararat above the surrounding plain, more than four thousand metres from the valley of the Aras to the highest peak, is perhaps unequalled in the world, and does much to enhance the magnificence of the mountain and the grandeur of the view. It is no wonder that this majestic mountain was thought to be the resting-place of Noah's Ark and the centre from which mankind once again spread throughout the world. As one reads in Genesis:

And God remembered Noah, and every living thing, and all the cattle that was with him in the Ark; and God made a wind to pass over the earth, and the waters assuaged. The fountains of the deep and the windows of heaven were stopped, and the rain from heaven was restrained; and the waters returned from off the earth continually; and after the end of the hundred and fifty days the waters were abated. And the Ark rested on the seventh month, on the seventeenth day of the month, upon the mountains of Ararat.

The story of Noah's landing here was part of the Armenians' tradition even before the Christian period, and after their conversion a purported piece of the Ark was enshrined in a sanctuary called 'Jacob's Well', on the north-eastern slope of Great Ararat. Visions of the Ark resting on top of Ararat have lured travellers here for the past century and a half, and mystics have returned with what they fancied were pieces of the vessel, or with tales of having seen it buried beneath glacial ice. One of the most stirring accounts of these visionary climbers is that of the British scholar James Bryce, who scaled Ararat on 11 September 1876, giving this emotional description of what he saw and felt as he looked out across the world below:

Below and around, included in this single view, seemed to lie the whole cradle of the human race, from Mesopotamia in the south to the great wall of the Caucasus that covered the northern horizon, the boundary for so many ages of the civilized world. If it was indeed here that man first set foot on the unpeopled earth, one

could imagine how the great dispersal went as the races spread
themselves down from these sacred heights along the course of
the great rivers down to the Black and Caspian Seas, and over the
Assyrian plain to the shores of the Southern Ocean, whence they
were wafted away to the other continents and isles. No more
imposing centre of the world could be imagined.

Six kilometres east of Doğubayazít is one of the most unusual
monuments in Turkey, the **Ishak Pasha Sarayí**. Built on a platform
which projects out from the top of a deep gorge opening on to the
Ararat plain, this extraordinary palace was built in the latter part
of the eighteenth century by a dynasty of feudal lords, the Çildiroğlu,
who at that time ruled eastern Anatolia and the Transcaucasus
under the Ottomans. Some sources say they were Georgians, some
Armenian, and still others Kurds, and in fact they may have been an
amalgamation of all three. The palace is attributed to Ishak Pasha,
who was made Vezir in 1789, but it was probably begun by his
father, Beylül Pasha, and was certainly completed by his son, Mahmut
Pasha. Ishak Pasha's power made him virtually independent of the
Sultan, and from this impregnable eyrie he controlled the lucrative
caravan trade along the Silk Road, which followed much the same
route as the modern highway to Iran. He amassed enormous wealth,
much of which he lavished on this palace, a combination of fortress
and oriental pleasure-dome. The palace is of no definite architectural style, combining elements of imitation Selcuk, mock-
Georgian, neo-Armenian, and baroque Ottoman art, but though it
is an eclectic anachronism the result is pleasing and highly original.

Across the gorge from the palace you see a mosque raised on a
high podium above the ravine, with the ruins of an ancient fortress
on the crag behind it. The mosque was perhaps built by Selim the
Grim in 1514, at the time of the Sultan's campaign against Shah
Ismail of Persia. On 23 August of that year the Sultan's army
decisively defeated the Persians at the battle of Çaldíran, thirty
kilometres to the south of Doğubayazít, and the great provinces of
Diyarbakír and Kurdistan were then permanently annexed to the
Ottoman Empire.

The fortress above the mosque has been identified by inscriptions
on its walls as being Urartian in origin, though reconstructed by the
Selcuks and Ottomans. The Urartians were almost unknown in
history until the last century, save for a few passing references to
them in the Bible, but since then archaeologists have unearthed
many of their former towns and fortresses. This has led to the

deciphering of their language, the discovery of their history, and the collection of their superb works of art in museums throughout the world. The word 'Urartu' is preserved in the Old Testament in the corrupt form 'Ararat', which in the Latin version became 'Armenia'. The Urartians first appear in history in the ninth century BC, when they are mentioned in the annals of the Assyrian King Shalmaneser III (860–25 BC).

Most of the surviving Urartian sites in Turkey are found to the south of Mount Ararat, principally in the region around Lake Van, where the capital of their kingdom was located. There are no good roads leading south from Doğubayazít along the Russian border, so in order to reach Van one must drive back westward to Ağrí and then turn left on the road which goes south to Patnos. As you approach Patnos you see ahead the beautiful snow-capped cone of Süphan Daği (4434 metres), the second highest peak in Turkey, rivalling Ararat in its grandeur. Then at Patnos you turn left on to the road which leads south-east to Van, reaching the shores of the lake at Erciş.

For those with time to explore there are a number of Urartian sites along this last part of the route, including two near Patnos and two more in the vicinity of Erciş. The present community of **Erciş** is relatively new, established here after the original site on the lake shore was inundated by a sudden rise of the water level in 1838. In the Middle Ages this place was called Arjesh, and Marco Polo referred to it as one of the three great cities of Armenia; however, it was sacked by the Georgians in 1209 and thereafter it declined to the status of an insignificant village. A cuneiform inscription of King Argistis II (713–685 BC) was discovered here in recent years, and the similarity of his name to that of the medieval town strongly suggests that this was one of the cities he founded.

As you come out of Erciş you see on your right the **Kadem Hatun Pasha Türbesi**, a mausoleum built in 1458 for the mother of a Karakoyunlu emir. The road then goes around the north-eastern corner of Lake Van, and at Bendimahi it crosses a river and runs down along the eastern shore of the lake. Between Erciş and Bendimahi four Urartian sites have been identified; three of these are close to the shore road and can easily be found if there is time to spare.

Twenty-five kilometres beyond Bendimahi you pass Timar, where you see offshore an islet called **Adír Adasí**, on which are the remains of a medieval Armenian monastery. A few kilometres farther along on the lake shore are the ruins of **Amik Kalesi**, a medieval Arab fortress. The road then veers inland and curves southward, and soon you see ahead the great rock of Van at the south-eastern end of the lake.

The modern city of **Van** is some distance inland from the lake shore. It occupies the site of what was once the garden suburb of the **ancient Tushpa**, capital of Urartu.

The Urartian state rose to eminence quite rapidly at the end of the ninth century BC, while Assyria, weakened by continual wars and internal disorders, was unable to oppose her adversary's advance. At the end of the ninth century the Urartians began to enlarge their territory, conducting campaigns throughout eastern Anatolia and the Transcaucasus. The period of Urartu's greatest splendour began in the reign of Menua (*c.* 810–786 BC), when it became the largest and most powerful state in western Asia. Throughout his kingdom, as attested by numerous inscriptions on the Rock of Van and elsewhere, Menua built towns, fortresses, palaces and temples, constructed canals, aqueducts and irrigation systems, and laid out farms, gardens and vineyards, bringing to flower the land which in ancient legend had been the site of the Garden of Eden.

The rise of Urartu continued throughout the reign of Menua's son, Argistis I (*c.* 786–64 BC), when the kingdom spread as far as the Mediterranean and Urartian works of art began to appear in Phrygia, Greece, and Italy. The situation changed during the reign of Argistis's son, Sarduris II (*c.* 764–35 BC), when the Assyrians revived and began to recover their lost dominions. In 743 the Assyrian King Tiglath-Pileser III won a victory over the army of Sarduris II, and eight years later he marched to Lake Van and besieged the fortress on the rock. As the Assyrian king wrote in his annals for the year 735 BC: 'I shut up Sarduris of Urartu in Turushpa [Tushpa], his capital city. I made a great slaughter in front of the gates of the town, and opposite the town I set up an image of my royalty.'

The well-fortified stronghold on the Rock of Van withstood the siege, though the lower town and the garden suburb were destroyed as the Assyrians marched into the heart of Urartu. The victory of Tiglath-Pileser III over Sarduris II almost destroyed Urartu, though the Urartians struggled to maintain their lands as they fought with the Assyrians throughout the following century. But this continual warfare fatally weakened both states and made them increasingly vulnerable to the new powers, most notably the Medes, who were beginning to come to the fore in western Asia. The Assyrian Empire came to an end with the fall of Nineveh in 612 BC, and about twenty years later Urartu fell to the Medes. The last surviving Urartian works have been dated to about 590 BC, and archaeological work at Van and other sites indicates that they were all destroyed by fire and the sword.

The Urartians were succeeded in eastern Anatolia and Trans-caucasia by the Armenians, who founded their first kingdom under the Orontid dynasty in the fourth century BC. Van became one of the principal cities in Armenia and retained its importance throughout the classical and Byzantine periods. During the tenth century AD the Artsunis of Vaspurakan, rivals of the Bagtarids, established an independent Armenian kingdom with its capital at Van. The first ruler of this kingdom was Gagik Artsuni, who founded a dynasty which ruled the area around Lake Van for a century and a half. But the Artsunid kingdom eventually suffered the same fate as that of the Bagtarids. In 1021 the last King of Van, Sennacherib-John of Vaspurakan, ceded his kingdom to the Byzantines, who themselves lost it to the Selcuks fifty years later after the battle of Manzikert. Unlike Ani, Van continued to be an important city right up to the present century, and its population remained predominantly Armenian. But the old city below the Rock of Van was utterly destroyed during the First World War, and the entire Armenian population either perished or fled.

The old city of Van has never been rebuilt, and there are now only some scattered ruins to testify to the fact that the site was inhabited for nearly three thousand years. One of the structures remaining in the lower city is the minaret of the Great Mosque, built by the Karakoyunlu Emir Yusuf between 1389 and 1400. Not far from this stand a pair of rather handsome *türbe*, which somehow survived the destruction visited upon the remainder of the lower city.

A good deal remains of the ancient walls and towers of the citadel on the great rock of Van which range in date from ancient Urartian through medieval Armenian and Selcuk to late Ottoman. There are many interesting inscriptions on the walls. The oldest is that of King Sarduris I of Urartu, and there is one three centuries later in date commemorating the conquest of Van by Xerxes (485–65 BC). Many of the Urartian inscriptions are in the so-called Caves of Khorkhor, which were apparently built as catacombs for the burial of the early Urartian kings.

The citadel commands a superb view of **Lake Van**, with the symmetrical snow-streaked form of Süphan Daǧí mirrored in the waters along its northern shore. This is by far the largest lake in Turkey – 3764 square kilometres – about six times as large as Lake Geneva. Its waters are charged with large concentrations of chlorides and sulphides of sodium and potassium, which leaves a not unpleasant feeling on the skin after bathing. Above all, the lake is surpassingly beautiful, an azure blue inland sea ringed around by the lordly mountains of eastern Anatolia.

One of the most important Urartian sites in Turkey is to be found three kilometres north-east of the town centre of modern Van, approached by the main road which goes out to the Iranian border via Özalp. This is **Toprakkale**, a flat-topped hill some seventy metres high on the right of the road. The Turkish name means Earth (*Toprak*) Castle (*Kale*), and on closer inspection one finds that the hill is actually made up of the remains of massive mud-brick walls and the debris of the structures that stood inside the fortress. Excavations have revealed that this was a royal residence and fortress begun by the Urartian kings in the early years of the seventh century BC.

Travellers with time to spare can use Van as a base for visiting the Hakkâri, the remote and mountainous south-eastern corner of Turkey, a wild region which has only been open to foreigners for the last decade or so. The first sizable village you come to is **Güzelsu**, which is dominated by the formidable **Hoşap Kale**; this mighty fortress was originally constructed in the fifteenth century and was completely rebuilt in 1643 by Sarí Süleyman Bey. The castle stands on a crag above the Hoşap River, which is here spanned by a handsome twin-arched bridge of cut stone; according to the dedicatory inscription at the centre this was constructed in 1500 by one Zeynel Bey. One can presume that both of these *beys* were local Kurdish war-lords and robber barons, for one is here in the heart of ancient Kurdistan.

The first large town is **Başkale**, after which the road runs along the rugged valley of the Great Zab, a tributary of the Tigris. You then drive along the right bank of the Zab as it takes you deep into the mountains of Kurdistan, until you finally arrive in **Hakkâri**, the principal town of the region.

Here one is in quite a different world, ringed round by tremendous mountains with several peaks over four thousand metres high, almost completely cut off from the rest of Turkey. Until half a century ago the Hakkâri had a large population of Nestorian Christians, members of a schismatic church which split off from the Patriarchate in Constantinople in the fifth century, but all of them either fled or perished in the years immediately following the First World War. Now only the tribal Kurds remain, living a nomadic and pastoral life which has not changed in its essentials since Urartian times. They are a fiercely independent mountain people with their own language and culture, often given to banditry and rebellion, ready to head for the hills with their families and animals when the Turkish army or gendarmerie are sent against them, savage foes but loyal friends, looked down upon with contempt by the citified people of western Turkey, but capable, hard-working and creative when an opportunity is presented them. They refer to all strangers, Turks and foreigners alike, by the word with which they have characterized all intruders into Kurdistan for the past two thousand years: they simply and contemptuously call them Rumi, which means Romans.

From Van you now drive south around the eastern end of the lake. Thirty-two kilometres out of Van you cross the Şemiran Suyu, the Waters of Semiramis, the great irrigation canal dug in the eighth century BC by King Menua of Urartu. Eight kilometres beyond the canal you come to the small town of Gevaş at the south-eastern corner of Lake Van. Outside the town a road leads to Gevaş Iskelesi, the embarkation point for the isle of Akhtamar. Near the road to the pier is the **Halime Hatun Türbesi**, a very pretty mausoleum built in 1358 for a Karakoyunlu princess.

The island of **Akhtamar** is about three kilometres from the southern shore of the lake. At its western end there is a bold crag of grey limestone which slopes rapidly down to the level eastern half of the islet, site of the incomparable Church of the Holy Cross.

During the early Middle Ages Akhtamar was used mainly as a place of refuge by the Armenians of the Lake Van region. Then in the second decade of the tenth century King Gagik I Artsuni made it one of the principal seats of his kingdom, fortifying the island and building a palace on the summit of the hill at its western end. The dates generally accepted for the construction of the **Church of the Holy Cross** are 915 to 921. It is a relatively small structure, 14.8 metres long and 11.5 wide, built of carefully joined pink sandstone facing an inner core of rubble concrete. The plan is of the centralized type which had been traditional in Armenia since at least as far back as the seventh century. The large central square, covered by a dome on a high drum, opens into four semi-circular exedrae along the main axes, and along the diagonals there are four small niches in the form of three-quarter cylinders. The dome is ultimately supported by the eight piers that stand between the axial exedrae and the diagonal niches; from there four pendentives open out to support the drum. The niches at the east end give access to two side chambers which flank the eastern exedra but do not open into it. The eastern exedra and its arch combine to form the sanctuary, whose raised floor is reached by way of four steps on either side. The south exedra housed the royal gallery over the entrance on that side; this was originally reached by an outer staircase, destroyed in the nineteenth century when the present belfry was constructed. The church is well lighted by eight windows in the drum and sixteen others in the exedrae and niches. The principal entrance is through the west exedra, and there are also portals in the north and south exedrae.

The exterior of the church only partially reflects the geometrical forms of the interior. The east and west ends are rectangular, the eastern façade being wider because it encloses the apse and the two side chambers. Both of these façades have deep, wedge-shaped recesses, those on the western end marking the width of the exedra, while the eastern ones show the articulation of the apse and the side chambers. The contours of the north and south façades are much more varied, with polygonal walls surrounding the exedrae and the niches; these add greatly to the beauty of the exterior through the constantly changing patterns of light and shade that play across the planes of the façade.

The most unusual and attractive feature of the church is the rich display of figural and ornamental sculpture which adorns its façades. A frieze of animals is carved in high relief directly under the roof; lions, foxes, dogs, hares, gazelles and a horse pursue one another in rapid motion, interrupted here and there by the figures of birds and by human masks. A scalloped band girds the base of the drum, and a second animal frieze is carved under the eaves of the roofs of the exedrae and niches; here, in addition to the creatures mentioned above, there are oxen, panthers, ibexes and snakes, occasionally punctuated by fighting or confronted animals, floral designs and human masks. A metre below this there is another frieze called the vine scroll, a fabulous creation in which various humans, beasts and birds carry on their multifarious activities while entwined in a burgeoning grapevine, a Breughel-like scene sculptured in an encircling relief around the church. Another ornamental band of pine cones enveloped in palmettes girds the lower level of the walls, about a metre above the ground. The spaces between the vine and palmette scrolls are filled with a rich array of human figures and animals, some of which are carved in the round. Arched bands, decorated with vegetable scrolls, crown the windows of the drum and of the church, as well as the triangular recesses of the east and west façades.

Among the many figures and scenes represented on the lower level of the façade, four are particularly notable. On the west façade the portraits of Gagik and Jesus flank the central window, with the King presenting a model of his church to Christ. On the south façade there are several scenes from the life of Jonah, including one in which his companions cast him out of a caique into the gaping jaws of a very merry whale. On the east half of the south façade there is a prominent scene in which David is about to slay Goliath. Perhaps the most memorable of all the sculptures is to be seen to the left of the window in the central section of the north façade. Here Adam and Eve stand on either side of the Tree of Life and are about to eat its forbidden fruit; they have heavy thighs and great pendent bellies, looking as if they had dined very well in the Garden of Eden.

The interior of the church was adorned throughout with murals; much has vanished and what remains is often faded and in rather poor condition, nevertheless it gives one a good idea of the original decorative scheme. The drum of the dome was decorated with a cycle representing the story of Adam and Eve, beginning with the introduction of Adam into the Garden of Eden and ending with their expulsion. Portraits of bishops were painted on three zones, one above the other, in the diagonal niches and on the outer faces of the pilasters. Interlacing floral designs cover the angular walls formed by these pilasters and the exedrae and niches. Scenes from the Gospels were represented in the remaining part of the church, namely in the four exedrae and the piers which support the barrel-vault in front of the west exedra.

Nothing remains of the palace built on Akhtamar by Gagik, who was crowned here as King of Vaspurakan in 908. As the chronicler Thomas Artusini described the scene:

Mounted on a horse with gilt trappings, he shone like the sun amidst the stars; large companies of soldiers, armed from head to foot, stood to the right and the left; the weapons clashed, the trumpets resounded, the horns blared, the flutes shrilled, the lyres gave forth melodious sounds, psalteries and banners preceded and followed him, and the soldiers of the royal army let out a mighty shout which shook the earth. With such pomp was he installed.

Returning to Gevaş Iskelesi, you now drive along the southern shore to **Tatvan**, a town at the south-western corner of Lake Van. Here passengers bound for Iran by rail are transported across the lake to Van, so you have the unexpected pleasure of finding a clean and comfortable hotel run by the Denizcilik Bankasí, the Turkish Maritime Lines. This makes Tatvan a good base for exploring the northern shore of the lake and the surrounding region.

Tatvan lies at the foot of **Nemrut Daǧí** (3050 metres), one of the two famous mountains of that name in eastern Anatolia. Those with time to spare can arrange to climb up to **Nemrut Gölü**, an extraordinary crater lake 2400 metres above sea-level, just to the south of the main peak of Nemrut Daǧí. This is one of the largest craters in the world, some seven kilometres in diameter, comparable in size to the famous Crater Lake in Oregon. The northern rim of the crater is more than seven hundred metres above the level of the lake, which fills the western half of the crater, the eastern half consisting of old lava streams covered with pumice and bristling with sharp crags – an altogether unforgettable sight.

Another interesting excursion from Tatvan is to the **ruins of Ahlat**, some forty kilometres by the road which runs along the northern shore of the lake. Ahlat was originally an important Armenian town, but it fell to the Arabs in the mid-eighth century, and then was held successively by the Byzantines, Selcuks, Ayubid, Kharizmid, Kurds, Selcuks again, then the Mongols, the Akkoyunlu, the Karakoyunlu, and finally the Ottomans. During Ottoman times it declined in importance and today the site is utterly abandoned, the population having moved to a new site some kilometres to the east along the lake shore.

Ahlat is second only to Kayseri in the number and variety of its tombs. A dozen mausolea, some of them ruined, some of them in perfect condition, have survived from the pre-Ottoman period. The largest and most splendid of these is the one you see to the right by the lake shore as you approach Old Ahlat. Built in 1273, it is a cylindrical structure nearly seven metres in diameter on a square podium with cut-away corners, surmounted by a conical roof resting on stalactite cornices. There is a door on the east side and windows on the other three cardinal points, with round-arched niches between them. Two other fine mausolea of the same period, the Çifte Türbe, are smaller versions of this one; they were built in 1279 for various members of the family of a Selcuk emir. The Erzen Hatun Kümbeti, a handsome tomb built for a Karakoyunlu princess in 1396, is an almost exact replica of the Halime Hatun tomb at Gevaş. Yet another Ahlat mausoleum of a rather different type is the Bayíndír Türbesi, built in 1492 for an emir of the Akkoyunlu. Here the cylindrical body of the *türbe* opens on the south through a decorative portico of rather heavy but attractive columns. From the Ottoman period there remains the fortress built on the lake shore in the sixteenth century.

The most haunting aspect of this ghost city is its vast Moslem cemetery, a veritable petrified forest of lichen-covered gravestones dating back to Selcuk times, many of them finely carved and adorned with calligraphic and floral designs. This is surely one of the most romantically beautiful graveyards in the world.

Thirty kilometres east of Ahlat you come to **Adilcevaz**, a large village on the shore of Lake Van directly below Süphan Daği. Here you see the remains of a Selcuk castle by the lake, and on a hilltop above a valley to the west are the cyclopean walls of an ancient Urartian fortress called Kefkalesi. Excavations have revealed that this must have been a major Urartian town, perhaps the Quallania mentioned in the annals of King Sargon of Assyria.

There is little of interest to see in the remaining stretch of the north coast between Adilcevaz and Erciş, where you began the circuit of Lake Van. You are advised, therefore, to return to Tatvan, where the hotel of the Denizcilik Bankasí provides an excellent place to rest before starting the long journey back to the west.

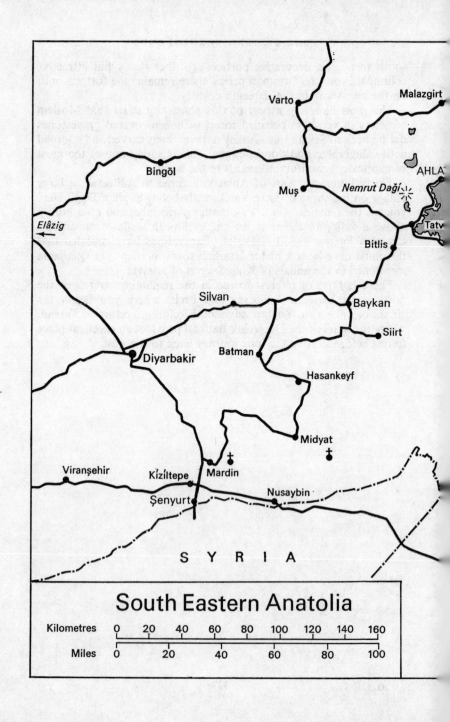

South Eastern Anatolia

Kilometres	0	20	40	60	80	100	120	140	160

Miles	0	20	40	60	80	100

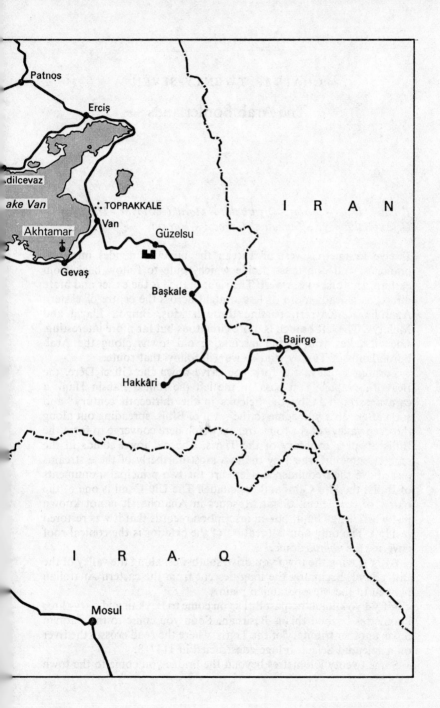

Patnos

Erciş

dilcevaz

ake Van

Akhtamar

.·. TOPRAKKALE

Van

Güzelsu

Gevaş

Başkale

I R A N

Bajirge

Hakkâri

I R A Q

Mosul

CHAPTER TWENTY-SEVEN

The Arab Borderlands

❧

Tatvan – Bitlis – Silvan – Diyarbakír – Mardin –Midyat – Hasankeyf –
Urfa – Sultantepe – Sumatar Harabesi – Harran

Twelve kilometres west of Tatvan the highway divides into two
branches, and one must decide which route to follow back from
eastern Anatolia to the west. The right branch is the easier and more
direct, as it leads more or less straight across the centre of eastern
Anatolia to Kayseri, passing through Muş, Bingöl, Elazíğ and
Malatya. The left branch is more circuitous but far more interesting,
since it takes you to the fascinating old towns along the Arab
borderlands of Turkey, and so we will follow that route.

Turning south at the fork you drive down the Güzel Dere, the
Beautiful Valley. You pass on the left the ruined Pabsin Haní, a
caravansarai built by the Selcuks in the thirteenth century; and
soon afterwards you come to the town of **Bitlis**, spreading out along
the deep valleys of the four streams which here converge to form the
Bitlis Suyu, a tributary of the Tigris. The old town stands in the
narrow canyon formed by the two most northerly of these streams
just above their confluence. Here are the two principal monuments
of Bitlis: the Ulu Cami and the citadel. The Ulu Cami is one of the
oldest of the Selcuk Great Mosques in Anatolia; it is not known
just when it was built, but an inscription records that it was restored
in 1150. The only unusual feature of the exterior is the conical roof
covering the *mihrab* dome.

After leaving the town you drive south-west along the valley of the
Bitlis Suyu, beginning the long descent from the eastern Anatolian
plateau to the Mesopotamian plain.

Fifty-two kilometres past Bitlis you come to Baykan and sixty-three
kilometres beyond this is Besirhan. Soon you come to the Batman
Suyu, another tributary of the Tigris, where the road crosses the river
on a splendid Selcuk bridge constructed in 1147–8.

Some twenty kilometres beyond the bridge you come to the town of **Silvan**, formerly known as Mayyafarikin. Silvan is thought by some scholars to be the **site of Tigranocerta**, the capital founded in the first century BC by the Armenian Emperor Tigranes the Great, son-in-law of Mithradates Eupator. However, no direct evidence has been put forward to support this claim, other than a few coins of Tigranes found in the vicinity, and in any event nothing remains of the city which was designed to rival Nineveh and Babylon. The town was rebuilt around AD 400 and renamed Martyropolis, commemorating sainted Christian martyrs whose remains had been transported there from Persia and enshrined. During the reign of Justinian the Great (527–65) the city was girded with a powerful defence wall and became an important garrison post on the marchlands between Byzantium and Persia. A few towers and sections of curtain wall of this defence system can still be seen at the western side of old Silvan, where the road from Bitlis enters the town through an ancient gate. The principal monument of the medieval Moslem town is the very grand Ulu Cami, built during the years 1152–7 by Najm al-Din Alpi, Emir of the Artukid Turks at that time.

About an hour's drive past Silvan the road descends towards an arid plain, and you see ahead the great city of **Diyarbakír**, surrounded by dark basalt walls on an eminence above the Tigris. This is one of the oldest cities in southern Anatolia, inhabited since the Bronze Age and fought over by every conqueror who has passed this way. In classical times it was known as Amida. It was annexed to the Roman Empire in AD 297. Half a century later the Emperor Constantius fortified it along the lines of the present defence system, and the walls were rebuilt and strengthened by several subsequent rulers of Byzantium, most notably Justinian. The city fell to the Arabs in 639 and was allotted to the Beni Bakr clan, from whom it took its present name – Diyarbakír – the Place of the Bakr. Nevertheless, the old name lingered on in the form of Kara Amid, Amid the Black, because of the great basalt walls which so impressed the various Moslem armies that besieged the town. The city was held in turn by the Umayyad and Abbasid Arabs, the Marwanid Kurds, the Artukid Turcomans and the White and Black Sheep, and it was even held briefly by the Persians before it was finally annexed to the Ottoman Empire in 1515 by Selim the Grim.

The **walls** of Diyarbakír are among the oldest and most impressive in Anatolia, and their numerous inscriptions and figural reliefs form a veritable museum of medieval stonework. The walls still stand more or less intact for almost their entire length of five and a half kilometres, save for two short stretches which were demolished

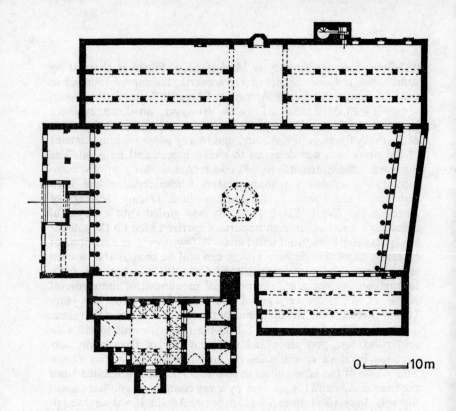

Ulu Cami, Diyarbakír

half a century ago. The walls were originally studded with seventy-eight defence towers, of which all but five are still standing to some extent. The original walls date back to Roman times, but after the capture of the city by the Selcuks in 1088 they were completely rebuilt by Sultan Malik Şah. The walls were restored again in 1208 by the Artukid Emir al Malik al-Salih Mahmud, who added several powerful bastions at salient points for additional protection.

The main road from Bitlis enters Diyarbakír to the right of the **Harput Gate**, one of the four main portals of the medieval town. This gate, which is remarkably well preserved, was known to the Arabs as the Bab el Armen, the Gate of the Armenians, perhaps because it led to the Armenian quarter of the town. After entering the Harput Gate you find yourself on Izzet Pasha Caddesi. This has obviously been the main street of the city since Roman times, and it still gives one the feeling of being in a great provincial Moslem capital, for the busy market area resounds with a babble of Turkish,

342

Kurdish, and occasionally even Arabic and Syriac: the peasants of all of south-eastern Anatolia congregate there as they have for centuries past.

At the beginning of the avenue you pass on your right the **Peygamber Camii**, an Ottoman structure built in 1524. This is one of seven Ottoman mosques built in Diyarbakír in the sixteenth century, the majority of them in the first decade after the conquest of the city by Selim the Grim in 1515.

Just beyond Peygamber Camii a street on the left leads off to the inner **citadel**. This is thought to be the original fortress constructed in Amida in the middle of the fourth century by Constantius, son and successor of Constantine the Great. It is separated from the city by a wall with eighteen towers, all of which remain partially standing. Inside the citadel are the ruins of the pentagonal keep of the inner fortress, and to the south-east of this is the Citadel Mosque, built in 1160 by the Artukid. In 1961–2 an excavation in the citadel unearthed the foundations of the former palace of the Artukid, built in the first half of the thirteenth century.

About three hundred metres farther along Izzet Pasha Caddesi you pass on the left a fine *han* built in 1575–6 by Hasan Pasha, Grand Vezir in the reign of Mehmet III. A little farther on you come to the main square of the town, at the western end of which you see the **Ulu Cami**. This is the very first of the Selcuk Great Mosques in Anatolia, built by Sultan Malik Şah in 1091–2, just three years after his conquest of Diyarbakír.

You enter through a great round-arched portal in the east side of the mosque, above which is an inscription and the figures in low relief of two lions attacking a pair of bulls. After passing through the doorway and the eastern arcade you find yourself in a vast rectangular courtyard with two *şadirvans* in the centre. To the left of the courtyard is the prayer hall; its high central bay rather resembles a Gothic cathedral, particularly with its square campanile-like minaret. The east and west sides of the courtyard are bounded by a two-tiered arcade of engaged columns, with a series of rooms on the upper floor at each end. At the north-west corner of the courtyard there is a small *mescit*, and in the north-east corner an arcade of ancient columns opens into the Masidiye Medrese. This was built in the reign of the Artukid Emir Sökmen II (1198–1223), and is adorned with a *mihrab* of black basalt.

The prayer hall consists of the high central bay flanked by three transverse bays formed by two rows of six columns each, with many of the columns and capitals obviously re-used from some ancient edifice. The effect is very grand indeed, and one is reminded of the Great Mosque in Damascus, on which the Ulu Cami here is so obviously modelled.

A door in the far left corner of the courtyard takes you out on to the street which runs past the west side of the mosque; if you turn left here you will see ahead at the next corner a medieval school of theology, the Zinciriye Medrese, built at the beginning of the reign of the Emir Sökmen II; it is now an archaeological museum.

Returning to Izzet Pasha Caddesi you now come to the main crossroads with the avenue which runs east-west between Yeni Kapí and the Urfa Gate. Looking to the left you see the **Kasím Padişah Camii**, built by an Akkoyunlu emir shortly before that dynasty lost Diyarbakír to the Ottomans. There are a number of Ottoman mosques down the avenue to the right and on the streets which lead off from it. About halfway along on the right side you see the **Kara Cami**, or **Black Mosque**, and directly behind that **Safa Cami**, which is attributed by some to Uzun Hasan (1435–78), the great leader of the White Sheep. Still another Ottoman mosque stands to the right of the avenue just before it reaches the Urfa Gate; this is the **Melek Pasha Camii**, built in 1591 when the founder was governor of Diyarbakír.

Continuing along Izzet Pasha Caddesi, you soon see to the right the **Bayram Pasha Camii**, built in 1572. Godfrey Goodwin, in his monumental *History of Ottoman Architecture*, calls this 'the most important Ottoman mosque in Diyarbakír ... It is indeed the prince of provincial mosques, as splendid in its decoration as it is in its proportions within the limits of the severe local style.'

At the end of Izzet Pasha Caddesi, just to the left of the Mardin Gate, stands the splendid **Deliller Haní**, thought to date from the sixteenth or seventeenth century. A short distance behind it is the **Hüsrev Pasha Camii**, built in the 1520s when Hüsrev was governor of Diyarbakír. He had the distinction of being Sinan's first patron, and the great architect built his first mosque for the Pasha in Aleppo in 1536–7 when he was governor there.

From Diyarbakír you drive south-east towards the Syrian border, crossing the hills between the Tigris valley and the Mesopotamian plain. Ninety-four kilometres along you turn left for **Mardin**, while the main highway continues for another thirty kilometres to the Syrian border at Nusaybin.

Mardin stands on the last line of hills leading down to the Fertile Crescent, and it has far more the appearance and atmosphere of an Arab town than one in Turkish Anatolia. The town is spread out along the south slope of a hill overlooking the arid plain of northern Syria, extending some two and a half kilometres in the east-west direction along the slope and only five hundred metres or so up and down the hill. The houses are all built of stone, with a good many arches and arcades, and they perch above one another tier on tier.

The hill culminates in a very steep and rocky eminence, whose flat summit is ringed by the walls of the medieval citadel. This is one of the most impregnable citadels in Anatolia, and it withstood for a time the assaults of such conquerors as Saladin, Tamerlane and Selim the Grim. The town, known in antiquity as Marida, was relatively unimportant in the Roman and Byzantine eras, despite its strategic location. It was taken by the Arabs in 640 and then fell in turn to the same powers who ruled Diyarbakír to the north. As a result, one finds in Mardin monuments ranging in date through the whole of the medieval Turkish period.

The Diyarbakír road approaches from the north and enters the town at its western end. As you near the town you see on a ridge to the left the ruined Telhan Kalesi, a bastion in the outer defence walls which surrounded the lower city and connected up with the walls of the citadel.

Before entering Mardin, you might visit an important monument which stands a little way outside the town to the south-west. This is the **Kasím Padişah Medresesi**, built in about 1500 by an Akkoyunlu emir. The building here was patterned on an earlier *medrese* of Isa Bey, another emir of the White Sheep, which you will see in the town itself.

After entering the town you turn left on the main street, which runs the full length of the town from west to east about halfway up its slope. About six hundred metres along on the right you pass the **Latifiye Cami**, founded in 1371. Soon after that you come to the main square, the Cumhuriyet Meydaní, and if you take the street which leads in the same direction across the way you come to the **Ulu Cami**. This was built by the Artukid emirs in the period 1176–86, and exhibits some features which became characteristic of sacred architecture in Mardin, most notably the fluted dome. Unfortunately, the mosque was badly damaged by an explosion during the Kurdish rebellion of 1832, and in subsequent restorations it has lost much of its original character.

You now return to the main street and continue going eastward for a short distance. Just past the Başak Hotel a flight of steps leads uphill to the citadel. Finally, above the last row of houses, you come to the most important monument in Mardin, the **Isa Bey Medresesi**.

The design and layout of the *medrese* are quite unusual, and the result is original and grand, particularly the southern façade.

At the western side of the *medrese* a path leads uphill to the **citadel**. You enter through an arched gateway above which there is an inscription and the figures of two lions in relief. The inscription mentions the names of Osman Bahadír, founder of the White Sheep dynasty, and his son Hamza Bahadír, and it has been dated to shortly after the conquest of Mardin by the Akkoyunlu in 1431. The principal remains inside the citadel are the ruins of a mosque and what appears to be a royal residence of the Akkoyunlu period. From the ramparts there is a superb view of Mardin and of the Mesopotamian plain to the south.

Those with time to spare might want to take a trip to the Tur Abdin, the plateau which lies along the borderland between Turkey and the north-eastern corner of Syria. This was a great centre for monasticism and Christian learning early in the Byzantine period, and even today there are half a dozen active monasteries in the region. The two most renowned are **Dayr Zafaran (the Saffron Monastery)**, five kilometres east of Mardin, and Mar Gabriel, some twenty-five kilometres east of **Midyat**, a town midway between Mardin and Cizre, a border post on the common boundary of Turkey, Syria and Iraq. Dayr Zafaran is the ancient patriarchal see of the Syrian Orthodox Church, though none of its patriarchs has been resident in Turkey for the past half-century. These Syriac-speaking Christians are called Jacobites, after Jacobus Baradeus, Bishop of Edessa. In the sixth century Baradeus broke with the Patriarchate of Constantinople because of his Monophysite doctrine; that is, he believed that the divine nature in Christ predominated over his humanity. This split with the Greek Orthodox Church became permanent after south-eastern Anatolia was lost to the Byzantine Empire, conquered first by the Persians, then the Arabs, and finally the Turks, so that for fourteen centuries the Jacobites and other eastern Christians were isolated in a Moslem world. They were almost lost to history until the beginning of modern times, and then they were decimated in the massacres and mass deportations which took place in Anatolia half a century ago. Today there are about forty thousand Jacobite Christians still living in Turkey, about half of them in Midyat and the surrounding villages in the Tur Abdin. They worship there in their ancient churches and monasteries as they have for fifteen centuries past, still celebrating their mass in the original Aramaic, the language of Christ.

When in Midyat one might make a farther detour to **Hasankeyf**, a village forty-four kilometres to the north on the left bank of the Tigris. The village takes its name from the medieval town of Hisn Kayfa, whose extensive ruins are to be seen on the other bank of the river. This has been identified as the ancient Cepha, an important frontier post on the border between the Byzantine Empire and Persia. It fell to the Arabs in 640, at the same time as Mardin, and was ruled in turn by the same succession of Moslem powers. It remained an important city throughout the Middle Ages, but then in Ottoman times it declined to the status of a mere village. One sees there today the ruins of the Byzantine citadel, a palace of the Artukid period, several ancient mosques, a *türbe*, and the impressive ruins of a bridge across the Tigris, which early travellers remarked upon as being the grandest in all of Anatolia.

From Mardin you now return to the Diyarbakír road and drive south for some twenty kilometres, after which you turn right on to the highway for Urfa. A short way along you pass the village of **Kízíltepe**. This has been identified as the site of the medieval Moslem city of Dunyasir, of which only the ruins of the Ulu Cami built by the Artukid and two *türbe* now remain.

The first town of any size you come to is **Viranşehir**, thirty-seven kilometres from Kízíltepe. This has been identified as the ancient Constantina, of which there remain only its basalt defence walls and towers, an impressive ruin some two kilometres long. These were originally built in Roman times and repaired in the sixth century by Justinian.

Ninety kilometres past Viranşehir you come to **Urfa**, a large town on the Mesopotamian plain, dominated by an ancient citadel on an eminence to the south-west. The origins of the city go back to the Bronze Age, though the town does not appear in history until the Hellenistic era. The town was refounded in the latter part of the fourth century BC by veterans of Alexander's army, who renamed it **Edessa** after their native city in Macedonia. Early in the third century BC Seleucus I Nicator raised the place to the status of a city, calling it Antioch, though the name Edessa continued in popular use. (To distinguish this from the more famous city on the Orontes Seleucus referred to this as Antioch 'the half-barbarous'.)

Edessa became a famous centre of religion and scholarship in the early centuries of the Byzantine Empire, and it played an important role both in the spread of Christianity and in the survival of classical Greek learning. Many works of Greek science and philosophy were here translated into Syriac, and in that form later made their way to Islamic universities, where they were in turn translated into Arabic.

At the beginning of the Renaissance these works made their way to Europe and were translated once again, this time from Arabic into Latin, providing a vital stimulus for the revival of learning in the West.

Edessa was taken by the Arabs soon after their victory over the Byzantines at the Yarmuk in 636. The Byzantines recaptured the city in 1032 and held it until 1087, when it was taken by the Selcuks, who gave it in fief to a local Armenian lord named Toros. Early in February 1098, at the beginning of the First Crusade, Baldwin of Flanders entered the city with eighty horsemen and was welcomed enthusiastically by the populace, who made him co-ruler with Toros. Four days later the mob overthrew Toros and acclaimed Baldwin as their ruler. Thus began the so-called County of Edessa, the first of several Crusader states which were formed in the Middle East at that time. The short history of this principality ended on Christmas Eve in 1144, when Edessa fell to Imad al-Din Zengi, the Selcuk governor of Mosul and the founder of the Zengid dynasty. After Zengi's death in 1146 the former ruler of Edessa, Count Joscelin, retook the city for a few days before it was recaptured by Zengi's son and successor, Nur al-Din, who put the Christian males to the sword, sold the women and children into slavery, and sacked and destroyed the city. The fall of Edessa made a deep impression on the West, and led Pope Eugenios III in 1145 to proclaim a Second Crusade. In his Papal Bull he extolled the knights of Christian Europe to 'gird themselves courageously to oppose the multitudes of unbelievers who are rejoicing that they have obtained a victory over us . . . to defend the eastern church . . . to snatch from their hands the many thousands of captives who are our kinsmen.'

But the city remained in Moslem hands as the Second Crusade was eventually directed elsewhere. In 1234 Edessa was taken by the army of the Selcuk Sultan Alâeddin Keykûbad, and in 1260 it fell to Hulagu, the Great Khan of the Mongols. And so the 'Holy City of Edessa' was separated from the rest of the Christian world, virtually to disappear from history until its rediscovery by Western travellers in the last century.

Despite its long and eventful history Urfa has very few ancient monuments. The most prominent of these is the **citadel**, which stands on top of a rocky eminence at the south-western corner of the town. Most of its present structure dates from the medieval Turkish period, but in origin it undoubtedly dates back to the Hellenistic era. Surviving from that period are two tall columns with Corinthian capitals in the centre of the citadel; they are known locally as the Throne of Nimrod.

At the foot of the citadel to the north is the sacred spring known to the Greeks as **Callirhoe**. This is the source of the water which fills the long rectangular pool some two hundred metres from the foot of the citadel. On the north side of the pool is the attractive Abdür-rahman Medresesi, founded in the late seventeenth century. At the western end of the pool you see the Makham al-Khalil Medresesi, founded in 1211–12 and restored several times since then.

The pool and the waterways which lead to and from it are filled with sacred carp which no one is allowed to catch. There are many local legends concerning these holy fish, but most are connected in one way or another with Abraham. For that reason the pool is known in Turkish as Birket Ibrahim, the Pool of Abraham.

Another prominent monument in Urfa is the **Ulu Cami**, whose enormous minaret is a landmark in the town centre. It was founded in the mid-twelfth century by Nur al-Din, son and successor of Zengi, and it is patterned on the Great Mosque which his father founded in Aleppo.

There are a number of interesting sights to be seen in the region south of Urfa; these are approached by the road which goes to Akçakale, the customs post on the Turkish-Syrian border.

Fifteen kilometres south of Urfa you turn left on to a dirt road which heads towards a high mound overlooking the arid plain, behind which is the hamlet of **Sultantepe**. Excavation of the Sultan-tepe mound has revealed the existence of an Assyrian settlement which flourished here in the eighth and seventh centuries BC. The most interesting discovery was of a hoard of tablets written in Assyrian and Sumerian hieroglyphs, which have greatly increased our knowledge of Assyrian history and culture. They include epical texts, among which is the *Epic of Gilgamesh*, wisdom literature, literary texts and prayers, historical and economic texts and letters, medical and mathematical texts, including a child's exercise book for the year 750 BC, and texts on astronomy and astrology. The texts range in date from 750 to 610 BC, ending abruptly just two years after Nineveh was destroyed and the Assyrian Empire ended. Some of these can be seen in the Ankara Museum.

After leaving Sultantepe you continue along a track which leads in much the same direction as that on which you approached. After a drive of about ten kilometres you come to **Sumatar Harabesi**, a watering place usually surrounded by the tents of nomadic shepherds. Here you should obtain a guide to lead you to the remarkable pagan sanctuaries in the surrounding region.

The main site consists of a natural mound, about fifty metres high, to the west and north of which stand eight groups of ruins forming a rough arc at a distance of four to eight hundred metres from the central mound. Six of these ruined buildings have one feature in common – a subterranean grotto, whose entrance points exactly in the direction of the central mound, which appears to have been a sacred site.

On the northern summit of the mound there are two figures carved into the rock, and beside them there are several inscriptions in Syriac. These and other inscriptions have revealed that this was a sanctuary of the Sabians, a people whom the medieval Arabs regarded as a separate religious group in the same category as the Jews and Christians. According to Arab sources, they were wor-shippers of the Sun God Helios, the Moon God Sin, and five planetary deities; thus the central mound has been identified as a sanctuary of Helios, and the other ruins as temples dedicated to the Moon God and the five planets. The Sabians worshipped their celestial gods here and at the nearby city of Harran, which was the centre of a cult which became quite widespread in the medieval Arab world, lasting until as late as the twelfth century AD. Orthodox Christians and Moslems looked upon them contemptuously as heathens who practised unholy and barbarous rites, an attitude shown in this lurid description of the Sabian shrines by the medieval chronicler Jacob of Sarug:

> On the tops of the hills Satan had built palaces to the goddesses, and in the high places erected temples to idols . . . On one hill were slaughtered sacrifices to Satan, on another was built an altar to Hermes; and one valley was called the Vale of Herakles . . . There was no hill that was not moist with the blood of sacrifices, and no high place that was empty of libations. Youths in multi-tudes were given as sacrifices, and maidens slaughtered to female idols and to the sun and the moon and Venus and the other luminaries.

From Sumatar Harabesi you return via Sultantepe to the main road and continue driving south. Eighteen kilometres along you turn left for **Harran**, crossing the arid Jullab plain, a bleak, open expanse broken here and there by conspicuous mounds formed by the accumulated debris of ancient settlements. Frequently you see a village beside one of these mounds, using the same brook, well, or seasonal water hole which undoubtedly attracted the first settlers on these sites. The modern villages are spread more or less uniformly across the plain, each of them a group of mud-brick houses roofed with several crude domes which give them the appearance of giant bee-hives. These 'bee-hive' villages are found all along the border area between Turkey and Syria, all inhabited by semi-settled Arab nomads. The way of life of these primitive communities has not changed in its essentials since biblical times; the nomads gradually give up their wandering and settle here on the edge of the Mesopotamian plain, just as the family of Abraham did when they came to Harran four millennia ago. As one reads in the Book of Genesis:

And Terah took Abram his son, and Lot the wife of Haran his son's son, and Sarai his daughter-in-law, his son Abram's wife; and they went forth with them from Ur of the Chaldees, to go into the land of Canaan; and they came unto Harran and dwelt there.

The site of Harran is enclosed by a stone city wall which survives in a ruinous state, its principal gateways still recognizable. The best preserved of these is the **Aleppo Gate**, on the western side of the city, which bears an inscription including the name Saladin and the date A.H. 588 (AD 1192), the last year but one in the life of that great Kurdish warrior.

The most prominent monument in Harran is **Qal'at**, a fortress at the south-eastern corner of the defence walls. The only other monument of note is the ruined **Ulu Cami**, which stands just to the north of the mound at the centre of the city. This was once known as Cami al-Firdaus, the Mosque of Paradise, thought to have been founded by Marwan II (744–50), the last Umayyad Caliph, who in the closing years of his life made Harran the capital of his empire. In its present state the mosque dates from the reign of Saladin (1138–93).

The mound at the centre of the city is the site of the original settlement at Harran, which in classical times was known as Carrhae. This is one of the oldest cities in Anatolia, and it is mentioned all through Mesopotamian, Roman and medieval history. The city gave its name to the battle of Carrhae, fought near here in 53 BC, when the Parthians destroyed an army led by Crassus in what a historian has described as 'the most serious and degrading defeat ever suffered by Roman arms'. There is a tablet from Mari, dated to about 2000 BC, which records a peace treaty made in the temple of the Moon God Sin at Harran. This was the first of several such treaties sealed in the Temple of Sin during the second millennium BC between various rulers in the Middle East, all of them expressing their reverence for 'the great god who dwells in Harran'. The temple was restored by several Assyrian rulers in the first half of the first millennium BC, and it continued to be a popular shrine throughout the Roman and medieval periods. The Emperor Caracalla was assassinated here in AD 217 after celebrating his birthday in the Temple of Sin, and in 363 the Emperor Julian the Apostate came here to pay his respects to the Moon God shortly before his death.

The celestial cult of the Sabians flourished here throughout the Middle Ages, and Arab chroniclers mention the Temple of Sin till as late as the twelfth century. But in 1260 Harran was destroyed by the Mongols and never thereafter rebuilt. Only a few nomadic Arab tribesmen lived on amid the ruins, as they do today, in a cluster of bee-hive houses in the south-eastern corner of the city, unaware of the tides of history that have swept over this place in the last four thousand years. As one reads in the Book of Genesis, completing the story of Abraham's residence in this ancient place:

> So Abram took Sarai his wife, and Lot his brother's son, and all their substance that they had gathered, and the souls they had gotten in Harran; and they went forth to go into the land of Canaan; and into the land of Canaan they came.

CHAPTER TWENTY-EIGHT

Southern Anatolia and the Hatay

✤

Urfa – Birecik – Carchemish – Gaziantep – Adíyaman – Nemrut Daği – Antakya – Iskenderun – Toprakkale – Ceyhan – Yílan Kalesi – Adana – Tarsus

The main highway from Urfa leads westward towards Gaziantep, running more or less parallel to the Syrian border. Eighty-four kilometres west of Urfa you come to **Birecik**, a town on the left bank of the Euphrates. This, the ancient Apamaea, has been a strategic ford and bridgehead since Seleucid times, for it stands on a narrow stretch of the Euphrates at the point where it begins to become navigable. It was known to the Franks as Berthe and was an important fortress in the Crusader County of Edessa. On a hill to the north-west of town you see the ruins of a medieval fortress partially rebuilt by the Crusaders in the twelfth century.

Birecik is one of the world's two remaining nesting-places for the bald ibis, a noble freak of a bird which is now almost extinct. The bald ibis leaves Birecik in July to winter at its only other home, in Morocco, and returns to its ancestral nests here on the Euphrates in the middle of February. The return of the bald ibis has since time immemorial signalled the end of winter and the coming of spring, and has thus been celebrated by the villagers in a joyous festival, surely the most unique in all of Turkey. Turkish conservationists are trying to preserve this vanishing species, but in 1973 there were only twenty-five mating couples and each year the number diminishes. And there are old villagers here who believe that spring will not come if the bald ibis does not fly back to the Euphrates as its herald.

Fifteen kilometres west of Birecik there is a turning to the left for the frontier village of **Karkamíş**. The village is near the ruins of **ancient Carchemish**, but because of its proximity to the frontier one must obtain permission from the security police and proceed to the site with a military escort. Carchemish is the most famous of the Neo-Hittite states which emerged in Anatolia after the fall of

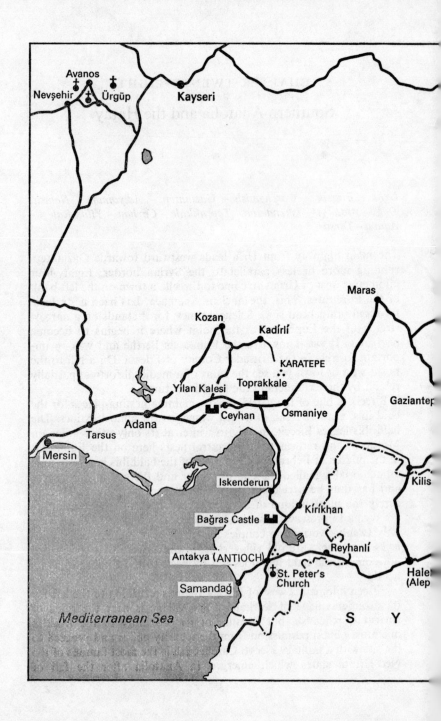

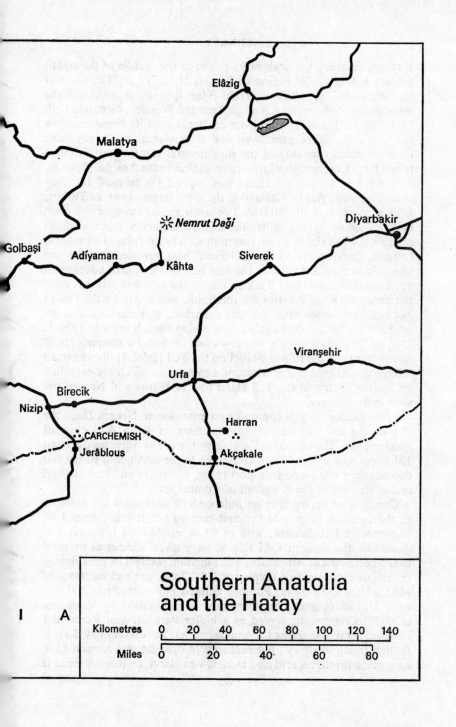

Southern Anatolia
and the Hatay

Kilometres 0 20 40 60 80 100 120 140

Miles 0 20 40 60 80

Elâzig

Malatya

☀ *Nemrut Daği*

Diyarbakir

Golbaşi

Adíyaman

Kâhta

Siverek

Viranşehir

Urfa

Birecik

Nizip

Harran

CARCHEMISH

Jerâblous

Akçakale

I A

Hattusa, reaching the peak of its power in the middle of the eighth century before finally falling to Sargon II in 717 BC. The site was first excavated just before World War I, when it attracted the attention of such luminaries as Sir Leonard Woolley, Gertrude Bell, D. C. Hogarth and T. E. Lawrence. Because of its remoteness the site is seldom visited nowadays, and most visitors to Turkey must be content with looking at the monumental statues and orthostat reliefs from Carchemish which are on exhibit in the Ankara Museum.

A drive of forty-eight kilometres beyond the turn-off for Carchemish brings you to **Gaziantep**, the sixth largest town in Turkey, with a population of 300,000. The town stands on a broad plain and is flanked by two hills; the eastern eminence is an artificial mound, the Tell Halaf, which is surmounted by the ruins of a medieval fortress. Excavations on the Tell Halaf have revealed that the site was inhabited as far back as the first half of the fourth millennium BC. During the medieval Turkish period the city was called Antep; the prefix Gazi, or Warrior for the Faith, was added by the Grand National Assembly after the city's Turkish Nationalist defenders held out for ten months against a besieging French army in 1920–1. Despite its great antiquity the town has no historic monuments of note other than the ruined citadel on the Tell Halaf. It does have an interesting archaeological museum, however, in which are exhibited antiquities found on the Tell Halaf and in Hittite and Neo-Hittite sites in the vicinity.

From Gaziantep you can make an excursion to **Nemrut Daği**, the site of the extraordinary tomb-sanctuary of King Antiochus of Commagene. The best base for visiting the site is **Adíyaman**, a town 191 kilometres by road from Gaziantep to the north-east, where you can obtain a guide and transport to the sanctuary on Nemrut Daği and other sites of the Kingdom of Commagene.

Commagene emerged as an independent state upon the collapse of the Seleucid Empire in the first century BC. It was founded by Mithradates I Kallinikos, who in 80 BC established his capital at Arsameia, the modern Eski Kâhta, sixty-seven kilometres by road to the north-east of Adíyaman. The kingdom reached its peak during the reign of Antiochus I Epiphanes (64–32 BC), son and successor of Mithradates I. In 64 BC Pompey entered into a treaty of alliance with Antiochus, and from then until its annexation by Vespasian in AD 72 Commagene served as a buffer state between Rome and Parthia. Strabo described Commagene as 'an exceedingly fertile, though small, territory', but centuries of drought and erosion have now made it into an arid and treeless wasteland. In Roman times it was the wealthiest of the small principalities on the eastern marches, with abundant resources of timber and cattle, controlling at Samosata a strategic bridgehead on the Euphrates where important military and trade routes converged.

Forty kilometres east of Adíyaman you come to the village of Kâhta, which some travellers prefer as a starting point because of its closer proximity to Nemrut Daǧí. Accommodation is available in the village, and if you spend the night there you can begin the ascent early the following morning. There are also primitive lodgings on the peak itself, for those who would rather make the ascent in late afternoon and rise at dawn. Either way, you should try to be on the peak at sunrise to see this incomparable monument in all its splendour.

Eleven kilometres beyond Kâhta you pass the Karakuş tumulus, the burial place of the queens and princesses of Commagene. It is surrounded by three groups of commemorative columns, some of them still surmounted by fragmentary statues and reliefs. The tumulus takes its name – Karakuş, the Black Bird – from the headless figure of an eagle, the symbol of Zeus, which perches on top of one of the columns.

Eight kilometres farther on you come to the Cendere River, the ancient Chabinas, which is there spanned by a Roman bridge. Each end of the bridge was originally flanked by a pair of commemorative columns, all but one of which are still standing. Latin inscriptions record that the bridge was erected by four cities of Commagene in honour of Septimius Severus (194–211); the four columns honoured the Emperor, his wife Julia Domna, and his sons Caracalla and Geta. It is thought that the missing column honoured Geta, and that it was removed after his murder by Caracalla in 212.

Seven kilometres beyond the bridge you come to Eski Kâhta, a Kurdish village on the banks of the Kâhta Çayí, the ancient Nymphaios. The village stands beneath Yeni Kale, the New Castle, a fortress built by the Mamelukes in the fourteenth century, probably on the foundations of an Armenian citadel. On the other side of the river there is an eminence called Eski Kale, the Old Castle, on top of which are the ruins of Arsameia ad Nymphaios, the ancient capital of Commagene. Excavations on Eski Kale have unearthed the remains of fortifications, the foundations of a palace with a mosaic floor, and a *hierothesion,* or tomb-sanctuary. A splendid relief found in the sanctuary has now been erected *in situ*; it shows a royal figure identified as Mithradates I Kallinikos shaking hands with Herakles. Nearby there is an inscription, the longest in Greek ever discovered, which records that the *hierothesion* was built in honour of Mithradates by 'the Great King Antiochus, God, the Righteous, Epiphanes, the Romanophile and Hellenophile, son of King Mithradates and Queen Laodike, daughter of Antiochus Epiphanes'.

The Antiochus Epiphanes mentioned in the inscription was one of the last Seleucid kings, and was assassinated in 96 BC. Through him, his namesake Antiochus of Commagene traced his ancestry back to Seleucus I Nicator, founder of the Seleucid Empire. On his father's side he traced his ancestry back to Darius the Great, and thus in his own mind Antiochus of Commagene represented the fusion of two of the great dynasties of East and West and their deified kingships.

After leaving Eski Kâhta you cross the Kâhta Çayí, after which the trail winds around the southern slope of the Ankar Daĝlari and then goes up to the peak of Nemrut Daĝí, 2200 metres above sea-level. There you are confronted with one of the most awesome sights in the whole of Anatolia, the megalomaniacal **hierothesion of Antiochus of Commagene**, with the gigantic heads of a dozen gods scattered around the base of the King's enormous tumulus on the mountain top.

The conical tumulus on the peak is constructed of fist-sized stones and is some fifty metres high and a hundred and fifty metres in diameter at its base. The tumulus forms the centre of the *hierothesion*, with terraces to the north, east and west. The east terrace was the principal sanctuary of the *hierothesion* because it faced the rising sun. At the eastern edge of the terrace there is a pyramidal Persian fire altar, and on the north and south it is bounded by low walls faced with orthostats. The orthostats on the north side were decorated with reliefs depicting the imperial Persian ancestors of Antiochus, while those on the south side represented his royal Greek antecedents. Unfortunately, only scattered fragments remain of what Antiochus called 'the heroic company of my ancestors'.

The west side of the east terrace is bounded by a double podium on top of which there were five colossal deities enthroned between two pairs of giant lions and eagles. These figures combined the pantheons of the Greek and Persian worlds, the divine ancestors of the deified Antiochus, each of them an amalgam of several deities. At the left side of the terrace sat the Sun God, a syncretism of Apollo, Mithra, Helios and Hermes. Beside him was enthroned Tyche, the Goddess of Fortune, the only one of the figures whose head is still in place. In the centre of the podium sat Zeus-Ahurmazda;

next to him was enthroned Antiochus deified as *Theos Epiphanes*, 'the God made manifest', and at the right side was Herakles-Artagnes-Ares. An inscription on the throne of Antiochus describes the shrine as being 'on the topmost ridge of his kingdom, in close proximity to the heavenly throne of Zeus', and it also tells of how he 'undertook to make this place a common throne-room of all the gods'.

The west terrace is arranged in much the same manner, except that there is no fire altar and the seating arrangement of the gods is different. Here, too, the heads of the gods have been toppled from their figures and are scattered about the terrace. They have been set upright in place in recent years and now present an extraordinary spectacle, each of them taller than a man. On both terraces Antiochus is represented as a beardless young man rather resembling Alexander the Great, with the imperious look of a deified king who ruled in both the terrestrial and celestial realms. Antiochus himself is presumed to be buried beneath the tumulus, but excavations have thus far failed to discover his tomb.

Returning to Gaziantep, you now take the highway which leads westward towards Adana. Seventy-five kilometres along you turn left on to the main Maraş-Antakya road and begin driving south. This takes you into the Hatay, that part of Turkey which projects down past the north-western corner of Syria along the eastern end of the Mediterranean. One hundred kilometres along you pass a turning to the right for Iskenderun, a route to which you will return after visiting Antakya.

Four kilometres past the turning a road leads off to the right to **Bağras Castle**, four kilometres to the west along an asphalt road. The castle is thought to have been built by the Byzantines in the tenth century, and was taken by the Crusaders in 1097 during their siege of Antioch. Later it was held in turn by the Saracens, Crusaders, Armenians and Mamelukes, before finally falling to the Ottomans under Selim the Grim in 1516.

After returning to the main road you continue driving south, rounding the eastern side of Lake Amik. At the southern end of the Amik plain you finally come to **Antakya, ancient Antioch**, one of the most historic towns in Turkey. The town stands mostly on the left bank of the Orontes, occupying less than half of the southernmost area of the ancient city. To the east is the eminence known to the Greeks as Mount Sipylus, on top of which you can see remnants of the defence walls of Antioch, giving some idea of the vast extent of the ancient city.

Antioch and its sister city of Seleucia ad Pieria were founded by Seleucus I Nicator, both of them dedicated within a year after his victory over Antigonus the One-Eyed at the battle of Ipsus in 301 BC. Seleucus, who already controlled Babylonia, now gained Syria and Mesopotamia as well, thus reigning over a vast and heterogeneous realm. He therefore abandoned his former capital of Seleucia-on-the-Tigris and built a new one closer to the centre of his empire.

Seleucus laid his first foundations on the Syrian coast in April 300 BC, when he established the port city of Seleucia ad Pieria just north of the Orontes. The following month he founded Antioch ad Orontes some thirty kilometres inland. Seleucia ad Pieria served as the capital until 281 BC, when the old Emperor was assassinated, after which his son and successor Antiochus I Soter moved the capital to Antioch. For the next two centuries Antioch remained the capital of the Seleucid Empire, which at its peak included most of what is now Turkey and Iran. The Seleucid realm collapsed after the conquest of Syria by Tigranes the Great in 83 BC, and two decades later it was annexed to the Roman Empire. In 64 BC Pompey made Antioch capital of the Roman province of Syria, and for the next three centuries it was surpassed in the Hellenistic world only by Rome and Alexandria, with a population which may have approached half a million.

A long line of Roman and Byzantine emperors in turn adorned the city with magnificent public buildings. During the early Byzantine period it rivalled Constantinople in size and splendour, and perhaps surpassed it in intellectual brilliance. But the site had two serious flaws, and these ultimately brought about the downfall of ancient Antioch. First, it was subject to frequent and devastating earthquakes. Secondly, the site was difficult to defend, and as the power of Rome began to wane Antioch became increasingly vulnerable to attack by its enemies to the east and south. In the middle of the third century AD the city was twice taken and sacked by the Persians, and on the latter occasion it was almost totally destroyed by fire. In 540 Antioch was captured and burned down again by the Persians, and shortly afterwards it was rebuilt on a reduced scale by Justinian. Early in the seventh century the Persians completely overran Asia Minor and Syria and almost brought about the downfall of the Byzantine Empire. The Persians captured Antioch in 611 and held it until the Byzantines regained the city in 628. But in 638 the Byzantine army was annihilated on the Yarmuk by the Arabs, who then conquered all of Syria, taking Antioch in the same year. Antioch remained in Arab hands until it was recaptured in 969 by Nicephorus II Phocas, 'the Pale Death of the Saracens'. It then served as an outpost of the Byzantine Empire for more than a century, until in 1084 it was captured by the Selcuks. In 1098, after a long and bloody siege, the city was taken by the Crusaders under Bohemund and became capital of the Frankish principality of Antioch. This Latin state lasted until 1268, when the city was totally destroyed by the Mamelukes under Baibars. Antioch never recovered from this disaster, and during the Ottoman period travellers reported that it was little more than a broken-down village, with a few hundred houses scattered among the ruins of the ancient city.

After World War I Antioch was part of the territory placed under French mandate by the League of Nations, but in 1939 a referendum resulted in the Hatay being annexed to the Republic of Turkey. In the years since then Antakya, as it came to be called, has gradually been recovering from centuries of decay and neglect, and today it is a pleasant and fairly prosperous provincial town. But the numerous catastrophes it has endured have utterly destroyed all of the celebrated monuments of Antioch, and there is little evidence today to indicate that this was once one of the great cities of the ancient world.

Excavations in the 1930s revealed that the main street of Antakya, Kurtuluş Caddesi, follows the course of the famous colonnaded street of ancient Antioch. Two Roman miles in length, more than ten metres wide, flanked by a splendid colonnade with triumphal arches at either end and a nymphaion in the central forum, this was probably the first and grandest of such monumental thoroughfares in the Roman world. The colonnaded way in Antioch is thought to have been constructed in 30 BC by King Herod of Judea, who thus honoured Augustus on his triumphal visit to Antioch after his victory at Actium over Antony and Cleopatra the previous year.

During the same excavations a large number of superb mosaic pavements were discovered in Antioch and its vicinity, particularly in the ancient suburb of Daphne. These are now on exhibit in the **Archaeological Museum of Antakya**, along with antiquities from other sites in the Hatay. These mosaics have been dated from the second century AD to the sixth, filling in what had been a serious gap in our knowledge of mosaic decoration in the late Roman period.

The **site of ancient Daphne** is near **Harbiye**, a village eight kilometres south of Antakya on the highway to Syria and the Lebanon. One kilometre south of the village you come to the springs and waterfalls for which Daphne was celebrated all over the ancient world. As one might expect, numerous legends were associated with this beautiful and sacred place. According to one myth, Apollo's pursuit of Daphne took place here, and the very laurel (*daphne* in Greek) into which the maiden was transformed was shown to pilgrims in Seleucid times. Here, too, stood the mourning cypress into which the youth Cyparissus was changed when he died of sadness after accidentally killing a pet stag. Because of its surpassing beauty, the gods are said to have used this vale for the Judgement of Paris. The sacred springs were reputed to be the abode of nymphs; and in one of them, the Castalia, there resided an oracle of Apollo. Seleucus was inspired by these and other legends and miracles to establish here a sanctuary of Apollo which became the principal adornment of his empire, the centre of a suburban shrine and pleasure-dome which was celebrated throughout the ancient world. The Seleucid rulers and later several Roman emperors built temples and palaces here, and still later the Byzantine emperors added churches and monasteries, making this a shrine whose fame rivalled that of Ephesus. It was probably in Daphne that Antony married Cleopatra in 40 BC, and here he received King Herod and confirmed him as ruler of Judea. Here, too, were held the Olympic Games of Antioch, the successor to the games of ancient Olympia, a series of athletic and cultural contests which became the most famous festival in the Roman world. But all of this came to an end as Daphne was engulfed in the catastrophes which ultimately destroyed Antioch, and today only a few scattered columns remain of the great shrine. The lovely springs and waterfalls remain, shaded by laurels and mourning cypresses, and the place is a favourite resort of the residents of modern Antakya.

The **site of Seleucia ad Pieria** is situated near Samandağ, a seaside town twenty-eight kilometres to the south-west of Antakya. The actual site is at **Mağarcík**, a hamlet overlooking the long beach which stretches north from the mouth of the Orontes. Little now remains of Seleucia, save for some ruined walls and gates and some very impressive canals and underground water tunnels. Here again you must use your imagination to recall that this was once one of the greatest and most populous ports on the Mediterranean.

On the way back from Samandağ to Antakya you see to the south the peak which in antiquity was known as the **Miraculous Mountain**. On the summit of this mountain there are two ruined churches dedicated to St Symeon Stylites the Younger, who in 521, at the age of seven, ascended a column to spend the rest of his life there in fasting and prayer. This ascetic saint was named for and emulated the original St Symeon Stylites, first and most famous of the pillar-sitting saints. St Symeon the Elder was born about 390, and at the age of twenty-seven he mounted a column thirty miles east of Antioch and began a life of asceticism, living on a series of columns each taller than the one before until his death in 459. As his fame grew, numerous pilgrims from all over the Christian world flocked to see Symeon on top of his pillar, and from his perch he exerted an enormous influence which at times cowed patriarchs and emperors. After the earthquake of 458 the populace of Antioch camped around his pillar for fifty days, praying to the saint to intercede with God for their salvation, but when he died the following year they took it as a sign of divine disapproval and thought that their world was coming to an end.

The most famous monument in the immediate vicinity of Antioch is the **Church of St Peter**, which is reached by taking the road which leads towards Aleppo and turning off to the right two kilometres out of town. The church is in a grotto on a hillside overlooking the fields and orchards on the left bank of the Orontes.

The present church was constructed in the thirteenth century by the Crusaders, though local tradition holds that this was one of the very first Christian sanctuaries in Antioch, founded by St Peter himself. Peter is known to have been in Antioch between AD 47 and 54, and, together with Paul and Barnabas, his efforts led to the establishment of the first Christian community there. This was the first congregation that included Gentiles as well as Jews, and was particularly important in establishing the ecumenical character of the early Church. Contemporary chroniclers report that it was in Antioch that the followers of Jesus were first called Christians, and the Acts of the Apostles describes how these disciples met in various houses in the town for teaching and fellowship, for the breaking of bread, and for communal prayer.

About a hundred metres beyond the church there is a curious relief carved into the cliff face; it consists of a large bust of a woman with a veiled face, and on her right shoulder there is a smaller draped figure. The sixth-century chronicler Ioannes Malalas called this the Charonian, and tells a curious story about its origin. According to Malalas, it was carved on the orders of Antiochus IV (175–63 BC) to placate the gods at a time of plague. The relief is presumably named for Charon, the legendary boatman who ferried souls across the River Styx into the underworld.

After leaving Antakya you drive back north and take the turn-off which leads to Iskenderun. This takes you over the path known in ancient times as Portae Syriae, the Syrian Gates, where a fortress commanded this historic route between the Amik plain and the Mediterranean. Once over the pass you come to the village of Belen, a pleasant place to stop for lunch before driving on to Iskenderun.

Iskenderun, the former **Alexandretta**, stands at the head of a deep gulf at the north-eastern end of the Mediterranean. The town (Alexander=Iskender in Turkish) is named after the original port on this site, Alexandria ad Issum, founded by Alexander the Great after his victory at the battle of Issus in 333 BC. The port was soon eclipsed by the nearby Seleucia ad Pieria. After World War I the town became capital of the Sancak of Alexandretta, a French mandate until the Hatay was annexed to Turkey in 1939. In recent years Iskenderun has grown considerably and is now the principal seaport on the Mediterranean coast of Turkey. The modern town has nothing of interest for the traveller, but its attractive seaside promenade is a pleasant place to while away an hour or two before driving on to the north. And it is wonderful to look upon the blue sea again, after driving hundreds of miles across the harsh landscape of eastern Anatolia.

Ten kilometres north of Iskenderun you come to **Saraseki**. Here, beside the sea, are the ruins of a fortress called Kíz Kalesi, the Maiden's Castle, and also the remains of a tower called Baba Yunus, or Father Jonah. The tower, which appears to date from the Seleucid period, takes its name from a local legend that this is the place where the whale finally spewed out Jonah.

Nine kilometres farther along you come to **Yakacík**, the former **Payas**, a village surrounded by gardens on the shore of the gulf. In the olive groves south of the village there are numerous fallen columns and dressed stones, the remains of the Seleucid town of Baiae. On the shore stands a ruined castle built by the Crusaders at the beginning of the thirteenth century and repaired in Ottoman times. There are also the remains of a mosque and a caravansarai built in the middle of the sixteenth century by Süleyman the Magnificent. These date from the time when Payas was an important port and the terminus of the caravan route from Mesopotamia to the Mediterranean.

Soon after passing Yakacík the road curves northward and leaves the Mediterranean shore. You now drive through the plain of Issus, where in the early autumn of 333 BC Alexander the Great defeated the Persians under Darius III, thus opening the way for the Macedonian army to penetrate south into Syria.

Fifty kilometres beyond Iskenderun you come to a turning to the right for Yeşilkent. Beside the road are the ruins of an aqueduct and other structures which have been identified as the remains of the Seleucid town of Epiphania. This was founded in about 175 BC by Antiochus IV Epiphanes, the most brilliant and complex of all the Seleucid kings; in his time he was known as Antiochus the Mad.

A short distance beyond the Yeşilkent turning the road divides, the right fork leading to Osmaniye and Gaziantep, and the left to Ceyhan and Adana. Taking the left fork, you soon come to a turn-off to the right for Toprakkale, a village dominated by a great castle on top of a huge mound. This castle first appears in history during the reign of Nicephorus II Phocas (963–9), who used it as a base during his campaigns against the Arabs. During the twelfth century it was held in turn by the Byzantines, Armenians and Crusaders, and in the following century it was captured and destroyed by the Mamelukes and never thereafter rebuilt.

Soon after the Toprakkale turning you join the road from Gaziantep to Adana and drive west across the great Cilician plain. This region was one of the cradles of Anatolian civilization; a survey published in 1951 by the British School of Archaeology in Ankara identified 150 ancient settlements in the region between Toprakkale and Mersin, ranging in date from the Neolithic and Chalcolithic periods through the Bronze Age and the Hittite era up to classical times. This vast plain was formed by alluvial deposits brought down by the Ceyhan and Seyhan, the two great rivers of Cilicia. The Ceyhan, the most easterly, flows down from the Anti-Taurus Mountains, the range which bounds Plain Cilicia to the north, while the Seyhan has its source in the Taurus Mountains. Medieval Arab geographers called these two streams the Rivers of Paradise.

A good base for exploring this area is Ceyhan, a town on the left bank of the Ceyhan River a short distance south of the Gaziantep-Adana highway. Two worthwhile excursions can be made from here to Anazarbus and Karatepe, both of which are approached by the road going north from Ceyhan to Kozan and Kadirli. Anazarbus was the last capital of the Armenian kingdom of Cilicia until its final downfall in 1375; the ruins are extensive and worth seeing for those who have the time to spare. Karatepe has been identified as the Neo-Hittite city of Asitwanda, founded in the twelfth century BC. A number of monumental sculptures and orthostat reliefs have been restored and replaced *in situ*, making this one of the most unique outdoor museums in Turkey. Both of these sites can be seen easily in a day's outing from Ceyhan.

Another interesting excursion from Ceyhan is to Yílan Kalesi, the

Castle of the Snake. This is on the right bank of the Ceyhan, some six kilometres along the old road from Ceyhan to Misis. The castle takes its name from the hoary old Turkish legend that in ancient times this was the residence of the King of Snakes. Yílan Kalesi has never been thoroughly studied, but it is believed to have been built in the late twelfth century by King Leo II of Lesser Armenia. It is one of the most impressive of all the medieval castles of Cilicia, its ruined walls and towers crowning a dramatic crag above the Ceyhan, looking like the setting for a production of *Dracula*.

Twenty-one kilometres past the turn-off for Ceyhan there is another turn-off for **Misis**, a town on the right bank of the undulating Ceyhan. Misis has been identified as the **ancient Mopsuestia**, known to the Crusaders as Mamistra. The ancient name of the town came from the tradition that it was founded by Mopsus, one of the three legendary seers of the ancient Greek world, who led remnants of his 'mixed multitudes of peoples' here to Cilicia after the fall of Troy.

After passing the turn-off to Misis you continue on the last stretch of the road to **Adana**, the fourth largest city in Turkey, with a population now approaching half a million. Adana stands on the banks of the Seyhan River in the very centre of the vast Cilician delta, and the wealth of that rich plain has made it the most prosperous provincial city in the country. The history of Adana goes back to the beginning of the first millennium BC, and, like most other Turkish cities, it has been fought over by all of the many powers that have marched across Anatolia. Here again there is little evidence of its historic past remaining in the modern town, though there is an interesting museum exhibiting finds from the many archaeological sites in the Cilician plain. The most prominent ancient monument is the Taş Köprü, a bridge across the Seyhan built by Hadrian and repaired by Justinian. The principal Turkish monument is the Ulu Cami, built in 1507 by Halil Bey, the Emir of the Ramazanoğlu Turks who ruled Cilicia before it was conquered by the Ottomans under Selim the Grim in 1516. The tiles in the mosque and in Halil Bey's *türbe* are among the finest in Turkey, rivalling those in the Rüstem Pasha Camii in Istanbul.

From Adana it is a short drive across the valley of the Seyhan to Tarsus, the end of this and an earlier itinerary along the coast of Rough Cilicia. From Tarsus you can head north through the Cilician Gates and across the Taurus into central Anatolia; and from there drive on across the plateau to Ankara and Istanbul, to complete the long journey around this ancient and extraordinary land.

Appendices

❧

Throughout this guide, modern Turkish spelling has been used for Turkish proper names and for things which are specifically Turkish. Modern Turkish is rigorously logical and phonetic, and the few letters which are pronounced differently than in English are indicated below. All letters have but a single sound and none is totally silent. Turkish is very lightly accented, most often on the last syllable, but all syllables should be clearly and almost evenly accented.

Vowels are pronounced as in French or German; i.e. *a* as in r*a*ther, *e* as in m*e*t, *i* as in mach*i*ne, *o* as in *o*h, *u* as in m*u*te. In addition, there are three other vowels which do not occur in English; these are *ı* (undotted), pronounced as the *u* in b*u*t, *ö* as in German or as *oy* in ann*oy*, *ü* as in German or as *ui* in s*ui*t.

Consonants are pronounced as in English, except the following:
c as *j* in *j*am; e.g. *cami* (mosque)=jahmy
ç as *ch* in *ch*at; e.g. *çorba* (soup)=chorba
g as in *g*et; never as in *g*em
ğ is almost silent and tends to lengthen the preceding vowel
ş as in *s*ugar; e.g. *çeşme* (fountain)=che*sh*me

PRACTICAL SUGGESTIONS

Climate
Turkey is a vast country with an extremely varied topography and climate, so that advice on the best season for travelling depends on where one is going. Istanbul and western Anatolia have a very temperate climate; seldom is it oppressively hot in summer and the temperature rarely drops below freezing in winter, though the mid-winter rains can be very gloomy. The Aegean coast has the most delightful climate in the country, save for the rainy winter months, and along the sub-tropical Mediterranean coast one can

swim for at least nine months of the year. The Black Sea coast is rainy and humid, the price it pays for the verdant forests which cloak the region. The central Anatolian plateau has an extraordinary range in climate, with the range becoming even more extreme as one goes farther east. Very heavy snowfall in the mountainous parts of eastern Anatolia makes it virtually impossible to travel to many places there during the winter months, and in the south-east the summer heat is almost unbearable. Generally speaking, the best time to visit most parts of Turkey is in late spring and early summer, when even the barren Anatolian plateau turns green and when wild flowers blossom among the ruins of ancient cities. But in old Istanbul one can enjoy oneself during all seasons of the year, for if it gets too hot in summer one can dine out in a restaurant on the Bosphorus, cooled by zephyrs from the Black Sea, and if the winter rains begin to dampen your spirits you can always take refuge in a *hamam*, where you can steam away an afternoon as sensuously as a sultan in his bath, or almost.

Mosques, Museums and Archaeological Sites
In Istanbul and other large cities museums are open (except where noted) every day except Monday; the hours are generally 9.00 to 5.00 or 5.30. Archaeological sites are generally open from 9.00 till an hour or so before sunset, but there are innumerable sites that are unfenced and can be visited at any time. Mosques open at the time of the first occasion of daily prayer, just before dawn, and close after the evening prayer, an hour or so after sunset. The great mosques in Istanbul and other large cities remain open in the intervals between the five occasions of daily prayer, but others are liable to be closed during those periods. Normal etiquette should be observed and appropriate clothing worn when visiting a mosque; one should remove one's shoes at the threshold and refrain from disturbing the faithful at their prayers.

The following are the hours for the principal museums in Istanbul:
Aya Sofya (Haghia Sophia): regular times
Aya Irene (Haghia Eirene): regular times
Topkapí Sarayí: open Monday, closed Tuesday; 9.30–5.00
Yerebatan Saray: open Monday, closed Tuesday; regular hours
Mosaic Museum: closed both Monday and Tuesday; regular hours
Archaeological Museum: regular times
Museum of the Ancient Orient: closed both Monday and Tuesday; regular hours
Museum of Turkish and Islamic Art: regular times

Fethiye Camii (Church of the Pammakaristos): closed Wednesday; open other days 9.30–4.30

Kariye Cami (Church of St Saviour in Chora): open Monday, closed Tuesday; regular hours in winter; in summer 8.30–5.15

Dolmabahçe Palace: closed for restoration

Rumeli Hisarí: regular days; open 9.30–5.30

Transport (for the non-motorist)

The Turkish National Airways (Turk Hava Yollarí, or THY) have a network which connects more than twenty cities in Turkey. Fares are low and services frequent. This is the most convenient way to travel to remote places in the east of Turkey, such as Van.

The Turkish Maritime Lines (Denizcilik Bankasí) run regular passenger ships along the coasts of the Black Sea, the Aegean, and the Mediterranean, as well as ferries in the Bosphorus, the Sea of Marmara, and Lake Van.

The railway from Europe, the route of the famous and now-defunct Orient Express, terminates at Sirkeci Station in Istanbul. Those wishing to continue on into Anatolia by rail must take a ferry across to Haydarpaşa Station on the Asian side. From Haydarpaşa there are several express trains daily to Ankara; our own favourite is the night sleeper, which offers old-fashioned European service and comfort. From Ankara there are two main lines running eastward through Anatolia, one to Kars and the other to Tatvan and thence by ferry to Van.

There are bus services between all of the cities and large towns in Turkey. Pullman bus services between major towns are more expensive but safer and more comfortable. Travelling by bus is undoubtedly the best way to become acquainted with the country and its people, for your fellow passengers will include the full spectrum of Turkish society, as well as the occasional gypsy and his dancing bear.

Taxis are plentiful in all cities and towns, though one should always agree on the fare in advance. (Ask the hotel clerk for advice on fares.) The *dolmuş*, or shared taxi, operates between fixed points and you pay only for the seat you occupy. Tours by Pullman bus or minibus can be arranged at most travel agencies in Istanbul, Ankara, Izmir and major resort centres.

Offices of the Tourism Bureau provide a free road map of Turkey that is reliable and up to date. Asphalt highways are marked in black and stabilized gravel or macadam roads are shown in red, while secondary roads of inferior quality are coloured orange.

Almost all of the itineraries in the present guide are on asphalt roads, and in the few cases where others are used appropriate advice and precautions have been given.

HOTELS

Istanbul and other large cities and towns of Turkey are well equipped with hotels, ranging from luxury establishments to simple hostels. Also, in recent years a large number of motels and pensions have been built along the Aegean and Mediterranean coasts and near some of the major archaeological sites. Most of these are listed in the Hotel Guide to Turkey, which can be obtained free of charge at any office of the Tourism Bureau. In general, Turkish hotels are clean and reasonably priced, though as you go farther east into Anatolia you would be wise to choose hotels in the higher categories. In the simpler Anatolian hostels guests often pay only for the beds they occupy. Therefore, if you want a private room in such places you may find that you will have to pay for all of the several beds in your room, otherwise you may find that the gypsy and his dancing bear are your room mates. Rooms can be rented in private houses in such seaside towns as Side and Bodrum, but elsewhere in Anatolia this is not usually possible.

RESTAURANTS AND TURKISH COOKING

Turkish cuisine is one of the most distinguished in the world, and few others can compare with it in quality and variety. Istanbul, with its cosmopolitan character, is particularly well endowed with good restaurants catering to every taste and social class, ranging from humble working-men's cookshops to de luxe restaurants with elaborate Turkish and international menus.

Turks usually begin their meal with cold hors d'oeuvres (*soğuk meze*), which are brought to you on a groaning tray from which you can select whatever your heart desires. You can then order various hot hors d'oeuvres (*sicak meze*), selected from a glutton's dream of gastronomic delicacies. If you are not completely stuffed by this time you can go on to order various kinds of meat (*et*) or fish (*balík*), which you can choose from the display window in the refrigerator (where you will see exhibited such exotic titbits as sheep's brains and testicles). Most Turks prefer to digest their food with *raki*, a powerful anise-based drink which is usually mixed half-and-half with water, but timid travellers might be advised to try one of the many brands of good Turkish wine (*şarap*). Turkish beer (*bira*) is also quite good, and there are a number of places, such as Istanbul's Passage of Flowers, which serve an old-fashioned German brew in giant glasses called Argentines. *Afiyet olsun*! (Bon appetit!)

SHOPS AND MARKETS

The most renowned of Turkey's markets is Istanbul's Kapalí Çarşí, the Covered Bazaar, but Bursa and Edirne and other cities also have colourful and interesting market quarters. The shops in and around the Kapalí Çarşí are particularly good for finding unique goods which are distinctively Turkish. The products for which the Covered Bazaar is noted are: copper and brassware, jewellery, Turkish embroideries, oriental rugs, Turkish carpets (*kilim*), pottery, glassware, ceramics, alabaster, onyx, meerschaum, leather, suede, and antiques. Many shops display signs saying that their goods are sold at fixed prices, but in many venerable places one can still enjoy a session of old-fashioned oriental bargaining over cups of Turkish coffee or glasses of tea.

HOLIDAYS

The following are the national holidays when most shops, offices, banks and museums are closed for all or part of the day:

January 1: New Year's Day
April 23: National Sovereignty Day and Children's Day
May 1: Spring Day
May 19: Freedom and Sovereignty Day
August 30: Victory Day
October 29: Anniversary of the Founding of the Turkish Republic
November 10: Anniversary of Atatürk's Death

In addition there are a number of Islamic holidays which are based on the lunar calendar, occurring eleven days earlier each year. Ramazan is a month of daytime fasting, equivalent to the Christian Lent. This is immediately followed by Şeker Bayram, the Sugar Holiday, a joyous time similar to Easter, and forty days after comes Kurban Bayram, the Feast of Sacrifice, when those who can afford it slaughter a ram for their first-born son and then spend the day feasting.

371

GLOSSARY

The following are some technical terms and Turkish words that are used frequently in the text. The words enclosed in parentheses are the forms which those Turkish terms take when they are modified by a preceding noun; e.g. Yeni Cami, the New Mosque; but Sultan Ahmet Camii, the Mosque *of* Sultan Ahmet

ada (*adasi*): island
agora: market-place; the civic centre of an ancient Greek city
bouleuterion: senate-house of an ancient Greek city
bulvar (*bulvari*): boulevard
cami (*camii*): mosque
capital: the topmost member of a column
çarşi (*çarşisi*): market or bazaar
cavea: auditorium of a Greek theatre
cella: the inner sanctuary of a Greek temple
çeşme (*çeşmesi*): fountain
dağ (*daği*): mountain
deniz: sea
dere (*deresi*): stream or valley
dershane: lecture-hall of an Islamic school of theology
diazoma (plural diazomata): aisle in a Greek theatre
eski: old
geçit (*geçti*): mountain pass
göl (*gölü*): lake
hamam (*hamami*): Turkish bath
han or *kervansaray*: inn or hostel for merchants and travellers
hisar (*hisari*): castle or fortress
hüyük: mound
imam: the cleric who presides over public prayers at a mosque
irmak: river
iskele: quay
kale (*kalesi*): castle or fortress
kapi (*kapisi*): gate or door
karum: Assyrian trading colony
kilise (*kilisesi*): church
köprü (*köprüsü*): bridge
korfez: bay or gulf
köy: village
külliye (*külliyesi*): building complex including a mosque and all of its pious foundations

kümbet: Selcuk mausoleum

liman (*limani*): harbour

medrese (*medresesi*): Islamic school of theology

megaron: Bronze Age building

mektep (*mektebi*): Ottoman primary school

mescit: a small mosque or place of prayer

meydan (*meydani*): square or town centre

mihrab: niche in a mosque indicating the direction of Mecca

mimber: pulpit in a mosque

müezzin: cleric who gives the call to prayer from the minaret of a
    mosque

nehir (*nehri*): river

oda (*odasi*): room or chamber

opisthodomus: rear chamber in a Greek temple

orchestra: the dancing-floor in an ancient Greek theatre

ova (*ovasi*): plain

paradoi: side entrances to a Greek theatre, passing between the
    stage-building and the auditorium

pazar (*pazari*): bazaar or market

pronaos: front chamber in a Greek temple

şadirvan: mosque fountain for ritual ablutions

saray (*sarayi*): palace

sebil: street fountain used for the distribution of water to passers-by

şehir (*şehri*): town

sokak (*sokaği*): street

stoa: a porticoed building

su (*suyu*): water or stream (a stream is sometimes called *çay*, which
    means tea)

tekke: dervish monastery

temenos: temple enclosure

türbe (*türbesi*): mausoleum

yeni: new

yol: road or path

CHRONOLOGICAL TABLE

BC

Palaeolithic Period (prior to 7000 BC)

? – 7000 – Cave dwellings at Karain; primitive stone implements
    and weapons

Neolithic Period (c. 7000–5500)

c. 7000 – First settlement at Hacílar; earliest evidences of agriculture in Anatolia

c. 6500–5500 – Çatal Hüyük becomes first cultural centre in Anatolia; earliest known religious shrines, pottery, frescoes and statuettes

Chalcolithic Period (c. 5500–3000)

c. 5500 – Sophisticated painted pottery and figurines at Hacílar and Çatal Hüyük

c. 5000–3000 – First settlements at Alacahüyük, Alişar, Canhasan and Beycesultan

Early Bronze Age (c. 3000–2000)

c. 3000 – First settlement at Troy

c. 2500–2000 – Flourishing of Hattian culture

Late Bronze Age (c. 2000–1200)

c. 1950 – Assyrian merchant-colony at Kültepe; first written records in Anatolia

c. 1900 – Founding of Hattusa by Hittites

c. 1700–1450 – Old Hittite Kingdom

c. 1450–1200 – Hittite Empire

c. 1260 – Fall of Troy

c. 1200 – Destruction of Hattusa

Anatolia's Dark Age (c. 1200–700)

c. 1200–1100 – Foundation of Neo-Hittite states at Carchemish, Karatepe and Zincirli

c. 1100–1000 – Migration of Greeks to Aegean coast of Anatolia

c. 900 – Rise of Urartian culture in eastern Anatolia

c. 900–800 – Rise of Phrygian, Lydian, Carian and Lycian cultures in western Anatolia

c. 800 – Foundation of Pan-Ionic League and rise of Greek culture in western Anatolia

717 – Carchemish and other Neo-Hittite states fall to the Assyrians

c. 700 – Cimmerians destroy most cities in western Anatolia

Archaic Period (c. 700–479)

c. 700 – Birth of Homer in Smyrna

c. 667 – Foundation of Byzantium

c. 650–600 – Miletos establishes colonies at Sinope, Amisus and Trebizond

c. 600–500 – Beginnings of Greek science and philosophy in Ionia

561–46 – Reign of Croesus of Lydia

546 – Croesus defeated by Cyrus the Great; Ionia subjected by Persia

512 – Byzantium taken by Darius
499 – Ionian cities revolt against Persia
494 – Ionian revolt is crushed and Miletos burned
490 – Persians defeated at Marathon
480 – Xerxes invades Greece; Persians defeated at Salamis
479 – Persians defeated at Plataea and Mycale; Persians evacuate Greece and Ionian cities regain freedom

Classical Period (479–323)
478 – Ionian cities join the Delian Confederacy
431 – Beginning of the Peloponnesian War
404 – End of the Peloponnesian War
401 – Xenophon and the Ten Thousand begin their expedition
386 – Ionia subjected once more by Persia
356 – Birth of Alexander the Great
336 – Accession of Alexander
334 – Alexander crosses the Hellespont and defeats Persians at the Granicus
323 – Death of Alexander

Hellenistic Period (323–130)
323 – Outbreak of war between the Diadochi, Alexander's successors
318–17 – Antigonus controls Asia Minor
301 – Battle of Ipsus and death of Antigonus; Lysimachus rules Anatolia and Seleucus gains northern Syria
300 – Founding of Antioch
281 – Battle of Corupedium; Seleucus defeats Lysimachus and occupies Anatolia; assassination of Seleucus
276–5 – Gauls invade Anatolia and are defeated by Antiochus
261–41 – Reign of Eumenes I and rise of Pergamum
230 – Alliance of Rome and Pergamum; Pergamenes defeat Gauls
223–187 – Reign of Antiochus III, the Great
188 – Treaty of Apamea ends Seleucid rule in Anatolia; expansion of Pergamene Kingdom
133 – Death of Attalus III of Pergamum; Rome inherits his kingdom

Roman Period (130 BC–AD 330)
130 – Organization of Roman province of Asia
100 – Mithradates VI Eupator becomes sole ruler of the Pontic Kingdom
88 – Asia Minor rises up against Romans; Mithradates invades Greece
83 – End of Seleucid Empire

80 – Foundation of Kingdom of Commagene
74 – Death of Nicomedes of Bithynia; Rome inherits his kingdom
64 – End of Mithradatic Wars; Romans control most of Anatolia
40 – Antony and Cleopatra marry in Antioch
30 – Augustus makes triumphal visit to Antioch after his victory at Actium over Antony and Cleopatra

AD

40–56 – Paul's missionary journeys; establishment of first ecumenical Christian community at Antioch
72 – Commagene Kingdom annexed by Rome
114 – Armenia annexed by Rome
196 – Byzantium taken by Septimius Severus
263–70 – Goths invade Asia Minor
313 – Edict of Milan; toleration of Christianity in Roman Empire
324 – Constantine defeats Licinius and becomes sole ruler of Roman Empire; begins to build new capital at Byzantium
330 – Constantinople dedicated as capital of Roman Empire

Byzantine Period (330–1453)
392 – Edict of Theodosius I banning paganism
527–65 – Reign of Justinian the Great; zenith of Byzantine power
626 – Avars and Slavs besiege Constantinople
628 – Heraclius defeats Persians and saves Byzantine Empire
636 – Arabs defeat Byzantines on the Yarmuk and penetrate into Asia Minor
677 – Arab fleet attacks Constantinople
717–18 – Arabs besiege Constantinople
726–80 – First Iconoclastic Period
813 – Bulgars besiege Constantinople for first time
831–43 – Second Iconoclastic Period
923 – Bulgars take Adrianople and besiege Constantinople
963–9 – Nicephorus Phocas victorious over Arabs and regains Cilicia and Cyprus
1054 – Schism between Greek and Roman churches
1071 – Byzantines defeated by Selcuks at Manzikert; Turks overrun Anatolia
1071–1283 – The Sultanate of Rum; Selcuks dominant power in Anatolia
1096 – Beginning of First Crusade; Latin armies enter Anatolia for first time
1176 – Selcuks annihilate Greeks at Myriocephalon; Byzantium loses last chance to expel the Turks from Asia Minor

APPENDICES

1203 – Beginning of Fourth Crusade; Latins attack Constantinople
1204 – Latins sack Constantinople; dismemberment of Byzantine Empire; Lascarids set up Byzantine capital in Nicaea; Comneni found Empire of Trebizond
1240 – Ottoman Turks make first appearance in western Anatolia; Mongols invade eastern Anatolia
1242 – Mongols defeat Selcuks at Kösedağ and destroy their power in Anatolia
1261 – Michael VIII Palaeologus retakes Constantinople and restores Byzantine Empire
1324 – Death of Osman Gazi, founder of Ottoman dynasty
1326 – Ottomans under Sultan Orhan take Prussia and establish their first capital there
1354 – Prince Süleyman leads first Turkish force into Europe
1363 – Turks under Murat I capture Adrianople and later move their capital there
1389 – Turks defeat Serbians at Kossova
1396 – Beyazit I defeats Crusader army at Nicopolis
1397 – First Turkish siege of Constantinople
1402 – Tamerlane defeats Turks at Ankara and captures Beyazit I; Mongols overrun Anatolia
1422 – Second Turkish siege of Constantinople
1444 – Turks crush Crusader army at Varna
1448 – Turks defeat Hungarians at second battle of Kossova
1453 – Turks under Mehmet II conquer Constantinople; Constantine XI, last Emperor of Byzantium, dies in battle; name of city subsequently becomes Istanbul

Ottoman Turkish Period (1453–1923)
1453 – Istanbul becomes capital of the Ottoman Empire, which now comprises most of Greece, the southern Balkans and western Anatolia
1517 – Selim I captures Cairo and assumes the title of Caliph; the Ottoman Empire has by now expanded into southern Europe, eastern Anatolia, Syria, Palestine, Egypt and Algeria
1520–66 – Reign of Süleyman the Magnificent; zenith of Ottoman power
1571 – Turks conquer Cyprus; Christian powers defeat Turkish fleet at battle of Lepanto
1578–1666 – 'The Rule of the Women'; ineffective sultans give up control of the Empire to their women and Grand Vezirs
1666–1812 – Period of intermittent wars between Turks and Euro-

377

pean powers; Ottoman Empire loses much territory in southern Europe

1821 – Greeks begin War of Independence

1826 – Mahmut II destroys Janissary Corps

1832 – Greece achieves independence; Ibrahim Pasha of Egypt invades Anatolia

1839–76 – The Tanzimat Period; programme of reform in the Ottoman Empire

1877 – Establishment of first Turkish parliament; dissolved the following year by Sultan Abdül Hamit II

1908 – Constitutional rule and parliament restored

1909 – Abdül Hamit deposed

1912–13 – Balkan Wars; Turks lose Macedonia and part of Thrace

1914 – Turkey enters World War I as ally of Germany

1915 – Turks repel Allied landings on Gallipoli peninsula

1918 – Turks surrender to Allies; Istanbul occupied by Anglo-French army

1919 – Sivas Congress; Atatürk leads Turkish Nationalists in beginning of struggle for national sovereignty; Greek army lands at Smyrna

1920 – Establishment of Grand National Assembly of Turkey with Atatürk as President; Greek army advances into Asia Minor

1922 – Turks defeat Greeks and drive them out of Asia Minor; Sultanate abolished

1923 – Treaty of Lausanne establishes sovereignty of modern Turkey, defines its frontiers, and arranges for exchange of minority populations between Greece and Turkey

Modern Turkish Period (1923 to present)

1923 – Establishment of the Turkish Republic with Atatürk as first President

1924 – Abolition of Caliphate

1925–38 – Atatürk's programme of reforms to modernize Turkey

1938 – Death of Atatürk

1945 – Turkey enters World War II on side of Allies

1946 – Turkey becomes charter member of the United Nations

1950 – Turkey enters Korean War as part of United Nations force

1973 – Bosphorus Bridge built between Europe and Asia; opened on fiftieth anniversary of the founding of the Turkish Republic

BYZANTINE EMPERORS

Constantine the Great, 324–37
Constantius, 337–61
Julian the Apostate, 361–3
Jovian, 363–4
Valens, 364–78
Theodosius the Great, 379–95
Arcadius, 395–408
Theodosius II, 408–50
Marcian, 450–7
Leo I, 457–74
Leo II, 474
Zeno, 474–91
Anastasius, 491–518
Justin I, 518–27
Justinian the Great, 527–65
Justin II, 565–78
Tiberius II, 578–82
Maurice, 582–602
Phocas, 602–10
Heraclius, 610–41
Constantine II, 641
Heracleonas, 641
Constantine III, 641–68
Constantine IV, 668–85
Justinian II, 685–95
Leontius, 695–8
Tiberius III, 698–705
Justinian II (second reign), 705–11
Philippicus Bardanes, 711–13
Anastasius II, 713–15
Theodosius III, 715–17
Leo III, 717–41
Constantine V, 741–75
Leo IV, 775–80
Constantine VI, 780–97
Eirene, 797–802
Nicephorus I, 802–11
Stauracius, 811
Michael I, 811–13

Leo V, 813–20
Michael II, 820–9
Theophilus, 829–42
Michael III, 842–67
Basil I, 867–86
Leo VI, 886–912
Alexander, 912–13
Constantine VII, 913–59
Romanus I (co-emperor), 919–44
Romanus II, 959–63
Nicephorus II Phocas, 963–9
John I Tzimisces, 969–76
Basil II, 976–1025
Constantine VIII, 1025–8
Romanus III Argyrus, 1028–34
Michael IV, 1034–41
Michael V, 1041–2
Theodora and Zoe, 1042
Constantine IX, 1042–55
Theodora (second reign), 1055–6
Michael VI, 1056–7
Isaac Comnenus, 1057–9
Constantine X Ducas, 1059–67
Romanus IV Diogenes, 1067–71
Michael VII Ducas, 1071–8
Nicephorus III, 1078–81
Alexius I Comnenus, 1081–1118
John II Comnenus, 1118–43
Manuel I Comnenus, 1143–80
Alexius II Comnenus, 1180–3
Andronicus I Comnenus, 1183–5
Isaac II Angelus, 1185–95
Alexius III Angelus, 1195–1203
Isaac Angelus (second reign), 1203–4
Alexius IV Angelus (co-emperor), 1203–4
Alexius V Ducas, 1204

TURKEY

*Theodore I Lascaris, 1204–22
*John III, 1222–54
*Theodore II Lascaris, 1254–8
*John IV, 1258–61
Michael VIII Palaeologus, 1261–82
Andronicus II Palaeologus, 1282–1328
Andronicus III Palaeologus, 1328–41
John V Palaeologus, 1341–91

John VI Cantacuzenus (co-emperor), 1341–54
Andronicus (IV) (co-emperor), 1376–9
John (VII) (co-emperor), 1390
Manuel II Palaeologus, 1391–1425
John VIII Palaeologus, 1425–48
Constantine XI Dragases, 1449–53

* *Ruled in Nicaea during the Latin occupation of Constantinople*

OTTOMAN SULTANS

Orhan Gazi, 1324–59
Murat I, 1359–89
Beyazit I, 1389–1403
(Interregnum, 1403–13)
Mehmet I, 1413–21
Murat II, 1421–51
Mehmet II, the Conqueror, 1451–81
Beyazit II, 1481–1512
Selim I, the Grim, 1512–20
Süleyman I, the Magnificent, 1520–66
Selim II, 1566–74
Murat III, 1574–95
Mehmet III, 1595–1603
Ahmet I, 1603–17
Mustafa I, 1617–18
Osman II, 1618–22
Mustafa I (second reign), 1622–3
Murat IV, 1623–40

Ibrahim, 1640–8
Mehmet IV, 1648–87
Süleyman II, 1687–91
Ahmet II, 1691–5
Mustafa II, 1695–1703
Ahmet III, 1703–30
Mahmut I, 1730–54
Osman III, 1754–7
Mustafa III, 1757–74
Abdül Hamit I, 1774–89
Selim III, 1789–1807
Mustafa IV, 1807–8
Mahmut II, 1808–39
Abdül Mecit I, 1839–61
Abdül Aziz, 1861–76
Murat V, 1876
Abdül Hamit II, 1876–1909
Mehmet V, 1909–18
Mehmet VI, 1918–22
Abdül Mecit (II) (Caliph only), 1922–4

SOME BOOKS ON TURKEY

The following is a brief and selective list of books about Turkey, past and present. This is not meant to be a bibliography, but an introduction to the history, art, architecture, archaeology, and other aspects of the many cultures which have flourished in this land over the past ten thousand years.

HISTORY AND ARCHAEOLOGY

Prehistoric Anatolia

Kurt Bittel, *Hattusa, the Capital of the Hittites*, Oxford University Press (1970). A popular description of the Hittite capital by one of the archaeologists who first excavated the site.

Carl Blegen, *Troy and the Trojans*, Thames and Hudson, London (1963). An account of Troy and its culture by the archaeologist who continued the pioneering work of Schliemann and Dörpfeld.

O. R. Gurney, *The Hittites*, Penguin Books, London (1968). A detailed modern work on the history and culture of the Hittites.

Seton Lloyd, *Early Anatolia*, Penguin Books, London (1956). A good introduction to the culture of prehistoric Anatolia.

James Mellaart, *Çatal Hüyük*, Thames and Hudson, London (1967). A fascinating book by the archaeologist whose discovery of Çatal Hüyük revolutionized the study of prehistoric Anatolia.

Greek and Roman Periods

A. R. Burn, *The Pelican History of Greece*, Penguin Books, London (1966). An introductory general account.

John Cook, *The Greeks in Ionia and the East*, Thames and Hudson, London (1962). An introduction to the early history of the Greek colonies in Asia Minor.

Peter Green, *Alexander of Macedon*, Penguin Books, London (1970). An excellent and very readable modern biography.

F. E. Peters, *The Harvest of Hellenism*, Simon and Schuster, New York (1970). A history of the Near East from Alexander the Great to the triumph of Christianity; the best modern introduction to this complex and important period.

Byzantine Period

Charles Diehl, *Byzantine Empresses*, Alfred Knopf, New York (1967). Biographical sketches of some of the fascinating women in Byzantine history.

Sirapie der Nersessian, *The Armenians*, Thames and Hudson, London (1979). An introduction to medieval Armenian history and culture.

Georg Ostrogorsky, *History of the Byzantine State*, Blackwell, Oxford (1968). The standard work; a masterpiece.

Steven Runciman, *Byzantine Civilization*, Edward Arnold, London (1933). The best and most readable introduction to Byzantine culture.

Steven Runciman, *The Fall of Constantinople, 1453*, Cambridge University Press (1965). A superb account of the last days of Byzantium.

A. A. Vasiliev, *History of the Byzantine Empire*, 2 vols, The University Press, Madison, Wisconsin (1961). A general work which covers the whole span of Byzantine history.

Ottoman Period

Claude Cahen, *Pre-Ottoman Turkey*, Taplinger, New York (1968). A scholarly study of Anatolia in the centuries preceding the rise of the Ottomans.

Halil Inalcík, *The Ottoman Empire: The Classical Age, 1300–1600*, Weidenfeld and Nicolson, London (1973). An outstanding work by one of Turkey's leading historians.

Raphaela Lewis, *Everyday Life in Ottoman Turkey*, B. T. Batsford, London (1971). A very interesting book about daily life in Ottoman times.

N. M. Penzer, *The Harem*, Spring Books, London (1965). A fascinating account of life in the Great Palace of the Ottoman Sultans.

Tamara Talbot Rice, *The Seljuks in Asia Minor*, Thames and Hudson, London (1961). An introduction to Selcuk history and culture.

Stanford J. Shaw and Ezel Kural Shaw, *History of the Ottoman Empire and Modern Turkey*, 2 vols, Cambridge University Press, London (1976–7). The only modern work which covers the whole span of Ottoman history; indispensable.

Lord Kinross, *The Ottoman Centuries*, Jonathan Cape, London (1977). A popular history of the Ottoman Empire. Very readable.

Modern Turkish Period

Lord Kinross, *Atatürk: The Rebirth of a Nation*, Weidenfeld and Nicolson, London (1964). A biography of the Father of modern Turkey.

Bernard Lewis, *The Emergence of Modern Turkey*, Oxford University Press (1968). A thorough study of the intellectual and social movements that transformed the Ottoman Empire into the modern Turkish Republic.

Geoffrey Lewis, *Turkey*, Ernest Benn, London (third edition 1965). A short outline of modern Turkish history and politics.

ART AND ARCHITECTURE

Ekrem Akurgal, *The Art of the Hittites*, Thames and Hudson, London (1962). An excellent study of prehistoric Anatolian art by one of Turkey's leading scholars; superbly illustrated with colour plates.

Oktay Aslanapa, *Turkish Art and Architecture*; Faber and Faber, London (1971). A thorough study of almost every aspect of Turkish art and architecture.

Fanny Davis, *The Palace of Topkapi*, Scribners, New York (1970). A very thorough study of the Great Palace of the Ottoman Sultans, including its buildings, institutions, works of art, history and way of life; beautifully illustrated.

Godfrey Goodwin, *A History of Ottoman Architecture*, Thames and Hudson, London (1971). A monumental study of Ottoman architecture and the rich culture which produced it; a handsome book with numerous illustrations; highly recommended.

Richard Krautheimer, *Early Christian and Byzantine Architecture*, Penguin Books, London (1965). The standard reference work.

Michael Levey, *The World of Ottoman Art*, Thames and Hudson, London (1971). The best modern introduction.

Cyril Mango, *Byzantine Architecture*, Harry N. Abrams Inc., New York (1976). An excellent and attractive study of Byzantine architecture.

D. S. Robertson, *Greek and Roman Architecture*, Cambridge University Press (second edition 1971). A scholarly introduction.

TRAVEL AND LOCAL COLOUR

Most of the great nineteenth-century travellers are now out of print, though copies turn up now and then in secondhand bookshops; the best are Beaufort, Chandler, Fellows, Hamilton, Leake, Lynch and Newton. (A handsome new edition of Chandler's travels has recently been published by the Trustees of the British Museum.) One old classic to look for is Miss Pardoe's *Beauties of the Bosphorus*, illustrated with beautiful prints by Bartlett. Another is Dwight's *Istanbul Old and New*, illustrated with numerous photographs that show the old city at the end of its last golden age.

The following travel books about Turkey are in print:

Evliya Efendi, *Narrative of Travels*, Johnson Reprint Co., New York (1968). (A reprint of the early nineteenth-century English translation by von Hammer.) A fascinating chronicle of life in the Ottoman Empire in the mid-seventeenth century, written by a colourful character who was at the centre of events at that time.

John Freely, *Stamboul Sketches*, Redhouse Press, Istanbul (1974). Essays on arcane and bizarre aspects of the Istanbul scene; illustrated with photos by Sedat Pakay, one of Turkey's most original photographers.

Freya Stark, *Ionia, a Quest* (1954); *The Lycian Shore* (1956); *Alexander's Path* (1958), John Murray, London. Evocative descriptions of Asia Minor by one of the last of the great travellers to the Near East.

Gwynn Williams, *Eastern Turkey: a guide and history*, Faber and Faber, London (1972). A description of parts of Turkey about which little has been written in modern times.

GUIDEBOOKS

The most complete guide to all of Turkey is the 1970 English translation of the *Guide Bleu*, Librairie Hachette, Paris; however, caution should be exercised in using this guide for there are numerous errors, many of which have been copied from earlier works. In recent years a number of more literate and scholarly guides have been written; the best of these are the following:

Ekrem Akurgal, *Ancient Civilizations and Ruins of Turkey*, Haşet Kitabevi, Istanbul (third edition 1973). An excellent guide to more than one hundred archaeological sites ranging from the Bronze Age to the Roman era.

George Bean, *Aegean Turkey* (1966); *Turkey's Southern Shore* (1968); *Turkey Beyond the Maeander* (1971); *Lycia* (1978), Ernest Benn, London. Far and away the best guides to the Graeco-Roman sites in western and southern Asia Minor; superbly written by a great scholar.

Hilary Sumner-Boyd and John Freely, *Strolling Through Istanbul*, Redhouse Press, Istanbul (second edition 1974). The best and most complete and up-to-date guide to the antiquities of Istanbul.

Hilary Sumner-Boyd and John Freely, *Istanbul; A Brief Guide to the City*, Redhouse Press, Istanbul (1973). A condensed pocket-book edition of the above work.

BOOKS BY MODERN TURKISH AUTHORS

Yashar Kemal, *Memed, My Hawk* (1961); *The Wind From the Plain* (1963); *Anatolian Tales* (1968), Collins, London. Yashar Kemal was born in 1922 to a poor peasant family in south-eastern Anatolia, the countryside that supplied the background to his first novel. He has on several occasions been nominated for the Nobel Prize for Literature, most recently in 1978.

Nazim Hikmet, *Selected Poems*, Jonathan Cape, London (1967); *The Moscow Symphony*, Poetry Europe Series, Rapp and Whiting, André Deutsch, London (1970). Nazim Hikmet was born in 1902 in Salonika, when that city was still part of the Ottoman Empire, and he died in exile in Moscow in 1963, where he had fled after having served thirteen years in a Turkish prison because of his political beliefs. He is generally acknowledged to be the finest poet who has ever written in modern Turkish.

Irfan Orga, *Portrait of a Turkish Family*, Macmillan, London (1957). An interesting account of life in a Turkish family during the period of transition from empire to republic.

Mahmut Makal, *A Village in Anatolia*, Valentine, Mitchell, London (1954). A sensitive description of Anatolian life by a village schoolteacher.

Ahmet Emin Yalman, *Turkey in My Times*, University of Oklahoma Press, Norman (1956). The life and times of a man who was Turkey's most eminent journalist.

Aziz Nesim, *Istanbul Boy*, University of Texas Press, Austin (1977). Delightful tales of Istanbul life by Turkey's most famous humorist.

Nermin Menemencioğlu (in collaboration with Fahir Iz), *Turkish Verse*, Penguin Books, London (1978). An anthology of Turkish poetry from the fourteenth century to the present day.

Index

❧

Abaga, Khan of the Mongols, 257
Abas I, King of Armenia, 318, 319
Abdül Aziz, Ottoman sultan, 87, 88
Abdül Mecit, Ottoman sultan, 27, 87, 88
Abraham, 351, 352
Abydos, 111
Achilles, 119, 120, 124
Acı Göl, 192
Adana, 366
Adapazarí, 296
Adilcevaz, 337
Adír Adasí, 329
Adíyaman, 356
Aeneas, 124
Aeolia and the Aeolian Greeks, 125, 136, 137, 140, 142, 166, 203
Ağa Limaní, 213
Agamemnon, 113, 115, 119, 124
Agamemnon, Baths of, 147
Agdistis, Phrygian god, 291
Ağrí, 329
Ağrí Dagí (see Mount Ararat)
Ahi Şerafettin, 281, 282
Ahlat, 336, 337
Ahmet I, Ottoman sultan, 41, 48
Ahmet II, Ottoman sultan, 65
Ahmet III, Ottoman sultan, 42, 59, 71, 85, 237
Aizanoi, 294, 295
Akçaabat, 303
Akçakale, 303
Akçay, 123
Akhtamar, 333–335
    Church of the Holy Apostles, 333–335
Akköy (Ionia), 162, 163
Akköy (Cappadocia), 243
Akkoyunlu, Turcoman tribe, 317, 336, 341, 346
Aksaray, 235, 236
Aksu, 199
Alabanda, 175, 176
Alaca Çayí, 322
Alacahüyük, 261, 268, 269, 277, 278, 279

Alâeddin Keykubad I, Selcuk sultan, 196, 197, 208, 209, 224, 225, 226, 228, 234, 237, 247, 249, 250, 252, 256, 292, 295, 349
Alâeddin Keykubad II, Selcuk sultan, 226, 227
Alagöz Dağí, 326
Alahan monastery, 221
Alanya, 207–210
Alçítepe, 112
Alexander the Great, 113, 142, 144, 148, 161, 166, 170, 176, 184, 193, 199, 201, 204, 218, 275, 286, 288, 289, 348, 364
Alexander, Byzantine emperor, 30
Alexandria Troas, 120, 121
Alexius I Comnenus, Byzantine emperor, 96
Alexius I Comnenus, Emperor of Trebizond, 304
Alexius III Comnenus, Emperor of Trebizond, 313
Ali Ağa, 136
Ali Bey Adasí, 124
Ali ibn Saltuk, founder of the Saltukid dynasty, 316
Alinda, 175, 176
Alişar, 277, 278
al-Malika al-Adilyya, Selcuk empress, 250
al-Malik al-Salih Mahmud, Artukid emir, 343
Alparslan, Selcuk sultan, 321
Altínkum, 165
Amasya, *259–261*, 297
Amazons, 136, 301, 302, 303
Amik Kalesi, 329, 330
Amik, plain and lake, 359
Anacreon, 147, 148
Anamur Castle (Mamure Kalesi), 211, 212
Anastasius, Byzantine emperor, 45, 54, 55
Anatolian Earth Mother, 277, 278, 291
Anazarbus, 365

387

Andriaki, 183
Andromache, 118
Andronicus I Comnenus, Byzantine emperor, 143, 144
Andronicus II Palaeologus, Byzantine emperor, 76
Anemurium, 211
Ani, 318–325
Ankara, 272–282
  history, 272, 273
  Ahi Elvan Camii, 281
  Alâeddin Camii, 276
  Arslanhane Camii, 281
  Atatürk Memorial (Anít Kabir), 282
  Bedesten of Mahmut Pasha, 276
  Citadel (Kale), 272, 275, 276
  Hací Bayram Camii, 275
  Julian's Column (Minaret of Belkis), 274
  Museum of Anatolian Cultures, 276–280
  Old Parliament, the, 273
  Roman Baths, 273
  Temple of Augustus, 274 275
Antalya, 196–198
Antalya, Gulf of, 183–198
Antandros, 123, 124
Anticragus Mountains, 179
Antigonus the One-Eyed, King of Macedonia, 93, 120, 142, 259, 360
Antioch (modern Antakya), 359–361
  Church of St Peter, 363
Antiochis ad Cragum, 211
Antiochus I, King of Commagene, 356, 358
Antiochus IV, King of Commagene, 221
Antiochus I, Seleucid emperor, 181
Antiochus II, Seleucid emperor, 181
Antiochus IV, Seleucid emperor, 211, 363, 365
Antiochus VII, Seleucid emperor, 208
Antiphellus, 182
Anti-Taurus Mountains, 365
Antoninus Pius, Roman emperor, 146
Antony, Marc, 218, 219, 361, 362
Aphrodisias, 187–189
Aphrodite of Cnidos, 174
Aplgharid Pahlavuni, Armenian prince, 323
Apollo, 119, 160, 175, 182, 362
Apollonius of Perge, 199
Apysyrtis, Medea's brother, 309
Arabs, 16, 55, 214, 242, 275, 292, 319, 329, 330, 341, 345, 347, 348, 351, 352, 360, 365
Ararat, Mt (Turkish Ağrí Dağí), 319, 321, 322, 326, 327, 328

Aras Nehri (ancient Araxes), 317, 326, 327
Arcadius, Byzantine emperor, 45
Archimedes, 199
Argistis II, Urartian king, 329, 330
Argonauts, 302, 303
Aristakes Lastivert, Armenian poet, 324, 325
Aristotle, 122
Armenians, 16, 75, 208, 212, 215, 216, 256, 314, 315, 317, 318, 319, 321, 322, 323, 324, 328, 329, 331, 333, 335, 336, 341, 343, 359, 360, 365, 366
Armenian dynasties:
  Arascid, 319
  Artaxiad, 319
  Artsuni, 331, 333, 335
  Bagtarid, 314, 317, 318, 319, 321, 322, 326
  Orontid, 319, 326, 331
  Rubenid, 215, 216
  Vaspurakan, 331, 333, 335
  Zachariad, 321, 322, 323, 324
Armenia, Kingdom of, 317, 318, 319, 321, 322, 326, 331, 333, 335
Armenia, Lesser Kingdom of (Cilicia), 208, 212, 215, 216, 365, 366
Arpa Çayí, 322, 326
Arrian, 113, 288, 303
Arslan Taş, 293
Artemis, 152, 153, 160, 182, 255
Artemisia, Queen of Caria, 170, 176
Artukids, 341, 343, 346, 347
Artvin, 309
Asad al-Din Ruzapa, Selcuk emir, 234
Ashot I, King of Armenia, 319, 326
Ashot II, King of Armenia, 319
Ashot III, King of Armenia, 319
Ashot IV, King of Armenia, 319
Asia, Roman province of, 120, 129, 152
Aşík Veysel, 251
Aşkale, 315
Asklepios, 134
Aspendos, 201, 203
Assos, 121, 122
Assyrians, 16, 44, 250, 251, 263, 264, 278, 330, 350, 356
Atatürk, Kemal, 84, 87, 253, 282
Athenaeus, 125
Athenians, 111, 112, 180, 181, 203
Attalus I, King of Pergamum, 128, 131, 199, 291
Attalus II, King of Pergamum, 129, 131, 196
Attalus III, King of Pergamum, 129, 196

Augustus, Roman emperor, 246, 274, 361
Avanos, 239, 242, 243
Avcílar, 242
Ayaş, 217
Ayasuluk, 152, 159
Ayatekla, 213
Aydín, 176, 186
Aydíncík, 212
Aydíníd Turks, 159
Ayvacík, 121, 123
Ayvalík, 124, 125

Baba Dağ, 187
Babaeski, 104
Babylonians, the, 44
Bacchylides, 147
Bafa Gölü, 166
Bağras Castle, 359
Baibars, Mameluke sultan, 257, 261
Baiea, 364
Bakír Çayí, 125
Balat, 162, 163
Baldwin, Count of Flanders, 348
Balíhisar, 290
Barnabas, co-founder of Sumela, 312
Basil I, Byzantine emperor, 29
Basil II, Byzantine emperor, 28, 319
Başkale, 332
Bass, Prof. George, 171
Bayburt, 314
Bayíndír Bey, Akkoyunlu emir, 336, 337
Baykan, 340
Bayrami dervishes, 275
Beaufort, Sir Francis, 212, 213, 214, 216, 217
Behramkale, 121
Bektaşi dervishes, 222, 292
Belen, 364
Belisírama, 237
Bell, Gertrude, 223, 234, 356
Berenson, Bernard, 224
Bergama, 125, 135
Beşkonak, 203
Beyazit I, Ottoman sultan, 88, 95, 96, 98, 100, 135, 148, 266, 276
Beyazit II, Ottoman sultan, 57, 58, 60, 61, 257, 260, 261, 307
Beyazit Pasha, Grand Vezir, 261
Bilecik, 295, 296
Binbir Kilise, 223
Bingöl, 340
Bingöl Mountains, 317
Birecik, 353
Bithynia, 92, 96, 102, 295, 296
Blegen, Prof. Carl W., 115, 118
Bodrum (ancient Halicarnassus), 168, 170–173
Castle of St Peter, 170–172
Boğazkale (formerly Boğazköy), 262–266, 278
Boğsak, 212, 213
Bohemund, 218, 361
Bolu, 283
Bosphorus, the, 19, 22, 33, 81, 86–89
Boyabat, 297
Bozüyük, 295
Briseis, 124
Brutus, 179, 180
Bryce, James, 327, 328
Bül Bül Dağí, 152
Bulgars, the, 104
Burdur, 192
Bursa, 96–102
history, 96
Archaeological Museum, 100
Bedesten, 98
Çekirge, 99, 100, 102
Citadel, 98
Eski Kaplíca Hamam, 100
Koza Han, 98
Muradiye mosque complex, 98, 99
Murat I Hüdavendigâr mosque complex, 99, 100
Museum of Turkish and Islamic Art, 101
Orhan Gazi Camii, 97, 98
Sipahiler Çarşísí, 98
Tomb of Murat II, 99
Tomb of Orhan Gazi, 98
Tomb of Osman Gazi, 98
Ulu Cami, 96
Yeni Kaplíca Hamam, 106.
Yeşil Cami, 100, 101
Yeşil Türbe, 101
Buruncuk, 137
Byron, Lord, 111
Byzantine Empire, 15, 22, 30, 78, 79, 104, 199, 208, 214, 215, 276, 315, 318, 319, 331, 336, 341, 360
Byzantine Empire of Trebizond, 304
Byzantium (see Constantinople)

Cabeira, 257, 258
Caicus River, 128, 132
Çamlíhemşin, 309
Çanakkale, 15, 111–114
Çandarli, 135
Canhasan, 222, 223, 277
Cape Cavalierè, 212
Cape Helles, 113
Cape Sigeum, 119
Cappadocia, 234–243
Caracalla, 273, 352, 357
Carchemish, 274

Çardak, 192
Caria and the Carians, 16, 152, 166, 167, 168, 170, 174, 176, 187, 192
Casanova, Giacomo, 83
Çatal Hüyük, 223, 277
Çavdarhisar, 294
Çavuşin, 242
Cayster River, 152, 153
Celaleddin Karatay, Selcuk emir, 198, 226, 227
Celaleddin Rumi, the Mevlana, 107, 222, *228–230*
Ceramus Gulf, 174, 177
Çeşme, 148
Cevri Kalfa, 42
Ceyhan River, 365
Charon, 363
Chimaera, the, 184
Chios, 148
Christians, 152, 153, 189, 190, 363
Chryseis, 119, 124
Cicero, 120
Çildiroğlu, Kurdish-Turkish clan, 328
Cilicia Campestris (the Plain), 210, 212–219
Cilicia Tracheia (the Rugged), 210–212
Cilician Gates, 218, 220
Cimmerians, 153, 286, 290
Çine, 175
Çine Çayí, 175
Cius, 96
Cizre, 340
Claros, 149, 150
Claudius, Roman emperor, 95
Clazomenae, 148
Cleopatra, 218, 219, 361, 362
Climax, Mt, 198
Cnidos, 173, 174, 177
Çobandede, 317
Colophon, 141, 149
Comana Pontica, 255, 257
Commagene, Kingdom of, 356–359
Constans II, Byzantine emperor, 341
Constantine the Great, Byzantine emperor, 28, 48, 51, 52, 55, 58, 85, 93, 307, 343
Constantine VII Porphyrogenitus, Byzantine emperor, 52
Constantine IX, Byzantine emperor, 31, 321
Constantinople, 19, 22, 25, 27, 28, 29, 30, 31, 32, 47, 49, 51, 52, 53, 54, 55, 56, 57, 58, 59, 75, 78, 79
Constantius, Byzantine emperor, 104
Çorlu, 103
Çorlulu Ali Pasha, Grand Vezir, 59
Çoruh Nehri, 314
Çorum, 261

Corycian Castles (Kíz Kalesi), 215, 216
Corycian Caves, 214, 215
Corycius, 215, 216
Crassus, Roman general, 352
Croesus, King of Lydia, 144, 152, 275, 286, 289
Crusades and Crusaders, 16, 30, 49, 51, 56, 71, 93, 97, 104, 196, 214, 215, 220, 275, 304, 348, 349, 353, 359, 361
Çubuk Pass, 193
Çumra, 223
Cybele, cult of, 152, 160, 175, 277, 291
Cyme, 136, 203
Cynossema, 112
Cyrus II, Persian emperor, 144, 179, 275, 286, 289

Dağ, 193
Damlataş Cave (Alanya), 210
Dandolo, Henricus, Doge of Venice, 30, 31
Danishmend, founder of the Danishmendid dynasty, 247
Danishmendid Turks, 247
Daphne, 361, 362
Dardanelles (Hellespont), 110–114, 118, 119, 120
Darius III, Persian emperor, 364
David of Trebizond, the Grand Comnenus, 304
David Comnenus, Emperor of Trebizond, 304
David IV, King of Georgia, 321
Davut Ağa, Ottoman architect, 107
Dayr Zafaran (the Saffron Monastery), 346, 347
Dazimon, 255
Değirmendere (Ionia), 149
Değirmendere (Pontus), 312
Demetrius Cantemir, 39
Denizli, 189
Derinkuyu, 238
Diadotus Tryphon, the Voluptuary, 208
Didyma, 163, 165
Diogenes Laertius, 136, 137
Diyarbakír, 341, *343–345*
Doğubayazít, 327, 328
  Palace of Ishak Pasha, 328
Domitian, Roman emperor, 191
Dörpfeld, Wilhelm, 115

Ebu Said Bahadír, Khan of the Mongols, 229
Eceabat, 111, 112, 113
Ecelkapíz Çayí, 144, 145
Ecumenical Councils, 93, 154
Edirne (ancient Hadrianople), 15, 94, 96, 99, 104–110

Edirne [cont'd]
  history, 104
  Antiquities Museum, 107
  Archaeological and Ethnological
    Museum, 107
  Bedesten, 104, 105
  Beyazit II mosque complex, 108, 109
  Bridge of the Conqueror, 108
  Bridge of Mihal Gazi, 109
  Bridge of Süleyman the Magnificent,
    108
  Caravansarai of Rüstem Pasha, 105
  Edirne Sarayí, 108
  Eski Cami, 104
  Kavaflar Arasta, 107
  Kírkpínar Wrestling Festival, 108
  Kule Kapísí, 105
  Mihal Gazi Hamamí, 109
  Mihal Gazi Pasha, 109
  Muradiye mosque complex, 107, 108
  Murat I Camii, 109
  Şahmelek Pasha Camii, 109
  Sarayiçi, 108
  Selimiye mosque complex, 104, 106,
    107
  Sokollu Mehmet Pasha Hamamí,
    110
  Üç Şerefeli Cami, 104, 105, 106
Edremit, 129
Edremit, Gulf of, 122–124
Efes (see Ephesus)
Eğridir, 192
Eirene, Empress of Byzantium, 93, 240
Eirene, wife of John II Comnenus, 31
Elazíğ, 340
Elmalí, 183
Endymion, 167
Entiope, Queen of the Amazons, 303
Ephesus, 152–160
  history, 152, 153
  ancient houses, 158
  Arcadiane, 156
  Archaeological Museum, 159–160
  Baths of Scholastica, 157
  Church of Haghia Maria, 154
  Citadel of Ayasuluk, 152, 159
  Commercial Agora, 154
  Curates Street, 154
  gymnasia, 154
  Harbour baths, 154
  House of the Blessed Virgin
    (Panayia Kapulu), 160
  Isa Bey Camii, 159
  Library of Celsus, 154
  Magnesia Gate, 158
  Nymphaion, 158
  Odeion, 158
  Prytaneion, 158
  stadium, 154
  State Agora, 158
  Temple of Artemis, 152, 153
  Temple of Domitian, 158
  Temple of Hadrian, 158
  Temple of Serapis, 154
  theatre, 154
Epiphania, 365
Erciş, 329
Erciyes Dağí, 238, 243, 246
Erdemli, 217
Eretnid Turks, 256
Erim, Prof. Kenan, 187
Ermenek, 211
Ertuğrul Gazi, founder of the Otto-
    man dynasty, 295, 296
Erythrae, 149
Eski Foça, 136
Eski Hisar, 174
Eski Kâhta, 356, 357, 358
Eski Kale, 113
Eski Malatya, 279
Eskişehir, 293
Euclid, 199
Eudoxos of Cnidos, 174
Eugenios II, Pope, 348, 349
Eumenes I, King of Pergamum, 128,
    129, 131
Eumenes II, King of Pergamum, 129,
    132, 190
Eumenes III, King of Pergamum, 131
Euphrates River (Turkish Firat), 353
Euromos, 167, 168
Eurymedon River, 208
Evliya Efendi, 32, 33, 66, 86, 100, 109,
    275, 308, 309
Ezine, 120
Ezinepazarí, 120

Faustina I, wife of Antoninus Pius, 146
Faustina II, wife of Marcus Aurelius,
    142
Fellows, Sir Charles, 186
Fener Burnu, 303
Fethiye, 178, 179
Feyzullah Efendi, Şeyulislam, 173
Finike, 183
Finike, Gulf of, 184
Firat Nehri (see Euphrates River)
Firuz Ağa, 57
Fossati brothers, architects, 27, 28
Frederick Barbarossa, 220, 221

Gagarians, the, 302
Gagik I Artsuni, King of Armenia,
    319, 322, 323, 331, 335
Gagik II Artsuni, King of Armenia,
    319

Gaius Julius Aquila, 154
Gaius Julius Polemaenus, 154
Galatia, Roman province of, 291
Gallipoli (Turkish Gelibolu), 110, 111
Gallipoli campaign, 112, 113, 114, 282
Gauls, the, 129, 275, 286, 287
Gazanfer Ağa, Chief White Eunuch, 72
Gaziantep, 356
Gazipaşa, 211
Gedik Ahmet Pasha, Grand Vezir, 208
Gediz Nehri, 137, 144
Gemlik, 96
Genoese, the, 24, 81, 82, 135, 137, 160, 302, 303
Georgians, the, 318, 321, 329
Germaniyid Turks, 294
Geta, son of Septimius Severus, 357
Gevher Nesibe Hatun, Selcuk princess, 247, 248
Geyre, 187, 189
Giresun, 302, 303
Giresun Adası, 307
Giyaseddin Keyhûsrev II, Selcuk sultan, 207
Giyaseddin Keyhûsrev III, Selcuk sultan, 297
Gök Irmak, 297
Gök Su, 213, 220, 221
Golden Horn, the, 19, 22, 33, 81, 84, 85
Goodwin, Godfrey, 344, 345
Gordion, 280, 286–290
Gordion Knot, 288, 289
Gordios, King of Phrygia, 286
Görele, 303
Göreme, 236, 239, 241
Graces, the Three, 214
Greek-Turkish population exchange, 160
Greek-Turkish War, 94, 140, 253, 283, 304, 313
Gryneum, 136
Gülbahar Hatun, mother of Selim I, 306, 307
Gülbahar Hatun, mother of Beyazit II, 257
Güllübahçe, 160
Güllüdere, 242
Güllük, Gulf of, 169
Gülnus Emetullah, Valide Sultan, 85, 86
Gümüşhane, 314
Gümüşlük, 173
Gyges, King of Lydia, 144, 149

Hací Bayram Veli, 275
Hací Bektaş, 222, 292
Hacílar, 192, 277
Hadrian, Roman emperor, 94, 104, 105, 131, 134, 182, 197, 218, 294, 303, 304, 366
Häkkâri, the, 332, 333
Halicarnassus (see Bodrum)
Halifat Gazi, Danishmendid emir, 260
Halil Bey, emir of the Ramazanoğlu Turks, 366
Halime Hatun, Karakoyunlu princess, 333, 336
Hamitoğlu Turks, 196, 197
Hamza Bahadír, Akkoyunlu emir, 346
Hanfman, Prof. G. M. A., 145
Hannibal, 182
Harbiye (ancient Daphne), 361, 362
Harran, 350, 351
Harşit Çayí, 303, 314
Hasan Dağí, 236, 237, 238
Hasankale, 317
Hasankeyf, 347
Hasanoğlan, 278
Hasan Pasha, Grand Vezir, 343
Hatay, the, 359–364
Hattians, the, 16, 262, 263
Hattusa (see Boğazkale)
Hattusilis I (Labarnas II), 263
Hattusilis III, 44
Havsa, 104
Havza, 297
Hayrettin, Ottoman architect, 108, 110
Hebut, Hittite god, 264, 265, 266, 267
Helen of Troy, 118, 119
Heracleia-under-Latmos, 166, 167
Heraclius, Byzantine emperor, 275
Hermeias of Atarneus, 121, 122
Hero, 111
Herod, King of Judea, 361, 362
Herodes Atticus, 121
Herodotus, 111, 125, 137, 142, 170, 179, 286, 290
Herostratus, 153
Hierapolis, 190, 191
Hisarlík, 114, 115
Hittites, the, 16, 262–268, 278, 279, 280, 313, 353, 356, 365
Hogarth, D. G., 356
Homer, 114, 115, 124, 137, 142, 150, 160, 165, 179, 184, 185
Honaz Dağí, 192
Hopa, 309
Horoz Tepesi, 255
Hoşap Kalesi, 332
Hoşap Nehri, 332
Hüdavend Padişah Hatun, Mongol princess, 316
Hulagu, Khan of the Mongols, 349
Hurrians, the, 16
Hüseyin Ağa, Chief White Eunuch, 261
Hüsrev Pasha, 345

INDEX

Iasus, 168
Ibrahim the Drunkard, 64
Ibrahim the Mad, Ottoman sultan, 31, 32, 39, 40, 46
Ibrahim Pasha, Süleyman's Grand Vezir, 52
Ibrahim Pasha of Egypt, 238
Ibrahim Pasha of Nevşehir, 71, 237
Iconoclastic Period, 29, 240
Ida, Mt, 119, 120, 123, 124
Ihlara, 236
Ildír, 149
Ilíca, 148, 149
Ilyas Bey Camii (Balat), 163
Imad al-Din Zengi, 348
Imroz, 119
Ince Liman, 111
Incíraltí, 147
Ionia and the Ionian Greeks, 136, 137, 141, 142, 144, 151, 161, 162, 165, 166, 301
Iotape, 211
Isaurians, 213, 221
Ishak Pasha of Doğubayazít, 328
Ishak Pasha Sarayí, 328
Isidorus of Miletos, 27, 162
Iskenderun (formerly Alexandretta), 364
Ismail, Shah of Persia, 328
Isparta, 192
Issus, battle of, 364
Istanbul, 15–89
 Ahmet I Camii (Blue Mosque), 48, 49
 Alay Kiosk, 46
 Alexander Sarcophagus, 44
 Amcazade Hüseyin Köprülü complex, 72
 Anadolu Hisar fortress, 88, 89
 Anadolu Kavaği, 89
 Ancinia Juliana, Byzantine princess, 72
 Archaeological Museum, 43–45
 Arch of Theodosius, 59
 Arnavutköy, 88
 Aspar Cistern, 73
 Atatürk Museum, 84
 Atik Ali Pasha Camii, 58
 Basilica Cistern (Yerebatan Saray), 25, 52
 Bebek, 88
 Beyazit Fire Tower, 61
 Beyazit II mosque complex, 60
 Beykoz, 89
 Beylerbey Palace, 87
 Binbirdirek Cistern, 52
 Blachernae Palace, 56, 79
 Bosphorus Bridge, 87

Bosphorus University (see Robert College)
British Embassy, 83
Bucoleon Palace, 55
Burmali Cami, 71
Byzantine sea-walls, 55
Çağaloğlu Hamamí, 25
Çemberlitaş Hamamí, 58
Çiçek Pasají (The Passage of Flowers), 83, 84
Çinili Kiosk, 43, 45
Constantine's Column, 58
Çorlulu Ali Pasha complex, 59
Dolmabahçe Palace, 87
Edirne Gate, 79
Eyüp, 84, 85
Fatih Cami (Mosque complex of Sultan Mehmet the Conqueror), 73
Feyzullah Efendi Medresesi, 73
Firuz Ağa Camii, 57
Forum of Theodosius the Great, 59
Fountain of Ahmet III, 36
Galata Bridge, 19, 85
Galata Tower, 82
Galatasaray Lisesi, 83
Gazanfer Ağa Medresesi, 72
Great Palace of Byzantium, 47, 53, 55, 56
Greek Orthodox Patriarchate, 75
Gülhane Park, 46
Haghia Eirene, 36, 43
Haghia Sophia, 25–32, 47, 48
Hasseki Hürrem Hamamí, 47
Hippodrome, 45, 47, 48–52
Hüseyin Bey Yalísí, 88
Ibrahim Pasha's Palace, 52
Istanbul University, 62
Kapalí Çarşí, 60, 61, 62
Kara Mustafa complex, 59
Kíbríslí Yalí, 88
Kílíç Ali Pasha Camii, 87
Kilyos, 89
Koca Sinan Pasha complex, 58
Köprülü Camii, 58
Köprülü Library, 58
Kücüksu Palace, 88
Kyriotissa, church of the, 70
Leander's Tower, 85
Marcian's Column, 73
Mehter Band, 84
Mihrimah Camii, 79, 80
Military Museum, 84
Molla Çelebi Camii, 87
Mosaic Museum, 52
Mosaic Peristyle, 52
Museum of the Ancient Orient, 43, 44
Nuruosmaniye Cami, 61

393

Istanbul [cont'd]
Nusretiye Cami, 87
Opera House, 84
Ostrorog Yalísí, 88
Palace of Antiochus, 57
Palazzo Venezia, 83
Pammakaristos, church of the
(Fethiye Cami), 74, 75
Princes' Isles, 85, 86
Robert College, 88
Rumeli Hisar fortress, 88, 89
Rumeli Kavağí, 89
Russian Embassy, 82
Rüstem Pasha Camii, 23, 24
Sahaflar Çarşísí, 60
St Anthony of Padua, church of, 83
St George, Patriarchal church, 57
St Mary Draperis, church of, 83
St Mary of the Mongols, church of,
75
St Polyeuctes, church of, 72
St Saviour in Chora, church of
(Kariye Cami), 75-78
Sts Sergius and Bacchus, church of
(Küçük Aya Sofya), 54
Saray Burnu, 33
Saríyer, 89
Şehzade Camii, 71
Selim I Camii, 73, 74
Şile, 89
Sokollu Mehmet Pasha Camii, 53,
54
Spice Bazaar (Mísír Çarşísí), 23
Süleymaniye, the (Mosque complex
of Süleyman the Magnificent), 62-
67
Museum of Turkish and Islamic
Art, 66
Swedish Embassy, 82
Sweet Waters of Asia, 88
Sweet Waters of Europe, 19
Tarabya, 89
Tekfursaray, 79
Theodosian walls, 79
Tomb of Mahmut II, 57
Topkapí Sarayí, 33-43, 47
Harem, the, 40-43
Tunel, 82
Üsküdar, 85, 86
Atik Valide Camii, 86
Fountain of Ahmet III, 85
Iskele Camii, 85
Şemsi Pasha Camii, 86
Yeni Valide Camii, 85
Valens Aqueduct, 70, 72
Yoros Castle, 89
Izmir (ancient Smyrna), 137, 140-143
history, 140

Agora, 142
Archaeological Museum, 143
Bazaar, 143
Baths of Diana, 141
Bayraklí, 141
Kadifekale (Mt Pagus), 140, 142
Izmir, Gulf of, 136
Iznik (ancient Nicaea), 92-96
history, 93-94
Haghia Sophia, 94
Istanbul Kapísí, 94
Lefke Kapísí, 94
Roman theatre, 95
Yenişehir Kapísí, 95
Yesil Cami, 94, 95
Zaviye of Nilufer Hatun, 94, 95
Zaviye of Yakup Sultan, 95
Iznik Gölü, 92
Izzeddin Keykâvus II, Selcuk sultan,
192
Izzeddin Kílíç Arslan II, Selcuk sultan,
276

Janissaries, the, 36, 71, 87, 143, 237
Jason, 302
Jews, the, 24, 146
John I Tzimisces, Byzantine emperor,
242
John II Comnenus, Byzantine emperor,
31, 105
John VI Cantacuzenos, Byzantine
emperor, 95
John-Sembat III, King of Armenia, 319
Joseph of Galilee, 274
Julian the Apostate, Roman emperor,
274, 352
Julius Caesar, 258, 259
Justinian the Great, Byzantine em-
peror, 19, 25, 27, 28, 43, 48, 49, 53,
54, 93, 94, 100, 159, 247, 290, 304,
313, 341, 348, 360, 366

Kabaağaç, Cevat Şakir, 173
Kâhta, 357
Kâhta Çayí, 357
Kale, 314
Kalidiran, 211
Kalkan, 182
Kalonoros, 207, 208
Kanes, 250, 251
Kanlídivane, 217
Kanytelis, 217
Kaplan Dağí, 170
Karaburun, 148
Karahüyük, 250
Karain Cave, 193, 276
Karakoyunlu Turks, 317, 336, 341, 346
Karaman, 221, 222

Karamania, Roman province of, 224
Karamanid Turks, 208, 212, 221, 224
Kara Mustafa Pasha, 59, 109
Karcasu, 187
Kars, 317, 318, 321
Kartal, 92
Kaş, 182
Kaymaklí, 328
Kayseri (ancient Caesarea), 246–250, 257
  history, 246
  Archaeological Museum, 249, 250
  Bazaar, 247
  Bedesten, 247
  Çifte Medrese, 247
  Çifte Kümbet, 250
  Döner Kümbet, 249
  Hatuniye Medresesi, 247
  Huant Foundation, 249
  Köşk Medrese, 250
  Kurşunlu Cami, 247
  Melek Gazi Medresesi, 247
  Sírçalí Kümbet, 250
  Ulu Cami, 247
  Vezir Han, 247
  Walls, 247
Kefkalesi, 357
Kekova, 183
Kelkit Çayí, 257
Kemalpaşa, 143
Kemer, 179, 185
Keşan, 110
Kethuddin Melek Şah, Selcuk prince, 254
Keyhato, Khan of the Mongols, 316
Keyhûsrev I, Selcuk sultan, 258
Keyhûsrev II, Selcuk sultan, 196, 197, 247, 249, 255
Keyhûsrev III, Selcuk sultan, 225, 227, 257, 282
Keykâvus I, Selcuk sultan, 224, 225, 247, 253, 254
Keykâvus II, Selcuk sultan, 225, 227, 234
Kherei, King of Lycia, 180
Kílíç Ali Pasha, 87
Kílíç Arslan I, Selcuk sultan, 220
Kílíç Arslan II, Selcuk sultan, 226
Kílíç Arslan IV, Selcuk sultan, 226
Kilitbahir, 112
Kíz Kalesi (Cilicia) (see Corycian Castles)
Kíz Kalesi (The Hatay), 364
Kízíl Ahmet Pasha, 247
Kízíl Çukur, 242
Kízíl Irmak, 242, 243, 253, 297, 301
Kízíltepe, 347
Knights of St John, 170, 213

Knolles, Richard, 213, 296
Koca Çay, 179
Koca Sinan Pasha, 58, 59
Kocayatak, 200
Köhnüş Valley, 293
Konya, 220, 223–234
  history, 223, 224
  Alâeddin Camii, 224, 225
  Archaeological Museum, 227
  Hasbey Darülhafízí, 227
  Ince Minare Medresesi, 226
  Iplikçi Camii, 227
  Karatay Medresesi, 226
  Mevlana Tekke, 228–231
  Sahip Ata mosque complex, 227
  Selimiye Camii, 228
  Şerefettin Camii, 227, 228
  Sírçalí Medrese, 227
Korkuteli, 183, 193
Kössem, Valide Sultan, 39, 43
Kovkalesi, 314
Kubaba, Phrygian goddess, 277, 280
Küçük Çekmece, 103
Kültepe, 250, 278
Kumkale, 119
Küplü, 295
Kurds, the, 315, 326, 327, 328, 332, 333, 336, 341, 346, 351
Kütahya, 293, 294
Kwaca Yakut, Emir of Erzurum, 316

Labarnas, Hittite king, 263, 278
Labarnas II (Hattusilis), Hittite king, 263
Labraynda, 168, 169
Lala Mustafa Pasha, 317
Lamas Çayí, 189
Laodicea, 189
Lapseki, 111
Larisa, 137
Latmian Gulf, 162, 166
Latmos, Mt, 166, 167
Lawrence, T. E., 356
Laz, the, 308, 309
Lazarus, King of Serbia, 99
Leake, Captain, 292, 293
Leander, 111
Leo I, Byzantine emperor, 73
Leo II, King of Lesser Armenia, 366
Leo VI, Byzantine emperor, 28, 30
Lesbos, 121, 122, 123, 124
Leto, 160, 182
Letoon, 181
Licinius, Roman emperor, 164
Limonlu Kalesi, 217
Limyra, 183
Loryma Peninsula, 177
Loti, Pierre, 85

Love, Prof. Iris, 174
Lüleburgaz, 103, 104
Lycaonia, 222, 235
Lycia and the Lycians, 178, 179, 180, 181, 182, 183
Lydia and the Lydians, 16, 144, 145, 149, 152, 199, 286
Lysander, Spartan general, 111
Lysimachus, King of Macedonia, 93, 120, 128, 152, 154

Ma, Anatolian Earth Mother, 255
Macauley, Rose, 308
Maçka (Pontus), 312, 314
Maden Şehir, 223
Maeander river and valley, 161, 162
Mahmut I, Ottoman sultan, 25
Mahmut II, Ottoman sultan, 36, 42, 57, 62, 87
Mahperi Huant Hatun, Selcuk empress, 249, 255, 258
Malatya, 340
Maltepe, 111
Mamelukes, 216, 225, 246, 257, 359
Man, Anatolian Moon goddess, 206
Manavgat, 206
Manlius Volso, Roman general, 287, 291
Manuel Comnenus, Byzantine prince, 304
Manuel Comnenus, Emperor of Trebizond, 305
Manzikert, battle of, 208, 321, 331
Marcian, Byzantine emperor, 72, 73
Marco Polo, 314, 329
Marcus Aurelius, Roman emperor, 142, 202
Marcus Aurelius Polemo, high priest of Olba, 221
Mardin, 345, 346
Marmara, Sea of, 19, 22, 23
Marmaris, 177, 178
Marwanids, 341
Marysas, 175
Medea, 309
Media and the Medes, 330
Mehmet I, Ottoman sultan, 98, 100, 105, 256, 260, 261
Mehmet II, Ottoman sultan, 33, 37, 45, 56, 61, 73, 79, 84, 88, 108, 112, 208, 224, 247, 276, 304, 308
Mehmet III, Ottoman sultan, 23, 32, 59
Mehmet IV, 23, 59
Mehmet Ağa, Ottoman architect, 48
Mehmet Bey, Hamitoğlu emir, 196, 197
Mehmut, Prince, son of Süleyman, 71
Melek Gazi, Danishmendid emir, 260
Melendiz River, 237

Meles River, 142
Mellaart, Prof. James, 223
Menteşe Turks, 163, 169
Menua, King of Urartu, 333
Menüçahir, Selcuk emir, 323
Mersin, 210, 218
Mesut I, Selcuk sultan, 225
Mevlevi dervishes, 197, 222, 228–231
Mezitli, 217
Michael III, Byzantine emperor, 29, 275
Michael IV, Byzantine emperor, 31
Midas, King of Phrygia, 286, 290, 292, 293
Midas Şehri, 292, 293
Midyat, 340, 346
Mihrimah, Ottoman princess, 24, 65, 79, 80, 85
Milas, 168, 169
Miletos, 161, 162, 300
Miraculous Mountain, the, 362
Misis, 366
Mithradates I Callinicus, King of Commagene, 356, 357
Mithradates VI, King of Pontus, 257, 258, 259, 297, 300, 301
Mithradatic Wars, 258, 259, 300
Mongols, 16, 93, 97, 145, 216, 246, 250, 253, 255, 256, 257, 261, 275, 276, 294, 315, 316, 322, 336
Mopsus, 199, 201, 366
Mugis al-Din Tuğrul Şah, Saltukid emir, 314
Muğla, 177
Mu'in al-Din Süleyman (the Pervane), Selcuk emir, 256, 257, 301
Murat I, Ottoman sultan, 95, 99, 100, 101, 104, 122, 196
Murat II, Ottoman sultan, 105, 107, 108
Murat III, Ottoman sultan, 23, 32, 41, 53, 58, 59, 86
Murat IV, Ottoman sultan, 39, 40
Mursilis II, Hittite king, 263, 279
Muş, 346
Musa Çelebi, son of Beyazit I, 104
Mustafa I, Ottoman sultan, 32
Mustafa II, Ottoman sultan, 72
Mustafa, Prince, Süleyman's son, 65
Mustafapaşa, 239
Mut, 221
Mycale, Mt, 160, 161, 162
Myndus Peninsula, 170
Myra, 182, 183
Myrina, 136
Myrina, Queen of the Amazons, 136

Nabuchadrezzar, King of Assyria, 44

Namurtköy, 341
Namurtköy Limaní, 136
Narlí Kuyu, 214
Nazili, 187
Nelson, Lord, 177
Nemesis, 206
Nemrut Daǧí (Lake Van), 336
Nemrut Daǧí (Adíyaman), 356
Nevşehir, 236, 237
Newton, Sir Charles, 170
Nicephorus I, Byzantine emperor, 109
Nicephorus II Phocas, Byzantine
    emperor, 242, 360, 361, 365
Nicomedes I, King of Bithynia, 93, 297
Nightingale, Florence, 88
Nika Revolt, 27, 43, *48*, *49*, *51*, 53, 55
Niksar, 257
Nilufer Hatun, wife of Orhan Gazi, 95
Notium, 149, 150
Nur al-Din, son of Zengi, 348, 349
Nurbanu, Valide Sultan, 58, 86
Nureddin Şen Timur, Mongol emir,
    257
Nysa, 186, 187

Odun Iskelesi, 120
Odysseus, 185
Oǧuz Turks, 295
Okuz Mehmet Pasha, 160
Ölceytü, Khan of the Mongols, 261,
    316
Olympus, 184
Ordu, 302
Ören, 124
Orhaneli Çayí, 294
Orhan Gazi, Ottoman sultan, 92, 93,
    94, 95, 96, 108
Orontes River, 359, 362
Ortahisar, 239, 243
Ortygia, 166
Osman I, Ottoman sultan, 96, 295
Osman II, Ottoman sultan, 38
Osman Bahadír, founder of the
    Akkoyunlu dynasty, 346
Ottomans and the Ottoman Empire,
    15, 22, 33, 36, 37, 57, 59, 60, 64, 65,
    67, 74, 93, 96, 97, 99, 104, 105, 110,
    196, 199, 201, 212, 214, 224, 246,
    276, 282, 294, *295*, *296*, 328, 336,
    337, 341, 359
Ovid, 181, 182

Pakran, 326
Pamphylia and the Pamphylians, 185,
    193, 199, 201, 204
Pamukkale, 190, 191
Panayir Daǧí, 152
Panionium, the, 142, 161

Paphylagonia, 297
Paris of Troy, 118
Parthians, the, 352, 356
Pasinler, 317
Patara, 182
Patnos, 329
Pausanias the Traveller, 136, 151, 165,
    180, 291
Peçin Kale, 169
Peloponnesian War, 111, 112, 113
Pergamum, 125-135
    history, 128-131
    Altar of Zeus, 132
    Archaeological Museum, 135
    Asklepieion, 133, 134, 135
    gymnasium, 133
    library, 131
    lower agora, 132
    Red Court, 128
    Temenos of Athena, 131
    Temple of Demeter, 133
    Temple of Zeus-Asklepios, 134
    theatre, 131
    Trajaneum, 131
    upper agora, 132
Pergamum, the Kingdom of, 291
Perge, 199, 200
Pericles, 111
Perikles, King of Lycia, 183, 184
Peristrema Valley, 236
Persia and the Persians, 93, 144, 162,
    163, 165, 174, 181, 189, 199, 203,
    275, 286, 289, 315, 319, 328, 347,
    360, 364
Pessinus, 290, 291
Pharnaces I, King of Pontus, 258, 259,
    300, 302
Phaselis, 184, 185
Philetaeros, King of Pergamum, 128,
    131
Philippicus Bardanes, Byzantine em-
    peror, 110
Phocaea and the Phocaeans, 137
Photius, Byzantine Patriarch, 29
Phrygia and the Phrygians, 16, 192,
    264, 280, 283, 286, 288, 289, 290, 291,
    292, 293
Piasus, King of the Pelasgians, 137
Pinara, 179
Pindar, 177
Pisidia, 192
Pitane, 135
Pithana, King of Kussura, 278
Plantagenet, Edward, 171
Plato, 121
Pliny the Younger, 95
Plutarch, 148, 179, 180, 218, 219
Polatlí, 283

Pompey, 204, 208, 218, 253, 276, 356, 360
Pontic Mountains, 303, 308, 314
Pontus, the Kingdom of, 255, 257, 258, 259, 301
Porsuk Çayí, 283
Porto Genovese, 184
Poseidon, 119, 185
Pozantí, 220
Priam, King of Troy, 118, 119
Priene, 161
Procopius, 19, 28
Protosileaus, Argive hero, 113
Provençal Isle, 213
Prusias I, King of Bithynia, 96
Ptolemy V Epiphanes, King of Egypt, 181
Purchas, Samuel, 230, 231

Ramazanoğlu Turks, 366
Raymond of Aguilers, chronicler of the Crusades, 92
Rhodes, 177, 184
Rhodian Peraea, 177
Rice, Prof. Talbot, 305
Rize, 309
Robert College, 88
Romanus III, Byzantine emperor, 31
Rome and the Romans, 16, 22, 93, 103, 120, 129, 152, 179, 180, 184, 185, 196, 199, 208, 218, 253, 259, 274, 275, 287, 291, 297, 352, 356, 366
Roxelana, 47, 52, 64, 65
Royal Persian Road, 144, 283, 286
Rukneddin Kíliç Arslan IV, Selcuk sultan, 256
Runciman, Sir Steven, 220, 221
Russians, the, 104, 148, 304, 315, 318
Rüstem Pasha, Grand Vezir, 24, 65, 100

Sabians, the, 350, 351, 352
Sagallasus, 192
Sahip Ata Fahrettin, Selcuk vezir, 226, 227, 249, 254
Şah Cihan Hatun, Selcuk princess, 249, 250
St Barnabas, 367
St Basil, 236
St Euphemia of Chalcedon, 57
St Francis of Assisi, 70, 71
St Gregory the Illuminator, 323
St Ignatius Theophorus, 29
St Ignatius the Younger, 29
St John the Apostle, 128, 152, 159, 180, 189, 190
St John Chrysostomos, 29
St Luke, 274
St Nicholas of Myra, 182, 183

St Paul, 152, 154, 218, 274, 363
St Peter, 363
St Philip, 191
St Symeon Stylites the Elder, 362, 363
St Symeon Stylites the Younger, 362, 363
St Thecla, church of, 213
Sakarya Nehri, 283, 295, 296
Saladin, 345, 351
Saltukid Turks, 314, 316
Samandağ, 362
Samasota, 357
Samsun, 301
Saraseki, 364
Sardis, 144–147
Sarduris II, King of Urartu, 330
Sargon II, King of Assyria, 286, 356
Sarí Süleyman Bey, Kurdish emir, 332
Şarkíşla, 251
Saros Gulf, 110
Sarpedon, 178
Scamander River, 119
Schliemann, Heinrich, 115, 118
Scopas, 170
Selene, daughter of the Moon, 167
Selcuks, 16, 93, 95, 96, 192, 196, 199, 208, 209, 210, 212, 214, 224, 225, 226, 227, 228, 229, 231, 232, 233, 234, 246, 253, 255, 256, 257, 261, 281, 294, 318, 321, 331, 336, 343, 348, 361
Seleucus I Nicator, Seleucid emperor, 128, 165, 174, 213, 218, 348, 358, 360, 362
Seleucia ad Pieria, 360, 362, 364
Selge, 203
Selim I, Ottoman sultan, 73, 74, 218, 249, 292, 304, 307, 328, 341, 345, 359, 366
Selim II, Ottoman sultan, 32, 53, 65, 86, 106, 228
Selimiye (Pamphylia), 203–206
Selimiye (Cappadocia), 227
Selinus, 211
Selinus River, 125, 128
Sembat II, King of Armenia, 319, 322, 323
Şemiran Suyu (The Waters of Semiramis), 333
Semiz Ali Pasha, Grand Vezir, 104
Şemsettin Cuwaymi, Mongol emir, 254
Şemsi Pasha, 86, 247
Sennacherib, King of Assyria, 218
Sennacherib-John, King of Armenia, 331
Septimius Severus, Roman emperor, 22, 48, 58, 191, 357
Sertavul Pass, 221

Sestos, 111
Seyhan River, 365
Seyit Battal Gazi, 292
Seyitgazi, 292
Shalmaneser III, King of Assyria, 329
Side, 203–206
Siğacík, 147
Siirt, 340
Silifke, 213, 214, 220
Silivri, 103
Silk Road, the, 328
Sillyum, 200, 201
Silvan, 341
Sinan, Ottoman architect, 24, 27, 32, 41, 47, 53, 62, 64, 67, 71, 79, 80, 85, 86, 87, 94, 103, 104, 105
Sinop (ancient Sinope), 259, 297, 300, 301, 303
Sinop Cape, 300
Sipylus, Mt, 359
Sivas, 253, 254
  history, 253
  Çifte Minare Medrese, 254
  Darüşifa of Keykâvus I, 253, 254
  Gök Medrese, 254
  Muzaffer Bürücirde Medresesi, 253
  Toprak Kalesi, 253
  Ulu Cami, 254
Sivrihisar, 296
Smyrna (see Izmir)
Softa Kalesi, 212
Soğanlí Valley, 239, 243
Söğüt, 98, 295, 296
Söke, 160
Sokollu Mehmet Pasha, 53, 104, 110
Soli, 217, 218
Solymnus, Mt, 185, 198
Spartans, the, 111, 112
Strabo, 136, 137, 186, 187, 211, 259, 260, 300, 309, 356
Stratoniceia, 174
Striker, Prof. Lee, 70
Süleyman the Magnificent, 24, 47, 52, 53, 62, 64, 65, 67, 71, 74, 79, 94, 103, 171, 228, 304, 364
Süleyman II, Ottoman sultan, 65, 110
Süleyman, Emir, son of Beyazit I, 164
Süleyman Pasha, son of Sultan Orhan, 108
Sultanhisar, 186
Sultantepe, 350
Sumatar Harabesi, 350, 351
Sumela monastery, 312, 313
Sumerians, 44
Sungurlu, 262
Süphan Dağí, 329, 331, 337
Sürmene Kastil, 309
Susanoğlu, 214

Syme, 177
Syrian Gates, 363
Syrian Orthodox Church, 346, 347

Tamerlane, 93, 94, 97, 105, 145, 163, 276, 345
Tarsus, 218, 366
Taş Kule (Eski Foca), 136
Taşucu, 213
Taurus Mountains, 193, 220–223
Tekirdağ, 103
Telmessus, 178, 179
Teos, 147, 148
Terme, 301, 302
Terme Çayí, 301
Termessus, 193
Teshub, Hittite god, 264, 265, 266, 267, 279
Texier, Charles, 262
Theodore Metochites, 75, 78
Theodore I Lascaris, Byzantine emperor, 93
Theodosius I, the Great, Byzantine emperor, 51, 315
Theodosius II, Byzantine emperor, 25, 79, 154
Theophano, Byzantine empress, 242
Theophilus the Unfortunate, Byzantine emperor, 55
Thierry, Nicole and Michele, 236
Thomas Artusini, Armenian chronicler, 335
Thrace, 103, 104
Thucydides, 112, 180
Tigranes the Great, Armenian king, 218, 360
Tigranocerta, 218, 341
Tigris River, 341, 347
Tmolus, Mt, 144
Tokat, 255–257
  history, 255
  Ali Pasha Camii, 256
  Bedesten, 256
  Gök Medrese, 256
  Pasha Hamamí, 256
  Sümbül Baba Zaviyesi, 257
  Türbe of Abdül Kasím, 256
  Türbe of Nureddin Şen Timur, 257
  Voyvoda Haní, 256
Toprakkale (Van), 332
Toprakkale (Cilicia), 365
Topuz Dağí, 243
Torul, 314
Trabzon (ancient Trebizond), 303–309
  history, 303–305
  Byzantine walls, 307
  Citadel, 308
  Gülbahar Hatun Camii, 305, 306

Trabzon [cont'd]
Panaghia Chrysokephalos (Fatih Camii), 307
St Eugenios, church of (Yeni Cuma Cami), 308
Trajan, Roman emperor, 131
Tralles, 186
Trebizond (see Trabzon)
Triarious, Roman general, 258
Troad, the, 114–123
Trojan War, 118–120
Troy, 114–120, 124
Tudhaliyas II, Hittite king, 263
Tudhaliyas IV, Hittite king, 268
Tunca River, 108
Tur Abdin, 346, 347
Turgutlu, 144
Turkish Republic, 272, 273, 283
Turumtay, Selcuk emir, 260
Tushpa, capital of Urartu, 336
Typhon the Monster, 215

Üçhisar, 239, 242, 243
Ulu Dağ (Mt Olympus of Bithynia), 102
Ulu Yol, the Great Selcuk Road, 234
Umar bin Savci, Germaniyid emir, 294
Ünye, 302
Urartu and the Urartians, 16, 280, 328, 329, 330, 331, 332, 333, 337
Urfa, 348, 349, 353
history, 348, 349
Abdürrahman Medresesi, 349
Citadel, 349
Makham al-Khalil Medresesi, 349
Pool of Abraham, 349
Ulu Cami, 349
Ürgüp, 236, 238, 239
Uzuncaburç, 214

Valens, Byzantine emperor, 72, 93, 104
Van, 300, 331
Van Gölü (Lake Van), 329, 330, 331, 333, 335, 336, 337
Venetians, the, 24, 83
Vespasian, Roman emperor, 181, 356
Vezirköprü, 297
Via Egnatia, 103
Viranşehir (Cilicia), 217
Viranşehir (Urfa), 347, 348
Virgil, 124

Whittemore, Thomas, 27
Wilbraham, Capt. Richard, 322
Williams, General Sir Fenwick, 318
Wood, J. T., 153
Woolley, Sir Leonard, 356

Xanthus, 179–181, 182
Xenophon and the Ten Thousand, 303, 314, 315
Xerxes, 111, 275, 331

Yakacík, 364
Yalova, 92
Yason Burnu, 302
Yatağan, 174, 177
Yazílíkaya (Boğazkale), 262, 267, 268
Yazílíkaya (Phrygia), 292
Yeni Foca, 131, 136
Yenişakran, 135, 136
Yeşil Irmak Nehri, 255, 257, 258, 259, 260, 261, 301
Yeşilkent, 364
Yílan Kalesi, 365, 366
Yunus Emre, Turkish poet, 222
Yürgüç Pasha, Ottoman vezir, 256
Yürüks, Turcoman nomads, 123, 197, 315

Zab Suyu, 332
Zeus, 119, 167, 291
Zigana Dağ, 314
Zile, 258
Zilve, 242

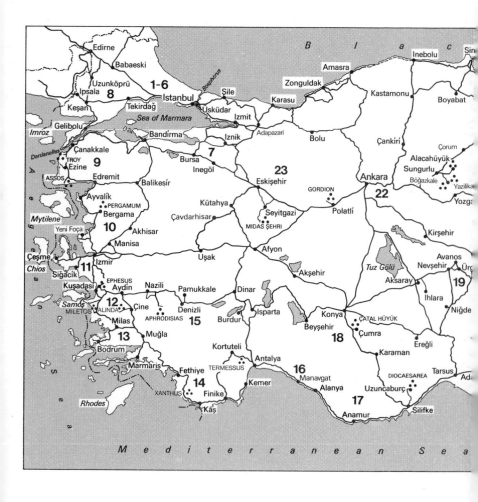

BLUE
LABYRINTH

DOUGLAS PRESTON and LINCOLN CHILD are the number one bestselling co-authors of the celebrated Pendergast novels, as well as the Gideon Crew books. Preston and Child's *Relic* and *The Cabinet of Curiosities* were chosen by readers in a National Public Radio poll as being among the one hundred greatest thrillers ever written, and *Relic* was made into a number one box office hit movie. Readers can sign up for their monthly newsletter, The Pendergast File, at www.PrestonChild.com and follow them on Facebook.

Also by Douglas Preston and Lincoln Child

Agent Pendergast Novels

Relic
Reliquary
The Cabinet of Curiosities
Still Life with Crows
Brimstone
Dance of Death
The Book of the Dead
The Wheel of Darkness
Cemetery Dance
Fever Dream
Cold Vengeance
Two Graves
White Fire
Blue Labyrinth

Gideon Crew Novels

Gideon's Sword
Gideon's Corpse
The Lost Island

Other Novels

Mount Dragon
Riptide
Thunderhead
The Ice Limit